Genêt

Genêt

A Biography of

Janet

Flanner

Brenda Wineapple

TICKNOR & FIELDS

New York

1989

For information about permission to reproduce selections
from this book, write to Permissions, Ticknor & Fields,
215 Park Avenue South, New York, New York 10003.

Library of Congress Cataloging-in-Publication Data

Wineapple, Brenda.
Genêt, a biography of Janet Flanner / Brenda Wineapple.
p.   cm.
Includes bibliographical references.
ISBN 0-89919-442-7
1. Flanner, Janet, 1892–1978 — Biography.   2. Authors,
American — 20th century — Biography.   3. Ameri-
cans — France — Paris — History — 20th century.
4. Paris (France) — Intellectual life — 20th century.
I. Title.
PS3511.L285Z94   1989
814'.52 — dc20   89-5215
[B]   CIP

Printed in the United States of America

D   10 9 8 7 6 5 4 3 2 1

My thanks to the Collection of American Literature, Beinecke Rare Book and Manuscript Library, Yale University,
and to the Estate of Gertrude Stein, for permission to quote
from an unpublished letter of Gertrude Stein to Janet Flanner. Excerpts from the Djuna Barnes letters to Janet Flanner
are reprinted by permission of The Authors League Fund,
New York, and The Historic Churches Preservation Trust,
London, as literary executors of the Estate of Djuna Barnes.
The excerpts from Glenway Wescott, "The Frenchman Six
Feet Three," copyright © 1942 by *Harper's Magazine,* all
rights reserved, are reprinted from the July 1942 issue by
special permission. The quotation from the first issue of
The New Yorker is reprinted by permission; copyright 1925,
1953 The New Yorker Magazine, Inc.

The author has made every effort to locate all owners of
photographs and copyrighted material and to obtain permission to reproduce them. Any errors or omissions are
unintentional, and corrections will be made in future print-
ings if necessary.

To Fannie S. Duckman and Jacob W. Silverman

Contents

List of Illustrations

Following pages 108 and 236

Preface

I never met Janet Flanner. At first I knew her only by those matchless sentences of hers, elegantly constructed arcs studded with sharp, shining insights. I knew almost nothing of her life except that for over fifty years she lived in Paris — alone, I assumed — in a hotel room littered with books and seasonal flowers. From that room she delivered, every two weeks, a public letter signed with the name readers of *The New Yorker* had come to anticipate: Genêt.

I knew she'd gone to Paris in the early twenties, one of the many Americans of her generation, mostly midwesterners like herself, in search of a better, more civilized shore; I knew she stayed long enough to be called America's answer to Tocqueville. Typing quickly, using no more than two fingers, a lit cigarette always within arm's reach, she gave her readers a small, savory taste of all things French, from the death of Anatole France to the fall of Charles de Gaulle.

I wanted to know more about this woman whose wavy, short-cropped hair had begun to whiten before she turned thirty, who was proud of her tiny feet and well-shaped hands but disliked the nose that seemed out of proportion to the rest of her face. I wanted to know more about the woman who hoped she might at least look like Voltaire someday. I wondered how she, born in Indianapolis at the turn of the century, had come to reject what she'd been raised to expect. I wondered what kept her in Paris decade after decade, an American woman on her own, chronicling the weekly mood of a foreign country. And I recalled what seemed at first an offhand remark by Norman Mailer, about to be introduced to Genêt; what was it like, he mused, to hold the same job for fifty years?

In working on this book, I have asked many questions, met many people, touched many documents: cards, clippings, a pass to the 1935 *Reichsparteitag* rally in Nuremberg; marriage certificates, death certificates, the handwritten will of a solicitous father who killed himself; passports that looked like diplomas; yellowed postcards from Constantinople, the ink unfaded on the correspondent's side; a list of books borrowed in 1923; an uncashed check from Pablo Picasso, the signature evidently of greater consequence to the recipient than the amount; V-mail discreetly censored; a long, flat box filled with layers of photographs that once had been carefully labeled and pasted onto the leaves of a scrapbook, recently dismantled. I held in my hands letters written in a hurry, no longer fresh, still immediate. I remember sitting in a library, carefully refolding the thin green typing paper one of Janet Flanner's friends always used, and I remember my shock one day many months later when the same friend answered my query on those same green sheets. I told her; it made her feel a bit posthumous, she said.

One fall afternoon, in search of the country house where Janet Flanner spent much of her adult life — that she lived alone in a hotel room all those years was only partly true — I followed the Route of Forty Pennies to the small village of Orgeval, near Paris. After a series of turns and reversals while trying to recall a handwritten map I'd seen in Texas, and no longer convinced I'd be able to recognize the house or its fabulous garden, I suddenly spotted it: two stories, stone, bleached, rectangular, empty. The windows were without screen or glass, their cerulean blue shutters open to the sky. The gate was painted the same clear color. I walked to the back of the house and stood by the locked gate. As I peered into the garden, I could smell the rotting apples and pears that had fallen, overripe, to the ground. Two lawn chairs were set among the weeds.

If we re-create the past by sifting through inert papers, hoping to animate them, the past enters us as well. When I went to Crown Hill Cemetery in Indianapolis, notebook in hand, and stood over the graves of Janet Flanner's family, I panicked: I should have brought flowers. What, after all, was I doing here? And why had I come? Because six years ago I had begun to read through the collection of papers Janet Flanner had deposited at the Library of Congress. There

I discovered a slice of history, complicated and alive — a chronicle of achievement, of opportunities lost and made; of luck and self-doubt; of expatriation, homelessness, commitment, and betrayal; and, finally, of women devoted to one another for a lifetime. This was Janet Flanner's story, and I thank her for opening it to me.

Acknowledgments

I owe a great deal to a great many:

To the National Endowment for the Humanities for the fellowship that enabled me to devote a full year to writing this book.

To the many who extended various kindnesses as well as patience with all manner of questions: Berenice Abbott, Roger Angell, the late Carlos Baker, Sybille Bedford, Rosamond Bernier, Célia Bertin, Simon Michael Bessie, Gardner Botsford, Kay Boyle, Benjamin Bradlee, Jr., Fanny Myers Brennan, John Broderick, Brian K. Buchanan, Stephen F. Buchanan, Virginia Spencer Carr, Alice Caulkins, Anne Chisholm, the late Elizabeth Jenks Clark, Chris Connelly, Doda Conrad, Rosalind Coward, the late Malcolm Cowley, Thomas Quinn Curtiss, Linda Davis, David Diamond, Honoria Murphy Donnelly, Stanley Eichelbaum, Clifton Fadiman, M. F. K. Fisher, Noel Riley Fitch, Peter F. Fleischmann, Hugh Ford, Philip Hamburger, Emily Hahn, Mathilda Hills, E. J. Kahn, Jr., Christin Keller, Scott Keller, Joan Leech, Mary McCarthy, Michael McManus, William Maxwell, Helen Kirkpatrick Milbank, Ruth M. Mills, Worrall Mountain, Edith Oliver, Robert Phelps, Ned Rorem, May Sarton, Mr. and Mrs. Percy Seitlin, the late Diane Forbes-Robertson Sheean, Allegra Stewart, Virgil Thomson, the late Edwin Tribble, Richard Vonnegut, George Wickes, Pat Wilkinson, Warren S. Wilkinson, Helen Wolff.

To the many others who answered query letters, provided addresses, supplied information, or simply wished me good luck.

To the many archives, and especially to the librarians and researchers, that made this project possible: at the Library of Congress, Charles Kelly, David Wigdor, Mary Wolfskill, and the staff of the Manuscripts Division, and Mary Ison and the staff of the Division of Prints and Photographs; Nancy Johnson, American Academy and Institute of Arts and Letters; Daria D'Arienzo, Amherst College Library; Bonnie Hardwick, the Bancroft Library, University of California at Berkeley; Amy B. Sheperdson, Mugar Memorial Library, Boston University; Leo M. Dolenski, Katharine White Papers, Bryn Mawr College Library; at the University of Chicago, Marlene Tuttle of the Office of University Alumni Affairs, Daniel Meyer at the Joseph Regenstein Library, and Maxine Sullivan at the Office of the University Registrar; the research division, Columbia Broadcast System; at Columbia University, the staff of Special Collections at Butler Library and the Oral History Research Collection; Bibliothèque Littéraire Jacques Doucet of Paris; James Bissett of the Manuscript Department of William R. Perkins Library, Duke University; Sara Willis and the staff of Houghton Reading Room, Harvard University; Rebecca Campbell Gibson at the Lilly Library, Indiana University; Connie McBirney and the staff of the Indianapolis Historical Society Library; the *Indianapolis Star;* Patty Matkovic, Noraleen Young, and the staff of the Indianapolis State Library; Martin Antonetti at Mills College Library; the staff of the Museum of Broadcasting, New York City; the research division of National Broadcasting Corporation; the Berg Collection, New York Public Library; the Fales Library, New York University; Robert A. Tibbetts of the Ohio State University Libraries; Hilary Cummings at the University of Oregon Library; Lucille C. Dunne, secretary for the alumni, Park Tudor School, Indianapolis; Jean F. Preston of Special Collections, the Harvey S. Firestone Library, Princeton University; Judith L. Ratcliffe of the *Ridgefield Press;* Louisa Bowen, David Koch, and Elizabeth Neally at the Morris Library, Southern Illinois University at Carbondale; Cathy Henderson, the Harry Ransom Research Center, University of Texas, Austin; Nancy Mackechnie, Mary McCarthy Papers, Vassar College Library; the Beinecke Library, Yale University.

To the incomparable Thora Girke, secretary to the Department of English, Union College, for her years of devotion, and to her able and good-humored staff of students, especially Lori Estes, Gregory Faye, Sara Fike, Andrea Goldberg, Kathleen Glastetter, and Shawn Morton. I would also like to thank the Interlibrary Loan staff of Shaffer Library, Union College, and the Union College Humanities Faculty Development Committee for their consistent and generous financial support of this book.

To my colleague William Murphy, for the admirable example he set as well as his unstinting encouragement and interest; to Merton M. Sealts for his unabated warmth and enthusiasm; to Walter B. Rideout for thoughtfully sending me his first edition of *The Cubical City;* to the Mellon Foundation and the New York University Humanities Council for sponsoring a Humanities Seminar for Visiting Scholars; to Professor Kenneth Silverman, who expertly led the seminar with gentle, probing questions; and to all the other biographers there, true and generous comrades.

To my friend Kathleen Hill, who commented with characteristic sensitivity on early portions of the manuscript. To Rosemarie and Peter Heinegg, for their innumerable kindnesses and the room of my own. To those new friends I was fortunate enough to make because of this project.

To the family of Janet Flanner, a special debt of gratitude. In particular, her sister, the late Hildegarde Flanner Monhoff, with her shrewd sense of the past, re-created much of her early childhood, made sure that various records were available to me, and answered letters and telephone calls without hesitation. Her son, John Monhoff, literally opened his house to my husband and me for several days and offered not only his invaluable private collection of papers but also his warm hospitality and genial support. This book would have been impossible without the consideration, generosity, and indulgence of both Mr. Monhoff and his mother.

To Brian Gallagher, for his friendship over the years and, in particular, for introducing me to Elise Goodman, my agent, whose enthusiasm is largely responsible for the birth of this project.

At Ticknor & Fields, to Katrina Kenison for her consistently constructive criticism and, more than anything, for her vision; to Cork Smith and Frances Kiernan, for their consistently sound advice and their ability to make Katrina's decision to leave publishing easier to bear; to Laurie Parsons, for her invaluable assistance with photographs; and to Peg Anderson, for her scrupulous and skilled copy editing, my deepest thanks.

And most of all to my husband, Michael Dellaira, that perceptive and tough reader, the tireless answerer of tiring questions, a kind friend and fellow traveler, a man of wit and wisdom and unfailing laughter.

Genêt

1

Young Girl
1892-1909

They say that my grandmother often picked you
And placed your quaint perfume
At her tight girdle.

My grandmother
Did Vergil into French
And then had seven children.

. . . I shall not pick you,
Dianthus.

"Young Girl," Hildegarde Flanner, 1921

A T THE TURN of the century, the houses of Indianapolis's prosperous middle class lined the broad streets stretching fashion-
ably north of the city's center. Here Frank and Mary Flanner lived
among lace curtains, fringed lamps, plaster busts, and portieres; here
Janet, their second daughter, was born on March 13, 1892. Six years
later the Flanners moved ten blocks farther north on Pennsylvania
Street to a larger, better-located home, where they stayed but a year.
Just before their third daughter, June Hildegarde, was born, in 1899,
the family moved again, this time to a stately new house with ten

acres of cherry orchard on North Meridian Street, at the northern-most edge of the city. They were an upwardly mobile family.

The three Flanner girls grew up in a household very much like that of their neighbors: staid, at least in its public demeanor; committed to the conventional pieties; and loyal to the unrelenting optimism William Dean Howells dubbed the "smiling aspects of American life." Their city, known as the "Athens of the Midwest," was civic-minded, proud, and increasingly prosperous. The discovery of natural gas in central Indiana had largely counteracted the frightening results of the Panic of 1873. And if one's financial future wasn't altogether certain, the modestly wealthy middle class could always anchor itself in its refined sense of culture. One could live comfortably in Indianapolis. There were clubs and professional organizations, theater, music, and edifying public lectures. In the summer one could go boating; in the winter, skate on the frozen canals.

Frank Flanner, Janet's father, a stocky man, not too tall, bald, and sporting a very large, bristly mustache, was known as a congenial fellow of "profound human sympathy."[1] In photographs his bright but doleful eyes stare directly, even a bit pleadingly, at the camera. According to Janet's sister Hildegarde, their father possessed a good mind, was generous, and wanted the best that money could buy for his family, his friends, and his community. So, too, did the beautiful, sensitive, and cultivated Mary Ellen Hockett Flanner, Janet's mother, who schooled her daughters in English poetry and good manners, admonishing them to enunciate clearly and make sure they always carried a clean handkerchief. In her photographs Mary Flanner looks straight into the camera, meeting the viewer with an intense stare. Or, posing demurely, she holds a flower to her face, her eyes cast downward.

Stepping out, the Flanners made a handsome pair — Frank in his top hat and high collar, Mary in elaborate dresses made to order by George Philip Meier, a renowned Indianapolis designer. Both were respected, active members of the community. Frank belonged to the Taxpayers' League, the Commercial Club, the Knights of Pythias, and, later, to the Columbia Club and the Indiana Gun Club; Mary, to the Art Association and the Women's Research Club. But she was best known as a published poet who directed amateur performances and tableaux vivants at the YMCA.

At home Frank and Mary provided their three daughters with all the advantages they could afford. The girls were given music lessons — Janet was "put to" the violin, said Hildegarde, but the lessons didn't "take."[2] Mary Emma, Janet's older sister by five years, was an accomplished pianist and was sent for a few years to a boarding school where she rode her own horse. "We all had a wonderful childhood," recalled Hildegarde. "We were not rich, and we were not poor. And we did not lead dull lives. Mother was always putting on some kind of dramatic performance for family and friends, and Father had taste and liked to buy things, imported things, which he considered beautiful."[3]

Frank Flanner earned a modest income, Hildegarde claimed, in real estate speculation. Janet told most people the same thing, proudly recalling the settlement house he had helped start. What the Flanner sisters often neglected to add was that their father earned his living primarily as a mortician. His establishment, owned jointly with his brother-in-law Charles J. Buchanan, was considered to be Indianapolis's finest. Flanner and Buchanan ran the public ambulance service and owned the only crematory in the state. An item in a local paper indicates its prominence: "A newcomer to our fair city asked what she might do to become adjusted socially and correctly in our city. The reply was join the Riviera Club, send your children to Mrs. Gates' Dancing School, and be buried by Flanner and Buchanan."[4]

In 1905, when Janet was thirteen, the Flanners left the cherry orchard and moved closer to the city's center, first to an apartment and then to a new home on North Capitol Street. As far as the community could tell, the move marked no change in their fortunes. All three girls were attending Tudor Hall, a respected private school; their mother was by then well known as a poet, playwright, and graceful platform reader; and Frank was actively involved in the settlement house named for him. In 1910 the entire family went to live in Berlin for a year, a move that involved considerable expense. But on February 17, 1912, some six months after their return to Indianapolis, the community was shocked to learn that Frank Flanner had killed himself in his own mortuary.

When Frank Flanner died, his mother, Orpha Annette Tyler Flanner, was eighty-eight and had outlived all but one of her seven children.

More than half a century earlier she had lost her husband, Henry Beeson Flanner, to the Civil War. Janet remembered her much-loved grandmother as a wonderful storyteller who entertained her children and grandchildren with tales of her eccentric husband and his odd relatives. Young Janet devoured the stories, in which Orpha usually was the central figure. Born in 1824 in Penn Yan, New York, to the respectable Dr. William Tyler and his wife Sarah, the black-eyed baby grew to be a restless, rebellious child — inquisitive, intrepid, and often in trouble with her mother, who disapproved of Orpha's "shameful" behavior. Orpha asked too many questions and talked to too many strangers. Her father, a stubborn man, was willing to punish his entire family to restrain her. One night Orpha and her cousin cut off her long hair and tossed the curls out the window. The next morning Dr. Tyler found his daughter's tresses, which he loved, scattered about the front yard. Although the family was about to move from Penn Yan to North Carolina, he refused to leave until Orpha's hair had grown back.[5]

Eventually the Tyler family settled in the Quaker community of Raysville in Henry County, Indiana, and Orpha was sent to the Indianapolis Female Institute, run by the Misses Axtell. Although the Axtell sisters taught mathematics, natural sciences, history, English, music, drawing, and foreign languages, Orpha mostly remembered that for several hours each day the schoolgirls were tied to a wooden plank to correct their posture and were frequently reminded to pronounce their "prunes and prisms" to bring a beautiful expression to the lips. But after her first term Orpha sadly returned home with poor marks in carriage and deportment. Weeping, she had begged her implacable teachers to change her grades, but they would not compromise their high standards.

Orpha's sorrow was quickly forgotten when she met her family's young boarder, Henry Flanner, who had come to Raysville in 1842 to teach school. The twenty-one-year-old Quaker got along well with the Tylers, finding them "quite an intelligent family, polite and obliging."[6] By the end of June 1843, he and Orpha were married and had returned to the place of Henry's birth, Mount Pleasant, Ohio. Orpha eagerly anticipated the move, for she despised Indiana; according to her daughter, "she felt it was a disgrace to live there, so uncouth and uncultured were the people."[7] But Orpha didn't find life among the

Quakers of Ohio much better. She was expected to feed and lodge everyone — as many as forty people — who came to the famous yearly meeting, even though Henry had been expelled from the group for having married her. And the young couple had moved in with Henry's two aunts, Rebecca and Annie Beeson, who had raised him. The family story was that upon seeing the infant Henry shortly after he was born, the sisters were so delighted that they took him home and never brought him back.[8]

The aunts had set up housekeeping together on a small farm. According to Orpha, Rebecca Beeson had been married to a "ne'er do well," Isaac Brown, and Annie Beeson had repeatedly refused all her prospective suitors, including the eleven who proposed after she was sixty. Devoted Quaker preachers, the two sisters looked forward to the yearly meeting as the social event of the season. Preening in front of the mirror, they would take hours to dress. When they were finally satisfied with themselves and their bonnets, the two gangling sisters would leave for meeting, where they stood for hours with their knees bent so as not to appear too tall.

The sisters raised Henry as their own until he was old enough to attend the nearby Friends' boarding school, well known for its rigid supervision of children. Henry was something less than a model student. Loving music and not comfortable with the strict Quaker regimen, he would sneak out each night to practice his fiddle, hidden in a nearby barn. When he learned of a concert to be held in Wheeling, West Virginia, he would climb out his window and down a nearby tree, walk ten miles to the ferry, and then cross the Ohio River to hear it. Soon his classmates were following him out the window to the barn, where Henry taught them to play various instruments. Such behavior did not long escape the notice of the Quaker teachers. Henry was frequently punished, but his aunts' intervention (and their community standing) kept him from being expelled outright.

After Henry brought Orpha back to Mount Pleasant to live, they spent much of their time on horseback, combing the countryside for specimens of unusual plants. Orpha recalled that Henry worked in the fields part of the day — he wasn't much of a farmer — and then the two of them would gather and then press and catalogue their plants. They named their first child Linnaeus after the Swedish botanist, they corresponded with naturalist Asa Gray, and they branched out into entomology. They grew potatoes, harvested apples and grapes, and after supper played the violin and piano. In the evenings, they gathered around the fire to instruct the children in Latin, Greek, and French. Henry was especially fond of Homer. But the Flanners were in constant and ever-increasing debt, and the family was growing. Pregnant for almost all of the first seven years of her marriage, Orpha gave birth to five children in quick succession; in 1854 the sixth, Janet's father, named William Frank after Dr. Tyler, was born.

Restless, Henry decided that his ambitions needed wider scope. He dreamed of starting an academy to "help the world to knowledge and inspire a greater love for fine things of life."[9] In 1856, when Frank was two, Henry booked passage on the steamer "Silver Wave," bound for St. Louis, to look for a community in need of teachers. Settling on Dent County in the border state of Missouri, he bought five hundred acres of land. The following year, the property in Mount Pleasant was sold, and Orpha, the six children, and Aunt Annie (Aunt Rebecca had died) moved to the Missouri property, where Orpha and Henry planned to build the Lake Spring School.

The Flanners — or at least Henry — might have satisfied their ambitions in Missouri had they arrived either much earlier or much later. The community they had come to educate was sympathetic neither to their admiration for Lincoln nor to their northern values. Less than four years later, the Flanners, now with seven children, were back in Mount Pleasant. As Henry reported it, "As Lincoln's election approached, days of trouble came! Free state men could not obtain justice in the courts. Some were run off. Others persecuted. Specks in the political horizon, gave evident Signs of a great Struggle Between the North and South. We could not sell, trade, or do anything but *leave*. . . . Things grew worse and more so, daily! I had lost my health, a sun stroke was near fatal. We all (my family) escaped with our *Lives!* nothing more."[10]

In fact, Henry was given twenty-four hours to vacate the premises or be tarred and feathered. When the family returned to Mount Pleasant, they were scorned by the Quaker community. "Say what you please of Quakers," said Frank's sister Anna many years later, "they do respect wealth, and here was my father who had sold his property and squandered it on a fool's errand, on a hair-brained mission in Missouri and now returned with nothing and seven children. Who was to care for them! Friends of former days refused to speak to them. My mother was always greatly embittered because of this treatment. They did not think my father had done a commendable thing in trying to help other people, and life was made very hard for him."[11]

Henry, in desperation, accepted a conscripted neighbor's offer: he would be paid $525 to enlist in the Union army as a substitute. He hoped to be a bandmaster — or at least play the fife. But less than six months after being sworn in, he fell ill. His feet and legs swelled, and he coughed all through the night. In a letter to Orpha he mourned the fate of his children: "Poor babies . . . I regret that their father is worthless."[12] He begged his wife to "cling to your money as to Life. It is everything in this world," adding, "I am a Broken down Wreck of manhood, of no use to any body, and a *hate* to myself." Completely demoralized, he was discharged and sent home to Mount Pleasant, where he died in May 1863.

Orpha and her children were left destitute. She could not claim the property in Missouri, because Morgan's Raiders had burned the courthouse where the deed was filed; she did not receive Henry's army pay because his unit had been disbanded. Living in Mount Pleasant among God-fearing Quakers was becoming increasingly intolerable. Her brother wrote from Indianapolis to say that she should move there, hinting that Henry had been another ne'er-do-well. Glad to leave Mount Pleasant, Orpha took her children, except for the two oldest, Linnaeus and Albert, to Indianapolis, believing that she would find a job teaching botany and music. When that failed, she opened a boardinghouse on the corner of New York and Meridian streets and began trying to sell her beloved herbarium to raise money. Years later her daughter Anna wrote that despite its poverty and privations, her childhood had been a happy one. But it's not hard to imagine the difficulties the Flanner children faced — Anna herself was teased by the other children in town about having to take in boarders; she felt embarrassed that her bread was sweetened with brown sugar, not white.[13] Charles was working his way through high school, hoping to go to college, and Orpha hardly had time for her youngest children, Tyler, Frank, and Anna, who were tended by their kind-hearted sister Emma until she married and went to live in Georgia.

Frank and Anna helped around the boardinghouse as much as possible. Frank would rise early to deliver papers and then return home to sweep the halls, porch, and sidewalk before serving the boarders their breakfast. After school he delivered papers again and then carried coal to the boarders' rooms. Saturdays he worked all day. By the time he was sixteen, he had dropped out of school, but he continued to study Latin so that he could begin teaching it. He and Tyler took charge when Orpha went to Georgia to visit their pregnant sister Emma.

In 1872 the family suffered two more blows. First, Emma, living in Georgia with her husband, died during childbirth. The young Flanner children, especially Frank, had adored their older sister, who had given them the maternal attention Orpha could never afford. Orpha, who had gone to Emma's to help with the birth, decided, grieving, to stay on. No one in the family was able to explain what happened next, or exactly when it happened, but Tyler took ill with influenza and feverishly wandered off, never to be seen again. These tragedies clearly affected Orpha, who decided to renounce her former life. In a long document consecrating herself to the service of the Lord, she declared her herbarium a product of sin, since she had broken the Holy Sabbath days to collect her plants. Praying that all her "deep-seated bitterness" be changed to love, she offered up to the Lord her knowledge of flowers, as well as each of her children, as proof of her devotion. Orpha returned to Indianapolis in 1874. Frank, the only Flanner son left in Indianapolis, continued to support his mother and his sister. A personable young man, able to quote Homer with ease, he would spend the rest of his life almost desperately trying to bring wealth, comfort, and stability to his family. By all external measures, he was quite successful.

Whether he recognized it or not, Frank Flanner had seen the character of his country change. He had been born on a midwestern farm where goods, from homespun to crops, were produced primarily for home consumption. When he returned with his family to Ohio after their sojourn in Missouri, he came back to circumstances changed not only by his father's failed mission and questionable community standing, but by the fact that midwestern farming could no longer exist as it had. The railroads, as well as an intricate system of waterways, brought new markets for farmers, new machinery, new forms of consolidation. When the Flanners moved from owning their land to renting, they were moving, like so many others, away from the world of the small independent farmer into the world of commercial trade.

By 1890 electricity was being used to power the streetcars of Indianapolis, a model city, which, as one resident put it, was now growing more like a sturdy oak than a mushroom.[14] To a young city dweller, reared on hard work and self-reliance, material success must have seemed the inevitable reward for business savvy mixed with a bit of virtue and cultivation. Frank Flanner had reason to hope that one day he would be able to assert himself as a modestly well-to-do, charitable, and cultured citizen. By owning his own business and by attaching himself to land — not for agriculture but for profit — he could realize the dreams that were not, ultimately, unlike his idealistic father's.

Once his sister Anna finished high school and began to teach, Frank set about acquiring a business of his own. The Kregelo family took him in as an apprentice to his chosen trade of undertaking. How the would-be Latin teacher became interested in this line of work is not known, but certainly he was familiar with the issues of poverty, death, and burial. One of the first things Orpha had done in Indianapolis was to buy a small plot in the well-groomed Crown Hill Cemetery. This gesture, by a woman who had barely a penny to her name, may well have influenced Frank, who later determined that everyone, rich or poor, must receive a decent burial, no matter how little they were able to spend on a casket.[15] In any event, using some of his mother's Civil War pension, Frank went into partnership with John Hommoun in 1881 to run the city ambulance and bury the city's dead. When his sister Anna married Charles Buchanan in 1884, he invited his brother-in-law to buy out Hommoun's share and join him in the undertaking business. The firm became Flanner and Buchanan.

After Anna married, Frank continued to live with his mother, and again they decided to take in boarders. In 1886 twenty-three-year-old Mary Ellen Hockett, a birthright Quaker from Muncie, Indiana, arrived. Frank, with his future secure, proposed to her not long after; on June 2, 1886, he wed the lovely former schoolteacher, who had come to Indianapolis with her own dreams of success. Exactly nine months later, their first child, named for Mary herself and Frank's nurturing sister Emma, was born.

Little is known of Mary's earlier years. However, it seems clear that she rather resented family life and didn't easily take to motherhood, considering it the major obstacle to her career.[16] And despite her Quaker upbringing, she had long dreamed of the theater. The makeshift school productions of her youth had shown her how glamour, passion, and high-toned seriousness could attach to the small compass of the stage. She never quite forgot how it felt to star as Little Eva, and no Quaker scruple would ever deter her, she decided. That she was often told she possessed theatrical talent, poise, and beauty simply reinforced her determination. "She was a religious woman," commented her daughter Hildegarde dryly, "whose true vocation was the theatre."[17]

A real professional opportunity apparently came her way sometime after Mary moved to Indianapolis, but she turned it down. According to Hildegarde, her mother "had the good sense to know that she was no Sarah Bernhardt," but Janet, using biographical events in her novel *The Cubical City,* suggested that her mother met Frank the same winter she was given a chance at the footlights, distracting her from her true vocation.[18] Not everyone in the community agreed that Mary had so easily put aside her ambitions.[19] The family's neighbors on North Pennsylvania Street believed "Mrs. Flanner always felt the world had missed a great tragedienne actress when she failed to tread the boards."[20]

Mary herself occasionally blamed her children: her "three talented daughters," she often told Hildegarde, had "robbed her of all her talent."[21] This clearly made an impression on the daughters. Janet, for one, told her mother much later that since children had ruined her mother's life, she would not have any.[22] In saying this she probably managed to conciliate her mother — and to punish her at the same time.

Mary was a woman in conflict. A study in contrasts, she was demanding, intelligent, ambitious, and disgusted by anything improper, carnal, or fleshy — even the sight of meat on her plate. She wanted her daughters to be educated and believed they should set their goals as high as possible. She wanted for them what she was unable to obtain for herself — a wider world, a larger audience, a bigger theater for her aspirations — but her fears made her cling to a position she disliked, that of wife and mother. And so she depended on the proprieties she rebelled against.

After marriage, she continued to write poems and publish them in local papers — some of her poetry was later included in *Poets and Poetry of Indiana* (1900) — and she did not entirely relinquish the theater. Although not destined to become another Maude Adams, she did all she could to bring the great names of the theater to the smaller circle of Indianapolis. She began to write and produce one-act plays, and she left home now and then to study voice and speech in Chicago, Madison, Cincinnati, and Boston. Eventually she was booked by a professional agency to give platform readings of Shakespeare, Browning, and a sampling of her own poems in states as far away as Texas.

Mary vented some of her frustrations with family life in her one-act comic plays. In one of them, *Bargain Day,* published by Samuel French in 1911, she satirized the tranquil life of an average middle-class couple. Hamilton McDowell, an "ordinary business man," is forced to come home for lunch because the downtown restaurants are jammed with conventioneers, tourists, and foolish shoppers lured by "idiotic bargain sales."[23] His routine disrupted, he can't understand why his wife, Nellie, "a sweet little home body," isn't there to feed him. Nellie soon appears, laden with bundles, and shows her impatient husband the spoils of her spree. Then she and Hamilton discover to their horror that Nellie, in her shopping frenzy, left their baby at the department store.

The story ends happily. The overwrought couple calls the store, and the baby is soon delivered by a messenger with a heavy German accent. But the play is not over until the McDowells learn more about the implications of their folly. The messenger, carrying two children, one white and one black, insists that the McDowells couldn't possibly be the parents of the child they claim. "I haf a white one and a black one but I hain't got me no dago!" he declares, refusing to give up their baby. Understanding, the McDowells straighten their clothes and smooth their mussed hair to prove they are, after all, fit

parents. The messenger then gives them their child, and in relief the
McDowells take a solemn vow. Nellie will never go bargain hunting
again, and Hamilton won't come home for lunch.

It's obvious Mary Flanner rebelled against the domestic role al-
located her. Yet to resist it, she herself frequently hid behind a
childishness somewhat like Nellie's while remaining quite aware of
the power of plaintive fragility. However, her mother-in-law, a self-
proclaimed "tough old squaw" who preferred sleeping by herself in
a tent to sharing a cottage on the summer property of her children,
regarded her daughter-in-law as lax and flighty and was apparently
not shy about saying so, much to the annoyance of Mary.[24] After the
first months of Frank and Mary's marriage, Orpha went to live with
the more congenial Buchanans, who also disapproved of Mary. But
the two families were close, united by business and by the strong
affection between Frank and his sister Anna and their devotion to
their mother. When Janet's family moved to the new house on North
Meridian Street, Frank immediately set Orpha's family shield in the
stained glass window above the hand-carved black walnut stairway.

The Flanners and the Buchanans mutually owned property at Tippecanoe Lake, where they spent summers together, and they shared
the tastes of their social set: they respected foreign culture, they
traveled, they attended church, they patronized the arts. Mary sometimes held her amateur theatricals in the Buchanans' ballroom. These
were the circumstances into which Janet Flanner was born.

As a child, Janet was well acquainted with her mother's frustrations.
If she misbehaved, her mother would lock the mischievous five-year-
old in the closet, which fortunately had a window. The neighbors on
that side of the Pennsylvania Street house could see the tearful little
girl and would quickly come next door to try to get her released.
Mary Emma and Janet, calling these neighbors Aunt and Uncle,
found them warmer and kinder than their sometimes regal and always
histrionic mother.

Janet was a precocious child, outspoken and strong-willed, who
liked to do things her own way. By the time the family moved to
Meridian Street, when Janet was seven, she knew how to shoot a
rifle. Her father had given her one, and she could shoot a snake or
a flying squirrel, skin it, and dry the skin. Once at Christmastime,

the turkey for Christmas dinner escaped and flew up to the tower of her aunt's house. No one knew what to do or how to get it down until Janet came along. She aimed, as always, to hit the middle, and brought the dinner down. In this and everything she did, her sister claimed, she was precise, concentrated, and to the point.[25]

The first seven years of Janet's life were exciting ones for the prospering Flanners. Mary was writing poetry, and Frank was busy with local civic affairs. Reared on tales of his father's and grandfather's missionary zeal and sensitivity to social injustice, he was open to the reformist spirit of his times. When Booker T. Washington, already recognized nationally, arrived in Indianapolis in 1896, he was denied accommodations at the downtown hotels. The Flanners, hearing of this outrage, invited him to be their house guest — even though this meant certain ostracization from local social clubs. Janet well remembered the pain this caused her father. She also remembered that the Flanners' black servant, whom Mary dismissed for refusing to serve their guest, decided to stay when he heard that Washington was famous. Sitting that night on Washington's knee, Janet privately thought that he was kind but ugly; when he asked her if she was afraid of him because he was very, very black, the four-year-old promptly asked why she should be — that made no difference.[26]

When approached in 1898 with the idea of establishing a settlement house for the blacks of the community, Frank, an ardent admirer of Lincoln, was clearly receptive. He set aside some land of his own for the project and gathered a group of men, including Franklin Vonnegut and Colonel Eli Lilly, to help finance it. The settlement project, first located in the small double house that Frank had donated, faltered during its first few years from lack of funds and leadership, but its struggle only strengthened its founders' belief in "sacrifice and steadfastness of purpose coupled with vision and progressive planning for the future."[27] The early Flanner House — the name was changed when it incorporated in 1903 — included a day-care center, where the children were cared for by women in white aprons; a hand laundry so that people would not have to stand outside in the mud or freezing cold to do their wash; and a rudimentary employment agency. One summer it provided stoves and kitchen space for canning produce.

Frank Flanner and his family were proud of the project, which seemed to be fulfilling its stated objectives: "the promotion of the social, moral and physical welfare of Negroes, particularly the young, in the establishment, and the pursuit of such philanthropy among Negroes as the trustees of the corporation deem practicable." In 1909 he donated additional property, but when he wanted to put in a "milk station" for the babies left there, the women laughed at him, saying, "Mr. Flanner, we've got plenty of our own for those babies."[28] Or so his daughter Janet later remembered, recalling the incident with both pride and amusement. Although she doesn't seem to have disparaged her father's social values, with their overtones of moral uplift, she was quite sensitive to an almost insulated quality in him, a refusal to think hard and practically about his schemes and their meaning. She had learned two of Orpha's lessons well: to respect hard-working women who fended for themselves and to mistrust starry-eyed idealism, even her own.

When Frank backed an invention that was something like a primitive computer, Janet pointed out to him that such a machine would cost thousands of bank clerks their jobs; he replied that he hadn't thought of that.[29] Whether or not she remembered these incidents accurately, they suggest Janet's wariness of her father's abstract schemes and their impractical applications. They made him remote, even comical. But Janet's remarks also suggest that she wanted to be regarded as more worldly than her father, whom she admired but perhaps perceived as not altogether fitted for this world.

The Flanner girls grew up fully aware of their father's business, but they seem to have been uncomfortable with it. According to one relative, children of funeral directors were frequently teased by other children and made to feel ashamed. Another relative heard that Mary herself was embarrassed by Frank's work and that her daughters adopted her feelings.[30] Although Mary of course knew his profession when she married him, she grew increasingly self-conscious and urged him to retire from it. This may have been the reason for Frank's speculative investments and his constant drive to make more money, even though the business was quite successful. Friends of the Flanners thought that Frank spent a good deal of time trying to please Mary.[31] Frank's business, they surmised, conflicted with Mary's aspirations and created an unrelenting friction between the couple.

In any case, in later life Frank's daughters often failed to name

Flanner and Buchanan as the source of their family's income, even though they knew that Frank was credited with having instituted many reforms in the business and was well known throughout the state. And his work did provide the Flanners with a comfortable way of life, with summers spent in Florida on property he owned or at the family cottage on Tippecanoe Lake, where they staged large Fourth of July celebrations and pageants.

When they moved to their country home on North Meridian Street, Frank typically would rise at six in the morning, before the others. From their separate bedrooms, his daughters could hear him preparing for work, singing some strange song about the fate of a whale that swallowed a torpedo fish. If Mary wasn't on the platform circuit, she would complete the domestic chores with the assistance of a cook, a laundress, and the family's groom. Later she might disappear into the sewing room, shut the door, and write or practice voice techniques. Twice a year a seamstress would come and stay for weeks at a time to help Mary prepare a new wardrobe for her readings. Then, having planned her program, she would leave on tour, determined that marriage and motherhood would not completely thwart her career.[32]

The girls seldom played together, being far apart in age, but as soon as they were old enough, whether they liked it or not, they were conscripted into Mary's home theater. Janet remembered playing the male leads. Grandmother Orpha generally disapproved of such frivolity. When she saw Janet appear in one production as a Principal Moonbeam Dancer, she admonished Mary about the number of petticoats the child was wearing: " 'Not enough,' snapped Grandmother. 'Too many,' snapped Mother."[33] The tension between Mary and Orpha was as real as Orpha's unswerving devotion to old-fashioned decorum. Janet was quickly learning that despite her mother's devotion to manners and convention, Mary was a renegade in her own way.

Janet's sister Mary Emma bowed out of these productions as early as she could. She changed her name to Marie before she was sixteen to declare her independence, and she insisted that the name be pronounced as if it rhymed with "starry." By all accounts she was an unhappy child, moody and withdrawn, perhaps jealous of her annoying younger sisters. And according to Hildegarde, Marie and

Janet shared some of the same traits, which didn't endear them to each other — they were both strong-minded, willful, and opinionated.[34] Their mother was not a very affectionate woman, and since she was quite ambivalent about the children who kept her at home, her first two daughters frequently found themselves competing for top billing. At an early age Janet learned to hold the family's attention when she talked, much as she herself was held spellbound by the stories of her grandmother Orpha. But it was the studious and musical Marie on whom the family first seemed to pin its expectations. And this was no doubt daunting to a girl who was so sensitive to criticism in her later life that she could not perform long-practiced piano pieces in public. Eventually she chose the Buchanans as her allies, and they returned her affection.

Marie, it seems, was closer to her father than to her mother and two sisters. As a small child, Hildegarde regarded her with fear and envy. Marie was occasionally left in charge when Mary traveled, and Hildegarde thought her eldest sister a tyrant: she complained to her friends at school that she'd been so frightened by her angry sister that she was afraid to go upstairs and fetch a red belt for her dress.[35]

If Janet too was domineering, she was also tender-hearted and generous to Hildegarde. Janet loved the small sister who, unlike Marie, was sweet and pretty and compliant. And she admired Hildegarde's literary gifts and believed that her baby sister's first sentence told of Macbeth's meeting with the witches: "They met me in the day of success." Hildegarde, however, remembered that she learned the line a few years later to win the approval and applause of what she called her "often chilly family."[36] Known as Baby for many years and treated accordingly, Hildegarde spent much of her life trying to please her mother, who, after being widowed, grew increasingly dependent on her youngest daughter.

Janet also was not indifferent to Mary's approval. Like Hildegarde, she knew at an early age that verbal cleverness was a way to win her mother's love and esteem. Janet was fascinated with words, which afforded access to the mysterious world of books her mother so loved. When Mary asked her what she wanted to be when she grew up, Janet answered quickly that she wanted to write. Mary, though momentarily delighted by her daughter's answer, asked the five-year-old to spell the word "author." Janet was stumped. And for many years afterward, Janet bent obligingly to Mary's will, ready to become the actress her mother wanted her to be.

Mary's emphasis on correct enunciation provided Janet with a victory of sorts during her first day at public school. She was the only one who knew how to pronounce the word "honor"; that she couldn't define it diminished some of her triumph but not her pride in her performance, which she recalled even sixty years later.[37] In the second grade she impressed the school authorities with her ability to read whatever was put before her with breathless, childish skill. Her father, less impressed, insisted she forgo the rewards of such precociousness and refused to allow his daughter instant promotion to the next grade, since she was weak in what he considered to be the basics of education: arithmetic and penmanship.

It was Frank who decided in 1903 that Janet, at age eleven, should leave public school and attend the newly opened, private preparatory school Tudor Hall. Marie, then in boarding school, and Hildegarde, when old enough, would eventually join her there. Frank was impressed with Fredonia Allen, the school's owner and first principal, as well as the Reverend James Cumming Smith of the Tabernacle Presbyterian Church, the school's first dean, who wished never to lose "sight of the broader aspect of education, . . . to prepare students for life" and, in particular, for college. Intent on bringing "the culture of the East to the Midwest," Fredonia Allen hired teachers from eastern schools and carefully supervised a program for her commuting and resident students. They attended concerts given by visiting orchestras, such as the Pittsburgh or Boston Symphony; went to the opera and theater to see *Madama Butterfly, Hamlet,* or *Ben-Hur;* attended teas, luncheons, and dances; and after the San Francisco earthquake of 1906 they held a euchre party to raise money for the victims.[38]

Dressed in a blue serge sailor suit known as a Peter Thompson, wearing black lisle stockings and high laced shoes, Janet Flanner looked like all the other girls. But unlike them, she wore a large white ribbon in her long hair as if to call attention to the chestnut-colored waves. She did not consider herself good-looking, lamenting especially the large nose her grandmother had said was her Tyler legacy, but she knew she had pretty feet and legs. And her long hair was important enough for her to protest its docking by developing a terrible earache. Her classmates, learning this, teased her, certain that they would not hurt her feelings, for Janet was known as a good sport. She was popular and lively, full of fun, high spirits, and sly humor.

At Tudor Hall Janet became increasingly aware of the subtle hallmarks of class. Social divisions were finely drawn between rich and not-so-rich, and the girls were conscious of every distinction between the cultured and the crass. To those who had enough money, what counted was refinement. For example, it was generally known that the Fletcher children (of the Fletcher National Bank and Trust) came to school in a muddy trap from the wrong side of town — despite their wealth.[39] Janet, however, rode to school each day in a well-painted, shiny pony cart bearing her monogram, J.T.F., which secured her position, at least externally, and gave her a vantage point from which she could discern the sham of vulgar wealth.

Janet's tethered pony patiently waited for its mistress, who, once inside the schoolroom, was made to read from the Bible for ten minutes before studying history or French or German or Latin. Janet fondly remembered her Cornell-trained Latin teacher, Miss Ann Browning Butler, who put the students to work constructing replicas of Julius Caesar's bridges in the assembly hall. They learned English grammar by diagramming sentences, which enchanted Janet; she later believed that her own writing style owed much to this logical training, although others attributed it to her mother's fine spoken prose.[40]

Janet liked Tudor Hall. Her grades were not high during her first years, but later she did moderately well in rhetoric and composition as well as in English literature. She disliked mathematics and, like her grandmother, never got high marks in deportment. But she often appeared in the class plays; she was on the basketball team; and in 1905 she was president of her class. Not as scholarly as her sister Marie, Janet had other interests. When she was fifteen, a Tudor Hall publication presented her story "The Adventures of Mynheer, the Prefect of Police, and the Guinea Pig," as a fine example of composition. The story was, in fact, a fine example of adolescence. In it Janet satirized authority and avenged herself on anyone who still did not think her an adult; she rewarded the commonsensical maturity of a young boy while ridiculing his pompous cousin the prefect. No one, Janet seemed to be saying, not her parents or her teachers or her sister Marie or her older cousins, could label her a child any longer.

Janet was sensitive not only to the earmarks of authority and class but also to the gloomy and often hypocritical moralizing that seemed to accompany good social standing. Among the worst offenders were the pious, well-heeled Protestants of Indianapolis, an important part of the city's social hierarchy. She long remembered the stiff, boring Sundays in the company of Bible-thumping relatives, who struck her as self-righteous and repressed, devoid of anything warm or human. Neither of Janet's parents, however, was strict in religious beliefs and practices. Mary Flanner cherished her Quaker legacy and disliked the stricter Protestantism of her mother-in-law Orpha and her Sunday school teacher sister-in-law, Anna Buchanan.

And Frank Flanner seemed to be a man in search of an orthodoxy. He left the Third Presbyterian Church, which he had joined in his youth, for the Mayflower Congregationalists, but he and Mary were won away from them by the Reverend Oscar McCulloch, pastor of the Plymouth Congregationalists and a brilliant orator. This articulate and inspirational spokesman of "light and life," as Frank called it, touched him with his passionate concern for justice in the here-and-now. "I am come," he would preach, "that they may have life, and that they might have it more abundantly." The Plymouth Congregationalists' liberal reconciliation of business, charity, worship, and evolution was attractive to Frank. And men like McCulloch inspired him with their humanitarian zeal, their feelings of responsibility toward the underprivileged, and their almost obsessional zest for work. President of the Indiana Benevolent Society and author of several reform bills, McCulloch helped establish the Children's Aid Society, a nurses' training center, and the Dime Savings and Loan — all before he collapsed and died from overwork at the age of forty-eight.

Janet said she lost her faith at fourteen, in 1906, when she began to consider herself an adult, different from her family and critical of them. Faith in their infallibility was doubtless the faith she lost. At about this same time the Flanner family fortunes were changing, even though superficially the changes seemed slight. They were moving; Marie was taken out of boarding school and enrolled in Tudor Hall; and Frank Flanner gave up the Congregational church for the Second Church of Christ Science. He seemed to move from church

to church as often as he traded houses. Despite his connections to
city and family, he had a homeless quality, which Janet apparently
sensed. To the community he was still an outgoing, thoughtful, and
jovial man, but those close to him could see that all was not well.
Word slowly leaked out that the Flanners' marriage was strained and
that Frank, tired, overworked, and very nervous, was speculating
with his money and often losing.

In later life Janet rarely spoke of these years except as a time of
great confusion, which came, no doubt, from her growing awareness
of her parents' troubles as much as from her own adolescence.
Around this time she developed another earache and then a severe
backache, which mysteriously plagued her until her first year of college.[41] She still appeared as energetic as ever. No one would guess
that at night her mother applied countless mustard plasters or that
the cook put a boiled onion in her ear to help relieve the pain.

According to Hildegarde, Janet was popular and well liked, a constant center of attention, and the record of her schooldays generally
confirms this. The school yearbook said of her that she "draweth the
strength of her verbosity finer than the staple of her argument." Her
picture was captioned: "Play such fantastic tricks before high Heaven/
As make the angels weep."[42] In her senior year at Tudor Hall she
became the yearbook's editor-in-chief; she participated in debates
on why girls should go to college and went to the requisite dances,
lectures, and parties. Although somewhat concerned about her
grades, which apparently disappointed her father, she had no real
reason to worry; in the spring of 1909, she marched in the commencement processional in a long white dress, carrying a long-
stemmed red rose. The pews of the Tabernacle Presbyterian Church
were decorated with large bouquets, and Hildegarde was chosen by
her sister to be a flower girl.

All the same, some crisis in the family had apparently occurred,
and Janet was aware of it. She was not going to college, at least not
right away. Somewhat unexpectedly, the Flanners had decided to
travel abroad.

2

This Hard Gemlike Flame
1910-1918

WHEN JANET RECALLED her first trip to Europe, taken when she was seventeen, she said she'd experienced something, an aesthetic delight, that she formulated as an inner promise — I shall return.[1] The trip awakened a desire, or "passionate yearning," as Janet called it later, for "the beauties of Europe, the long accretions of architecture and poetry and civilization and education, the beautiful gardens, the beautiful palaces, the towns made with what they call promenades so people can promenade about. I was consumed by this necessity, a kind of magnificent malady, a fever to take part, if only as an onlooker."[2] Her first trip abroad stirred her imagination and her feelings and awakened her to the promise of — aesthetic and sexual — pleasures, often indistinguishable from one another.

In 1909, a young Tudor Hall graduate who wasn't going directly to college and wasn't ready to marry might well go to Europe to continue her education. This is what Marie Flanner did. By the time Janet finished high school, Marie had been in Berlin for about a year, studying music with Mark Twain's son-in-law, Ossip Gabrulovich, a Russian pianist celebrated for his interpretation of Chopin. It was an enviable situation, and Janet would have liked to do something comparable. She hadn't made specific plans for college, though she vaguely intended to go, and she was eager to get out of Indianapolis and see the world.

Fortunately, just after she graduated, her parents decided to take the family abroad for two years. They intended to stay at Marie's pension in Berlin and then travel to France perhaps, and certainly to England. These countries, especially Germany, were those most frequently visited by their friends; discriminating Indianapolis citizens were so fond of Munich that they called it their little "Hoosier Colony."[3] Hildegarde, now ten, could study with a governess, Frank and Mary reasoned, and Frank would have a much-needed rest.

Janet was thrilled. Since childhood she'd been filled with romantic stories about Europe, home of the writers her mother so loved, the subject of countless lectures at Tudor Hall, the exotic setting for the lush popular novels of Robert Chambers. Now it had become almost tangible to the impressionable Janet, who avidly read her sister Marie's letters. Servants were sent scuttling about the house on North Capitol Avenue to ready the family for their adventure: clothes had to be ordered and packed, letters of introduction sought. Frank ordered red leather luggage for Janet. Then there were farewells and parties, and finally the day came when the four Flanners and their several trunks left for Indianapolis's noisy, cathedrallike Union Station.

Yet for all the preparations and anticipation, there was, according to Hildegarde, something ill-conceived about the trip. In retrospect she called it "not well-planned" and wondered why they stayed in Berlin so long instead of going to other cities. Marie, she said, certainly resented her family's descending on her en masse, and Frank was moody and difficult. Finally he went off to the Adriatic by himself and had what Hildegarde remembered as a "wonderful time."[4] Mary remained in Berlin but felt so awkward and displaced that she spent most of her time in her room sewing. Her only real social triumph occurred when she managed to transform one of her dresses into something décolletage, after the example of the Kaiserin, Augusta Victoria, to wear to the opera.[5]

Janet fared much better. Exhilarated by her new surroundings, and with her Tudor Hall German, she adapted to Berlin's social life much more easily than her parents did. Although she later maintained that she disliked Berlin and that its soggy, dark streets did not satisfy her hunger for beauty, the entire experience left lasting images — the Kaiser's annual military review, a lavish affair, with a zeppelin flying overhead as hysterical crowds cheered; the tortoiseshell lorgnons of what she called the "fantastically effeminate" German officers, who habitually pushed women off the street and into the gutter;[6] and a new friend, a young woman named Carlotta Nehring.

Janet disliked beer and militarism and the rudeness of soldiers, all of which she associated with Germany, but she found Carlotta, the wife of a German officer, enchanting. Little is known about Carlotta, who was apparently not much older than Janet, but Hildegarde remembered her as lovely and "fashionable" and that she and Janet spent a good deal of time together at the theater or the opera. Janet was infatuated.[7] Long after she left Berlin she carried Carlotta's picture, eventually pasting it in her scrapbook, where it stayed for the rest of her life.

The atmosphere of Berlin was unlike any Janet had experienced. All around her, sex and sexual practices were openly discussed — or exhibited — in ways unimaginable at home. Various sexual theories, particularly those of the German neuropsychiatrist Richard von Krafft-Ebing and the English writer Havelock Ellis, were being widely debated at the time. Krafft-Ebing argued that homoscxuality was a physiological disorder, not a moral one, and included lesbianism with male homosexuality in his discussions of sexual behavior. Ellis went one step further, proclaiming that homosexuals were not only not morally corrupt, but that they were not physiologically degenerate — and definitely should not be persecuted. (A defender of Oscar Wilde and a champion of many feminist issues, he nonetheless regarded lesbians, or "congenital inverts," as they were called, as potentially dangerous to society because they threatened the traditional balance of masculine and feminine social roles. But by and large, Ellis argued, they should be tolerated.)

At this time also, outspoken German feminists had recently joined forces with the lesbian groups that had flourished since the turn of the century to protest the extension of Paragraph 175 of the German Penal Code, which would incriminate homosexual acts between women.[8] There was no reason, the feminists argued, why lesbians — or anyone else, for that matter — should not be allowed to love whom they wished.

Janet may or may not have heard these debates, but she was increasingly aware of sexuality as an issue. She'd shed the Tudor Hall uniform and, like her mother, was aware of the nuance of dress; she observed the way men and women behaved toward one another in the streets and in the cafés, and the way men, especially the soldiers, assumed they were superior beings. Curious, talkative, and attentive, she was also more and more conscious of her own intense responses to the people she met. Janet seemed to sense in herself the awakening of something quite special. Later she hinted at these reactions, saying that during this trip she'd learned that in Europe one could feel romantic, one "could fall in love with life."[9]

Several years later, when Janet was struggling with the decision to leave her new husband for the woman she loved, she would remember seeing the dazzling Oléo de Merode dance at the Berlin Wintergarten during the winter of 1910. In "The Portrait of Our Lady," a short story written shortly after she returned from Berlin and revised just before her marriage fell apart, Janet portrayed her fictional dancer, Therese Manet, as a woman of great mystical beauty.[10] In the earlier version Therese is a remote symbol; after being seen once early in the story, the dancer disappears; later her image, pasted in the window of a Jewish home, saves the family from a pogrom. However, it's the structure of the early story that is interesting: persecution follows Therese's appearance.

A few years later Janet altered the story, making Therese Manet even more the erotic center. When she danced, Manet's detractors forgot her somewhat shady reputation, for every movement was spellbinding. "A dancing madonna" who was "curved as Gothic vaults are curved," Therese Manet sways before violins that sounded "like choristers' voices." Her hair, "which she parted in the center of her pear-shaped head, clung so tightly to her scalp you might have thought it had been painted there with black paint, then varnished for its gleams by some Christian artist, who found solace in morbid diptychs. Beneath her rich vestments (you were allowed only the sense of her limb), her foot hung as she danced, narrow like a moonstone mounted in leather and gold."[11] When she moved across the stage, she seemed "to be mounting the steps that led ascending to some glittering dais of the imagination where panels of embroidered velvet hung by an altar whose fretted marble and glowing vhalices [*sic*] she would finally pose, impregnable, unattained."[12]

Therese Manet inspires lust and possessiveness in the men who behold her, but to a young boy, "still good," who finds a picture of her in the street, she arouses an aesthetic pleasure that is pure in its erotic simplicity.[13] Janet's view of the dancer seems similar: in awakening desire, Manet must have represented something disturbing — and full of promise.

During the summer of 1910 the Flanners moved to a large country hotel on the Starnberger See near Munich, but then abruptly canceled the rest of their travel plans. As both Janet and Hildegarde later told the story, the family was forced to return home when their father's money unexpectedly ran out.[14] Frank Flanner had apparently lost about $5,000 backing an invention something like a teletype machine.[15] Although he still owned a good deal of property, and the mortuary business was expanding, the loss was a terrible blow to him.

Back in Indianapolis, he became increasingly distraught, and no one really knew why. He confided to a friend at the Indiana Association of Undertakers that he'd gone to Europe "on account of his affliction with nervous prostration." The friend, seeing that Frank was drawn and tense, suggested retirement: give up "the effort to gather in more shekels," he advised. Frank paused as if he were making some inner calculation, then turned to ask, "But how?"[16]

The energetic man most people knew as good-natured, kind, and reliable became despondent, irascible, and so distracted that he once led a funeral procession the wrong way on a one-way street — not a remarkable event in itself but one his family later recalled as proof of how disturbed he was.[17] Although he gave up his position on the state Board of Trade, pleading illness, he did remain somewhat involved in civic affairs and was constantly concerned about the well-being of Flanner House. Yet he felt frustrated; everything he'd tried to accomplish came to nothing. He tried to solicit help for the son of the Flanners' laundress, a black boy who'd killed someone in a quarrel, but the boy was found guilty. When the youth was sentenced to hang, Frank, who'd come to hear the verdict, stood up, his face red, and helplessly shouted, "Goddam you, Judge." The judge declared Frank in contempt of court and fined him ten dollars.[18]

On Saturday morning February 17, 1912, Frank stopped on his way to work at several druggists, making a purchase at each one. Not long after he arrived at the Flanner and Buchanan establishment at 320 North Illinois Street, he told his nephew that he was tired and was going to lie down. He took his packages into the chapel, mixed their contents together in a cup, drank the concoction of prussic acid, strychnine, carbolic acid, and morphine, and lay down on the davenport. His nephew found the body about thirty minutes later.

"Familiar with Death Through Career; Finds It by Own Hand," read the front-page headline that evening. Mary released a few details to the eager press: that his family had been watching him carefully, for he occasionally talked of suicide; that he had spent the previous evening pacing but had seemed fine and cheerful that morning; that he had been despondent for over a year about an "illness of long standing."

However, such explanations didn't prevent Frank Flanner's suicide from becoming a local scandal and an event that Janet would grimly remember for the rest of her life. Although the papers cited a long-standing physical illness as the cause of his nervous disorders and, ultimately, his death, most people didn't believe it. (Hildegarde and her family years later admitted they'd never heard he'd been sick.)[19] People looked for scapegoats and villains in the now-publicized family melodrama. Many believed that Mary had pushed her husband too hard. An unhappy woman, they said, ashamed that her husband was a funeral director, she demanded he earn his income in some other way and still provide for his family in the accustomed style. According to others, the unfortunate couple was sexually incompatible, and Frank was having an extramarital affair. Still others blamed the Buchanans for not having supported either Frank's philanthropic work or his grandiose dreams of improving Indianapolis. They believed Charles had shouldered the more improvident Frank out of an important business deal. A few surmised that the failing health of his mother, Orpha, recently paralyzed by a stroke, had further contributed to his "nervous condition."[20]

Twelve years later, in her novel *The Cubical City,* Janet created her own version of events, modeling the kind and intelligent James Poole after her father. Poole is an idealistic real estate entrepreneur who dreams of turning midwestern suburbs into landscapes filled with gardens, terraces, and fountains. His Rotarian dreams are crushed, however, when his mercenary business partner squeezes him out of the property he planned to develop. In ill health and unable to take consolation from either religion or medicine, the fatalistic Poole kills himself.

As if rationalizing his decision to die, Janet heaps more illness, defeat, and loneliness on Poole than one character could possibly bear and treads lightly on James and Agatha's marriage, hinting only that James had always felt unloved and that despite his protective feelings toward Agatha, his marriage didn't figure much in his plans one way or another. Yet Poole comes across as a vibrant, sympathetic, and deeply troubled figure, quite different from his delicate and passionless wife. "Nature outside of flowers was unnecessary to her," Janet comments about the woman who gave up her one chance at stardom when she married and ever after lived within the paper world of books.[21]

Although she obliquely suggests possible problems in the marriage, Janet directly indicts Poole's business partner, a two-dimensional villain who cares only about wealth and appearances. In fact, Janet did believe that her uncle Charles Buchanan maneuvered Frank out of property that rightly belonged to both men, thus contributing greatly to Frank's death. Hildegarde recalled that Janet said some "very surprising things in her outspoken way" about the Buchanans' unjust treatment of their father.[22]

In fact, in her novel Janet implicates all of James Poole's family in his death — even the ones who bore no direct responsibility for it — portraying a complicated situation filled with pain, anger, blame, and guilt. Poole's daughter, a sexually active young woman, blames herself for her father's suicide; as in "Portrait of Our Lady," the expression of sexuality meets with punishment. Having allowed her sexual dalliances to take precedence over family obligations, she feels she, too, has somehow betrayed him.

If the shadow of Poole's suicide fell over everyone it touched, Janet no doubt felt unconsciously as much to blame for her father's suicide as Delia Poole felt consciously. Yet she was also angry; she kept no photographs of her father, and on the rare occasions when she talked of him, she invariably mentioned that he had been a failure in his personal relations. At the age of eighty, she suggested that her father himself had abrogated his responsibilities. "No one has a right to take their own life," she emphatically told the writer George Wickes.[23] They were discussing the memoir she'd recently written in which she recalled some of her conversations with Ernest Hemingway, whose father had also killed himself. Yet on another occasion she said she had told Hemingway that suicide is "permissible" as an "act of liberation from whatever humiliating bondage on earth could no longer be borne with self-respect."[24] But Janet never, at the time of his death or later, regarded her father's suicide as an act of heroic liberation.

To her the "life instinct" was "unconquerable," or so she would write to the editors of *The Little Review* on a 1929 questionnaire. "I have seen it conquered," she continued, "but only in circumstances which were intellectually unreliable."[25] Though it's hard to know exactly what she meant by "intellectually unreliable," she may have been referring to her father's death, implying he'd lost control of his reason. Whether this meant she grieved for him more or less is impossible to say.

Over the years Janet would remember her father with condescension, pride, compassion, and sometimes guilt, as the "poor, unappreciated, disliked" man "always left out where I am concerned,"[26] but she rarely talked about his death except to remark occasionally that she'd hardly cried at his funeral.[27] Twelve years later, Janet expressed some of her feelings this way: "Thank god you can only have one set of parents. . . . If you could have lots of them, like brothers and sisters and for each one have to go through this pain, no one could stand it."[28]

Whenever Janet "suffered speculative periods" in her life, she later told a friend, "flight is the result."[29] After her father's death she wanted to leave Indianapolis. Yet despite her longing for culture, excitement, independence, experience, and even a degree of anonymity, she wasn't willing to wander too far.

If she decided to stay in the Midwest, Chicago would be a logical choice. America's second largest city bristled with art and intrigue;

it was a hodgepodge of vulgarity, commercialism, refinement, and energy. And it was not too far from home. Chicago represented all the power and the contradictions of the new age — one could smell the stockyards even while sipping tea in Frank Lloyd Wright's finely constructed bookshop; Henry Adams had written that "education ran riot at Chicago." With its business buccaneers and rebellious young writers, its genteel lakefront society and urban squalor, Chicago had "all the electrifying and unifying power of a college yell," wrote novelist Henry Blake Fuller.

By 1912 young writers and artists were clustering there, often making the city their subject. Carl Sandburg was writing his Chicago poems, Sherwood Anderson was drafting *Windy McPherson's Son,* and Floyd Dell had become literary editor of the *Chicago Evening Post.* Harriet Monroe had begun *Poetry: A Magazine of Verse;* the iconoclastic Margaret Anderson had moved to the city, where she would start the peripatetic *Little Review* in 1914.

The city's new university was luring top names in all fields. Originally endowed in 1890 by John D. Rockefeller, who, as one university historian put it, was "undaunted by the crudities of the present," the university boasted an illustrious faculty that included John Dewey, George Herbert Mead, writers William Vaughn Moody and Robert Herrick, scientist Howard Taylor Ricketts, as well as Nobel laureate Albert Michelson.[30] The university promised them the freedom "to organize scholarly disciplines unencumbered by prevailing academic conventions or practice" in a city that was a "complete social laboratory."[31] (The city didn't always appreciate the university's attitude. When certain Divinity School scholars said the Bible needn't be taken literally, outraged citizens accused the university of harboring atheists.)

In his will Frank Flanner had carefully provided for his wife, his three daughters, and his mother, stipulating that Mary should freely spend the proceeds of his estate for education and travel, both for herself and the children. Despite his straitened financial circumstances, Frank left about $150,000 (or so Janet once calculated), more than enough to support his family and allow Janet to go to college, should she wish to go. She decided she did. Since Chicago appealed to her, and since its university automatically admitted Tudor Hall graduates without an entrance examination, Janet was able to enroll in the fall of 1912, some eight months after her father's death.

At twenty, Janet was just enough older than the other freshmen to feel more experienced and worldly. Like her classmates, she wore her dresses long and her hair, already showing a gray streak in the front, pulled up and covered with a wide-brimmed hat. She made friends quickly, especially among those in the junior and senior classes — Richard Myers and Alice-Lee Herrick, Ernestine Evans, and William Lane Rehm. Most of them would stay close friends over the years.

Trim and energetic, she loved to organize activities and excursions. She and her friends, clinging to the ropes attached to the sides of the buildings, would slide along icy Michigan Boulevard to the opera house to hear Mary Garden sing. Afterward they might dance until a late hour to a jug band at one of the city's clubs. They organized their own amateur dramatics, and Janet became an associate of the Dramatic Club, working behind the scenes on the all-male Black-friars' comic operas, as well as a charter member of a short-lived undergraduate literary magazine. On weekends she and her friends left the campus of smoky gray buildings to go to Alice-Lee's grand-father's home for Sunday roast beef. Witty, full of pungent conver-sation, and considered the most eccentric of the group, Janet was always welcome.[32] She entertained her friends with high-handed comments they remembered, even when they didn't know precisely what she meant. Declaring that she didn't "put much stock in a Jesus gang," she declined the invitations of the secret societies, formed in lieu of sororities, preferring to live independently at the Green Hall dormitory.[33] She did join several women's social societies, however, notably Kalailu and the Sign of the Sickle, although she wasn't fond of formal organizations or regulations. Or classes. She skipped them often, partly because of late-night dancing to ragtime music.

Janet loved being part of a rebellion against tepid, stuffy behavior. "There had always been a void between every generation and its offspring, of course," she wrote a few years later, "but certainly it seemed uniquely broad now."[34] Henry Mencken called the young women of her generation "flappers," describing them as "unshocked, even . . . feminist; reading Havelock Ellis and seeing Strindberg or Shaw."[35] Though she would hardly have called herself a flapper, Janet had already been exposed to Ibsen and Shaw, had already been to

Europe, had doubtless read Havelock Ellis, and enjoyed flouting convention. Like her friends, she found her mentors among those European authors who championed the sensuous, the spontaneous, the intuitive, and the aesthetic. She was reading Swinburne, whose alliterations were to shape her own early poetry, and Walter Pater, whose *Renaissance* she cited as a major influence all her life. "To burn always with this hard gemlike flame," he exhorted, "to maintain this ecstasy, is success in life. In a sense it might even be said that our failure is to form habits; for, after all, habit is relative to a stereotyped world, and meantime it is only the roughness of the eye that makes any two persons, things, situations, seem alike."[36]

Nonconformity, a fine-tuned sensibility, passionate eagerness, and burning love of the aesthetic — these qualities, and not one's scholastic record, measured success as far as Janet was concerned. At the end of her first quarter she passed German but received no credit for English composition or French. During the winter quarter she did better, mainly because she attended her classes, but that spring she didn't finish her course work in English, which she hardly attended anyway, and she barely passed political economy.

The next year wasn't much better. She failed political economy outright. However, she did receive the highest grade of her academic career in an English course, the one she hadn't completed the year before. But by the winter term of 1914, she was again repeating an English composition course and barely attending or passing psychology. In March of this term, seven days before her twenty-second birthday, she withdrew from the university and returned to Indianapolis.

Later Janet was apt to explain her withdrawal in various ways. To some friends she confided that she had been "sacked."[37] She told Mary McCarthy she'd been considered "lawless" on account of her late-night hours.[38] Or, putting the matter more elegantly, she'd say she "engaged in a struggle with the university in which the University was the victor."[39] Sometimes she told interviewers the decision to leave the university had been hers; jokingly, she said she'd withdrawn when they wouldn't give her credit for taking the same courses over and over again.[40] And, she added, she'd gone to college to study writing but discovered that only Robert Morss Lovett knew how to teach it.

Some of this was true. She did seem to enjoy her English courses when she attended them, but not much else in the academic life interested her. She wasn't engaged by her courses or by the faculty, except Lovett, although she did like the assistant dean of women, Sophonisba Breckinridge. An important member of the National American Woman Suffrage Association, Breckinridge had worked with the Women's Trade Union League on behalf of the strikers during the shirtwaist factory strike of 1909. Janet, who had gone off to college with the idea of studying both sociology and literature, respected her energy, her commitment, and the kinds of questions she asked. Working among Chicago's poor, Breckinridge wanted to know what caused crime. But Janet's admiration for Lovett and Breckinridge didn't extend to the university as a whole. As she explained to Mary McCarthy, she had "no patience" for its regulations; she was "too old" and had already "lived abroad for a year and a half."[41]

On other occasions Janet was quoted as saying she had to leave the university when her father committed suicide.[42] Although this wasn't literally true, since her father had died two years before, Janet had been more deeply affected by Frank Flanner's death than she liked to admit, and she may not have been quite ready to leave Indianapolis and her mother or to live up to her own and her family's expectations.

Mary Flanner had built a new house on North Illinois Street at the back of the cherry orchard property and had taken a nominal position with Flanner and Buchanan. She continued her husband's work with the Vacant Lots Committee, which encouraged the city's poor to cultivate gardens, she was still writing and organizing plays, and she was instrumental in the founding of the city's experimental and repertory theater. Marie had returned home from Europe, and Hildegarde was attending public high school. From Janet's point of view some things hadn't changed at all.

One can only imagine how she felt on returning home — how she regarded her failed college career and what she planned or hoped for her future. She made it clear to her family that she detested "Indianapolis manners and mores" and sounded as though she'd leave again as soon as the opportunity presented itself.[43] Although determined to separate herself from an environment and people she disliked, she had no immediate plans, though by now she was pretty sure she'd rather be a writer than the actress her mother wanted her to be.

Not long after her homecoming, Janet left for Philadelphia to work at a model Quaker girls' reformatory. At Sleighton Farm the inmates, divided according to their age and their crime, lived in little cottages along a main street among June-blooming red roses. The mock-pastoral environment, with its looming red brick mansion and village store, and without gates or walls, charmed Janet, who loved to hear the young girls sing in chorus — before they sneaked out at night.[44] Echoing Sophonisba Breckinridge, Janet was fond of explaining her months of employment there as a study in the causes of crime, and she was equally fond of saying that she left nine months after she came when she found the answer — poverty.

But her sister Hildegarde recalled that Janet didn't last long because she really wasn't all that reform-minded or willing to give herself up to social movements.[45] Another source, a friend of the Buchanan family, speculates that Janet went to Sleighton Farm because she was pregnant, which would also account for the suddenness of her departure from Chicago.[46] But there is no evidence to support this, and it seems best to assume that the combined influence of Sophonisba Breckinridge and Frank Flanner — as well as Mary's Quaker connections — took Janet to Pennsylvania. They did not, however, keep her there.

Thus far, despite her complaints about Indianapolis, Janet hadn't been able to stay away from it for very long. The trip to Europe had been cut short, as had her college career. Sleighton Farm, likewise, had not proved to be an avenue out of the Midwest. By 1916 she was back again, twenty-four years old and calling herself "Jeannette."

Even with a new name and the self-assertion this implied, there was little for Janet to do at home other than assist her mother with the newly established Little Theater and act in some of its productions. Janet wanted to write, and she wanted a job writing. In 1917, an acquaintance, Mary Jo Cosser, who was a good friend of Frank Tarkington Baker, the *Indianapolis Star*'s drama editor, suggested he hire Janet on the paper, which he did. According to a family friend, she was handed a bag of money and sent downtown to review the vaudeville and burlesque shows.[47] Then she would go back to the office and write brief notices. This was not the kind of job or the kind of theater Mary, with her taste for Yeats, thought appropriate for her daughter, but Janet loved it.

Janet liked to think of herself as an arbiter of all the arts. In late 1917 Baker promoted her to assistant drama editor, with her own bylined column (as Janet, not Jeannette, Flanner). The column, "Excursions and Impressions in the Field of Art" (later shortened to the more manageable "Impressions in the Field of Art"), was exactly that — a report on whatever works of art Janet saw, read, or thought about.

The column was often didactic. Announcing that art need be true only to the artist's spiritual vision, she said the work should fuse the "aesthetic traditions that went before and call out from his soul the sacred union of superior taste and imagination."[48] She took exception to Tolstoy's statement that art must be of service to the people, a formulation she found, like William Morris's views, too utilitarian. Moreover, she asserted that an appreciation of art could not be bought or taught; those who made art or appreciated it were in a class by themselves. Janet associated herself with the knowledgeable elite who appreciated the true value of art, something not affected by temporal matters: "it is a symbol of perpetually unfluctuating worth, a spiritual fact." She had little patience with puritans, who "hate the ability to make nature too beautiful," or with "common people," usually more concerned with "the price of beans than with art." But, she argued, the wealthy should never be condemned for their love of art or for their ability to pay high prices for it. The large sums art fetches simply demonstrate its true value. Of course, if art is bought only for its "financial reliability," then it "will be vilely demeaned."[49]

She was particularly contemptuous of the middle class which, in its ignorance, insisted art should be representational, that "bananas should look like bananas." At least the wealthy exposed their children to art, and the children of the poor were allowed to express themselves in "neighborhood art."[50] Yet not all self-expression met with her approval. To her way of thinking, the avant-garde editors of *The Little Review* were nothing more than middle-class positivists, "doctors in spite of themselves," who "rush into the halls of the world's esthetics, now sicklied oe'r, as though eager to put a thermometer down the throat of the Venus de Milo."[51] Satirizing their attempts to challenge existing definitions of art and formulate new ones, she wrote of Margaret Anderson and Jane Heap as if they were not her contemporaries but a pair of foolish youths seeking to patent their discovery of beauty in a typically loutish and American way.

By and large, Janet filled her column with deferential quotes from the art critics of the New York newspapers — the *Sun* and the *Tribune* — or with diatribes about what art is and isn't, most of which bear the stamp of Pater's aestheticism. Her moralizing reads as if written by someone too insecure, and too young, to be generous in her views. At the same time, it is not entirely without humor, especially when Janet takes art off its high pedestal. Describing the roof of the newly constructed Indianapolis library, decorated with ancient and modern luminaries, she wondered what might have happened if poet William Cullen Bryant, say, had been placed next to Sappho. What might she have said to him? Janet slyly asked, if only he would listen, "which he would not."[52]

In April 1917 the United States, spurred by Woodrow Wilson's plea before Congress to make the world "safe for democracy," entered the Great War. Although Janet deplored the idea of war, her youthful imagination was stirred by Wilson's high-minded rhetoric. She was excited and full of enthusiasm for a cause she equated with nothing less than a purification of spirit. The war, Janet often proclaimed in her column, might spell the end of civilization, but, on the brighter side, it might get rid of "ugly materialism."

When discussing the war, Janet curtailed much of her contempt for American philistines and focused instead on the Germans. She hadn't liked the Germans she'd encountered in Berlin and now, buoyed by anti-German sentiment in America, she had no reason to change her mind. To her, Germans were absurd, savage, and crudely insensitive to the finer things in life. Willing to accept a fake Leonardo da Vinci bust stuffed with calico rags as authentic because the Kaiser had declared it genuine, they refused to recognize the "true value" of art. Worse, they were bent on destroying the "standard of civilization" best symbolized by Reims Cathedral; in so doing, they were destroying the "sine qua non of that life which can, with truth, be called civilized."[53] On the other hand, she greatly admired the French;

in continuing to hold art exhibits, they demonstrated what Janet praised as the spiritual significance of war.

She argued that war, however horrible, was at least creating a new set of values — idealism and self-sacrifice — in America. Those who had been concerned with "nonessentials," who poured "too much strength and earnestness into unimportant, even carnal, channels," and who regarded beauty, truth, conduct, and spirit as matters of "leisurely avocation" to be discussed after business hours — they would all be changed.[54] War demanded self-sacrifice, idealism, and commitment, especially of women, who could benefit from this war by getting back to "fundamental values."[55]

Yet Janet wondered whether this also meant a loss for art and culture. This was an important question for Janet, who had been taught to regard women as the caretakers of all things spiritual. And the same women she upbraided for their "thoughtless hedonism" were the guardians of leisure and art. Those who entered the work force to become drones in the "beehive of activity" would give up the very things that made them different from bellicose, money-making, predatory men. What would the cost to art then be, and how would this change women? How could women work, for example, and continue to promote culture? How could women work and not become like the rapacious, insensible businessman they loathed? But how could a woman justify not working?

Janet answered some of her own questions by insisting that women were better served by work than by idleness, although they should not forfeit their cultural mission. For all their leisure time, women, she argued, had created little of lasting value. (Although Janet admired the writings of Sappho, George Sand, Harriet Beecher Stowe, and George Eliot, she considered them exceptions; most women had not created "anything of either utilitarian or artistic value."[56]) Now, called to service, they could work for an ideal rather than for the satisfactions of petty self-interest; they wouldn't have to be hedonists, at one extreme, or drudges, at the other.

Despite the lofty sentiments and idealistic rhetoric, a vein of contradiction ran through Janet's columns. While condemning frivolous living as vehemently as any puritan, and lecturing against hedonism, sloth, and "riotous living" (much as her University of Chicago teachers might have lectured her), at the same time she disdained business and, in general, the Protestant work ethic. Declaring that nothing was more fundamental than the creation and appreciation of beauty, she suggested that a life devoted to art, or to the art of living, was a life well spent. And yet, drawn as she was to the life of the aesthete, her conscience denounced it as immoral, for she valued hard work — to such an extent that she never felt she was working quite hard enough.[57]

Janet implicitly recognized this conflict, and in one of her more unusual newspaper pieces retold the story of the grasshopper and the ant, casting the grasshopper as a hedonist and the ant as an industrious puritan. The resourceful and frugal ant saved pennies, believed in progress, and lived only for the common good. The grasshopper, by contrast, was a "Frenchy sort of fellow," an individualist and artist, a great lover of beauty who preferred pleasure to work. While the ant cultivated his "grossly fertile lands," the grasshopper enjoyed love and life — he was a person of "bel esprit and great human affections" who'd rather starve than live like the practical and prosaic ant. He did starve. But Janet's hard-working ant came to an end that for Janet was equally gloomy — he became a socialist. Socialism might paternalistically provide us with bread, she declared, but one cannot live by bread alone.

In the end she couldn't really justify the grasshopper's death — however happy he was — even though it's clear she was partial to him. Instead she concluded her parable by urging the reader, and evidently herself, to try to resolve this conflict.[58]

Living at home was difficult, but Janet enjoyed writing for the newspaper for twenty-five dollars a week and a press pass that admitted her everywhere. She had kept in touch with her college friends, some of whom had stayed in Chicago. One in particular, William Lane Rehm, nicknamed "Rube," was an affectionate, kind young man from Chicago who had graduated from the university in 1914. Slow-moving, blond, and conventionally handsome, with a square, firmly set chin and wire-rimmed glasses that gave him a studious look, Lane seemed an unlikely match for Janet, at least according to their college friends.[59] Although he recognized humor in others, he had no great sense of it himself and was described as a Victorian, even a puritan, and a sentimentalist, not a romantic. This decent young man revered but could not quite fathom Janet Flanner.[60]

By April of 1918 Lane had unsuccessfully tried to enlist in every possible branch of military service, much to the bemusement of his friends, who were being shipped off reluctantly to fight the Great War. He had been living on and off in New York and apparently seeing Janet whenever he visited his mother in Chicago. That month they decided, very suddenly, to marry. On Thursday evening, April 25, 1918, relatives and friends gathered in the Flanner home for the ceremony, conducted by the Reverend Wicks of the Unitarian Church.

The wedding took everyone by surprise — Lane's friends do not mention it in correspondence written at the time, and Mary Flanner announced the betrothal only two days before the ceremony.[61] Had the event been planned, it would have been announced earlier, given Mary's attention to propriety, and it would have been arranged for a time when Hildegarde, at Sweet Briar College, could come home. Lane may have pressured Janet into an immediate marriage, believing that he might be called to service soon and wanting to have someone at home waiting for him. If so, Janet was willing. Or, like her autobiographical heroine in *The Cubical City,* Janet may have merged "passion with patriotism," and, her feelings confused by visions of heroic men nobly marching to the front, may have supposed that she and Lane "were to be in love and he was to go to war."[62] Years later she confided to a cousin that she married to get out of Indianapolis.[63]

The newlyweds left for New York City immediately after their April wedding, but by the end of May, Janet was back at home with her mother. It's not clear why she returned to Indianapolis, or even whether Lane was with her. (In the Indianapolis *Blue Book,* Janet was listed as Mrs. Janet Tyler Flanner Rehm, residing with her two sisters and their mother on North Illinois Street. Lane wasn't mentioned at all.) But it's not certain that anyone, even the newlyweds, suspected trouble in the marriage as yet.

Janet made it clear she was just biding her time in Indianapolis. Her office mate at the *Star,* where she resumed writing her column, recalled that she was obviously "using her experience as a springboard

from which she could plunge into the bigger field."[64] After asking
for and getting a five-dollar raise, she began writing another column,
"Comments on the Screen," sometimes called the first movie criticism ever written. It was not exactly movie criticism, even though
Indianapolis had become a testing ground for new movies, which
were shown in the city's luxury cinema palace, the Circle Theater.
Her screen comments were rather like those she made about art;
she summarized articles from film trade magazines and gave her
opinions; she occasionally mentioned film stars or directors of particular note, and she generally objected to certain parts of movies,
like bathing scenes, that were neither artistic nor dignified. Seldom
commenting on individual movies, she could be quite amusing when
discussing westerns, for example, with their swaggering heroes inevitably rapping on a bar, calling for a straight whiskey, and downing
what was in reality cold tea. The hero would stride confidently away,
as Janet put it, "mind made up. It was always made up by the time
he left the bar."[65]

Janet's mind was also made up; in August, two months after she
started her film column, she returned to New York and moved with
Lane into a small apartment at 125 Washington Place in Greenwich
Village. This time she wasn't going back.

3

She Whom the Gods Had Made
1918-1921

FOR ABOUT A YEAR Janet had inveighed against philistinism, ugliness, billboards, and business, telling *Indianapolis Star* readers that outside their hometown, men and women carrying the banner of art were marching to the beat of the future. Many of them had marched to New York, in particular, to Greenwich Village, which attracted no small number of restless, desperate young lovers of beauty. Soon after Janet moved there, full of the rhetoric of war and love and sacrifice, she learned two things. She was not in love with her husband, and she was unaccountably attracted to the women she met.

The newlyweds' apartment on Washington Place was small but serviceable, with enough room for Janet to work on stories and articles and for Lane, who wanted to paint, to take out his canvases in the evenings after returning from his job as a bank clerk. Nearby were small restaurants and cafés: Polly's Restaurant, where the cook and waiter periodically called the patrons "bourgeois pigs"; the Brevoort Hotel and Café on the corner of Fifth Avenue and Eighth Street; the Mad Hatter on West Fourth, the Village's first tearoom, frequented by women who smoked in public and talked about art by the giant stone fireplace. They were within easy walking distance of the stables recently converted into artists' studios near Washington

Square. At 23 Fifth Avenue Mabel Dodge held her famous Wednesday night salon, and on Eighth Street, Gertrude Vanderbilt Whitney held hers. By day notorious characters roamed the narrow Village streets. There was the hatless poet Harry Kemp, called the Byron of the Village whenever the title wasn't being used by someone else; the Baroness Elsa von Freytag-Lorinhoeven, a favorite of *The Little Review,* who was said to wear postage stamps on her cheeks and to shave and shellac her head; the self-promoting Guido Bruno, Village impresario; even Theodore Dreiser and Edna St. Vincent Millay.

The Village had been for some time a center of bohemianism and left-wing politics, art and radicalism, but many of its enthusiasts claimed that by 1918 its heyday had passed. Radical politics, once personified by John Reed and the socialist magazine *Masses,* had in one way or another been overtaken by the war effort. After Woodrow Wilson had asked the whole country — men, women, children — to mobilize, almost everyone appeared to be cheering. Some, like the editors and several contributors to *Masses,* went so far as to be indicted for violating the Sedition Act of 1917, but many Greenwich Villagers jumped on the war wagon. In the spring of 1917, during the Alley Festa, organized by Mrs. William Delano, Mrs. Harry Payne Whitney, and Frank Crowninshield, artists, writers, entertainers, and prominent society figures had gathered to raise money for the Red Cross and other war relief funds. They had covered MacDougal Alley with a red, white, and blue awning and hung banners, lanterns, war posters, and colored lights over the street. At the Festa's end, more than $500,000 in Liberty Loan bonds had been sold. (When someone once insinuated that Janet wouldn't know what to do with her money if she had enough to invest, she tartly answered she'd of course buy Liberty Bonds.)[1]

If war fever upstaged long discussions about the redistribution of wealth, the subjects of art, sex, and women's rights continued to interest those coming to the Village. And the Village was hospitable to the "New Woman," described superficially in the memoirs of the period as the sexually liberated, cigarette-smoking woman who insisted on paying for herself. According to Matthew Josephson, her "sophistication . . . was related to a whole series of social and artistic taboos recurring in the pattern of their talk. All that was judged 'conventional' and 'bourgeois' in social behavior fell under their contempt; similarly, in artistic matters, they upheld the realistic, and truthful, style, as against the 'sentimental,' which was associated with bourgeois weakness."[2]

This perspective was not necessarily the one Janet claimed, although she certainly shared some of the New Woman's aspirations.[3] She fully intended to assert her freedom, which included making her own friends and having her own social life, and she fully intended to live as independently as she could. She had an income from her father's estate. She and Lane Rehm had drawn up a prenuptial agreement specifying that neither would lay claim to the other's finances should they divorce. Lane, who was eventually employed by the banking firm of Brown Brothers Harriman, helped Janet with her investments and offered financial advice but never compromised her economic autonomy. By all accounts he was sympathetic to Janet's way of looking at things, and Janet in later years fondly recalled him as a good man — "too good for me."[4]

Her first months in New York were heady ones. There's no doubt that she was well liked and even achieved some small social prominence. A match for anyone at a time when, as Malcolm Cowley recalled, "everything was an excuse for talking," Janet quickly earned a reputation for being witty — and from none other than that discerning self-appointed judge in such matters, Franklin P. Adams.[5]

Under the byline F.P.A., Adams had already been so successful as a columnist for the New York *World* that he was making $25,000 a year. "The Conning Tower" chronicled the comings and goings of his friends, particularly those graced with "wit," and printed some of their contributions. Several of these friends had known each other before the war, and some had met in Paris during the war while working on the newspaper *Stars and Stripes,* which had attracted some of the army's "least alarming soldiers."[6] The group included Alexander Woollcott, the *New York Times* drama critic; Harold Ross, former reporter and eventually editor of *Stars and Stripes;* C. Leroy Baldridge, from the University of Chicago, and Baldridge's friend Hilmer Baukhage, also from the university, and a close friend of Janet's college friends Richard and Alice Lee Herrick Myers. Through Woollcott the group met Jane Grant, another *Times* reporter and one of the few women given assignments equal to the men's.

After the war most of this group returned to New York to continue their debunking of pretentiousness, middle-class conformity, and sentimental rhetoric. Several of them returned to their jobs, but others tried to continue the work they'd done during the war; Harold Ross, for example, intended to keep the spirit of *Stars and Stripes* alive with a magazine for veterans called *Home Sector,* a short-lived venture. Lane and Janet became ancillary members of this uptown group after meeting the others through their Chicago connections and at Neysa McMein's studio on Fifty-seventh Street.

Neysa (née Marjorie) McMein, who had come to New York from the Midwest with a vaudeville troupe, was at the time one of the highest-paid magazine illustrators in the country. A "Brünnhilde with a classic face," according to screenwriter Anita Loos, Neysa introduced herself to F.P.A., began to appear regularly in his column, and soon met several of the others who were later labeled the "Algonquin crowd."[7] Neysa was a bohemian of sorts, with a reputation for riding on parade elephants and running out of her studio to chase fire engines; she attracted people from the various New York art, literary, and theatrical worlds to her studio, where they would congregate to talk and exchange witticisms, or play poker, cribbage, and the two pianos.[8] The comings and goings seldom bothered Neysa, who rarely latched the door, left her easel, or wiped the paint from her face and clothes. In her sparsely furnished and unkempt studio, littered with coats, overshoes, pastels, and drawings, one could hear the El clattering on Sixth Avenue. There one might find Irving Berlin, Father Francis Duffy, Heywood Broun, Ruth Hale, Ruth Gordon, Jascha Heifetz, Robert Benchley, or Dorothy Parker, who lived across the hall. Neysa inspired devotion in Alec Woollcott, among others, and in Janet.

Janet was dazzled by Neysa's glamour, unpretentiousness, and generosity. She'd never met anyone quite like her — so accepting, tactful, intelligent, and so willing to be herself on every occasion. And she was impressed with the way the eclectic Neysa accepted and casually ushered Janet into her life. Janet often felt poor and obscure in the company of Neysa's friends, but not with Neysa, who'd gladly pay all Janet's expenses when they traveled together, as they occasionally did. Or Neysa would find a way to get the trip paid for. Thinly disguised as a maid, Janet went along with her on a magazine assignment to cover the 1920 Republican National Convention. In return for the privilege, Janet, holding a wastebasket suspended by a corset string, posed as a milkmaid for Neysa who, hired to paint a portrait of one of the convention's grande dames, was unable to draw without a model.[9]

No doubt it was through Neysa that Janet met many of those who followed Alec Woollcott's lead and ate lunch every day at the Algonquin Hotel, where manager Frank Case had arranged for them to sit together at a round table. The group included F.P.A., considered the group's "dean" because he had the steadiest income and largest audience; the theatrical press agents Murdock Pemberton and John Peter Toohey; the journalists Heywood Broun, Ruth Hale, and Jane Grant; the *Vanity Fair* writers Dorothy Parker, Robert Sherwood, and Robert Benchley; and the writers Marc Connelly and George S. Kaufman, soon to be successful collaborators. It was Woollcott who introduced the rough-hewn Harold Ross, later the founder and editor of *The New Yorker* magazine.

One ate at the round table by invitation only. Anita Loos, invited to join the "vicious circle," chose to decline their advances, following the lead of her heroes Henry Mencken and George Jean Nathan. Skeptical of the group's self-satisfaction and forced sophistication, Loos satirized them in *But Gentlemen Marry Brunettes,* writing that "every genius who eats his luncheon at the Algonquin Hotel is always writing that this is the place where all the great literary geniuses eat their luncheon" so that "everybody had an opportunity to talk about himself. . . . I think it is wonderful to have so many internal resources that you never have to bother to go outside yourself to see anything."[10] Janet's college friend Richard Myers wrote to Stephen Vincent Benét in 1925 about the Algonquin crowd: "How well do I remember it — and its regular habitués — all self-complacency, simply weltering in their ego, and those insufferable critics!!!! But the pie *was* good."[11]

Edna Ferber remembered them as a "hard-boiled crew: brilliant, wise, witty, generous, . . . just getting a firm footing on the spectacular success which was to become established in the ten or twelve years that followed."[12] Helen Hayes recalled that they were "as hard on each other as they were on everybody else. It was dangerous to expose anyone's dream to the death rays of their 'sophistication.' "[13]

Ferber agreed that the talk was frequently "biting and brutal," but enjoyed the spontaneity, the high standards, and their "tonic" influence on American letters: "The people they could not and would not stand were the bore, the hypocrite, sentimentalist, and the socially pretentious. They were ruthless toward charlatans, toward the pompous and the mentally and artistically dishonest. Casual, incisive, they had a terrible integrity about their work and a boundless ambition."[14]

Although she shared many of their values, Janet felt like a small-town girl among this group. For one thing, she didn't gamble, and on the few occasions when she did, she lost. But accompanying Neysa or invited on her own to some of their croquet parties along the Palisades, Janet did not long remain obscure. Marc Connelly remembered her "blazing personality" at Neysa's studio, where, looking young and serious in her dark elegant dress, she sat for one of Neysa's first full portraits.[15] In the spring of 1920 Frank Adams paid her a very high compliment when he dedicated a poem, "Thoughts in Hot Weather," to her: "When the bard is on the brink of / All the terrors that appall," he wrote, "It is sweet to sit and think of / You and nothing else at all."

Janet enjoyed their attentions and their humor; she genuinely admired Alec Woollcott and Jane Grant, and she considered Neysa one of her best companions. But changes in her personal life slowly took her away from this group, and though she would never completely lose touch with them, she was beginning to see that she could not live among them for long. Janet later confided to one of her friends that she'd been happy and attractive and well liked when she lived in New York, but another friend, the theater critic Thomas Quinn Curtiss, has surmised that she'd been depressed and confused a good deal of the time.[16] She reminisced that although she adored New York, she had needed to be away: "I was very . . . criminal," she explained. "Not very good to my husband."[17]

By the time Janet began frequenting Neysa's studio, the war had ended. On Armistice Day, November 11, 1918, she ran over to the studio of her friend the painter Mark Tobey with the news, then they joined the flag-waving crowds shouting on Sixth Avenue. Janet was still making new friends and exploring the small bookshops, used furniture stores, and quietly curved streets around their new home on Washington Place. But with the war over, life returned to routine. (Peace, as she would say in 1945, is not dramatic like war.)[18] The man she was married to no longer might have to risk his life for his country, and Janet suspected she'd confused her feelings for Lane Rehm with her romantic patriotism, almost as if her senses had been conscripted (or so she said of her heroine in *The Cubical City*).[19]

Much later she remembered this period as a time of great confusion. Not only did she realize she wasn't in love with Lane, she also began to acknowledge that she was physically attracted to women: "I was married," she remarked, "and so at sea in my disappointment in not being in love as I had been with women that I had no sense of recording any veracity of any sorts, my emotional push toward my lesbic approach to all life being so dominant that if I did not have it so vibrant a permanent problem in my daily life, I had nothing at all to replace it."[20] Years after she left New York, she still recalled some of the women who had intrigued her there, like Neysa and the violet-eyed, consumptive Mary Pyne, the Village beauty who had fascinated Theodore Dreiser; Janet watched Pyne but never met her.[21]

During this time, according to Jane Grant, Janet reportedly took a job on the New York *Sun* which, for undisclosed reasons, lasted just a week.[22] Mainly she stayed at home writing satirical poems, as labored in tone and subject matter as her *Indianapolis Star* pieces; bishops and cardinals represent a hypocritical morality full of "emblems of sloth and sinning," and charming, foolish aesthetes picturesquely dance with death. Her one published story, "In Transit and Return," is a conventional tale about a young boy who defies his manipulative mother, overcomes small-town shame, and graduates into long pants.[23]

In the unpublished "As It Was," however, she specifically addresses the issues preoccupying her: how women stirred her imagination.[24] Like "Portrait of Our Lady," the story describes a beautiful woman in lavish detail and compares her to the foolish and far less appealing men who either don't appreciate her or, worse, want to own her. This time the beautiful woman is none other than Eve. Lucifer is talking with his lazy friend God, who has recently finished creating the sun and is now languorously reclining on the grass. The sad-eyed

Lucifer chides God: "It has been days since you have really worked. Make something new, something fresh, something great. Stretch your hands as artist, God, and create. . . . Create beauty, fragile, troubling, which spills the scent of perfume as it walks." God asks what this new creation should be, and Lucifer answers from his heart: "Make a woman."

With Lucifer's assistance, God makes the creature Eve, who stands on "delicate feet, narrow ankles, clinging knees. It had a belly whose center was curiously carved and breasts rouged by feathers of rose. Its hair was a moss which stirred in the wind the two breathed, and its eyes were closed." Delighted, Lucifer begs God to make another. God reluctantly agrees as Lucifer excitedly begins to gather the necessary material, ignorant of the dirt falling in its midst. God, in a hurry, carelessly spins the dirt-smeared dust into thick thighs and shoulders, then drops moss in all the wrong places. They run out of clay; the new creature is a mess.

Disappointed, even disgusted, with the outcome — not a work of art like the first but a figure peculiarly resembling God himself — God takes the last bit of clay and flings it at the statue; still unformed, it clings. "Then the statue," Janet slyly tells us, "became nude." God, exhausted, will do no more and leaves to take a nap.

The adoring Lucifer spends the night weeping and caressing Eve until dawn when, having "spent his passion," he falls asleep. The next morning God finds Lucifer quite alone. "She whom the gods had made," Janet tells us, "departed with what they might not destroy."

In 1918 Solita Solano, a thirty-year-old writer, moved to New York. Dark-haired and exotic-looking, she was to become the first great — and in many ways undiminished — love of Janet's life. "Rarely does a day go by that I don't think of you," Janet wrote in 1974, almost sixty years after they had first met. "Yes, we have known each other very very long."[25]

On December 21, 1918, *Variety* welcomed Solita Solano to Manhattan. The former Boston journalist was the new drama editor of the New York *Tribune,* and, as *Variety* noted, she occupied a "unique position" there — it had been a long time since a woman headed the drama department. Miss Solano was eminently qualified for the job.

She'd been drama critic and editor for the Boston *Traveler* and *Journal,* she was a translator of some repute, she was widely traveled, and her own short fiction was being published. She was someone to be reckoned with.

Solita Solano came to the *Tribune* by a circuitous route. Born in Troy, New York, in 1888, she was christened Sarah Wilkinson, but she hated her Anglo-Saxon birth name, with its upstate family associations, and claimed she took her new name from a Spanish grandmother, although there is no record of such a person.[26] In any event, she passed her first sixteen years rather gloomily among the Wilkinsons of Troy.

When illness forced Almadus Wilkinson, Sarah's father, to retire from his Troy law practice at a fairly young age, he and his family withdrew to his father's summer estate in the small village of Johnsonville, north of Albany. There Sarah spent most of her childhood, which she did not remember as happy. Her mother took orders from the semi-invalid Almadus, who busied himself writing a stage adaptation of Shakespeare's *As You Like It* as well as crime fiction for the Troy *Daily Times.* A writer by avocation since his Harvard days, when he'd published short pieces in the *Advocate,* he nonetheless vehemently disapproved of his daughter's literary ambitions. He forbade Sarah access to his books, keeping his library locked.[27] Years later, in an autobiographical poem, Solita recalled, "Father said Too young, and see / The other things you've done / Is this a daughter? / Look at my good son. / Can't you act like your brother / Not worry your mother / Neat, sweet, and dutiful / No one asks you to be beautiful / No one wants you with a brain / A damnable thing for a woman."[28]

Solita, dark-haired and dark-skinned, grew up feeling that she was ugly. She seemed to lack the graces that might have charmed her mother and the knack for obedience that might have softened her father. First sent to the Emma Willard School in Troy, she was later remanded to the Sacred Heart Convent for more discipline. This simply whetted her appetite; she stole, she lied, she read Diamond Dick, she pawned her jewelry.

Then in 1903 Almadus Wilkinson died. In his will he gave over Sarah's portion of his estate to her two younger brothers to administer. Further, he stipulated that if Sarah married without her mother's written consent or, after her mother's death, without the consent of her younger brothers or their heirs, she'd lose her entire inheritance. In retaliation she eloped with Oliver Filley the following year. Filley had recently left the Rensselaer Polytechnic Institute in Troy to work as a supervising engineer for the Bureau of Public Works in the Philippines. In 1904 she celebrated her sixteenth birthday with him in Shanghai, away from what she described as the " 'inmates' and house" in Troy.[29]

For the next four years, in China, Japan, and the Philippines, Sarah surveyed land, plotted maps, and helped build some of the coral roads at Tacloban that MacArthur later used in the Second World War. She learned telegraphy and three Malay languages so she could interpret for her engineer husband. In Manila the couple figured prominently in the social life, often leading the cotillion at society and governmental functions and privileged enough to give Theodore Roosevelt's daughter Alice a ride in Sarah's victoria. But Sarah Wilkinson Filley began to detest colonial conversations. And her marriage was not working. She decided she must leave her husband. With the help of one of her servants, she climbed out her window one night and ran away. In 1913 the marriage was annulled, but she still lost her inheritance. Some years later she told novelist George Moore, who was captivated by Solita (he said he would always remember her teeth), about that "sad, early" marriage which, she told her disbelieving family, included beatings.[30]

By 1908 Solita had managed to get to New York City, where she decided to try to earn her living on the stage. She met her roommate, Pearl White, still a struggling beginner, at a Broadway theatrical agent's when they were both looking for jobs. The two women moved into a fleabag boardinghouse for theatrical people on West Thirty-eighth Street. Pearl, once she was hired by Pathé, could afford a new suit and hat, which Solita borrowed for all her interviews and auditions until she landed her own job with the Union Park Players and the Gardner Vincent Stock Company.

Solita was a passable actress with no illusions about her talent and no prospect of making money. As she later told the story, she was virtually penniless; when a friend in 1910 bought her a train ticket to Boston, she decided to leave New York and acting for the promise of a new career in journalism.[31] Before long, she was earning eighteen dollars a week as a rookie reporter for the Boston *Traveler*. Another friend recalls that Solita went to Boston to enroll in a famous French class and soon met a group of people who regarded her as a "shooting star."[32] In any event, she was selected to cover important trials like that of I.W.W. leader Joseph Ettors and developed a reputation for being frank, fearless, and competent. She was soon promoted to feature editor and then drama critic and editor. Every week she produced a four-page amusement section of theatrical gossip and comment, advertised as the "bright and breezy 'Green Room Glints.' " Her mother, she commented, began to forgive her "lurid Past."[33]

Busy and sought after, Solita was well known for her candor and her style. A small woman with large, blue-violet eyes who on occasion marshaled the woman suffrage parades in Boston, she was intrepid, outspoken, and given to large enthusiasms. When she interviewed her idol Sarah Bernhardt after a performance of *Camille*, Bernhardt gave Solita her tear-soaked handkerchief, which Solita kept for the rest of her life. The celebrated English actor Sir Herbert Tree was quite taken with Solita during his last American tour and begged her to join him in England. In a letter posted the day he died, he was still offering to pay her passage and employ her as his secretary, ostensibly to give her time for her own writing.[34]

Like Alec Woollcott, Solita Solano found herself fighting for the critic's right to be candid in her drama criticism.[35] In 1915, after Eugene Walter's play *Just a Woman* opened in Boston in one of the Shubert brothers' theaters and Solita gave it a very bad notice, the furious Shuberts canceled all their advertising, refusing to support a paper that carried her reviews. The *Traveler* stood firm. Ernest Gruening, then editor of the paper (he was later a U.S. senator and governor of Alaska), wouldn't fire her. Instead he told the Shuberts that if their boycott continued, several Boston papers, not just the *Traveler*, would drop their theater ads. The Shuberts retreated, called off the boycott, and Solita stayed with the *Traveler* until both she and Gruening moved over to the Boston *Journal* in 1917.[36]

Successful as she was, journalism was not her ultimate goal; she wanted to "write truly great fiction some day."[37] She began to write some stories, loosely based on her experiences in the Philippines, and by the end of 1918, when she moved to New York to join the

Tribune, she was corresponding with Mencken and Nathan of *Smart Set* magazine. Apologizing that "the Comstocks would fall on us with all arms and we'd be barred from the news-stands of 30 states," they said they could not publish one of her graphic early stories, even though they thought it "excellent."[38] They did, however, take her story "Little Grand Duchess" in 1918, and in 1920 one called "Vespers," a tale of a young, lonely girl stashed away in a convent school by her beautiful mother, who tells the child that though she's "not so ugly" as she was two years ago, she's still not pretty or accomplished enough to come home. Nathan wrote, " 'Vespers' is not a good story — it is an exceptionally good story."[39]

Once in New York, Solita began appearing in F.P.A.'s literary gossip column as "a fine black girl with a fair wit, and some hatreds I shared with her."[40] However, she cared little for Frank Adams and the entire Algonquin crowd, although she was fond of Dorothy Parker. Their humor was not to her liking, nor was their disregard for sentiment, romance, and metaphysics. Solita wanted something more — she wanted beauty and passion and rapture; she wanted, as she once put it, to "defy time's laws for love and loveliness."[41]

Janet Flanner and Solita Solano met sometime during the winter after the war. To Janet, Solita seemed worldly and wise, elegant, lovely, and experienced. She spoke Spanish and Italian fluently (in addition to the Malay languages she'd learned), she'd published several stories, she lived alone on East Ninth Street, and she was the drama editor of the *Tribune.* She was volatile, intense, often coquettish, warm and articulate, and at times she seemed very sad. And Solita fell in love with Janet, who adored her. She could confide in Solita, she could express her doubts about her marriage, and she could confess the secret she'd begun to discover — that her responses to women were stronger, fuller, perhaps more binding than anything she'd ever felt toward a man. Solita understood; she felt the same way.

The two women found that they both disliked their middle-class backgrounds, wanted to experience everything they thought had been denied them, and felt a bit lost in New York. The self-possessed Solita revealed herself to be vulnerable, even self-effacing, despite her worldly ways. And Janet, who wanted to be accepted in the world of her Algonquin acquaintances, also wanted to be free of their, and her own, provincialism. She and Solita saw in each other a hunger for all that was noble-minded, and they recognized that they both wanted something special from life. To Janet it must have seemed that Solita was already on her way to achieving it.

They met during a critical period in both their lives. Solita had just been demoted to reporter at the *Tribune* in spite of having enlarged the drama section from two to five pages and having increased its advertising. She assumed that she'd lost her post because she had again dared criticize one of the Shuberts' plays — not because Heywood Broun had returned. Thinking that no other paper would take her on as editor, and not willing to settle for anything less, she left the *Tribune* to work as a press agent for Winchell Smith and John L. Golden, the theatrical team that had just produced the enormously popular play *Lightnin.* It was a high-paying job, but she regarded it as demeaning. She'd entered, she said, an "epoch of distress, battling for lucre."[42]

Janet, too, was in distress. She'd become pregnant. No one is quite sure what happened subsequently — whether she miscarried or had an abortion — but it is clear that her marriage was failing, she couldn't find work, and she couldn't sell her stories.[43] She enjoyed the new life she and Solita were beginning to share, but it was a complicated one, and it threatened to separate Janet from the life she had assumed she'd have. Spurning that life was one matter; replacing it was another. If she and Solita were quite serious about being with each other, Janet knew she'd have to make some difficult choices, ones that would inevitably hurt others, especially Lane Rehm. Moreover, she knew it would be difficult, if not impossible, for her family or the people she called her friends to understand or accept her relationship with Solita.

Certainly the nervousness of the early days of their intimacy, with its clandestine meetings and shared confidences, alternated with simple pleasure in each other's company and a troubling awareness that theirs was a very private, isolated, and even frightening relationship. Neither of them could know what the future held; both knew that their relationship was socially unacceptable, yet neither could give up the intensity or the growing tenderness.

New York was beginning to feel claustrophobic, especially after

Janet's mother and her sister Hildegarde arrived from California in January 1921. They rented an apartment in an old row house, one of a group that had been taken over by the church Saint Mark's-in-the-Bouwerie. They planned to stay for at least two months before returning to Berkeley. Hildegarde had enrolled at the University of California at her mother's request, after Mary Flanner decided to make her home in the West. But for the time being they were settled in New York, and Janet must have felt more than ever the need to be away from her mother's probing, watchful eye.

In May Janet, Solita, and Neysa McMein became charter members of the Lucy Stone League, founded by Ruth Hale and Jane Grant to help women keep their own names in marriage. They met some of the other members — including Zona Gale, Charlotte Perkins Gilman, Susan Glaspell, Fannie Hurst, and Freda Kirchwey — at the league's first meeting in the Hotel Pennsylvania. Among these women Janet could find some degree of support for her relationship with Solita, but she wasn't interested in political alliances. She knew that if she and Solita stayed in New York, or even the United States, they would not be able to live as they wished.

The opportunity Janet and Solita had been waiting for came later that year, when *National Geographic* offered to send Solita on assignment to Constantinople by way of Greece. If Janet went along, the two of them could manage financially, they figured, for Janet was receiving a small income from her father's estate, and Solita had no doubt about her own earning abilities. If need be, she could help Janet get freelance assignments from the *Tribune.* Solita was adamant about their going; Janet later remembered Solita's insistence as somewhat "brutal," though she thanked her for it the rest of her life.

Janet now knew she would have to leave Lane, whom her mother liked enormously, once and for all.[44] In retrospect it seems that no one expected Janet and Lane to stay together, and no one was particularly surprised when she left. The separation and eventual divorce were presented as amicable, and friends generally remembered it that way. They believed it was Lane, and not Janet, who suffered.[45] Janet was not blind to his suffering, nor to the enormity of the choice she was making. For many years she continued to feel a great deal of remorse for the pain she caused him, to the point of believing she had acted "criminally." Philip Hamburger, Janet's colleague at *The New Yorker,* recalls her telling him, sometime after Lane's death in 1958, that she'd visited her ex-husband's grave. "It had triggered some emotion," remembers Hamburger. "She was close to tears."[46] Around that same time Janet received a letter from Lane's brother, who reminded her that "nothing you could have done, honestly and in good faith to your own good self, could have altered that relationship. And you must NOT permit any afterthought not only to gain dominance but even to emerge. Your life was mapped well in advance, you have clung to it and done nobly."[47]

At the time, however, she tried to break free as quickly and thoroughly as possible. To her sisters, her haste seemed almost ruthless, even selfish.[48] In the early summer of 1921 she sold the furniture in her apartment, including the family's cherry pieces handed down from Quaker cabinetmakers and her grandmother's old botany books. She avoided telling her mother and Hildegarde, in California, and Marie, who was living in New York at the time, that she planned to leave. She was apt to act almost precipitously, Hildegarde recalled, to accomplish what had to be done.[49] It was almost as if the decision to leave was so important that any hesitation or consultation might threaten it.

4

But, I Must Dare All
1921-1924

*After all everybody, that is, everybody who writes is interested
in living inside themselves in order to tell what is inside
themselves. That is why writers have to have two countries,
the one where they belong and the one in which they live
really. The second one is romantic, it is separate from themselves, it is not real but it is really there.*

Gertrude Stein, *Paris France*

I WANTED BEAUTY, with a capital B," Janet Flanner said when
asked why she chose to live abroad. "I was consumed by my own
appetite to consume — in a very limited way, of course, the beauties
of Europe." And, she added, "a dominant part of the aesthetic civilization" in Europe was "based upon the creative faculty of choice."[1]
The early 1920s, it turned out, were propitious for her choice.
Tourist-class passage from New York to Le Havre cost about eighty
dollars, and to the young American for whom Europe represented
all that was romantic and urbane, culture was available at an incredibly
low rate of exchange.

Janet and Solita chose to detach themselves from America, in
Janet's words, "to begin anew."[2] But she did not want to make a

total break with her American heritage; she wanted freedom from the sexual, personal, and professional restrictions of an America that was inimical, if not openly hostile, to her relationship with Solita. They did not wish to live in a vacuum; rather, they wanted to be part of a tradition, one that could offer them a meaningful social and historical identity.

Disembarking at Piraeus in July 1921, Janet and Solita took the tram into Athens. Janet averted her eyes as they passed the Acropolis because she wanted to wait and see it first at night. That evening they hired a cab and drove up to the ruins, where the full moon lit the ancient buildings and young lovers embraced among the fallen pillars. Janet was so overwhelmed that she couldn't bring herself to enter the temple. She never forgot that night.[3] Over fifty years later, looking at a photograph of the Parthenon, Janet wrote to Solita that it "brought back its civilization and ours. Few so ignorant as you and I delved with such reward into Greece — from its porch we looked out onto the sea the mariners sailed — . . . Thank you for Greece, my great first adventure in illumination."[4]

For three months they took photographs with the camera lent Solita by *National Geographic:* two young women in white dresses and white hats outside the temple of Nike; laughing and playing with goats in the countryside, surrounded by purple mountains; looking down on a city that looked like "an apronful of lump sugar dumped on to the brown dustcloth which is the Attic Plain."[5] They visited Sparta, Knossos, Eleusis; they composed lyrics, wrote travel pieces, read Sappho, and drank coffee in the cafés around Athens's Constitution Square as crowds cheered the marching Greek soldiers, dressed in red caps and blue skirts, sent off to fight the Turks.

On hearing the rumor that a Turkish leader had been captured, Janet wrote, Athens "rallied like a tired old opera singer to whom the management had sent out an emergency call and gave a magnificent performance."[6] The city turned into "a babel of roaring dialects, a cubist picture of waving arms and canes, sweating waiters, white shirt fronts and flags beneath the moonlit sky." Writing her first travel piece, "Hoi Polloi at Close Range," for the New York *Tribune,* she used some of the devices readers would later associate with her "Letter from Paris" — the ironic juxtapositions, the pictorial details, the winding sentences punctuated by unexpected metaphor. And it contains one of her major themes: the civilization of today, influenced by bourgeois self-interest, is moving away from an ideal. In Athens she found an aesthetic symbol for this ideal — the Acropolis, setting a standard of beauty and serenity for the rest of the world. But Athens, like the rest of the world, was slowly being modernized.

Her disaffection, although real, was also the literary fashion. Like many of her peers, Janet deplored the way the modern world cheapened and used the past. Like them, she despised the crudity and vulgarity of modern America. The writers she and Solita admired regarded the Great War as the modern world's attempt to put death on the assembly line.[7] Like many of them, Janet and Solita turned a cynical ear to the rhetoric of progress and prosperity.

After three months in Greece, including a rocky trip to Crete in a small ship laden with goats and rotting tomatoes, they entered the city of the Turks. Solita wrote of Constantinople that "modernity has left its mark everywhere, especially since the city's occupation by the Allies, and soon the pictorial appeal that now remains will be gone forever. It will be a clean, decent, civilized city — but no longer Constantinople."[8] Yet the battered and lonely ruins of Byzantium produced an ineradicable impression: "Modern Constantinople is forgotten as one tries to imagine what these barriers seemed like to the hordes of barbarians who came every few years, looked at those miles of moated and turreted walls, and then turned back. . . . Seen from the air, the walls look like a long saffron cord, knotted and laid along the green countryside."[9]

Like T. S. Eliot, whom they soon adopted as "our poet," Janet and Solita wished to see beyond the broken images of the present; they wanted to reach back to a world where they imagined they could live and love in freedom. Together they created a shared set of images for this world, and together they set about building it, calling themselves Romantics.

They both continued to write despite the minor hardships of travel — bedbugs, lumpy beds, a bout of dysentery ascribed to too many green melons. Solita completed articles for *National Geographic* on Greece and Constantinople as well as several for *The American Boy;* her articles were brilliant, William Showalter, her editor at *Geographic,* told her. He circulated the manuscripts he couldn't use and tried to get her an assignment in Russia. When he couldn't manage that, he suggested she go to Rome. There, with Janet in tow, Solita wrote another travel piece, submitted too late for publication in *Geographic* but sent on by them to *Travel.* She was on her way to becoming a celebrity of sorts.[10]

Janet was also writing, and two of the poems she composed around this time survive. In "On Keats and Shelley Buried in Rome," she contrasts the church's view of eternity with the two dead poets, now nothing but dust. The conclusion she draws is the obvious Romantic one — a poet's art "still would rise from loam," like the eternal beauty of nature, even if all churches collapsed and all books were burned. The other poem, "Lament in Precious Shape," neither imitates the Romantics so heavily nor bothers to indict the church, still a favorite target. Simpler and more direct than her other poems, it imitates the lyrics of Sappho.

Sappho clearly helped Janet define her voice and gave her a form in which she could express her new sense of freedom. "Lament" celebrates love in terms of loss; its tone is elegiac. Discovering love and beauty in the ruins of ancient civilization or among the fragments of an ancient voice is not only liberating, it reminds her of what the present lacks. "I am a cold empty urn," Janet writes, "That was once well cherished / By a girl with moving hands / With her gifts have perished." The beloved brought "Freesia that no bee had sucked," but after her death, the speaker enters an eternity of nothingness, "Where no doves have fluttered / Where no leaves have ever moved." Left alone, the speaker asks to be filled with her beloved's "faithless dust: / Never was flesh whiter. / She who loved life, let her feel / Still my form delight her."[11]

Janet was also developing a public voice. In Vienna during the spring of 1922, while Solita was again on assignment for *National Geographic,* Janet witnessed anti-Semitic demonstrations against Arthur Schnitzler and his play *Die Reigen.* She hadn't liked the play, but found the riots so upsetting that she wrote a long letter to Alec Woollcott at the *New York Times.* He printed it, even though it was a convoluted argument in which Janet affected the high-minded tone of one who disdains the taste of the common hordes. She argued that Schnitzler's play was not very good, and that its use of sex was boring and certainly not scandalous. On that account, it could have been left to die a natural death, but since rioters insisted on protesting the Jewish author, the play was getting much more attention than it deserved.[12]

Despite her contempt for the Austrians' anti-Semitism, Janet was enchanted by the elegance of Vienna, with its beautiful parks, great cathedral, and the palaces surrounding the tree-lined Ringstrasse. But the war had ravaged the imperial city, spreading social and economic misery amid the splendor. She and Solita visited the outskirts of the city, where they saw women and children foraging for scraps of food. They found the homeless, again mostly women and children, digging by hand the foundations for places to live. They saw under-nourished children and learned that most of them were tubercular; that inflation had made the currency virtually worthless; that the middle class, having already pawned its trinkets, emerald rings, and gold boxes, its books and its furniture, commonly ate the noon meal in community kitchens. As guests at one such mess for university professors, they saw one of the faculty neatly collect the crumbs remaining on the table after he'd finished his food. He then pocketed them to take home to his hungry family.[13]

Janet's views on the Great War were changing. No longer did she see it from the perspective of Indianapolis, where she had written that the war could purge America of its hedonism and return its people to fundamental values.[14] In Greece the feverish enthusiasm for war reminded her of the "gusto of baseball fans at the pasting up of each new war score."[15] Both women saw war as the outcome of political quarrels waged by male bureaucrats and politicians, a position Janet unflaggingly maintained. Men, she once observed, can make war, and they are absurd enough to believe they are superior for doing so.[16]

Neither Janet nor Solita was the disillusioned youth made popular by Scott Fitzgerald and later by Ernest Hemingway. Janet recalled that "we knew where we were heading,"[17] and that she didn't feel particularly anguished but was "eager to appreciate the beauties of . . . Europe."[18] Her discoveries and even her sense of disenfran-chisement had sources different from those claimed by the young men of her generation.[19] Although she cited the usual reasons for leaving America — puritanism, materialism, hypocrisy, standardization — she also added that "leaving home was part of our sense of

liberty. That's why we were able to begin anew. . . . We wanted something we weren't getting."[20]

As if to make the break with her old life complete, in 1923 Janet
drafted her first will. She bequeathed most of her possessions and
her money to her mother and sisters. To Neysa McMein she left her
silver bracelets; to Lane Rehm a pair of Italian mosaic earrings, to
be made into cufflinks. Calling Solita the one most able to judge
their worth, she asked that the manuscripts "remaining from years
of unsuccessful working" be given to her. Then she said she wished
to be cremated and her ashes scattered. But her name was to be duly
inscribed on her father's headstone; she wanted acknowledgment as
part of the family. If her family wished to keep the ashes, they were
to be kept in a Grecian-type urn and set upon the fragment of Doric
capital she had "rudely" taken from the Dionysian Temple at Eleusis.
On it should appear this translation from Sappho's "Anactoria": "But,
I must dare all, since one so poor . . ."[21]

When the editors of *The Little Review* in 1929 asked Janet what she
would "most like to be (in case you are not satisfied)," Janet answered
that "I should like to be a traveller proper to this century: a knapsack
and diary is no longer enough. A voyage suitable to the 20th century
is like no exploration into visible space ever taken before, must be
conducted with elaborate knowledge, scientific data, vaccinations and
most particularly, the superb modern mechanics which only a mil-
lionaire can rent. Poor people should not travel now. The day of
pilgrims is over."[22] Yet in 1921 she and Solita were in fact pilgrims
of a sort, paying homage to as many cities and cultures as they
could. Between the spring of 1921, when they first left New York,
and the fall of 1922, when they settled in Paris, they visited many
cities, including Athens, several Greek islands, Crete, Constantinople, Rome, Florence, Siena, Vicenza, Vienna, Dresden, and Berlin.
Though their funds were limited, their money went quite far in
Europe after the war.

But they could not travel forever. Implicitly, Janet and Solita were
looking for a home, and if they did not plan to settle in Paris when
they first left the United States, it was not long before they were
drawn there. By the fall of 1922, when Solita had finished all her
travel assignments, they had decided to stay in the French capital.

They first rented rooms in a pension at 8 rue Quatrefages, near the Jardin des Plantes and the soon-to-be-completed Mosquée, but they couldn't stand the noise of the construction or the sound of the piano student practicing down the hall. So they moved to the Hôtel Place Trianon, across the street from the chapel of the Sorbonne and decorated at night with lurid-looking red electric lights. Apartments were scarce, especially those that included gas heat and running water, and were more expensive than the modest small hotels, as coal stoves and kitchenettes were extra.

In early December 1923 Janet and Solita moved again, having found the place that would suit them, as it turned out, for the next sixteen years. This time they went to the small Hôtel Saint-Germain-des-Prés, a five-story walk-up in the sixth arrondissement, at 36 rue Bonaparte. They took a large, irregularly shaped room on the fourth floor — eventually they rented three other rooms on the floor — and paid less than a dollar a day. "Its charms," Solita recalled, "were certainly not in its amenities; those we built in ourselves much later."[23] A narrow hallway from the rue Bonaparte, furnished only with a bench, served as the reception salon; a half-room with a chair, table, and the hotel telephone functioned as a kind of lobby. On each floor four doors opened from the landing. The hotel's bathroom, "barely containing a tub and chair," commented Solita, was on the fifth floor. "The bath mat was five attached wooden slats. To have a bath, it was necessary to notify well in advance the one and only servitor — there was no maid — the *garçon de tous les étages;* he drew the water, laid one towel, small, on the chair, and marked down the equivalent of 20 cents in his little black book."[24]

Their room was sunny in the morning, and from their windows they could see the gaily decorated tops of the green city buses. There were two closets (one for books), several pieces of red furniture, and a fireplace that didn't work. The proprietors, Louis and Melanie Doré, owned a cat, permitted no cooking, and kept the halls clean and waxed. All the rooms were steam-heated, and though the heat cost extra, Janet figured that they were living quite cheaply. Shopping and cooking at home would be much more expensive than the roast beef and potatoes they could order in a modest restaurant for one franc seventy-five, or a little less than ten cents. Nearby was a bistro called La Quatrième République, where at lunchtime Janet and Solita drank homemade onionskin wine, ate boiled eggs, talked politics with the proprietor, and rented fresh napkins for thirty centimes a day. But Solita liked brioche for breakfast, and Janet liked to join her, for an extravagant three francs fifty, which they would try to balance by evening.

Behind the façade of rue Bonaparte, among the small shops, were the elegant homes of families who dated their proprietorship from the revolution. Around the corner on the rue Jacob was the Hôtel Angleterre, the first stop of Djuna Barnes and others from Greenwich Village who came to Paris. A block away from their hotel stood the oldest church in Paris, the Saint-Germain-des-Prés, and near it were the two well-known cafés, the Deux Magots and the Flore, "rapidly filling with the accents we hoped to leave behind," Solita wrote. Yet like many of their American compatriots, they frequently sat at the Left Bank cafés where they could talk for hours in English. Some Americans, like Natalie Barney and Sylvia Beach and later the British-born Nancy Cunard, entered the world of French books, theater, publishing, and debate. Others, like Scott Fitzgerald, never did. Janet and Solita wanted to try. They arranged to take language lessons twice a week to unlearn their bookish French.

As Margaret Anderson noted, speaking about herself as much as about the period, it was a time for personality.[25] Solita, still breezy, laughed if anyone referred to Cleveland as a city. With her large eyes "of an intense blue," as Janet noted, and with her dark hair cut short and shingled — she said she would have cut it like a man's but her ears would not lie flat — Solita was a striking figure, always smartly dressed and composed.[26] Janet also made a point of looking chic and handsome.[27] By 1923 she too had cut her chestnut hair, now rapidly graying, and wore it very short in back with little bangs over the ears that made her hair — thinning, she feared — look thicker. She decided this made her look at least five to eight years younger — quite pretty in fact, she assured her mother.

Attracted to the bohemian life, virtually the norm among recent arrivals to the Left Bank, Janet and Solita cultivated not only personality and style but a sense of purpose. They furnished their rooms with leopard print throws and pillows and bought a few items of furniture; Janet bought a large yellow armchair, which vaguely matched their dark yellow wallpaper, with its stripes and faded roses, and a small antique table for writing. They had no obligations or chores, except earning whatever money they wanted to spend. They were ready, said Solita, "to learn all about art and write our first novels."[28]

They rose at eight, had breakfast at the Deux Magots around nine, then took care of errands for the rest of the morning. In the afternoon and early evening they wrote. Later they drank mint tea and ate couscous in the fifth arrondissement or wandered over to the bookstalls on the quay. Occasionally they bought a few items at the flea market or browsed through the books and magazines at Brentano's, to keep up with the latest being published at home. Their neighborhood contained anything they might want: the post office was nearby on the rue des Saints-Pères; on the rue Jacob they bought the small articles they needed in Madame Chenu's notion shop. A few doors down was the tobacconist, who sold matches and American cigarettes. Across the street was the pharmacy, the flower shop, and the dry cleaner. They made friends with the shopkeepers, learned their personal habits, and became devoted to some, like Madame Alexandre, the sewing woman they called "Doodle," and her husband, their coiffeur. Very soon after their arrival, they paid their respects to Oscar Wilde, interred in the Père Lachaise cemetery. Janet carried one large black iris; she later said that a single flower, rather than a bouquet, seemed in keeping with Wilde's style.[29]

They took short holidays to explore the countryside of Normandy and Brittany, drinking bad cider and vermouth and sleeping in second-class hotels. They ate the regional buckwheat pancakes and visited all the churches recommended by Henry Adams, marveling over their arches and naves. Like several of their new acquaintances, they lived in genteel poverty. To Americans visiting Paris in 1922, however, Janet and Solita seemed just like tourists — or so Anita Loos thought when her husband John Emerson introduced her to a couple of "girls John picked up in his wanderings."[30] Soon, however, she was calling Janet and Solita two of her most valued friends. And shortly after their meeting, she was delighted when Janet decided to join her and John in Vienna.

Young and high-spirited, Janet and Anita were charmed by what they called the "undefeated gaiety" of the Viennese. At the Theatrical Club they met the playwright Ferenc Molnár and the singer Richard

Touher, then performing in a Franz Lehár operetta; they sat for hours over coffee with whipped cream in the Sacher Hotel, still managed by Frau Sacher, who had fed the nobility gratis during the war. They heard *Der Rosenkavalier* at the famed Opera House and agreed that life in Vienna was like a musical comedy.[31] "We were lively and hip," Anita Loos recalled, seriously adding, "Most of all, we took amazing good luck for granted."[32]

For all her urbanity, real or assumed, Janet appeared to herself as wide-eyed and restlessly eager to understand, appreciate, and participate. She did, however, feel that she was part of the thriving but self-conscious culture, which lived as much in the streets and cafés and small presses as in the galleries and theaters. American magazines explained what one could expect to find in Paris, why one went, what one did there.[33] Ezra Pound, writing a letter from Paris for *The Dial* in 1920, somewhat sardonically called the city the "paradise of artists irrespective of their merit or demerit" but added that at least "conversation still exists there."[34] American artist Elizabeth Eyre de Lanux, in Paris since 1918, met Janet and Solita at the Deux Magots soon after they arrived and wrote in her Paris letter for *Town and Country* that in 1922 "those who used to come to Paris once a year come once a season; those who stayed a month have chosen their quartier and signed a lease; . . . And this great migration is not exclusively due to the rigid enforcement of the 18th Amendment, nor entirely owing to the fall of the lira, the mark, the franc, the crown, the leu, the dinar and the drachma and other symbols (over here we call it all the rise of the dollar). There seems to be a widespread rumor that the art of living (whatever is meant by this elastic term) has reached higher points of perfection in Europe than it has at home. Art is an individual matter, and life does its best to keep up with it. The art of living, consequently, is for everyone to practice in his or her own way."[35]

In fact, so many were practicing it in Paris that Paris was good copy. Publisher and writer Robert McAlmon recalled that "articles were appearing in American magazines and newspapers about the life of the deracinated, exiled, and expatriated who lived mainly in Paris, leading, the articles implied, non-working and dissolute lives."[36] He tried to correct the record by compiling a long list of productive, not dissipated, foreign artists — 250 in all. But despite his efforts, the myth remained. Sixty years later, in 1984, Kay Boyle was still trying to dispel it.[37] Yet to many, Scott Fitzgerald and Nancy Cunard continued to symbolize the fate of the entire era known as the "jazz age" — figures of great charm, vitality, and promise dragged by excess into alcoholism, madness, and despair.

Yet despite the moralistic endings tacked onto the stories of the expatriates, no one tired of explaining the allure of Paris, both in the twenties and after. Paris was said to represent individuality, to welcome originality. In 1925 the Indiana sculptress Janet Scudder, a friend of Janet's, said that Paris gave everyone a special niche, and for journalist Sisley Huddleston, writing in 1927, Paris offered "everything that is obtainable . . . things of the spirit and things which minister to bodily needs, comforts, and pleasures. Everything there is to be seen anywhere is in some form to be seen in Paris. It is the microcosm of the universe."[38] It was a city of pleasure, offering the startling Ballets Russes of Diaghilev, with sets painted by Picasso and Léger and music composed by Stravinsky. It was nights dancing at the cabarets of Montmartre, afternoons of animated discussion around café tables. It was a home for those looking for companionship or a publisher; it was an absence of convention and an amplitude of feeling. Harold Stearns, in his 1935 memoir of Paris, said it was a place where one was content just to be alive.[39] Margaret Anderson, who moved *The Little Review* from New York to Paris in 1923, called it "the city of love, liberty, and light."[40] Descriptions of Paris in the twenties were no less clichéd then than now.

Friends of Janet's had already moved there. The scholarly Reverend Richard Doubs, former curate of Saint Mark's-in-the-Bouwerie and a friend of Marie's as well as Janet's, had transferred to the American Church of the Holy Trinity in Paris and lived around the corner from Janet and Solita. Neither minded his pedantry, since he devoted most of it to church architecture, one of their favorite subjects. Occasionally they would meet him at the Deux Magots for breakfast and then spend the rest of the day gazing up at arches in Sens or Auxerre, with Doubs their gentle tutor.

Richard and Alice-Lee Myers, Janet's college friends, had taken up residence nearby on the rue Visconti. Whenever sheet music arrived from America, they would invite Janet to come by and sing

with them in the husky alto they loved.[41] They also loved her salacious
humor. Whenever he came to town, Solita's friend Charles Bain
(Bastian) Hoyt, a wealthy young collector of Chinese ceramics, would
usher Janet through the Louvre's early sculptures and then take both
women out for champagne and dinner at one of the best restaurants.
Janet brought the vacationing Alec Woollcott to the tomb of Héloïse
and Abelard at Père Lachaise, where Woollcott promptly paid his
respects by putting two walnuts on the tomb.[42] Neysa McMein
amused Janet and Solita with her street market purchases — goatskin
rugs sold by unscrupulous vendors — and with her passion for the
fake jewels on the rue de Rivoli. When Neysa managed to get them
tickets for Stravinsky's Les Noces — one seat in the gallery and one
in the front row — she was confident that her friends wouldn't mind
sharing the better seat. They spent most of the performance running
up and down the gallery stairs.[43]

Although Janet knew most of the Left Bank literary celebrities
only by reputation, she was becoming familiar with the places they
frequented: the Dada-inspired Boeuf-sur-le-Toit, named by its co-
founder Jean Cocteau, drew an international crowd, one she called
the "most brilliant of a brilliant epoch." To her it wasn't a "snob
cabaret," as writer Richard Aldington called it, but one of the places
where friends might gather to hear her new friend Eugene MacCown,
a painter from Missouri, play jazz piano or listen to three of the Les
Six composers — Darius Milhaud, Francis Poulenc, and Georges
Auric — jam with Jean Wiener. She knew the Jockey, opened by
the painter Hilaire Hiler on the rue Campagne-Première, which Basil
Woon in his 1926 The Paris That's Not in the Guidebooks described
as full of "white-faced women with large nostrils and artificial eyes
and curious persons in velvet coats and windsor ties, who drink beer
and pose for the tourists."[44] She watched Josephine Baker dance in
La Revue Nègre wearing nothing more than a pink flamingo feather;
Janet too was caught up by the rage for Afro-American music heard
at the Bal Nègre, and she particularly liked the Bal Colonial on the
rue Blomet, featuring dancers from the French colonies who swayed
to "sophisticated jazz."[45]

Janet and Solita were not involved with the small magazines or
presses flourishing in Paris at the time, and they were not really
interested in the disputes and manifestos or the literary fracas sur-

rounding them. Dada, for example, did not appeal to these traditionalists, whose interests in literature did not include the avant-garde, except insofar as it rejected the "brutal vulgarity" of a writer like Dreiser.[46] If Janet went to the Montparnasse cafés, the Sélect, the Rotonde, and the Dôme ("an over-the-counter market" recalled Malcolm Cowley, "that traded in literary futures"), she did not consider herself part of this particular crowd, which she thought too radical and rowdy — and too young. She preferred to think of herself as "Saint-Germain-des-Près": older, more conservative, not so alcoholic and noisy, perhaps slightly arrogant.

Those two worlds intersected at Sylvia Beach's bookshop Shakespeare and Company on the rue de l'Odéon. Janet was fond of Sylvia and saw her frequently in the early twenties, as most of the Left Bank expatriates did, for Sylvia's bookshop and lending library was the colony's unofficial living room. "Has there ever been another bookshop like Shakespeare and Company? It was not just the crowded shelves, the little bust of Shakespeare, or the many informal photographs of her friends, it was Sylvia herself. . . . She found us printers, translators, and rooms," reminisced the writer Bryher (Winifred Ellerman).[47] Janet and Solita almost rented the unheated furnished apartment above Sylvia's shop for 500 francs a month, hand and bed linen included, but decided against it at the prospect of cold winter mornings.

Janet long remembered the day in February 1922 when Sylvia placed a blue-and-white copy of *Ulysses* in the window of the shop. Joyce's novel, Janet recalled, "burst over" the Left Bank "like an explosion in print whose words and phrases fell upon us like a gift of tongues, like a less than holy Pentecostal experience."[48] However, she regarded Joyce the man, as opposed to Joyce the artist, more cynically, attributing both his solitary habits and his somewhat shabby treatment of Sylvia, who'd published *Ulysses* in full, to what she called the selfishness of genius. She met Joyce only once, some years later, in the thirties. When Ernest Hemingway and his second wife, Pauline Pfeiffer, invited Janet and Solita to join them and Joyce for dinner at Michaud's, Ernest hardly spoke, he was so busy watching Joyce in a "stupor of silent worship," according to Solita. Joyce was drunk and Janet was bored, so she and Pauline left. Ernest excused himself from the table for a minute, and Joyce turned to Solita, addressing her for the first time. "Don't go," he implored and then said nothing else to her for the rest of the evening.[49]

Occasionally Janet and Solita entertained visitors, among them Scott Fitzgerald, who sometimes stopped by to discuss literature at two in the morning, drunk and never able to reach the fourth floor before the stairway light went out.[50] The young and eager Hemingway, who frequently dropped by, would sit in Janet's oversized yellow chair, which they called "Ernest's chair," she remembered. "It was the only one big enough to hold him, leaning back, laughing talking, his long legs crossed and cocked up in front of him."[51] The two of them would stroll over to the Deux Magots and sit for hours, discussing Stendhal or detective novels or how to write. One should write, Ernest told her, "so it feels good."[52] One night years later, over drinks at the Deux Magots, he bent forward. "Listen, Jan" — she said he always called her that, "like a member of my family" — he said, apropos of a piece she'd written on bullfighting: "I just want you to know that if a journalistic prize is ever given for the worst sports writer of the western world, I'm going to see you get it, pal, for you deserve it. You're perfectly terrible."[53]

Janet was generally shy about meeting well-known literary personages; she said she shrank away when introduced to Ford Madox Ford. She and Gene MacCown (who said he had been born in a prairie schooner) had gone to one of the dance halls near the Bastille, where they danced to bells and an accordion for twenty centimes. Afterward Gene invited her to a party at Ford's, unperturbed that he and Janet were dressed in heavy shoes, scarves, and sailor's pea-jackets; Ford's illustrious guests were in evening attire. It didn't matter. Janet and Gene danced, and Gene got very drunk. Janet met the Princess Violet Murat — rumored to be the lover of painter Marie Laurencin — the Dadaist Tristan Tzara, and the artist Mina Loy — whose writing Janet dismissed as "Gertrude Steinish" — and her daughter. She was introduced to Stella Bowen, Ford's Australian companion, and finally to the wheezing, overweight Ford himself. "What a privilege," she happily exclaimed.[54]

The world seemed full of possibilities and malleable enough to be shaped by her every desire. These were, Janet told Hugh Ford much later, vain and creative years, years of temper and great passion and abuse, of self-promotion and self-importance, hilarity, and for many, despite rumors to the contrary, hard work.[55] Janet and Solita were not bound by responsibilities or commitments, which Janet considered "leeches"; they could leave Paris whenever they wished, especially during the chilly winter months and the hot summer ones.[56]

In February 1924 they took the money they figured Solita's first novel, *The Uncertain Feast,* would earn and the money she had already made and left damp, cold Paris for Sicily, traveling by way of the Loire Valley, Marseilles, and Naples. Staying in Palermo for over a month in a small hotel without running water, they stood each morning on their balcony to watch the donkeys haul green cauliflower through the triangular square below. It was just the kind of picturesque vacation they wanted. They watched goats being milked, heard the sounds of oak bells and the hurdy-gurdy man; a young maid arranged for them to bathe unnoticed by the hotel proprietor and mended their pajamas without their asking.[57]

Janet had brought *The Cubical City* to work on, and Solita was working on her second novel, but neither of them got much work done, either in Sicily or in Rome, their next stop. At St. Peter's they wore black dresses and black veils; they ate well, dining as the guest of a rich friend who let them use the bath at his more expensive hotel every afternoon. Two weeks later in Florence, they met the Hungarian-American actor Leo Ditrichstein and his wife, who asked them to translate Sacha Guitry's play *Après l'Amour* into English and paid them $150. The Ditrichsteins prepared a private room in their villa for Janet and Solita, allowing them to work in solitude each morning from nine to one. In the afternoons, they all browsed the galleries until four, had ices on the Piazza Victor Emmanuel, and drove until seven in the Ditrichsteins' car, returning to eat sumptuous Tuscan dinners — risotto, hare with sweet and sour sauce, boiled asparagus tossed with butter and Parmesan cheese.[58]

Ditrichstein was so pleased with the translation that he suggested Janet and Solita join him in Vienna to do another. They decided to accept the first-class tickets he offered them — a member of his own party had become sick — and were in Vienna by June. Although they thought the second play wasn't worth their time or effort, they stayed on, having rented the same inexpensive apartment they had taken two years earlier, and rationalizing that room, breakfast, and lunch cost only two dollars a day. The Ditrichsteins took Janet and

Solita motoring, to dinner in charming restaurants, and to the theater
as their guests. But by August Janet and Solita were bored. They
played kegels in the basement of a small café most afternoons until
the weather turned cooler. Then they went back to Italy and on
home to Paris.

Although eager to talk about literature, Janet didn't often admit to
her friends that she was writing. Jane Grant recalled Janet declaring
that she intended to pass the rest of her life at the Deux Magots —
and maybe write a novel if the spirit moved her.[59] Janet's correspondence of this time indicates she wasn't spending all her time at
the cafés or at the Folies-Bergère; she was composing poetry, writing
a couple of articles she called "dreadful hack things" — she refused
to tell her mother where they were published — and slowly putting
together a draft of *The Cubical City.*

She often complained that she worked slowly and with difficulty.
Her pace made her feel wretched. But Solita, who had utmost faith
in Janet's talent, pushed her to complete it. "Janet's book is racing,"
she wrote Janet's mother, as if she were helping Janet convince Mary
that she was indeed working. "It's going to be beautifully written
and I'm sure the first publisher that sees it will snap it up. I know
of no one who writes more lovely prose than she; and the imagination
and imagery she gives to her writing is extraordinary and unique."[60]

When her mother asked how the novel was going, Janet reported
little progress, but she assured Mary that she was productive and
happy. In letter after letter, Janet recounted the pleasures and amenities of her new life, showing her mother she was justified in choosing
as she had. Her mother could hardly quarrel with her daughter's
choice, representing as it did the kind of life Mary always said she
wanted for her daughter, if not for herself.

Janet explained to her mother that at least her book would contain
nothing "cheap or claptrapetry."[61] She would not pander to a reader's
lagging attention with obvious devices to snag it; she concentrated
on style and cared little about plot.[62] Although she admired the
leanness of Sappho's verse and the lyrical prose of Henry James,
Janet wanted her novel to be lavishly sensual and stylistically surprising. Still immersed in the imagery of romanticism, she tried to

create atmosphere and character with colorful, pictorial, elaborate phrases.

Although she later dismissed *The Cubical City,* saying it was not really a novel, even declaring that it was no good at all (though sometimes she said it was well written), it remains an interesting example of her early style. More important, it is her symbolic farewell to America, written from the vantage point of her new home. And this autobiographical roman à clef was her only real attempt at a long, sustained work using unabashedly personal sources: her relationship with her parents, her father's death, her life in New York, and her reasons for leaving.

Janet's protagonist, Delia Poole, based loosely on Neysa McMein, is a successful commercial artist from the Midwest who lives in New York and looks for something she vaguely calls freedom. That freedom is not simply the right to take lovers; it is the ability to enjoy without remorse or recrimination the pleasures of the flesh, as men have traditionally done; society, Janet tells us, prevents women from doing the same. But Delia is largely unsocialized; primitive, sensuous, vain, and inarticulate, she is an anachronism, a woman living in the twentieth century but ignorant of its conventions. Her past is littered with lovers; she takes and discards whom she pleases when she pleases; she acts wholly upon instinct.

Beyond the story of Delia's worldly education, the novel presents her slow and painful recognition that she will never be free from the world's entanglements. Each relationship, with all its attendant responsibilities, traps Delia in a web of guilt, stealth, and deception. She cannot be herself without hurting others; to protect them, she deceives them; to protect herself, she deceives herself.

Delia's world is a world of betrayal, primarily sexual. Sexuality betrayed Delia's mother, luring her from her career on the stage to a wedded life she neither liked nor understood. Yet Delia's robust and "pagan" sexuality, unlike her mother's, leaves her vulnerable, for it is at odds with a world that fears and represses sexual desire, leaving only guilt in its wake. Ironically, Delia is betrayed by the very sexual instincts Janet calls natural and good. When Delia learns that her unhappy father has lost a significant amount of money in a failed real estate venture, she blames herself: she believes she "helped

sell" his precious property over "his head for sprays of fading free-
sias," flowers that symbolize Delia's sexual desires.[63]

The novel's plot is fairly simple. Delia is affianced to a young man
who is sent on business to the Philippines. Unable to wait for Paul's
return, she is unfaithful to him, more by chance than design; she is
a fairly passive woman who neither plans her infidelity nor remembers much about it afterward. When Paul returns and confronts her,
Delia feels that she is the one who's been betrayed. Delia tells him
she was always faithful in her feelings, though perhaps not in her
actions. "What people do is of no importance," she says. "It's what
one feels for them that counts." And, she adds, if she regrets anything,
her regrets are her own — "It was my life, not yours."[64] To her way
of thinking, she has merely exercised the privileges of youth and
freedom and flesh — privileges a woman is denied, she learns.

Delia is not simply an unintentional feminist confronting an out-
moded double standard. Delia accepts Paul after implicitly acknowl-
edging that she can't have what she really wants, which is a
relationship as passionate and meaningful as those she has had with
several women. These gave Delia the intimacy, intensity, and tenderness for which "love was the only accurate word" and meant much
more to her than any of her affairs with men.[65] But the relationships
could not last, because they were modeled on heterosexual relationships, and because a rigidly heterosexual society made no room for
them.

Nancy Burke once loved Delia better than anything in the world,
lavishing on her all the attentions of wife, mother, and friend. During
the early days of their friendship, Delia and Nancy shielded their
feelings from the world by taking an extended trip together, but they
could not isolate themselves forever. Inevitably, the outside world
intruded in the form of Delia's fiancé. The friendship between the
two women fell apart when the jealous Nancy became possessive
and conniving and weak.

In contrast to Nancy's demanding affections is the lusty tenderness
of Mercy Wellington, a disinterested collector of admirers. With
Mercy, Delia feels she is in the presence of someone who has risen
above proprietary relations. Older than Delia, the civilized, wise, and
mature Mercy has learned to keep her private life private by outwardly conforming to whatever is expected of her.[66] But although

she loves Delia, "loving women, to Mercy, was not practicable." Ever expedient, she follows the fashions of the social world; for her, female friendship "didn't have enough shape" to be taken too seriously.[67]

Delia admires Mercy, even envies her apparent freedom. Mercy hints to Delia that she, too, can be free, if she will marry and learn to exploit the privileges allowed the married woman and denied the single. But Delia can never be as cynical or as deliberate as Mercy, just as she cannot be as domestic and faithful as Nancy. Delia is unable to promise any woman what she can promise no man — sexual loyalty, domesticity, hypocrisy.

When Nancy leaves her, Delia feels a "wrenching as if something that had been lifted out had left its roots that could lament and wave in the inner cardiac air like mandrakes on a field at night because they had been cut."[68] Realizing that their friendship has ended, Delia, sinking into a "breast-like chair," grieves for the nurturing support Nancy, and all women, could give — if only they did not become like men. Men, too weak, too exploitative, too eager to possess, offer nothing to a woman like Delia. Ironically, in choosing to spend her life with a man, she need not give up a woman's nurturing support. She remains linked to her mother, but the price is high.

It is essentially because of her relationship to her mother that Delia finally decides to go through with a marriage to Paul. Having installed the widowed Mrs. Poole in her New York apartment, she frequently finds herself lying about her whereabouts, avoiding her mother's pointed questions. Eventually realizing she cannot escape Mrs. Poole, Delia capitulates to what she thinks her mother prefers. But her capitulation is not a simple matter. Janet suggests that Delia decides to stay bound to her mother: "Mother and child, Delia thought. Nothing ever managed to cut that tie. And no one ever wanted to cut it. Everybody clung. She knew."[69]

Janet consistently described Indiana as a hateful place, with its bourgeois standards, its lack of beauty, and its elongated, flat spaces. In *The Cubical City* the fields of Ohio appear "virile . . . procreative and breastless, idling out the cold winter under a patient domestic sky." This "male" landscape, with its stubble of corn in spring and its "beard of red clover" in summer, offered "nothing to the eye."[70] For Janet, America was a masculine place — unappealing, unsensuous, restricting.[71] She left this America for Paris, a city with "an old girl's countenance, shaded by a trollop's gay wig."[72] Europe offered her a different scope and range in which to discover and indulge herself and, unlike Delia, explore the "lusty tenderness" of female sexuality.

It is very likely that since adolescence, Janet had known she could not easily accommodate her sexual feelings to what was approved by family, friends, or the world at large. This awareness could not help but make her feel guilty and even hypocritical, leading as she must have, a kind of double life.[73] At the same time, choosing to leave a proper heterosexual marriage for a relationship with another woman must have been as dislocating and frightening as it was exhilarating. But her relationship with Solita allowed her to be, finally, more at one with herself.

There were fewer choices available to Delia than to Janet Flanner, though the two should be seen together to understand the difficulty of Janet's choices and the complexity of the feelings underlying them. Although Janet portrayed Delia sympathetically, she made it clear that Delia failed to understand herself. Janet admired what she called Delia's "healthy eroticism" but associated her untutored eclecticism and her ignorance of the past with the America she detested.[74] Delia could not hope to free herself by living solely in the present. To the extent that Delia was a hedonist, Janet was ambivalent about her. And to the extent that she could not free herself from the bond with her mother, Janet took pity on her. Conscious of the painful necessity of this kind of separation, Janet wrote many years later that "we do not want to be intimate enough with our family even to think of passion, for another, in their presence; it seems indecent. That is why, in longing, one can long freely only away from them and best among strangers."[75]

Janet and Solita doubtless kept the nature of their relationship from Mary Flanner, who asked few questions and delicately ignored what she preferred not to see. However, she must have suspected that the friendship was more than platonic. Yet, though Janet apparently concealed her private life — and protested to her mother that she, like Mary, considered sex vulgar — she was anxious for her mother and Hildegarde to share part of it. They already knew and liked Solita, who responded well to all Mary's small maternal affections when she and Janet visited Berkeley together in August 1923.

Mary made little slipper bags for Solita's shoes and bought her a pair of yellow lounging pajamas. A few months later, after fire swept through Mary and Hildegarde's home and destroyed everything they'd brought from Indianapolis — except four books, a few of Hildegarde's poems, and scattered pieces of jewelry — Solita joined Janet in trying to induce Mary to visit Paris: "We are planning places to show you and cafes where you may drink coffee on pleasant terraces and watch the life on the boulevard. I know you will adore Paris as we do. You ought to stay a long time. Perhaps you will like it well enough to wish to live here," Solita wrote. "We might even find an apartment big enough for four although you might not like to see so much of me. While in that case I'll live around the corner but no further away than that."[76]

Mary briefly considered moving to Paris with Hildegarde, and Janet encouraged her. But she decided against it — it's unlikely she considered the proposition very seriously — and in the next twenty-five years never even visited Janet there. She told Hildegarde she was too prone to seasickness to make the trip, but it's not clear what she said to Janet, who was obviously disappointed.[77] Perhaps Janet guessed that her mother preferred not having to confront her life directly. Mary may well have preferred that Hildegarde not confront it as well, for Hildegarde went to Paris only after their mother died. As a result, family reunions took place in California, New York, and, very occasionally, back in Indianapolis.

Mary continued to urge Janet to return home; Janet responded by arguing that living abroad was proof of her devotion, especially since she was in Europe to write the novels in which her mother played a major part. Her reasoning must have struck Mary as specious, but it was evident that Janet was happier in Paris than she'd ever been before. "Hardly any of us has been really happy in life and I am now," she confided to her mother. "And the contagion of mutual contact adding more unhappiness has, as we all can say, been tragic. It becomes finally nearly a battle for survival, where every passage at arms is paid for as much with tears as victory."[78]

Janet dedicated *The Cubical City* to her mother, whose picture hung over her bed.

5

Paris France
1924-1925

SOME FORTY YEARS after she and Janet first moved into their rooms on the rue Bonaparte, Solita walked down the street and peered into the lobby of their former hotel. "This is how a ghost must feel," she said to herself, "except in the puff of smoke that used to be the heart."[1] Janet, who sometimes chafed at Solita's unabashed nostalgia, savored the memory of their first years in Paris. "How could I look back over the twenties and not say they were lots of fun?" she asked Mike Wallace in 1973. "I had lots of fun."[2]

In later life Janet was not averse to bolstering the myth of Paris in the twenties with her own memories — reminiscences about the taste of French food or the cheap price of good wine, about the gracious mannequins parading their fashions at Longchamps, about dancing till dawn in cheap cafés and watching the sun rise in the markets of Les Halles over coffee and flowers. She remembered the streets crowded with desultory talk in a language that fell musically on midwestern ears. No doubt she romanticized her Paris and felt justified in filling it with a kaleidoscopic set of bright images, for it was there that she first entered the world she'd dreamed about. As she described it to her family, it was a world of freedom and work, an artistic milieu, and she and Solita felt they were too bohemian to live in any other.

In their world the central characters were women, many of whom had come to Paris to be rid of the social and sexual restrictions endured at home.[3] In America the passage of the woman suffrage amendment hadn't brought them real sexual and economic freedom, and although women in France did not have the right to vote until 1945, Paris offered many like Janet and Solita a certain latitude of movement. As American women in French society, they enjoyed the best of both worlds. At home they felt they were living a shadow life — ignored, censured, condescended to or despised because of their sexual preference; here they were suddenly a minority of a different kind: they were American women abroad. That they lived together, worked together, were openly sexual with one another was no longer the concern of friends or family.

The community of women was by no means homogeneous, despite points of contact such as Natalie Barney's salon or Gertrude Stein and Alice Toklas's studio or Sylvia Beach's bookshop. But within it one could find female artists, writers, publishers — groups of women who did not have to hide themselves or their sexual preferences or their anger at restrictions "that antagonized," as Margaret Anderson once said.[4]

Janet and Solita were not immediately taken up by any particular group, although they were clearly aware of the most celebrated one, the salon run by Gertrude Stein and Alice Toklas in the rue de Fleurus. Solita was not enamored of it, calling it a "well-sieved literary salon for those who were asked to come a second time."[5] Janet was apparently asked, and she liked Gertrude, whom she deferentially called Miss Stein during the first few years of their acquaintance. As soon as Janet met her, she later recalled, she knew Gertrude was a wonderful woman, with her handsome face like a Roman emperor's and hearty belly laugh. She always led the conversation, for "Gertrude led everything." Gertrude generated excitement and warmth, and she talked "with the greatest sense, coherency, simplicity, and precision."[6] Alice Toklas was different; evasive and creative, she reminded Janet of a "praying mantis among strawberry leaves."[7] Sitting behind the tea tray, which Janet confessed thinking the best place to be, Alice "stripped her truths down so close that they bled."[8]

Janet made most of these remarks years later. Little is known of her actual relationship with Gertrude and Alice. Gertrude, who was reported to have said that Janet looked like the buffalo side of an Indian nickel, was fond of the younger woman, eighteen years her junior. And she must have enjoyed the awe with which Janet regarded her, as an uncompromising and serious artist. That Janet didn't understand Gertrude's work — and eventually went so far as to call it "charming nonsense" — mattered less than that Gertrude had created it.[9] And so she always treated Gertrude the way Gertrude liked to be treated. Janet frequently called on Gertrude and Alice, bringing flowers; Virgil Thomson remembered Janet always buzzing in and out.[10] She made herself useful. Get a pencil and make an inventory of the paintings, Gertrude instructed, when she and Alice were moving to the rue Christine, and Janet obliged. Alice didn't think she did a very good job.

Nor did Alice think Janet read much of Gertrude's writing, although she must have. In 1927 she planned to write a profile of Gertrude (she later denied this, saying she never wrote about friends). Either *The New Yorker* did not accept it or she never finished it. However, years later she wrote the introduction to *Two: Gertrude Stein and Her Brother,* the first volume of Stein's work to be published by Yale University Press. When Thornton Wilder suggested Janet do it, Alice consented reluctantly; when Alice saw the result — a reminiscent, complimentary, and somewhat (but not entirely) anecdotal piece whose style mimicked Stein's — she was not altogether pleased.[11]

Another of Janet and Solita's new acquaintances was also uncommitted to any particular group. In fact, she was so highly individual that no group or movement could claim her for very long. A British-born shipping heiress contemptuous of her class, the tall and striking Nancy Cunard was considered extremely intelligent, volatile, generous, and strong-willed; it was whispered that she was the illegitimate daughter of novelist George Moore; at the very least she was his best friend. One fall evening in 1924 Gene MacCown arranged for Janet and Solita to meet the younger woman, whose thin silhouette they'd already glimpsed at Left Bank parties.[12] They waited expectantly at a Montparnasse café. Nancy, golden-haired and riveting, with eyes as blue as sapphires — "a cause for wonder anywhere except in the ambiance of that decade in which we danced," said Solita — arrived an hour late, "which was quite early for her to be late." The three women, Solita continued, "became a fixed triangle, we survived all the spring quarrels and the sea changes of forty-two years of modern female fidelity."[13]

Reputedly the model for Iris March in Michael Arlen's novel *The Green Hat* and for several of Aldous Huxley's hard, sexually independent characters, Nancy was the female figure most often selected to represent the twenties: talented, rich, and energetic, she seemed at the same time restless, melancholy, driven, and ultimately, wasted.[14] She was devoted to her writing, wanted to start a small press, and believed wholeheartedly in the kinds of freedom Janet and Solita talked about. When they first met, Nancy had already published two books of poems: *Outlaws,* which Janet admired and which had earned the respect of her friend George Moore, and the generally well reviewed *Sublunary.* Yet in spite of all her concrete accomplishments — her writing, as well as the output of her publishing venture, the Hours Press — Nancy Cunard remembered the twenties as years of pain and struggle. (The thirties, she once said, were her years.) And she was to despise the stereotyped views of the decade marketed later in her life. When several publishers begged her in the 1960s to write her memoirs, she refused. Everyone is crazy for another silly volume about the roaring twenties, she said; "I wish them all asthma."[15]

Her disapproval of bourgeois life was real and deep; her rebellion anguished and often self-destructive; her rage frequently uncontained. But when she thought of her early days in Paris, she also thought of Janet and Solita. And of all the women Janet and Solita met during their first few years in Europe, they felt closest to Nancy. Janet told her sister Hildegarde that Nancy was a great woman, a fine poet, and the best mind of any Anglo-Saxon woman in Europe — next to herself, she mischievously added.[16]

In a very few months, they were calling one another 1, 2, and 3 or the "three happily married women," referring to their earlier unhappy marriages as well as their new friendship. When away from one another they wrote, exchanging confidences, *bavardage,* and information, and signing their letters with a tripod or the fraction $\frac{1}{3}$. Nancy suggested Janet and Solita try the homosexual bar she had discovered near the Porte-St.-Martin; Janet and Solita told her about the night they went "brothelling" together; they shared a recipe for staying thin: work, worry, and sex. All three disdained "Litterachure," pomposity, the staid, and the sordidly commercial. They disliked people they called "impersonators"; they themselves were "real."[17] They read each other's work, commenting with care and enthusiasm. Janet considered Nancy's poem *Parallax* far better than Eliot's *Waste Land*. Nancy pressed Solita's novel *The Uncertain Feast,* which she thought excellent, on her friend Raymond Mortimer, a critic, and insisted that Janet let her read a draft of *The Cubical City*. Janet, at first a bit reluctant, finally gave it to Nancy — the only person other than Solita permitted to read a draft.

Janet spent a good deal of time at "the Grattery," her affectionate name for Nancy's Paris flat on the rue le Regrattier, decorated with blood-red walls and sketches by Wyndham Lewis. The flat was too cold for Janet's taste, but she enjoyed Nancy's frequent parties with their eclectic guest lists — George Moore, Havelock Ellis, Mary Reynolds, Marcel Duchamp, the young surrealist writer René Crevel. She and Solita often ate and drank there with Nancy before going on to a more public place to dance and listen to music. When Janet and Solita gave their first New Year's Eve party, they sat their ten guests in front of specially made placemats decorated with playing cards. Their beloved and elegant Nancy was seated as the queen of hearts.

Janet was never away from Nancy for long during those first years in Paris, even in the summer of 1925 when Janet and Solita rented a small house for a few weeks in le Lavandou in the south of France, a place originally discovered by the Surrealists. The terrace of their house, located next to a group of fishing huts, had a lovely view of mimosa trees, silvery olive groves, slim fruit trees, and the shiny coast. Solita especially liked the idea of having a real house with several rooms, a small kitchen, and a door that opened directly to the outdoors, but neither she nor Janet could tolerate even the smallest of household tasks. Unused to domestic chores, they were enraged by the drudgery of housecleaning and cooking and dishwashing.[18] And the house was dirty, dark, and ugly inside. With the mistral blowing, hot and relentless, they felt listless. Janet's lips split at the corners, and Solita took to bed with a chest cold.

Then Nancy arrived, bringing Virginia Woolf's *Mrs. Dalloway* and furiously cursing the wind, and the situation improved. They visited nearby friends; Gene MacCown had also rented a house, and the four would meet in a café in town to talk passionately about the books they wanted to write, the paintings they dreamed of painting. For hours they sat under red and blue umbrellas, idly catching locusts and saying little. On U.S.A. Night, the Fourth of July, Janet borrowed Nancy's white skirt and found blue artichoke flowers — no one knew what they were — to accompany the red poppies and white daisies strewn on their table. On Bastille Day Janet met Gene and René Crevel in Toulon and watched the fireworks. Then they went to the dance halls, and Janet stayed overnight in a small hotel Nancy had found near the harbor. Excitement came when Gene's house servant robbed him of his silk wardrobe. The boy was apprehended, and they all went to Toulon for the trial.

Gene started a portrait of Janet, which he dubbed the Great Stone Face, or Janet at Sixty, after the severity of her look. (Margaret Anderson, some years later, called it "agonized.") But Janet was happier than she remembered ever being, and she loved Nancy's company. They took long afternoon walks through the purplish heath, counting magnolia trees in blossom, or walked along the coast for hours during the evenings. One night as they sat by the side of the road, they caught a glowworm, and Nancy promised to talk as long as it glimmered. They got up two hours later. Janet remembered that night almost until the end of her life, and its memory gave her such pleasure that at times, she confessed to Nancy, she ached with nostalgia.[19] Figuring they would save money staying in a hotel — the alternative was hiring a cook or a housekeeper — Janet and Solita eventually gave their house to René Crevel. They stayed until late summer, returned to Paris, and resumed their routine.

Early in the fall Janet and Nancy went to the Fôret de Sénart for ten days. Lugging manuscripts, drafts of poems, and several books with them to a small roadside inn, they intended to work during the day and read in the evenings. They got little done: the mornings were too chilly, the hotel had no firewood, and each night at dinner the proprietor lectured them for hours on the treacherous economic policies of England and America. But during the warm fall afternoons, they wandered through the large hunting preserves, talking for hours. Nancy pressed the books she liked on Janet, like Woolf's *Modern Reader* and Ezra Pound's *Cantos.* Janet thought the *Cantos* filled with amazing beauty and violence as well as long, dull, incomprehensible, and silly passages, but she adored the Woolf and was grateful to Nancy for the selections. They exchanged small pieces of jewelry, and Nancy gave Janet some discarded clothes of her mother, Lady Emerald Cunard. Janet cherished the Vionnet gowns and was especially fond of Sir Bache Cunard's top hat, which she said she wore to the Magic City Mardi Gras costume ball the night Princess Violet Murat, dressed as a concierge, taught Janet to take snuff.[20]

Photographer Berenice Abbott remembers Janet and Nancy and Solita as always looking smart and elegant, never careless or dowdy; they knew, she says, that a woman had to dress well; these women were very savvy.[21] Generally Janet wore the huge seal coat trimmed in black skunk that had belonged to Bastian Hoyt's mother; he gave it to her, and she had it remade. He also gave her stockings with a gold stripe, which she often wore along with a black cloche hat she'd bought in New York. And in her hotel room she lounged in rose flannel Oxford bags made by her tailor

Filled with adventure and ambition, brushed by glamour, and living in one of Europe's most alluring cities, Janet and Solita felt the whole world spread before them. They believed they could be anything they wanted. That is what Janet seemed to imply the day she walked over to the small studio recently set up by Berenice Abbott at 44 rue de Bac, to be photographed in her Magic City costume — top hat, black velvet jacket, striped silk trousers. The costume was Janet's idea, recalled Abbott, who thought of Janet as somewhat formal, Solita less so.[22] For one of the photographs Janet sat on the floor cross-legged and stared directly forward, looking handsome and serious as Uncle Sam in a top hat decorated with a double set of masks.

Nancy's father died in the fall of 1925 while Nancy was visiting England. When she decided to stay on, "the three" sent gifts and letters back and forth. Eager to go to Winchester, Salisbury, and Stonehenge with Nancy, Janet visited her in February 1926. When she arrived, she discovered Nancy in bed with the flu, so Janet sat by Nancy's bedside, her back to the fire, and read aloud to her. Finally Nancy felt well enough to go to London and introduce Janet, as she'd promised, to the famous George Moore at his home on Ebury Street. Janet was very nervous, and Moore didn't help matters, being, as Nancy called it, in a "typical" mood. According to Nancy, "It was one of those days when George Moore wore an absolutely 'white' look concerning all subjects and persons and he was being rather formal. But he did not remain so 'til the end. He went into modern painting a little for our benefit, repeating what he had already told me: 'I cannot get even as far as Cezanne!' To Janet he now said: 'Well, it is no use my trying to understand certain kinds of painting. I have seen a portrait of Cezanne — a portrait of a peasant *by* a peasant. And I have also read some of Mr. Joyce's *Ulysses*. It cannot be a novel, for there isn't a tree in it!' "[23]

Janet was taken aback. She didn't take Moore's remark on trees in *Ulysses* ironically — not that it was — or comically, as Nancy had. Nancy tried to explain the remark by saying he'd made the same criticism of Fielding's *Tom Jones,* which both women had recently read. Janet wasn't mollified. She "thought he had a very curious way of speaking: that special accentuation of words like 'a' and 'the,' as if they counted a great deal," and his manners were worse than his critical opinions.[24] Moore told the two young women that he'd once gotten even with a woman who'd spurned him by kicking her in the rump. He was supposed to be a great author, and as Solita later told Daphne Fielding, Janet had not yet recovered from the literary influences of Henry James and Walter Pater.[25] Like her mother, whom she criticized for a similar quality, Janet still expected a lofty idealism, if not some wisdom, from the writers she admired. Nancy was the iconoclast, not Janet.

"Delighted you are coming to Paris so soon!" Solita wrote Janet's sister Marie in 1925. "We shall have many pleasant hours in the cafes, I trust, where the lid is off and all is merry."[26] Janet and Solita's relationship was no secret from Marie, who was also adept at keeping her private life private. Hired to teach at the David Mannes School of Music in New York just the year before, Marie had decided to take her first summer vacation in Paris and study piano with Alfred Cortot at the École Normale de Musique. In August she met Janet and Solita in le Lavandou and then returned with them to Paris, where she stayed for almost a month, had her hair cut, bought clothes, and got along well with her younger sister — "not always the case in our family," Hildegarde observed.[27]

Marie did a great deal to help Janet with her American investments during her first years in Paris. With Janet living so far away, the rivalry between them abated somewhat.[28] However, Janet and Hildegarde were still more comfortable with each other than either was with Marie. Janet, who called Hildegarde such pet names as Hildabill, my little pigeon, Bug, and Baby, was nonetheless somewhat condescending toward her younger sister, whom she ambivalently regarded as, like their mother, a dreamer too delicate for the coarseness of this world. Yet in some ways, Janet was as competitive with Hildegarde as she was with Marie. She considered Hildegarde in many ways the most talented of the three Flanner sisters. Already a prize-winning poet whose first volume, *Young Girl* (1920), had been roundly praised, she was publishing in magazines like *The Nation, The New Republic,* and *Poetry.* Janet enviously told Hildegarde that in Paris Janet Flanner was known merely as Hildegarde Flanner's sister. According to a friend of both women, Janet in later years jealously guarded her job at *The New Yorker* from Hildegarde, and as late as 1973 Hildegarde was reluctant to tell Janet she'd sent the magazine an article.[29]

Reflecting on her own career at the age of eighty, Hildegarde noted sharply that it "was not necessary to go to Paris in order to want to write poetry. For me, at least, it was necessary only to be aware of visible things against which there was no rebellion."[30] If Janet was considered the rebellious daughter, Hildegarde was the dutiful one. Even after her marriage to the architect Frederick Monhoff in 1926, Hildegarde stayed close to the mother whose "devouring affection" demanded her constant physical presence.[31] Mary lived with or adjacent to the Monhoffs for the rest of her life. Janet apologized to her young sister. Her own appetite for life, she acknowledged, was burdening Hildegarde with their mother.[32] But she did not intend to return. She was finding her place in a new community of women, one much different, it seemed, from the one her family represented. She wasn't going to give that up.

Both Janet and Solita wrote extensively in their novels about sexual freedom and the destructive nature of jealousy. They believed that all sexual responses were natural and healthy and that hypocrisy or possessiveness poisoned a relationship. That is what they were arguing in their prose, and that is what they aimed to practice. Their relationship was strong, loving, stable, and evidently not monogamous; they admitted others into their lives without disturbing the fundamental equilibrium. They trusted each other, they had become each other's family, and they believed that nothing and no one could alter their feelings.

In one respect they seemed not unlike Natalie Barney, the American-born heiress whose salon on the rue Jacob drew an international crowd. Natalie, who regarded sexual freedom as her inalienable right, was the best-known lesbian in Paris and a feminist intent on providing her friends with a modern-day Lesbos; there was nothing inhibited, repressed, or small about her. The "Amazone" of her friend Rémy de Gourmont's *Lettres à l'Amazone,* Natalie wrote and published *Pensées de L'Amazone,* reflections on lesbian life and love; she founded the Académie des Femmes, a female response to the all-male Académie Française; she introduced women artists to one another and promoted their work; and she provided a cultural as well as an erotic gathering place for women. Female guests often gathered in her garden to dance around a small Temple à l'Amitié.[33]

When William Carlos Williams was dragged to Natalie's by Ezra Pound, he was intimidated by what he saw: "I admired her and her lovely garden, well kept, her laughing doves, her Japanese servants," he recalled in his *Autobiography.* "There were officers wearing red buttons in their lapels there and women of all descriptions. Out of the corner of my eye I saw a small clique of them sneaking off together into a side room while casting surreptitious glances about them, hoping their exit had not been unnoticed. I went out," he concluded, "and stood up to take a good piss."[34]

Natalie's salon included members of the *Mercure de France* group (including Valéry and Gide), Colette, the Duchesse de Clermont-Tonnerre, Sacha Guitry, Bernard Berenson, and Romaine Brooks, as well as literary-minded expatriates like Gertrude Stein. Natalie Barney "collected people," Solita recalled, "and you could be sure of being dazzled any Friday (her day) you dropped in for tea."[35] A woman of charm and great social presence, according to Virgil Thomson, Natalie was a skillful and munificent hostess: she "spent money graciously, she kept a very luxurious table, she had not only the

Fridays but people were always going there to dinner and to lunch. She led an active generous social life. And people went there and stayed with her. And she helped to get their works published — she may even have paid a bit of money."[36]

Solita said Natalie's home looked something like an aquarium with underwater light, but she, like Janet, admired the food and entertainment. Natalie served cakes from Rumpelmayers and tiny cucumber sandwiches. She might provide music — George Antheil's First String Quartet premiered there — or pageantry — Colette enacted a selection from her play *La Vagabonde*. Her guests chatted about politics and art, and then, according to Janet, there would be "a new rendezvous among ladies who had taken a fancy to each other or wished to see each other again."[37]

Natalie was a magnetic presence. Claiming that American women were born with a Bible in their mouths, she eschewed sentimentality and monogamy.[38] She was a materialist, remarked one friend; she "usually saw no reason to make a fuss" — even over the death of an ex-lover.[39] Janet commented that Natalie was an essentially independent woman who was never captive.[40] Sylvia Beach described her charms as "fatal"; she felt no qualms about pursuing or rejecting lovers. In Djuna Barnes's privately published *Ladies Almanack,* a bawdy satire of the Barney salon, generally assumed to have been financed by Natalie and written for the entertainment of friends, Natalie appeared as the wise and lusty Dame Evangeline Musset, a proselytizing lesbian who loved women with abandon. Janet, who enjoyed the satire, nonetheless commented years later that Natalie was a perfect example of an enchanting person *not* to write about."[41]

Janet, though no prude, was much more circumspect than Natalie about her private life and in later years was reluctant to associate herself too closely with Natalie or the salon. Janet respected Natalie's style and generosity, but she claimed not to have known her well, nor did she see her alone: "If you weren't in love with her — which I certainly was not, . . . — you didn't know as much about her, and you couldn't appreciate her as much either."[42] Characterizing Natalie as a female pope who held some of her lovers in a kind of thrall, or so it seemed to outsiders, Janet in all likelihood objected to the way

Natalie seemed to commandeer the various women who were in love with her.

Although Janet said she used to "breeze in and breeze out" of Natalie's, she really stayed much longer, clustered with the other guests around the teapot in the little dining room. In *Ladies Almanack,* Janet and Solita appeared as two minor characters in the retinue, journalists called Nip and Tuck. Bettina Bergery recalled that by the thirties Janet was considered one of Natalie's Knights of the Round Table, an intimate friend who stayed at the teas longer than a half an hour, but even before, Janet and Solita were both regular visitors.[43] They knew Dolly Wilde and Elizabeth Eyre de Lanux and possibly met Djuna Barnes and Esther Murphy and Germaine Beaumont there.

Janet greatly admired one of Natalie's lovers, Dorothy Wilde, the handsome and witty niece of Oscar, who enjoyed appearing at costume parties dressed as her uncle. She and Janet danced most of one night together at the Mardi Gras Ball, Dolly shedding the talc she had sprinkled in her hair on Janet's coat. "Dear grey and white Janet," Dolly called her — Janet's hair had lost most of its color — "your hair is your fortune & there is a nuance about you that makes you rare & exceptional."[44]

Janet also admired Germaine Beaumont, the French writer who was rumored to be Colette's lover and, according to Solita, her protégée. A French journalist writing for *Le Matin* and *Les Nouvelles Littéraires,* Germaine modeled her work, said Janet, on the essays by Francis Bacon she'd read during her British schooling. But like Janet, she considered herself a novelist more than a journalist, and it was as a novelist that she was rewarded in 1931 with the coveted Prix Théophraste Renaudot. She too was devoted to Natalie, and she too, said Janet, became "a very very close friend of mine."[45] By the late twenties they were spending a great deal of time together. One year they spent two warm April weeks in Saint-Malo, a walled sea town on the Brittany coast, where they watched the archbishop of Rennes bless the codfishing boats during the Lenten festivities. And in 1930, for Janet's thirty-eighth birthday, Germaine treated her to a special dinner of caviar, champagne, and lobster at Prunier.

Janet's new friends, all living in close proximity, saw one another often. They discussed their work, their ambitions, each other. They flirted, met for drinks, danced, and talked until the early hours of the morning. Janet walked over to Natalie's on Fridays, and if Nancy wasn't giving one of her parties at the Grattery, she might drop by Dorothy Ireland's studio around the corner from the rue Bonaparte. Janet thought that the wealthy Ireland was a protégée of T. S. Eliot's patroness at the *Criterion,* Lady Rothermere; she often entertained with a large open bar (Janet assured her mother that one did not have to drink all that was offered), a gramophone, dancing, and introductions. Janet reciprocated by adding what she was told was her best commodity — her wit.

Janet claimed to grow tired of these parties, but she was fond of the women she was meeting, women like Djuna Barnes, who feared no man, said Janet: Djuna had the temerity to call T. S. Eliot "Tom" and was a writer of stature, second only, some believed, to the great Joyce — whom Djuna brazenly called "Jim."[46] Known as the Irish Colette, she first arrived in Paris from New York in the early twenties, having already written several plays and stories, among them the prize-winning "A Night Among the Horses" and a chapbook on female sexuality titled *The Book of Repulsive Women.* She was also recognized as a seasoned journalist, though she regarded journalism in much the same way Janet and Solita did, as mere income.

Djuna was quick-tongued, proud, and slyly funny, described by a fellow Greenwich Villager as having "red cheeks. Auburn hair. Gray eyes, ever sparkling with delight and mischief. Fantastic earrings in her ears, picturesquely dressed, ever ready to live and be merry: that's the real Djuna as she walks down Fifth Avenue, or sips her black coffee, a cigarette in hand, in the Cafe Lafayette."[47] Djuna in Paris was no less striking, wrapped in a long dark cape as she walked about the Left Bank. Natalie considered Djuna, with her pencil-thin nose, high cheekbones, upright carriage, and hair tightly wound under her hat, as beautiful as any woman sketched by Manet.

Having settled in a hotel on the rue Jacob around the corner from Janet and Solita, Djuna worked on her stories in bed every morning.[48] Janet always felt Djuna's work didn't receive the recognition it deserved, and she knew that Djuna spurned much of the attention she got. When her novel *Nightwood* was hailed as a great book in the thirties, Janet wrote Djuna to say how pleased she was; Djuna's cup must be filled to the brim, Janet said and then added, as if aware of something sycophantic in her own fulsome praise, that "knowing you you will find it not enough!!!!" Djuna, who saved the note, wrote "typical Flanner impudence" in the margin.[49]

What remains of the correspondence between Djuna and Janet, mostly dating from the fifties, shows Janet trying to respect Djuna's increasingly cloistered habits while coaxing her into an occasional meeting. Both Janet and Solita were solicitous of Djuna during those later years, sending her money and on one occasion buying her a new typewriter. Apparently they were equally solicitous in the twenties, at least whenever Djuna would accept their help. Janet recalled that Djuna had been fond of her in her haughty way. Djuna's biographer Andrew Field observed that though she "liked Janet well enough, for some reason she could never really feel close to her."[50]

Kathryn Hulme, later to write *The Nun's Story*, remembered her initial impression of Janet and Solita and Djuna. When she first saw them sipping martinis together at the Café Flore, it was late in the afternoon, the only time they mingled with outsiders. Hatless and chic, with an enviable self-assurance, they sat in their black tailored suits, raising their glasses with white gloves. Hulme thought they looked like three rather elegant Fates.[51]

Margaret Anderson, the beautiful and outspoken coeditor of *The Little Review*, was "so emotional and inarticulate," according to Alice Toklas, that she "gasped for breath."[52] Sinclair Lewis called her too remote from the common herd, too concerned with the exceptional rather than the average. But men like Lewis bored her, and Margaret Anderson would not suffer herself to be bored.

When she "sensed" that a modern literary movement was about to declare itself, she knew she must publish a review to sponsor it; this was a "logical" necessity.[53] Established in Chicago in 1914 to contain "the best conversation the world has to offer," *The Little Review* claimed to "make no compromise with the public taste." The magazine was always poor; by 1923, when Margaret and Jane Heap moved its operation to Paris, they had already taken it to California and New York in search of backers. They could not offer payment to the magazine's contributors — Gertrude Stein criticized *The Little*

Review for this — but they managed, nonetheless, to interest Floyd Dell, Sherwood Anderson, George Soule, and William Butler Yeats in contributing pieces to the very first issue.

Margaret and Jane were mavericks. Once, when all of the manuscripts they received struck them as mediocre or dull, they published thirteen blank pages. They didn't hesitate to publish Joyce's *Ulysses* serially when Ezra Pound, their foreign editor after 1916, sent them the first installment of a work they immediately recognized as Art. For three years they published sections of the novel, even when its cost drove Anderson to canvassing Wall Street for subscriptions and even after the United States Post Office declared three issues obscene and had them burned. In 1920 the Society for the Suppression of Vice issued an injunction against *The Little Review*. Anderson and Heap, with the assistance of John Quinn, Pound's patron, fought and lost; they were fined $100 for the publication of obscene literature and were led off to be fingerprinted. Characteristically, the fastidious Margaret turned the fingerprinting into an ordeal for the clerks, who thought it a simple procedure. (Djuna Barnes once complained that Margaret always used to wash the soap before using it.) Now Margaret protested not only that she didn't like the soap but that there weren't enough towels and that she must be brought a nail brush. "I managed to make them suffer for my indignity," she said, "until they were all in a state bordering on personal guilt."[54]

In the early twenties, while in New York, Margaret met and fell in love with the singer Georgette Leblanc, the former companion of dramatist Maurice Maeterlinck. In 1923 the two of them sailed to France, where Jane Heap soon joined them. In 1924, all three women temporarily lived at the communal Institute for the Harmonious Development of Man in Fontainbleau-Avon, renamed the Château de Prieuré by its founder, the Russian mystic Gurdjieff.

According to many of his detractors — and there were many — Gurdjieff was an opportunist who lured rich women willing to pay large fees for the privilege of scrubbing his floors and being insulted by him at dinner. Most, however, agreed that he was a charismatic figure; with his large eyes, shaved head, and long mustache, he looked the part of a worldly saint. Margaret was first exposed to Gurdjieff in New York when she attended his program of sacred Tibetan dances. These dances, which presumably conveyed esoteric knowledge, were just one of the techniques Gurdjieff used to enlighten his disciples. Self-knowledge and transcendence were to be achieved through hard physical work, discipline, searing self-examination, and constant discussion. The method suited Margaret, who loved conversation and argument.

Solita, invited by her new friend Margaret to join the group at the Prieuré, hoped to find a "superman of saintly countenance" but was initially quite disappointed. Gurdjieff's teachings bored her, and she was annoyed that women could not smoke in the study house. Margaret, insisting she try again, brought her to lunch with Gurdjieff, who muttered in broken English. "I rejected his language, the suit he was wearing, and his table manners," Solita recalled. "I decided that I rather disliked him."⁵⁵ However, she was intrigued enough to talk Janet into going with her to Jane Heap's Monday night lectures on Gurdjieff's philosophy. In the winter of 1927 they were meeting at Georgette Leblanc's flat. Jane would speak at length; Janet would try to punch holes in her argument. The dogged and clever Jane was a good adversary, but Janet remained unenlightened. She felt Gurdjieff's philosophy demanded the kind of intellectual submissiveness she associated with religious fundamentalism. Hildegarde recalled that Janet was impatient with anything that touched on the mystical or mysterious. She would demand rational explanations and run her opponent into a corner, scornful when they could only say "you just don't understand."⁵⁶ She preferred skepticism; it seemed more reliable, intellectually and scientifically.

It was Solita, rather than Janet, who became enamored of Margaret, finding in her quasi-mysticism and passionate devotion to beauty an outlet for her own desire to escape a life of mediocrity. None of Solita's three novels had sold well, and consigned once again to earning money from journalism, by 1927 Solita too wished for something otherworldly and romantic.⁵⁷ Janet, although still sympathetic to the quest for the hard gemlike flame, found Margaret's effusions tedious and soft. "Life on a cloud," as Margaret described her own, was not entirely inviting to Janet, who more and more liked to consider herself down-to-earth and realistic, commonsensical and sane. And despite Margaret's ethereal preoccupations, Janet sensed that her flamboyant beauty "enveloped a will of tempered steel." Janet was wary.

Janet had been skeptical about *The Little Review* during its first years of publication, when she satirized Margaret as a youthful positivist for her *Indianapolis Star* readers. Although Janet came to respect what Margaret achieved in her magazine, she still held herself aloof from its emphatic pronouncements and prescriptions. In addition, she knew that Margaret's and Jane's achievements required a kind of risk taking she did not want to engage in. Writing to e.e. cummings years later, she said she had never pushed a question to its limit, always preferring the moderate to the revolutionary, even in her youth.[58]

Later Margaret felt that she and *The Little Review* were ill served by Janet's "Letter from Paris"; Janet, she believed, could have done more to promote her magazine. She accounted for the increasing popularity of the Paris letter over the years by saying Janet simply gave the public what it wanted, cleverly stringing bon mots together. When Margaret wrote a novella and sent it to her friends for criticism, she didn't send Janet a copy, explaining that Janet "wouldn't have known what to say, unless it had already been published and praised by the critics. Then she would have written a panegyric. (I'm not being malicious; simply truthful.)"[59]

Yet for all their differences in attitude and temperament, Janet and Margaret were devoted friends, working closely together and admiring each other's accomplishments. Theirs, too, was a relationship of "modern female fidelity" as Solita had described her and Janet's friendship with Nancy. They were loyal to each other and tried to be as honest as possible. In 1929, Janet and Solita helped compile the last issue of *The Little Review* at their hotel, spilling Margaret's green ink all over their sheets. Margaret assisted Janet with everything, from the Paris letter to the adornment of her room; she once decided to enhance the fireplace by painting it red. Janet and Solita edited Margaret's first memoir, *My Thirty Years' War,* though Janet took care not to be too critical. She advised Margaret to concentrate more on the history of the magazine, its intentions, and accomplishments and less on its editors' housing problems — "your 30 year war with reality has momentarily become a 30 year war with realtors," Janet wrote her when she read the draft. Then she softened, explaining, "Solita says to say this because I think it."[60]

Janet said she truly loved Margaret; it was Georgette she couldn't stand. Georgette's singing made Janet want to jump into the Seine. Years later Janet confided to Solita that "those weekends when you expected her [Margaret] in your room had shakespearian quality and I must have been the most minor character — I loved you and her and disliked dear Georgette."[61] When Solita installed Margaret and Georgette, debt-ridden, in the hotel, sharing her time and even her money, occasionally buying Margaret the clothes she desperately needed and paying her bills, Janet was uncomfortable. After all, none of them knew of any real precedents for their sexual and emotional arrangements, and there were no obvious rules or institutions to follow.

Ironically, by the end of 1925, Janet had just begun to earn her own income and, although she may not yet have realized it, was becoming less dependent on Solita for entrée into the artistic world of Europe. More and more, outsiders regarded Solita as Janet's mistress, and Janet as the better writer.[62]

6

A Gentleman of the Press in Skirts
1925-1928

"Ah, America," said Louis Aragon the other day, "the country of skyscrapers and cowboys, railroad accidents and cocktail shakers. . . . " "No, no," I said, "that's an old-fashioned Frenchman's idea of America. America —" "Excuse me," he went on, "I got that idea from Americans-who-live-in-Paris; we invented the legend of America ten years ago, and now it's the Americans' turn at believing it."

Elizabeth Eyre de Lanux, 1925

ALTHOUGH HE found its style a bit precious, Solita's friend the publisher George Putnam praised the manuscript of *The Cubical City* in late 1924 and said he was committed to publishing it. Pleased and relieved, Janet continued to work. Yet she rarely spoke of it to friends, preferring them to think of her as indolent even though the people she admired, like Nancy Cunard and Djuna Barnes, certainly weren't. But Janet tended to make light of her work or undervalue it; only Solita knew that Janet had trouble sitting down and writing.

Published in 1926, *The Cubical City* received mixed reviews: the *New York Times* criticized its "florid rhetoric" but called the book vital and strong; the New York *Herald Tribune* liked the story but thought the language of the novel "overreaches itself to grasp at the unusual phrase."[1] The *Los Angeles Record,* calling Janet a "worthy competitor of Sherwood Anderson, John Dos Passos, Waldo Frank and Maxwell Bodenheim," declared *The Cubical City* "too masculine in thought and construction to invite comparison with any women novelists." Janet read this with interest and some amusement. But of all the reviews she saw, the one she most often cited was the *Boston Evening Transcript'*s, admonishing her for being "too brilliantly attuned" although her writing "reminds one in a less brilliant way of the quick witted phrases of Rose Macaulay." This last greatly disappointed Janet, who had been straining after Henry James.

The lukewarm reviews didn't discourage her from immediately starting a second novel, as Solita had done, which seemed to Janet a very good idea. She figured she could have the new one finished in a few months if she wrote about 4,000 words a day. And she had decided on the subject: another mother/daughter relationship, she wrote to Mary Flanner. This time the setting was California, the title "A State of Bliss." And she would omit the men early on; she agreed with Mary, who had apparently said they didn't compare to the women of *Cubical City.*[2] She completed what must have been a sketch for the novel, a story called "California — Dunt Esk," which pokes fun at the unrefined English spoken by Mary Flanner's hired help.[3] The story centers on Mary's decision to live in California and Janet's disapproval: there was no "culture" in the golden land.

But Janet couldn't sustain her enthusiasm for the new project, partly because her time was more and more taken up with the new job she'd accepted a year earlier. Much to her surprise, it was reshaping her life. The offer had come in the form of a request from Janet's friend Jane Grant, the *New York Times* journalist. Writing to Janet in June 1925, Jane explained that she'd been busy working on a project her husband, Harold Ross, had been "giving birth to." It was called, in case Janet hadn't heard, *The New Yorker.*[4]

Ross, as he was commonly called, was a moody and energetic young man who had been aching to start a magazine of his own, something like *Stars and Stripes.* He had liked working on a publication that was written for a small, well-defined group of readers — in that case, soldiers — by a similarly small and well-defined group, also soldiers.

After the war he wanted to continue in the same vein; he imagined a magazine, written for a small community, that would present information "honestly" without inflated rhetoric and without paying homage to conventional pieties.

Having tried unsuccessfully to do this with *Home Sector,* he had wandered from the *American Legion Weekly* to the humor magazine *Judge.* But he remained determined to start something different. Impressed by the repartee of his Algonquin round table compatriots and perspicacious enough to consider exploiting their wit in his own venture, he found a backer in Raoul Fleischmann, one of the occasional Algonquinites who frequented their card party, the Thanatopsis Poker and Inside Straight Club. Fleischmann's father had invented the "breadline," both word and concept, by giving away each day's unsold bread to the poor every night at eleven. Raoul, bored with the bakery and not the type to squander the family wealth on polo parties, agreed to help finance Ross's project.

The first issue of *The New Yorker* appeared on February 21, 1925. After the fashion of *Vanity Fair,* which also disdained what it called the "old lady from Dubuque," or provincial morality, *The New Yorker* announced itself as the voice of the young, the fit, the urbane, the cognoscenti: "It hopes to reflect the metropolitan life, to keep up with events and affairs of the day, to be gay, humorous, satirical but to be more than just a jester. It will publish facts that it will have to go behind the scenes to get, but it will not deal in scandal for the sake of scandal nor sensation for the sake of sensation. It will try conscientiously to keep its readers informed of what is going on in the fields in which they are most interested. It has announced that it is not edited for the old lady in Dubuque. By this it means that it is not of that group of publications engaged in tapping the Great Buying Power of the North American steppe region by trading mirrors and colored beads in the form of our best brands of hokum."[5] As if to show more precisely what it would do, the first issue sported Rea Irvin's drawing of a high-hatted, high-collared, old-fashioned dandy peering at a butterfly through a monocle.

The picture was certainly better than the magazine's contents, which contributors and readers alike agreed were awful. Even listing Heywood Broun, Ralph Barton, Marc Connelly, Edna Ferber, Rea Irvin, George Kaufman, Alice Duer Miller, Dorothy Parker, Lawrence Stallings, and Alexander Woollcott as advisory editors — the only dishonest thing he ever did, Ross said — could not guarantee the magazine's quality, boost its circulation, or offset its increasing debt. By spring, Fleischmann wanted to quit and did; he reconsidered, the story goes, when he overheard John Hanrahan, the magazine's business consultant, say Fleischmann was killing a living thing. Whatever happened, he decided to give the magazine eight months' probation.

If Ross was not sure exactly what he wanted — some amalgam of the old *American Mercury,* London's *Punch,* and Germany's *Simplicissimus* — he did know what he didn't want. Operating on instinct, uncanny skill, tactlessness, and a determination bordering on fanaticism, he hired and fired employees while he and Jane Grant scoured magazines, newspapers, and letters for anything that might suit. While looking for new material for the fall issues, Jane, recalling that Janet had once said she planned to spend the rest of her life hanging around the Deux Magots, decided that Janet ought to put her intentions to good use. She offered Janet a job as the new magazine's Paris correspondent.

There had already been a "Letter from Paris" in the first issues of the magazine, Jane said, but she and Ross had thought it superficial and glib; the contributor did not really know Paris. "Therefore, I am looking to you as my great white hope. Certainly you know your Paris, better than anyone I can think of, and while I know it is difficult to make long distance arrangements, I feel sure you can get the idea if anybody can. He [Ross] wants anecdotal and incidental stuff on places familiar to Americans and on people of note whether they are Americans or internationally prominent — dope on fields of the arts and a little on fashions, perhaps, although he does not want the latter treated technically; there should be lots of chat about people seem [*sic*] about and in it all he wants a definite personality injected. In fact, any one of your letters would be just the thing."[6]

For a weekly letter of about a thousand words, Ross offered Janet forty dollars per submission. It was not a huge sum, but it would go a long way in Paris. Janet's expenses were rising; her hotel had jumped its price, and food was more costly. And Ross was promising a steady job, at least so long as the experiment lasted, on a magazine that Jane Grant wrote would be "really good before long." (Janet was not impressed with the first issues.) Moreover, the offer gave her a chance to maintain ties in absentia to the New York crowd she admired but did not want to live among. And it provided her with a legitimate reason, even an injunction, to stay in Paris.

Harold Ross told Janet he wanted her pieces to appear anonymously, a policy he'd developed with regard to all the magazine's contributors. He did not want to advertise the magazine's content or its writers, and for several years — the apocryphal list of advisory editors notwithstanding — all the writers signed their pieces with pseudonyms. No names appeared on the magazine's cover. Ross's idea was that the magazine would speak for itself and would create what Lionel Trilling derisively called its writers' "corporate" existence, an interchangeable aloofness and humor and a low-key, if not altogether repressed, public-spiritedness.[7]

For the new Paris correspondent, charged with writing about the Paris that would be interesting to Americans and familiar with the tone set at the Algonquin, Ross came up with what he thought was a Gallicized version of Janet, or so Janet said. (She originally thought he might call her something like "flâneuse," the feminine form of *flâneur,* a loafer.) No one is really sure how or where he got the name Genêt — whether he knew, for instance, that Edmond-Charles-Édouard Genet (called Citizen Genet) was the first minister of the French Republic to the United States and no insignificant letter writer himself. In any event Janet, who credited Ross with having invented her, must have been flattered.

On September 13, 1925, Janet sent Ross her first manuscript. She didn't hear anything for over six weeks. Then Ross informed her he was publishing the letter in the magazine's October 10 issue. But he had decided to use the letters bimonthly, not weekly, and was now offering only thirty-five dollars per submission. Despite the changes, Janet was so excited that she wrote to her mother immediately, proudly adding that Mary could keep some of Janet's small income for herself.

Janet had studied the earlier Paris letters and had tried to make hers consistent with them, and Ross edited Genêt's first contribution, dated September 25, to sound as if it were written by the previous correspondent. Since last she wrote, Genêt laconically asserted, noth-

ing much in Paris had changed; "anyone who thinks anyone of consequence is back in town yet is a yokel." But her irony offset her
arrogance, so it seemed she was satirizing the pose she had adopted.
This attitude, in fact, was also implied by Rea Irvin's dandy — the
freedom to have it both ways.

Janet and the magazine took a somewhat patronizing tone toward
the uninitiated even while listing the "important" places to go, to
see, to know — places presumed not to be in the conventional sightseer's itinerary. Tips for readers included veiled advice on how to
live as the intellectual aristocracy did, tempered with the right dose
of self-mockery, making the writer seem involved with and knowledgeable about goings-on, while at the same time aloof from such
trivialities. An advertisement in an early issue self-deprecatingly appealed to this kind of snobbishness: "Do you know it is just as easy
to be *au courant* as it is to be a Baptist? By devoting twenty minutes
each week to *The New Yorker,* you become witty and conversant with
practically every subject there is. You not only understand what the
best plays mean, if anything, but you actually know the names and
numbers of the more prominent actresses and head waiters."

A vigorous advertising campaign and a promotional series called
"The Making of a Magazine," featuring a character called Eustace
Tilley (assumed to be the dandy of the first cover), helped to rescue
the failing *New Yorker* — with the fortuitous assistance of Ellin Mackay's popular article published in late 1925, called "Why We Go to
Cabarets, A Post Debutante Explains." By February 1926, its first
anniversary, the magazine had attracted significant advertisers, including Saks Fifth Avenue, Pierce-Arrow, and Paris designer Paul
Poiret; circulation was climbing, and the length of the magazine had
more than doubled. By 1927 Ross had added James Thurber and
Wolcott Gibbs to a staff that already included — in addition to Janet
Flanner — Ralph Ingersoll, E. B. White, Katharine Sergeant Angell,
Morris Markey, Dorothy Parker, Lois Long, and cartoonists Peter
Arno and Helen Hokinson. The format of the magazine was fairly
well established, as was its content: columns like "Notes and Comments," "The Talk of the Town," and "Tables for Two" appeared
regularly, as did a "Reporter at Large" feature, "casuals" — short,
informal prose pieces — and, of course, urbane cartoons. Art deco
titles introduced each prose piece and gave the magazine a visual

continuity consistent with its uniform editorial policies. Facts had to be straight, each piece had to be clearly written and informal, and in no case did the magazine advocate anything but a horror of pretension.[8]

In keeping with this policy, in her early Paris letters Janet strung together a glittering array of anecdotes, observations, and wry comments; this was part of their attraction, and it served the magazine's purpose. As a result Genêt's bimonthly "Letter from Paris" quickly assumed an attitude of shared understanding, not necessarily of particular places or events, but of that which was considered, by writer and reader, noteworthy, aesthetically satisfying, and amusing. It also implied a shared desire: to belong to a cultural elite, to know its tastes and habits, to witness, to count. It was these desires and assumptions on which *The New Yorker* was founded — the assumption of taste, the perpetuation of comfort, and the declaration, bordering on complacency, of worth.

Genêt reported on all the scenes — the street scene, the art scene, the fashion scene, the publishing scene; she thought of herself as a high-class gossip columnist and assumed her readers were familiar with her world and the people and places and issues inhabiting it, whether it was Colette's favorite restaurant, the opening of the new Surréaliste Gallery and the latest Chaplin movies, the prices paid at John Quinn's auction of modern art, the fashions at Longchamps, or the work of various painters, photographers, composers, writers, and small presses. She called attention to the publication of Mozart's letters to his wife and Pierre de Lanux's collection of lead soldiers. She told what constructivist films had been privately viewed and what measures were taken against the showing of Eisenstein's *Battleship Potemkin,* and who or what had recently died — Anatole France, Marshal Foch, *The Little Review.*

Her audience read about gay Parisian evenings spent on the "Hill" (Montmartre) listening to jazz or "Harlem" music; they were told which cabarets and small breakfast bistros catered to all-night crowds. Descriptions of masked balls and, by day, of women dressed in "androgynous simplicity," with low heels and cloche hats, gave the *New Yorker* reader a brief, incisive sketch of a highly stylized world. Genêt portrayed each event, person, place, against a background of muted disdain for American plumbing, household appliances, puritanism, and prosperity. She described the avalanche of "recently successful stock investors" that descended on "Yurrup" as "resembling in their thirst for licker and bargains the swarm of petty war-profiteers who with empty suitcases trooped into France along with Wilson's ideals."[9]

Hers was not to explain, expound, or evaluate; like *The New Yorker* itself, she preferred to be witty, distant, and uninvolved. Thus, when she noted that *Ulysses* was in its sixth edition, she assumed that her readers knew this was no ordinary novel. Mere mention of the book assured its importance. Her function, as she saw it, was not analytic. Ross conceived of her as a reporter, one who informed rather than educated. When reporting on Milhaud's "Les Choëphores," she said little of the music but instead told how composer Georges Auric had showed up at the Boeuf-sur-le-Toit and been wrongly credited with the unpopular piece. If she gave her opinions at all, she made them veiled and ambiguous. She called George Antheil's "Ballet méca-nique" wonderful but described it as the sounds made by three people, "one pounding an old boiler, one grinding a model 1890 coffee grinder, and one blowing the usual 7 o'clock factory whistle and ringing the bell that starts the New York fire department going in the morning."[10]

She did not always distance herself from the scenes she evoked; instead, she sometimes used herself as a point of reference to characterize and, implicitly, evaluate an experience. Referring to the 1925 Autumn Salon, she wrote, "After looking at the 3000-odd canvases, you go out with a feeling that one of your eyes may be orange and the other pink and that one of your shoulders is certainly six inches higher than the other."[11] She did not intend to analyze the show; she wanted to re-create, in part, her experience in the most amusing way possible.

To do this, she occasionally summarized opinions that caught her fancy; she admired Jules Romains's theory of the cinema, likening it to that of the unconscious. She quoted Cocteau's remark that "this is an age when movements are killed by being given names."[12] She commented on Montherlant's new book about bullfighting, *Les Bes-tiares,* saying that since he "so adores these unfortunate bulls that he can be happy only when killing them, his contempt for women doubt-less saves them a lot of similar pain."[13] Sometimes she recounted her own conversations. The waiter in her neighborhood restaurant couldn't understand American Prohibition, she told her readers, and wanted to know if it was a religion.[14] Or she reported on the exploits of friends: Nancy Cunard's Hours Press; the excerpt in *transition* of Djuna Barnes's *Ryder;* the music of Virgil Thomson and the paintings of Eugene MacCown; the comings and goings of Anita Loos, George Moore, Glenway Wescott, and Scott Fitzgerald. The early letters were generally most successful when Janet described events she herself had seen, flavoring them with sharp pictorial detail; at their worst, they consisted of where-to's, and how-to's loosely slung together.

Janet was fond of repeating that Ross wanted her to write about what the French thought, not what she thought. If Ross did send such explicit directives, they do not survive. Yet whether either of them defined the scope of the "Letter from Paris" is less important than that Janet *felt* her assignment should exclude the editorial, the impressionistic, and the personal as much as possible. At their best, her Paris letters told not just what the French were thinking — if they did that at all — but what she thought in precisely the way she wanted her thought known, through style. She wanted to appear crisp, incisive, good-humored, and intelligent. She wanted to seem down-to-earth, aristocratic, amused.

Reading about a dozen French newspapers a day, she credited them, and Ross, with teaching her how to write. The "exactitude" of the French language in the newspapers, and Ross's editorial passions — particularly for grammar — showed Janet how to trim the ornate from her style, balance her sentences, choose her images precisely, and make her descriptions as pointed as possible. She felt that she was learning discipline, where before she had none. And because Ross, as both editor and audience, demanded precision, Janet frequently said she wrote to please him.[15]

Most who worked for Ross saw beneath his gruff blustering a kindhearted, intelligent man who deeply respected his authors, and they were loyal to him partly because he so clearly shared their devotion to the craft of writing. In addition, he inspired trust and respect among those, like Janet, who regarded him as a father and themselves as talented, precocious children. It is unlikely, however, that anyone — especially Janet, who saw him infrequently — would have regarded him so highly if he were just an editorial figurehead. He received their love because he actively demanded the best from his writers and apparently labored over their manuscripts and because he was fair, generous, and a bit of a comic figure, with his rough-and-tumble manner, his peculiar haircut, and his incomparable, if incomprehensible, management style.

Janet also credited Ross in these early days with having created the "formula" for the letter from abroad: foreign correspondence, intimate style. Of course foreign correspondence had existed before *The New Yorker,* and news from Paris, especially in the twenties, was considered intrinsically interesting. In 1922 *Vanity Fair* ran a series by Edna St. Vincent Millay (writing under a pseudonym) called "Diary of an American Art Student," and Ezra Pound wrote an early Paris letter for *The Dial,* which later contained letters from Vienna, Germany, Italy, and Russia. Both Harold Stearns and Elizabeth Eyre de Lanux wrote from Paris for *Town and Country.* But, Pound polemicized, Stearns gloomily covered French politics, and Eyre de Lanux, in her "Letters of Elizabeth," did not hesitate to editorialize. Ross wanted something a little bit different; he got it in Genêt, who was neither gloomy nor editorial nor analytic. She was a prose stylist with a sharp, skeptical eye and a highly developed sense of the absurd.

Although the style "Genêt" was developing was unmistakably Janet's, Genêt was in a certain sense a composite figure, a collaboration that began with Janet and her friends in Paris and ended in New York, where the letter was edited. During these early days Janet established the routine that she would follow, more or less, for the next fifty years. She closeted herself in her hotel room for as long as forty-eight hours at a stretch. Solita, her official deputy, was working on her own variation of a Paris letter for the *Detroit Athletic Club News,* but often read Janet's copy aloud as Janet typed, or she both typed and edited for Janet. Later other friends, like Margaret Anderson, attended events Janet reported on, helped gather material, or suggested items, events, even points of view.

When the letter was finished, Janet brought her copy down to the Gare Saint-Lazare, where the French post office had a special desk set up on the mornings when the boat train connected with a fast New York-bound liner. After the copy arrived in New York and was edited, Janet often heard nothing until after it was in print. In the first few months of her employment, she felt that her copy was mangled by editing but acknowledged that much of the clipping had to be done to meet a production schedule she kept forgetting. She always seemed to send too much at the wrong time.

But she enjoyed the fairly constant praise she received, although she said she was irritated by requests for cheap glamour; how low-cut was the neckline of the hoi polloi, how many titles could be counted at the Ritz bar. Reminded that she was writing for intelligent people, she sometimes thought the magazine was interested only in petty snobberies.[16] Or so she told her mother, possibly to avoid censure from that direction.

When Janet was asked to write about things she thought were silly, or when embarrassing additions were made to her letter, she could remind herself that few people actually knew Genêt's identity; Genêt, after all, was a mask. For Janet, used to keeping her private life private, it was easy to assume this mask. In fact, Genêt gave her an institutional reason for concealing many of her opinions and feelings, as well as her personal life. This was a policy not only of necessity, given her audience, but of conviction, as shown by her reluctance to use the pronoun "I." As she once suggested to her friend the composer David Diamond, "The trick is never to say 'I.' You're safer with one or it. 'I' is like a fortissimo. It's too loud."[17]

Genêt was a public figure who prided herself on the pains she took with each Paris letter, deliberately crafting material into well-shaped vignettes edged in sharp humor. Style enabled her, Janet believed, to be objective and conscientious, bathetic and tart. And Genêt fit well into Janet's life, especially as it elevated many of her interests to the status of news. Capitalizing on expatriation, itself a commodity of the twenties, Genêt allowed Janet to meet a great number of people and attend a great number of events while staying at a distance, if she wished. The persona of Genêt, with its androgynous sound, allowed Janet to be, as she once quipped to a colleague, "a gentleman of the press in skirts."[18]

By providing money and mobility, Genêt let Janet participate in the world of so-called culture, good taste, money, and wit. At the age of eighty she reflected on this situation: "My satisfaction in living there was double: I felt I was living both at home and abroad — living surrounded with the human familiarity of American friends and acquaintances, and the constant, shifting stimulation that came from the native French."[19] And with this double life came a double vision. Genêt placed Janet inside history because she was there, as well as outside it, as an American in Paris, a woman, a spectator.

At the same time Janet dispatched her first Paris letter, Nancy Cunard wrote her and demanded, "Is he or not arriving?" Nancy was referring to Lane Rehm, who was coming to Paris, according to one source, to convince Janet to return to the United States.[20] Or so Janet feared.

Three years earlier, when Janet first made France her home, she had registered with the French police as separated from her husband. Since then, she had been somewhat lax about getting a divorce. As time went on, Lane and the life he represented seemed farther and farther away, and Janet might have been willing to let the situation drift. But her mother urged her to get on with the legalities, mostly for financial reasons; she wanted Janet's income protected, even though her daughter and son-in-law had signed a prenuptial agreement for just this reason. Janet had in fact left most of the financial arrangements to her mother and a cousin, but either she or Lane had to establish grounds for divorce. Janet, who was apparently filing, briefly considered desertion, but this wouldn't work since she was the one who had left. She and Lane had to get together to figure something out.

Early in 1926, Lane arrived in Paris. Janet was nervous when they met, but the scenes she had dreaded did not take place. She and Lane simply signed papers promising not to lay claim to each other's inheritance, worked out other legal matters, and arranged to use the fact that Lane had changed his residence so Janet could claim he deserted her. Relieved, she assured him they would never lose their affection for each other. She reported to her mother that he had been kind and helpful, a "dear boy" in fact. Someone sent word to the *New York Times,* which reported that Mrs. Janet Rehm was granted a decree of divorce.[21] On hearing the news, Nancy responded swiftly; one's friends are always glad for a divorce, she said.[22]

Mary Flanner may have assumed Janet would soon return home to stay, now that she was divorced and her first novel was finished. But if Mary hoped as much in the summer of 1926, she must have been disappointed, for Janet was going to California with Solita only to visit. And although she had written to her mother almost weekly, and sometimes more often, ever since she had been abroad, calling her "darling" or "darlingest," she frequently observed that they got along best when far apart. Apparently the visit that summer only reinforced that view. "A violent raw time you may have had," Nancy commented sympathetically to Janet shortly after she and Solita returned to France in the fall.[23] For the next three years, Janet managed not to go back to America. She and her mother occasionally mentioned Mary's visiting Paris, but discussion about Mary's living in France or Janet's returning permanently to the United States dropped out of their correspondence. And now she had her job at *The New Yorker* to anchor her in France.

When Janet and Solita moved to a small, inexpensive inn in the Loire Valley for the summer of 1927, Janet carefully wrote her mother that she wanted to work on her book away from the distractions of Paris; it was assumed that she couldn't work in California. She explained that she had gotten little done the preceding winter and spring and had been spending too much money, but in the small whitewashed village of Mosquer, living on thirty francs a day, she could live and work comfortably. Margaret and Georgette were nearby in one of the rundown and romantic chateaus they liked to rent; Margaret played Bach, Georgette wrote her memoirs, Janet and Solita worked in the morning and swam in the afternoon. They ate fresh sardines, boiled or mashed potatoes, fried sole, custard, plums, and cheese. Janet was content. She occasionally went to Paris to pick up items for *The New Yorker,* she took short trips to nearby villages. She scotched most of her new novel and started over again, intending to write something along the lines of a humorous autobiography. Using the same schedule as the year before, she estimated she could finish by spring if she wrote for six hours a day.

The Loire Valley was beautiful, but Janet's contentment didn't last. Soon after she returned to Paris, she again became discouraged, accusing herself of not knowing how to concentrate or think, of having no ideas and no insight. Increasingly, without even realizing it, she turned to Genêt. Nancy Cunard printed envelopes for her with the *New Yorker* logo; these would certainly impress her editors, Janet wrote to her mother, since they'd been fashioned by a lady's daughter. Janet was being facetious — up to a point. While to her family she might seem the rebellious black sheep, when Janet compared herself to friends like Nancy Cunard or Margaret Anderson or Djuna Barnes, she saw herself as bourgeois, neat, and timid. But she didn't completely mind, for she had rejected neither her literary models nor her belief in "culture" when she moved away from family and country. Deriding stuffy morality, for Janet as well as the magazine employing her, was not the same as supporting the subversive or the avant-garde, in art or in politics.

While Solita was spending more and more time with Georgette and Margaret, Janet often saw Nancy, who of late was busy with her farmhouse, Le Puits Carré, in La Chapelle-Réanville, about sixty miles from Paris. Nancy was about to start the Hours Press, which was to publish the work of George Moore, Norman Douglas, Arthur Symons, and Richard Aldington. Later she could boast she'd been the first to discover the young Samuel Beckett, when he entered her poetry contest at the eleventh hour. Having set up an old hand press in her remodeled stable, Nancy was learning to set type. Even Janet and Solita assisted, sweating in the new pressroom in ninety-seven-degree heat, with the first Hours Press publication, George Moore's *Peronnik the Fool.*

Nancy was spending much of her time with her lover, the writer Louis Aragon, editor of the Surrealist review *La Révolution Surréaliste.* He, too, was involved with the Hours Press, helping in the pressroom and later translating Lewis Carroll's *Hunting of the Snark* into French for Nancy to publish. In her Paris letter Janet frequently praised Aragon's writing; in private she said she didn't like him.[24] Janet was not particularly moved by Surrealism, despite her friendships with writers René Crevel and Pierre de Massot. When de Massot took her to see Antonin Artaud act in a small play, she disapproved of what she called his violently "anti-thespian" ideas of acting. Nor did Janet approve of the Surrealists' attitude toward women in general. As Nancy's biographer Anne Chisholm explains, "Women played a small part in the Surrealist scheme of things. For all their desire to live unconventionally and to shock the bourgeoisie, the Surrealists had highly conventional, even traditional, ideas about women."[25] Janet was well aware that these attitudes persisted, even among some of the most outspoken members of the avant-garde, to say nothing of the *New Yorker* readership.

Janet was relishing her public persona more and more. Genêt knew and cared about music, theater, smart cafés, literature, art, and

food — the finest civilization had to offer, according to her. Writing
to her mother, she still dismissed much of the magazine as slight,
and her own contribution as printed gossip, but she was grateful
nonetheless for the secure income.[26] Her work for *The New Yorker*
was meant only to underwrite her true vocation; she had come to
Paris to be an artist, and she hadn't quite given up.

However, her novel was progressing slowly, if at all. While writing
a couple of short stories in a desultory way, she worked primarily
on her Paris letter, using almost everyone she knew and everywhere
she went for material. When Neysa McMein came to Europe in the
spring of 1928, she invited Janet to accompany her to Venice and
Vienna, with all expenses paid. From these cities Janet duly reported
on Victor Cunard's new quattrocento palace and the aristocratic elegance of the Sacher Bar. Later in the summer Janet returned to
Venice with Solita, this time as Nancy's guests at the Palazzo Clary,
and her next Paris letter described, without a trace of sarcasm, the
all-night barge parties given for Nancy, with roving musicians, costumed gondoliers, and endless trays of fresh fish.

But Genêt could be condescending or could sound as if she feared
nothing, as if nothing were outside her frame of reference or sphere
of knowledge. Genêt became Janet's way of threading through a
society she both admired and disliked, one whose amenities attracted
her and whose values often repelled her. This made the public voice
of Genêt all the more appealing, for privately Janet still assumed she
and Solita were just an "innocent pair of green horns in all that
Venetian glass society."[27]

That summer, while visiting Nancy in Venice, they watched in
horror as Nancy taunted Aragon and he threatened suicide. "The
sight of Aragons trunk downstairs always meant he had packed to
leave *again* & had broke the elevator with his luggage," recalled
Janet.[28] The quarrels were terrible. As Solita reminisced, "To be in
the presence of Nancy was more like coming to grips with a force
of nature than being out for an evening's gossip and dancing after a
hard day's work."[29]

Soon they would all be seeing one another less; Nancy would
become more involved with politics, Solita with Gurdjieff, and Janet
with *The New Yorker*.

*

Mary Hockett Flanner,
circa 1900

Frank Flanner,
circa 1910

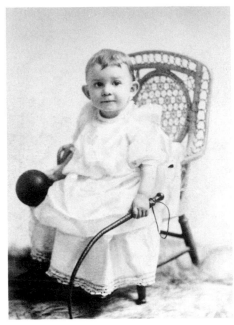

Janet Tyler Flanner

Janet at three, May 25, 1895

Mary as a young woman,
circa 1888

The Flanner home on North Meridian Street, Indianapolis

Mary Emma (Marie), twelve,
and Janet, seven

Janet at eighteen

Hildegarde Flanner at eighteen

William Lane Rehm

Jane Grant and Harold Ross

Neysa McMein in her New York studio, circa 1920

Solita Solano in 1923

Djuna Barnes and Natalie Barney

Margaret Anderson, early 1920s

Janet and Solita on Crete, 1921

Nancy Cunard, early 1920s

Janet at forty in 1932

Titled "Lost: A Renaissance," Jane Heap's farewell editorial in *The Little Review* in May 1929 claimed that "all of the arts have broken faith or lost connection with their origin and function."[30] The hoped-for renaissance sponsored by *The Little Review* had not occurred. And since artists, according to Margaret Anderson in her farewell editorial, did not really know what they were talking about, she and Jane Heap could no longer publish their magazine.

At the same time that these two were explaining why they chose to stop publishing and were receiving heartfelt farewells from writers like T. S. Eliot and Ford Madox Ford, *The New Yorker* was grossing more than two million dollars a year and earning over 20 percent of gross for its stockholders. It began to publish two editions, one for New Yorkers and one for out-of-towners. Although they were the same editorially, the advertisements and their rates differed; an advertiser could sign for the cheaper city edition or choose to reach a wider audience of 63,000.[31] *The New Yorker* had become a financial success and was on its way to becoming a national institution.

Janet was proud of the magazine and her association with it, and not solely because of its wide circulation or earnings. She was being paid fairly well. However, when the magazine accepted one of Kay Boyle's stories, Janet asked her how much she was getting paid. Boyle answered, "Two hundred fifty dollars," and Janet was outraged. "They don't pay me that," Janet stormed and, according to Boyle, immediately wrote Ross for a raise.[32] But more than economic satisfaction was the pleasure and privilege of being associated with writers she admired, like James Thurber, and editors like Katharine Angell and of course Ross himself. Together they believed that *The New Yorker* was not just another magazine; William Shawn, Ross's successor, later summed up the view they all shared, that *The New Yorker* "established a canon of taste, and laid the basis for a tradition of good writing."[33]

Lured by the prospect of making more money — Paris was increasingly expensive — and urged by her editors to send in other pieces, Janet decided to try her hand at a "Profile," a 3,600-word sketch of a living personality — one of the magazine's earliest features. The editors kept a backlog of eligible profile names, which were assigned, at first, to writers who knew the subject or who knew people who did. These writers were asked to write more of an essay than a series of vignettes and to take a point of view beyond that of the cheeky spectator. For Janet, whose method in the Paris letter involved concealing her point of view and trying to make her juxtapositions, contrasts, and examples suggest one, this was a challenge. And an opportunity.

When she had first met Isadora Duncan at Dorothy Ireland's in the winter of 1925, Janet thought the forty-seven-year-old dancer fat and frowsy — and one of the outstanding women of the twentieth century. On that cold December night Janet and Isadora got along well, Janet hardly believing she was talking to the woman she had seen spin across the stage of the Indianapolis Opera House ten years earlier. As they said goodbye, Isadora told her she was leaving for Nice the next day but would come to call when she returned. They clasped hands.

Isadora kept her promise, arriving at Janet's hotel one evening a few months later in an unpaid-for rented car. Isadora seldom could pay her own way, but that never stopped her. She would frequently invite a number of people for drinks and then find someone to take care of the bill. That night she found Janet, who didn't mind; she just made sure she was never caught again. But refusing Isadora was difficult. When Janet and Solita went one evening to see her at her room in the Hôtel Lutetia, Isadora held them "by force," recalled Solita, until she fell asleep. They took off their shoes, and when she began to snore, they quietly padded out.[34]

Begun in 1926, the profile of Isadora appeared in the issue of January 1, 1927. It characterized the dancer as a heroic woman whose art was beyond the comprehension of provincial morality — beyond the bourgeois stuffiness of those Americans bred, as Janet put it, on "Turkey in the Straw." Drawing on her own knowledge of and feeling for Greece, she portrayed Isadora as a living Greek sculpture swathed in Attic grace, beauty, and sensuality. Janet argued that she had thus become palatable even to the so-called refined Americans hungry for culture. Isadora, reared in the context of Janet's own upbringing, with its noisy Progressivism, had escaped it for an "exciting and fantastic" life, dancing all over the world to the tune of human liberty. But all her ideals "gained for Isadora was the loss of her passport and the presence of the constabulary on the stage of the Indianapolis

Opera House where the chief of police watched for sedition in the movement of Isadora's knees."[35]

Janet thought the profile quite good, and in many ways it is one of her best long pieces. Unaccustomed to the longer form, she sometimes overwrote and overdramatized, and in the other two profiles written in the late twenties — of designer Paul Poiret and writer Edith Wharton — she romanticized her subjects even more than she had the "tragic" Isadora.[36]

It was Isadora's personality, according to Janet, that helped render her art into a cult, and this was true of Poiret's egotistical mania as well. For that reason, she found Poiret as attractive as Isadora. Both were born too late; neither Dadaists nor Surrealists nor proponents, really, of the "modern," they hunted through the past to find an appropriate, perhaps Platonic, model of eternal beauty. For Isadora it was Greece, for Poiret the exotic East. Poiret, of course, was not averse to using modern technology to create his contemporary pleasure dome: for atmosphere at one of his costume balls, which he called La Mille et Deuxième Nuit, he chained parrots to bushes wired with electric lights.

Janet called Poiret a pirate and showed him to be a restless figure, scavenging across time for the design, the art, the books, the people, to satisfy his large and avaricious fancy. Dressmaker, perfumer, collector, boulevard actor, he too was out of step with his generation, always trying, Janet wrote, "to establish himself in other centuries as if for him time and history were optional."[37] Obstinately unsympathetic to changes in fashion and refusing to pander to the public taste, Poiret appeared in her profile as a courageous figure, even as he robed women in impractical eastern splendor, tyrannically barked orders at his staff, or nibbled chocolates. Like Isadora, Poiret publicly flaunted his dismissal of the penurious.

Janet excelled at describing the lush detail Poiret surrounded himself with. Edith Wharton, by contrast, did not offer Janet this kind of material. Another "outsider," Wharton did not live publicly and, unlike Duncan and Poiret, was born of the patrician class, whose manners she never quite lost. In a fairly unflattering and not altogether meticulous portrait, Janet reinforced the stereotype of the cold, implacable Mrs. Wharton organizing her day the way she organized her plots — with exacting, passionless skill. According to

Janet, she "saw the plot, but never the point. Born for ethics, she ignored the senses." She also ignored cathartic despair, "Baudelairean visions," and human indiscretion. Moving her characters like so many chess pieces, according to Janet, Wharton documented social decay with historical precision, gave the public what it wanted, and got richer. But Wharton earned Janet's respect for her permanent expatriation — "her most American act."

Common to all three profiles is Janet's obvious disdain for America and "Americanized" values. Isadora Duncan and Paul Poiret were romantic renegades transcending the provincial present, and Edith Wharton, who wrote scathingly of her patrician world, had retreated into an ordered "old-fashioned" world of fine sensibility: "She is a dignified little woman set down in the middle of her past. She says that to the greener growths of her day, she must seem like a taffeta sofa under a gas-lit chandelier. Certainly she is old-fashioned in that she reserves her magnanimity for special occasions."[38] Although Janet subtly criticized Wharton for pandering to the public Duncan and Poiret disdained and although she appeared proud and withdrawn, her quixotic devotion to the "truly literate" was made to seem touching. Wharton's delicacy may have been overrefined, but her nostalgia appealed to Janet, who was as skeptical about the passionate literary movements shoving Wharton aside as she was about Mrs. Wharton herself.

She seems to have been proudest of this profile, feeling more deferential toward Edith Wharton than toward either Isadora Duncan or Paul Poiret. Moreover, "Isadora" and the profile of Poiret, called "The Egotist," did not carry Janet's signature; they were attributed to "Hippolyta," queen of the Amazons, a name we may assume Janet chose. Her mother regretted that Janet had not signed the Poiret profile, and Janet apparently regretted it as well. She probably asked if she could use her own name in "Dearest Edith." This was the first time her name appeared in *The New Yorker* since she had begun writing for it four years earlier.[39] No doubt Janet wanted to show her respect for this sophisticated and somewhat unworldly woman, this friend of Henry James who, for all her faults and contradictions, still represented literature, culture, and civilization. And no doubt Janet wanted to be part of this special world.

When talking about her own generation, Kay Boyle once remarked that it was rebelling against "all literary pretentiousness, against weary, dreary rhetoric, against all the outworn literary and academic conventions. Our slogans were 'Down with Henry James, down with Edith Wharton, down with the sterility of "The Waste Land." ' "[40] Yet Janet, very much part of these times, had something eighteenth century about her, and she knew it.[41] Her tomb, she told Margaret Anderson, "will read, 'Hic jacet, 600 B.C. Greece; 1100 A.D. France and Italy; 1700–1800 England.' "[42] She loved elegance and grace and had an appetite for the finest, said her publisher and friend Simon Michael Bessie, adding that this was a paradox, given the trends of the twenties and the thirties of which she was a part.[43] She was not interested in breaking down culture but in preserving it.

After Janet submitted the Wharton profile to *The New Yorker,* Djuna Barnes told her that Katharine Angell had raved about it. But Katharine had also raved about Djuna's profile of James Joyce, which was not printed because the editorial board thought it too unusual. Janet's piece, more conventional and therefore more usable, earned her $165 — double what she received for the Duncan profile. She bought Solita crystal beads, sent her mother $100, and invested the rest in a new typewriter. And she gave up the idea of writing another novel. If she had started competing with Wharton earlier, she said, she might have gotten somewhere — apparently meaning that she had set her sights too high.[44] Or her mother had.

7

Noeline
1928-1933

THOSE WHO KNEW HER well say the beautiful Noel Haskins Murphy suffered three tragic losses in her lifetime.[1] In 1924, just four years after she married, she lost her husband to the belated claims of the Great War. Fred Murphy had been wounded, decorated, honored, horrified; his tank had been blown up, his friends killed, his sense of what was decent destroyed. In 1920 he went back to Europe with his young American bride because Europe had charmed him and because he hoped its physicians might be of help. "When I met Fred Murphy at dinner," Edmund Wilson recalled, "I thought him supercilious and didn't like him, because he kept contracting his eyebrows as if he were in pain. He was but I didn't know it." Murphy was one of those men, observed Wilson, "who have been rendered unstable and erratic by their war experience . . . badly shot up and then put together by surgeons, to survive for only a few years in the constant fear and danger of collapse."[2]

Murphy's stomach ulcers got worse, and his health rapidly deteriorated. In unrelenting, agitated pain, he would wake in the night, delirious, frantic, covered in perspiration. Noel, by his side, tried to quiet him. In May, a month before their anniversary, he died. Noel was inconsolable. Refusing to live more than thirty miles from Saint Germain-en-Laye, where Fred was buried, she bought a small farm nearby in the tiny village of Orgeval, slightly northeast of Paris. Even in 1940, when the Germans marched into Paris, she still wouldn't budge.

The Second World War, like the First, cast its shadow over Noel. In most ways, she was one of the lucky ones — fortunate enough to stay, relatively undisturbed, on her own land and to suffer only from backbreaking work and occasional hunger. By the war's end, Noel was over fifty; her voice had cracked and her small career as a singer was virtually over. This was her second loss; that the war also took away Janet was her third.

By early January 1932 Janet Flanner and Noel Murphy were in love. "Janet has a new lady-love — and is so engrossed in her that we see her rarely," Janet's college friend and fellow expatriate Richard Myers wrote to Stephen Vincent Benét.[3] Janet and Solita continued to live together at the Hôtel Saint-Germain-des-Prés, an arrangement that perplexed and amused outsiders. "Janet Flanner is now in love with Noel Murphy," Myers wrote, "but she still keeps house with Solita Solano. Solita has a house in the country where she is in love with another girl and where Janet visits. Noel doesn't visit in that house but has another friend, some French woman, where she visits until Janet returns from Solita's. X plus Y equals???"[4]

Janet had known Noel at least since the preceding summer, when the two of them and Noel's sister-in-law, Esther Murphy Strachey, drove to Berlin in Noel's small car. Janet was a great fan of Esther's, who had the finest historical mind Janet had ever come across, telling wonderful stories about all the Louis and recounting the Battle of Waterloo in a way that had you believing Napoleon had won it. Edith Wharton was another of Esther's passions, and her anecdotes may very well have helped Janet with the profile of Wharton. It was Esther who drove Scott Fitzgerald to Mrs. Wharton's home the afternoon he tried to insult the novelist, asking if she had ever heard of Karl Marx. (I have, of course, Wharton answered sweetly. His good friend Friedrich Engels gave me my copy of *Das Kapital*.)[5] Esther was planning to write a book about Wharton, and also one on Madame de Maintenon, which her friends assumed would be as intelligent and insightful as Esther's long monologues.[6]

Before that trip to Berlin in 1931, Janet may have seen Esther's lovely sister-in-law in passing; Noel occasionally dropped in on Natalie Barney's Fridays, and she was always the smartest woman at the new Crillon bar, said Solita. Janet and Noel were often invited to the same parties, like the huge dinner John Peale Bishop and his wife, Margaret Hutchins Bishop, neighbors of Noel's in Orgeval, gave on the occasion of their eighth anniversary. The guests, recalled Richard Myers, "were the usual horde they travel with — the nymphomaniac (the 'constant nymphomaniac' as Janet Flanner called her) — Lorna Lindsley; Helen Porter Simpson, Noel Murphy — (a rotten knocker) — Esther Murphy Strachey — one of the most grotesque creatures — but Irish and therefore witty — a Frenchman — who was obviously astonished at the conversation and an Irishman named MacDermott — whose wife looked like Jean and who has been married to everybody including Scofield Thayer and E E Cummings."[7]

A stunning woman with high cheekbones and hay-colored hair, the elegant Noel stood almost six feet tall — a veritable Viking, said one acquaintance.[8] Artist Pavlik Tchelitchew thought Noel a blend of Greta Garbo and Marlene Dietrich.[9] Frank to the point of seeming fierce, proud, and at times taciturn, Noel was someone people took notice of. Solita thought of her as "a careless, flamboyant Amazone in bright shorts and skirts — or something the peasants had never seen before, either for costumes or formidable motoring energy."[10] When old friends, such as actress Katharine Cornell, came to France to visit, Noel often whisked them through France and Belgium in her small Ford or entertained them in Germany, where she went at least once a year for singing lessons.

Noel's fine, high voice was "trained," Glenway Wescott once recalled, "as the French train their singers especially for the German repertory, with a golden tubular tone."[11] She preferred the songs of Schumann, Schubert, Debussy, and Strauss; she accompanied herself, if no one else was available, on the dwarf jazz piano she'd brought from New York, and she gave her several cats names like Brio and Largo. Her problem, Wescott suggested, "seemed to be that her exquisite physique was not stalwart enough for the volume of sound she had learned to produce. It made her pretty neck, which was like a water bird's, throb, and the note would slip."[12] Janet said that when Noel sang, she wiggled.

She seemed to live comfortably; she kept an enormous wine cellar and paid whatever she had to for good opera tickets. But she was careful about her money; sometimes her guests, especially Janet, complained that she kept her house damp and drafty; physical cold and deprivation, however, never seemed to bother Noel. Most of her friends assumed she was as poor as she was proud; Fred had not been able to leave her anything. His father had written to say he was thinking of selling the family business, the Mark Cross Company, and had asked his son to send back his shares of its stock. "Fred sent him all the shares, and then Fred died," Noel recalled, "so I didn't get a penny."[13] For six months Fred's father sent Noel $500 a month. Then he abruptly told her he couldn't pay her anymore. "It was just like discharging a servant," she observed.[14] However, Noel, the daughter of wealthy and socially prominent New Yorkers, apparently had her own income. And in 1928, when their mother died, Noel and her sister were left the balance of an estate that one paper reported valued at more than $10,000, but was probably far more.[15]

Janet used to tease Noel about her refined "Pahk Avenue mahner" — which was how Noel's upper-crust speech sounded to Janet's ears. Noel's mother, Henrietta S. Havemeyer Haskins, was the daughter of an old New York family associated with politics and high finance: Noel's grandfather was the wealthy sugar merchant Albert Havemeyer, and her great-uncle, William F. Havemeyer, had twice been elected mayor of New York City. Noel's father, Charles Waldo Haskins, a distant cousin of Ralph Waldo Emerson, was appointed in 1893 under the Joint Commission of the Fifty-third Congress to revise the nation's accounting system. He worked on legislation to regulate the public accountant's profession through a Board of Examiners appointed by the Regents of the University of the State of New York, became president of the examining board, and founded New York University's School of Commerce, where he was dean. He was also in charge of, among other things, the accounts of the West Shore Railway, which he may have gotten through his wife's family.

Henrietta Havemeyer Haskins was a widow by the time Noeline, her second daughter, born on Christmas Day in 1894, was nine. A wealthy woman, she was able to continue giving her children most of the material things they desired. But if the young Noel Haskins's upbringing was patrician, she had no intention of becoming one of

New York society's hostesses. At twenty-one she joined the newly
formed Washington Square Players, a group dedicated, so its man-
ifesto ran, to "hard work and perseverance, coupled with ability and
the absence of purely commercial consideration." The Players sponsored one-act plays of "artistic merit," chosen democratically by
everyone in the group. The Washington Square Players were soon
regarded by many as an "oasis of artistic refreshment," declared the
New York Times. Noel — calling herself Noel Haddon — starred in
the Players' second-season premiere of Philip Moeller's *Helena's Husband,* a spoof about the relationship between Helen of Troy and
Menelaus. Noel quickly became one of the most highly acclaimed
of the group, but in 1917, after two years with the group, she quit.
The United States was going to war, and Noel Haskins wanted to
go to London.

It was around this time that she indirectly met the charming Frederic Murphy through his sister Esther, who read Noel long sections
from the letters he was sending from the front lines. Sensitive, modest, witty, compassionate, and intelligent — Frederic was the shining
star of the Murphy family, no small feat in a family that also boasted
Esther and Gerald. Esther mesmerized people with her conversation
and her sharp intelligence. She seemed to remember everything she
read, everything that was said to her, and everything spoken just out
of earshot, a remarkable gift in one who dominated most conversations.[16] Brother Gerald and his wife, Sara, were later known as the
incarnation of all that was glamorous and elegant in American expatriates; according to Gerald's friend Scott Fitzgerald, who modeled
the hero in *Tender Is the Night* after him, Gerald Murphy had a talent
for personality. But Fred, almost a decade older than Noel, was the
finest man she had ever met.

Janet thought their story romantic, all the more so because eight
years after his death Noel hardly mentioned Fred; she merely
claimed, in a very matter-of-fact way, that she still loved him. Noel,
who forgot very little, was not a sentimentalist. Nor did she tolerate
sentimentality in anyone else. She found Hemingway's "false man-
liness" tedious, and she disliked Fitzgerald, always pinching someone
when he was drunk.[17] (Hemingway, who modeled a minor character
in *The Sun Also Rises* after Noel, said he liked her well enough but
she made him "nervous the way cats do some people."[18]) Noel

thought of herself as a "Victorian," meaning, most likely, that she did not brook self-indulgence, laziness, or intemperance. But with her somewhat remote aspect, her belief in hard work, and her unswerving loyalties, she embodied attitudes Janet found appealing. Janet began to pick up some of Noel's Park Avenue accent.

It was Noel's beauty that first drew Janet to her, and her personality made her seem desirably unattainable. As they drove through the Black Forest in the summer of 1931, Janet periodically traded the front seat with Esther for a glimpse of Noel's straight profile. The countryside she had missed in Germany years before with her family all seemed so picturesque and charming now. That was how Noel saw it, and Janet was beginning to see through her eyes. They left the car, Noel took off her driving gloves, and the three of them sat down to smoked pork and sweet red cabbage; they drank Moselle wine, stayed in small inns decked with petunias, and sipped martinis in Berlin's Jockey Club over quiet jazz. Faces turned when they walked into a cabaret; Janet saw how others looked at Noel, who didn't return the glances. And Noel was drawn to Janet, who made her laugh.

Theirs swiftly became a passionate relationship, apparently excluding everything and everyone else. Solita still edited much of Janet's work, offering the criticism and editorial advice that she was also beginning to give without pay to other friends, including Hemingway. She served as Janet's private secretary, even to packing her clothes when Janet left Paris on assignment or went to Orgeval for the weekend. Hers was a devotion that bordered on the self-effacing, it seemed to outsiders. However, their relationship, though stable, had never been an exclusive one; it was predicated on the "absolute freedom" Solita gave Janet, according to Margaret Anderson.[19] Though neither Janet nor Solita seriously considered altering their domestic arrangement, Noel soon assumed a central place in what looked to some like an entourage, and Janet was spending more time in Orgeval.[20] Early in 1932 Solita half-humorously complained that "Genêt . . . lives with me when she remembers it."[21]

Superficially, Noel seemed to resemble Solita, not in looks but in disposition. Both were described as "extravagant" personalities, flamboyant and somewhat histrionic; by contrast, Janet was perceived as milder, possessing a "quiet, positive dominance with no need to assert

her [self]."²² Solita was always telling people what she thought when
they didn't want to be told — something Janet criticized her for.
Virgil Thomson considered her a bit of a bully.²³ And Noel, too,
could be insensitive: she shocked one friend when she called the
Second World War the most exciting time of her life.²⁴ Even Janet
admitted that Noel's pronouncements occasionally sounded brutal;
according to Mary McCarthy, who met her much later, Noel could
be quite cutting.²⁵

Solita was becoming more and more involved with Gurdjieff and
his teachings. After he had closed the Institute at the Prieuré, she'd
been curious enough to join Jane Heap's study group, and soon she
became Gurdjieff's faithful secretary, transcribing much of what
went on during his lunchtime sessions at the Café de La Paix. Janet
or Noel would occasionally attend these sessions, and Noel once
brought Gurdjieff medicines from Germany. On delivering them,
she complained to him that she chronically suffered from headaches.
Liver, Gurdjieff said, and then upset her by saying that she reminded
him of a camel and a sparrow. "Now I look to see if you are male
camel or female camel. I not know yet. But I know even what kind
of *merde* you make. You ever see camel *merde*?"²⁶

Solita introduced Kathryn Hulme to Gurdjieff's teachings, telling
her that it was "the only important thing in Paris."²⁷ Janet, not inclined
to discipleship, didn't agree. In fact, in later years Janet resented
anything that might link her too closely with Gurdjieff and his group,
even the mention of her name and address in Kathryn Hulme's 1966
memoir, *Undiscovered Country.* "I had *not* known till I read the proofs
that you had included me & Solita by name & address & while it is
a tribute to friendship such as ours all is, cela me gene, because for
the varied contexts of yr (the phone rang & disturbed me, sorry) life
as you report it, I do not belong in this volume having been no
Gurdjieffite."²⁸ She refused to write a blurb for the book, explaining
that "to write in praise of your book would simply look like back-
patting in my estimation. This is a matter of professional conscience
with me and I could not separate myself from it really."²⁹ Janet had
gladly written a blurb for Hulme's earlier memoir, *The Wild Place,*
and Solita suspected that she now refused because of the association
with Gurdjieff's followers. When *Undiscovered Country* was published, Kathryn sent Noel a copy, but not Janet.

Although Noel and Solita were friendly, they weren't particularly close. All the same, Solita was invited to Orgeval and was soon a frequent visitor. Noel, happy to accommodate guests fleeing modern Paris for eighteenth-century country life (as Solita described it), kept her bright blue gate open and her three hand-painted guest rooms almost always full. She cooled champagne in her well, and if her guests insisted on reimbursing her for the hospitality, she charged them ten francs a day for food and drink. Margaret and Georgette, Louis and Mary Bromfield, Diane and Vincent Sheean, or Gertrude Stein and Alice Toklas often drove out for Sunday lunch and sat in the large back yard. If Gertrude and Margaret came on the same day, the arguments lasted until long after coffee was served. Margaret, for a change, was not allowed to dominate and didn't mind, delighted to have such a responsive adversary. Djuna Barnes occasionally came out to sunbathe in the nude. And once e. e. cummings spent a long afternoon there, calling his tall and lanky hostess Little Thimble.[30]

Days and nights in Orgeval were idyllic, soothing, even domestic. Solita called Noel's two-story stone house, surrounded by eight-foot walls, a refuge from the Depression. Janet apparently felt much the same way. In a Paris letter from the small village, she romanticized the Old World peasants swinging their scythes and flails while the whole family helped out, furnishing wine and cheese and flowers and music to celebrate the last day of the harvest. (At the same time, she poked fun, particularly at the peasants' notion of "progress"; they illuminated the church altar with electricity instead of the prettier candles they used at home.)[31] Noel made soup with herbs and vegetables from her garden; she filled the closets with lavender she grew herself, and she planted and carefully tended asters, dahlias, Madonna lilies, hyacinths, Canterbury bells, and zinnias in front of the house. Her roses were the size of saucers. But even if it hadn't been so idyllic, one friend pointed out, it wouldn't have mattered. Janet went to Orgeval primarily to be with Noel Murphy, whose beauty, Janet remarked more than once, was maddening.[32]

Early in 1932 Solita reported to readers of the *Detroit Athletic Club News* that Janet Flanner, who'd just lost her purse crammed with notes for a Paris letter, "says her life is no longer possible — what

with artists and writers being furious she doesn't write them up in
The New Yorker. Her stockings all have runs, the exhibitions are dull,
someone sat down on her best hat, she can't get her novel started."[33]
Janet still occasionally toyed with the idea of writing another novel,
but most of the incentives were gone: she'd never really begun her
second book; *Cubical City* hadn't sold as well as she'd hoped; Solita
had stopped writing fiction altogether. For her, starting and finishing
fiction was much more difficult than doing a *New Yorker* letter. One
of her good friends, a genuine admirer of her prose, assumed she
didn't get much writing done because she was plain lazy, but the way
Janet told it, something always interfered: a free-lance commission,
a scouting expedition for French books on behalf of the American
publishers Brewer and Warren, an event just right for *The New
Yorker.*

And Genêt absorbed time. More and more, *The New Yorker* was
using Janet as a general correspondent, which meant she was expected to cover anything going on in or near France. Happy to oblige,
she was earning money steadily. With her income and Solita's
hundred dollars a month for her *D.A.C. News* articles, they had
decided in 1928 they could afford to rent another room in their
hotel. They also installed a tub and a small gas burner and created
a suite of sorts, which they wallpapered and painted yellow. Janet
bought Solita a gramophone so that after the evening's work they
could softly play records late. Then they scoured the antique stores
and flea markets for new furniture, collecting in the next few years
a small picture of roses in a vase, a five-foot mahogany bookshelf,
and a Louis XV table, which Solita gave Janet for her birthday. "I believe I have found a niche," she wrote excitedly to her
mother.[34]

She wasn't referring just to her newly arranged rooms; she was
also talking about a project she'd undertaken, one that made her
think she had at last found her calling. When Ernestine Evans, a
college friend, arranged for Janet to translate Colette's *Chéri* for the
Boni brothers, she immediately accepted the offer of $150 and began
fantasizing about translating all of Colette's work into English. Wanting to write, yearning to do something genuinely creative, she
thought translating might be the answer. In translations, she reasoned, she could use her words to convey someone else's ideas —

the best of two worlds for someone like Janet, who believed she had no ideas of her own, or so she often lamented to her mother and Hildegarde.[35]

In 1928, sitting down at her new Erica typewriter, typing as usual with two fingers, Janet set to work translating, doubtlessly learning a great deal about style from the classical Colette. Once a week Germaine Beaumont checked her work for errors and helped with idioms; Solita edited for clarity and then did all the final copying. However, the next year, when Boni asked her to translate *Claudine à l'École,* Janet took the job reluctantly. Although Colette's writing represented the qualities Janet admired — rich vocabulary, accuracy, a sensuous love of nature, and a matchless clarity of presentation — she thought the second book a bad choice. The story was too long and it bored her; she found the work of turning the sensual *Claudine* into supple English prose tiresome. The result, predictably, was not as successful as her first translation, and as it happened, *Claudine at School* was the last Colette she translated. Moreover, the Boni brothers didn't publish it — it was taken eventually by Gollancz in London — and they put out only one more in the series, Jane Terry's translation of *Mitsou,* to which Janet wrote the introduction.[36]

Janet had not given up the idea of writing something more than journalism; if not translations of Colette and not fiction, she'd try a book of history. Influenced by Esther Murphy, Janet in early 1930 enthusiastically began researching a book on the women of the seventeenth century, which she tentatively titled "Without Men." She spent her mother's Christmas check on a twelve-volume set of Saint-Simon's history of Louis XIV's court, assuming it would give her a vantage point on her century; in March she took a bus to the Bibliothèque Nationale and filled out the forms necessary for a reader's card; over the summer she read up on the sixteenth century as well as the eighteenth, and for two months in the fall borrowed from Shakespeare and Company volumes on Madame de Maintenon, Elizabeth and Essex, and Henry VIII.

Nothing happened. She didn't write to her mother for several months, and when she apologized for the lapse, she explained that she couldn't bear sending a letter when she felt she was again disappointing them both. This behavior was an "old child-founded evasion," Janet wrote in the fall of 1931, "the old secrecy that goes on in every adolescent's heart and consciousness and which, in an ill-balanced nature like mine, deepens and broadens with time until at certain periods it is a gulf over which the generations cannot jump."[37] She thought the problem was that she was unable to do creative work. But, she added, she would not give up, and she was enthusiastic, once again, about a new project, a translation of Georgette Leblanc's memoir, *My Life with Maeterlinck.*

Never one to admire Janet's writing without qualifications, Margaret Anderson thought Janet had translated "down-to-earth" Colette beautifully but bungled Georgette's book. According to Margaret, Janet "never knew what Georgette was talking about. . . . When Georgette spoke of her 'tragedy of astonishment,' Janet thought she meant Maeterlinck's marriage to a younger woman! Solita and I had to rescue the translation from her and do it ourselves."[38]

Finding Georgette's writing baroque and woolly, Janet couldn't work as quickly as the publishers demanded without making dozens of errors. Solita and Margaret did in fact come to her rescue, and Georgette helped with the proofs. When it was all finished, late in the fall of 1931, Janet shared half of her $400 fee with Georgette and Margaret and split the rest with Solita. She had not found her niche after all.

The end of her brief career as a translator was doubtless a disappointment, and Janet may have wanted to avoid telling this to her mother; she may also have been avoiding Mary during these early days of her romance with Noel. If so, Noel also provided Janet with a new subject and, finally, news fit for Mary Flanner. Janet wrote a short story about Noel and sent it to *The New Yorker.* Katharine Angell White enthusiastically responded by suggesting an entire series. During the summer of 1931, while staying with Noel in Orgeval, Janet went to work, hoping that she could write a few stories and that they would help with her novel — or even become one.

The New Yorker published three of them.[39] "Tchatzu" and "Oh, Fire!" appeared in 1932, "Venetian Perspective" in 1934.[40] All chronicled the life of "Mrs. Daphne," named for the nymph who preferred a life "without men" and turned herself into tree bark when pursued. This fictionalized Noel Murphy appears as an American war widow of independent temper, a lovely and cultured, fairly well-to-do expatriate. Spurning her suitors, superior without being arrogant, she clearly is the object of her author's admiration.

In "Oh, Fire!" Mrs. Daphne, staying in Paris at her brother-in-law's studio, is momentarily flustered while composing a letter to a would-be suitor she met at Bayreuth. He's been persistent, and she doesn't know how to dampen his ardor in French, their common language. Fumbling over her verbs — wondering if she should use the French conditional or present tense — she smells smoke, notices the overzealous blaze in the fireplace, and confronts the officious concierge, who demands to see the necessary insurance papers. Mrs. Daphne, annoyed that her brother-in-law lent her a fire-prone flat, must then deal with the firemen, who are more interested in her writing table and its contents than the matter at hand. After some amusing exchanges, they extinguish the fire and leave. Mrs. Daphne notices her unfinished letter and drops it into the wet fireplace.

Mrs. Daphne's indifference to her many male suitors is also the subject of "Tchatzu," named for Noel's Russian maid. The story is a brief study in contrasts: the dark, romanticizing Tchatzu set against the fair, patrician Mrs. Daphne. The déclassé Tchatzu respects two things above all else, men and royalty; Mrs. Daphne, however, is impervious to the men, all of whom Tchatzu regards as princes who wish to marry her. Although Tchatzu generally regards women as inferior beings, she doesn't fault them for an accident of birth they cannot change. Her exception to this rule is Mrs. Daphne herself, who as an American should be able to change anything.

Janet presents Tchatzu as amusing, untutored, superstitious, and, in her own way, charming. Tchatzu ignores the world of politics, revolutions, theories, history; she speaks a Georgian dialect inter-mixed with some Polish, Russian, three English words, and fifty French, all mispronounced and used without tenses. However, the juxtaposition of Tchatzu and Mrs. Daphne amounts to little more than a slight character sketch of Tchatzu, mildly ironic, genial, a bit condescending. Both women are essentially stock characters, pan-tomiming their few lines with courtly aplomb. The story, like "Oh, Fire!" dances around the complex Noel Murphy, reduced for public consumption to appearing cold and dignified, and then around Tchatzu, similarly reduced and made to appear slightly ridiculous.

In the third of the series, "Venetian Perspective," Mrs. Daphne is compared with Bertha Bensdorp, a former Wagnerian opera singer whose continual thick-accented talk smothers everyone near her, especially her polite husband, Hans, a mild-mannered banker. Mrs. Daphne meets the couple in Venice and dines with them. Several days after she bids them farewell "from her blonde, perfumed height," she runs into Mrs. Bensdorp shaking with grief, her diamond and emerald jewelry quivering. Hans has left her. When Mrs. Daphne tries to console Mrs. Bensdorp, the latter turns and asks why a pretty widow like Mrs. Daphne is alone in the world. Find yourself a Hans, the comic Bertha advises, to love and to take care of; never let him get away.

All three stories use Mrs. Daphne as the norm against which the other characters are judged, and in all three the characters are differentiated by their command of language. Able to use four languages skillfully, Mrs. Daphne, unlike her foils, seems to control all situations. She falters only once, in "Oh, Fire!" when she attempts to extinguish her suitor's ardor. In fact the possible introduction of men into this harmonious, if comic, female world is the only thing threatening Mrs. Daphne.

Mrs. Daphne seems to find pleasure in her aloofness, something neither Mrs. Bensdorf or Tchatzu could ever understand. Hers is an austere, untouchable beauty, self-contained and a bit self-regarding. Like her mythological namesake, she disdains the world of men and their affairs, the world that killed her husband. But as Janet would eventually admit, the world of men was never far off, no matter how distant it might seem during those deep summer days in Orgeval. And to regard the world of men and their affairs as if it were theater, Janet would learn, was a perspective only the twenties allowed. It became abundantly and painfully clear in the next few years that there was no separate world for anyone — men or women, Georgian or American or French.

8

C'Était les Beaux Jours
1929-1934

IN THE FALL OF 1929, as she sailed from New York to France on the *Bremen,* dining on caviar and cold partridge, Janet gave little thought to the recent stock market disaster. *The New Yorker*'s arrangement with the Lloyd shipping line, which advertised in its pages, kept her well insulated; even without that, she regarded the crash as comeuppance for the fat American parvenu, not for her. In her December 4 Paris letter, referring to the "recent unpleasantness in Wall Street," she made it amply clear that Genêt and the French hadn't been affected by the stock market crash — at least not yet.

For Christmas she and Solita trimmed their tree with chocolate candy and invited guests over, as was their custom, for cocktails and pâté. Solita bought Janet a red leather handbag, and Nancy gave her a pair of green jade cups; Bastian Hoyt gave her $100 and Mary Flanner sent her annual holiday check, which, like all her checks, came in handy. Janet was not extravagant. She and Solita, keeping careful accounts, did not overspend — but they didn't save either: they ate well, bought new clothes, traveled fairly often. And when Kathryn Hulme put her Citroën roadster up for sale in the fall of 1931, Janet felt solvent enough to buy it.

Janet could not afford to be cavalier about money, but she knew she could pay the rent and still afford the luxuries she enjoyed —

fine restaurants, fresh flowers, a good bottle of wine. And this ease was reflected in her Paris letter, for Genêt treated financial matters as if reporting to those who had the taste, and the income, for luxuries. She alerted Americans to news of the exchange rate, warning them about increases in champagne costs, or provided them with current prices on paintings and other precious objects. Genêt was concerned with a style of life, and the Paris letter treated economics and politics as if they merely enhanced or detracted from the art of living. Genêt kept readers informed of the way the prefect of Paris regulated life on the Left Bank; she described the city's first Proletarian Exhibition (capitalist in style and Bolshevik in ideology); she reported that the French denounced "with dignity" the American boycott of Charlie Chaplin; but she did not mention the outburst of French reaction that same year to the trial and execution of Sacco and Vanzetti in Boston.

Not long after Janet returned to France in the late fall of 1929, she finished a *New Yorker* profile of the perfumer and financier François Coty. Published in May 1930, "Perfume and Politics" hinted that things might soon be different: no longer would the revolt against philistinism occupy a purely aesthetic theater; the economic and social crises of the thirties would affect everyone and show how art and politics were connected. As Janet pointed out in one of her Paris letters, politicians were beginning to give "lectures like *littérateurs* and the literary gentry are settling into politics."

Her profile touched on several political topics — Coty's "new" (her word) Fascism; his determination to crush Communism, and his "proletarian" newspaper *L'Ami du Peuple*. In a Paris letter she had once called Coty's paper "excellent"; now she brushed over it, mentioning only that it opposed Bolshevism, the British Labour Party, Lloyd George, and Édouard Herriot, France's former Radical prime minister. She skirted the matter of Coty's Fascist political affiliations and instead concentrated on his character, much as she had with Isadora Duncan, Paul Poiret, and Edith Wharton. To her Coty was a "realist" who "rightly" understood the relation between peace in Europe and sound economic policy, unlike the sloganeering politicians who reminded her of Woodrow Wilson. A moody and mysterious Horatio Alger — "creative," shrewd, comical — he was a "financial genius" who had created an enormously successful cosmetic business. Janet undoubtedly knew he was subsidizing antiparliamentary movements, but if she had any reservations about him, she dismissed them by making him appear ridiculous; he was simply like the "sympathetic and declamatory *saltimbanques* who from the top of a tight-rope offer marvelous cure-alls which have the high merit of relieving nothing but public tedium."[1]

Documenting virtually every stage of the perfume-making business, from the gathering of oils to the cutting of crystal bottles, she anchored the article firmly in Coty's business. This approach was consistent with the *New Yorker* profiles of the time. As Stanley Edgar Hyman would write in the *New Republic* in 1942, the *New Yorker* profile, certainly no political forum, got its effects "wholly from factual documentation, never from moral slant."[2] Although it's impossible to know how much Janet's editors directed her writing or to what extent they restricted her, Janet knew what they wanted, and she wanted to provide it. She was not inclined to analyze Coty's economic policies, political movements, or even his motives and aspirations.

The young photographer Horst Bormann, who first met Janet around this time, thought of her as an "American journalist learning her way," which meant to him that she was interested in "facts, facts, and more facts, all the way." Apparently she believed that facts revealed truth, that they were objective and knowable. And yet, Horst noted, she was "opinionated and argumentative. . . . She could laugh, even giggle sometimes, but she didn't have a light touch."[3]

Janet, decidedly a beginner when it came to writing about politics, relied on friends like Esther Murphy or Germaine Beaumont. Virgil Thomson presumed "it was Germaine who explained to Janet — who finally got it through her head — about the French political parties. Very few Americans ever understand the multiplicity and the nature of French political parties. But after Germaine had been around for a while, Janet could at least handle the subject."[4]

Thomson himself talked to her about music. Her friend the designer Mainbocher, an old friend of Neysa's, provided material on French dressmakers for an article in *Ladies' Home Journal.*[5] Natalie Barney often supplied the kind of detail that became a hallmark of Janet's writing, such as what Mata Hari wore the day she was shot (a "neat Amazonian tailored suit, specially made for the occasion," wrote Janet, "and a pair of new white gloves").[6] And although Germaine helped her unravel the complexity of French politics, Janet mainly preferred to use the anecdotal social material she gathered. She wrote most effectively and most enjoyed writing when she could describe what she herself observed, adding the arresting or telling detail perhaps gleaned from other sources. She was not interested in linking person, place, or event to politics or economics but in describing her subject economically, tartly, shrewdly: she told readers that the indefatigable Clemenceau "had asked to be buried upright" and that the hostess Elsa Maxwell was "not a social promoter" but "an evangelist under crystal chandeliers whose shout of 'Isn't this divine?' is the hilarious hallelujah of the saved."[7]

Among the staff of *The New Yorker* at that time Janet was not considered one of the best writers. Katharine White thought she wrote cryptically and far less well than someone like Louise Bogan, for instance. But White was sanguine: "We edit her obscurities out."[8] Janet knew this and was grateful, especially since she hadn't been nearly as successful with other magazines. Dick Myers, then an editor at *Ladies' Home Journal,* was unable to pull strings to get more of her pieces published. She'd hoped to parlay her $500 payment for the article on dressmakers into a $1,000 fee for future work. But an article on expatriates was rejected and nothing else was commissioned.

The reason may have been the stock market crash as much as anything else. Magazines like *Ladies' Home Journal* were cutting back. And so Janet became increasingly dependent on *The New Yorker,* which provided certain income, certain publication, and criticism tempered by a great deal of encouragement. In addition, it insulated her from what she feared might be true, not about the style of her writing but about its content. A comment by Natalie Barney had wounded her: Janet is amusing and bright, Barney reportedly quipped, "bright as a button. But," she added, "what is a button?"

Janet reported from Berlin in 1931, "There must be, it is true, terrible want in certain quarters of Berlin," but she didn't see much of it, and she certainly wasn't going to write about the little she saw.[9] Having gone to take the entertainment pulse of the city, she told her *New Yorker* readers that Berliners actually seemed more affable than she'd remembered them, their night life as lively, their food much better. She remarked on the new Pergamon Museum, rated the fare at the local movie houses, and gave the German capital high marks for courtesy to tourists; she had not come to Berlin, her report insisted, to cover political or economic conditions.

But by the next year it was impossible to avoid writing about the world economic crisis. In France industrial production had fallen, unemployment had risen, wages and salaries had been cut, governments were toppling. And the country still owed the United States payment (plus interest) of its war debts, even though the U.S. canceled Germany's debt. Premier Herriot, who insisted that France meet its obligation, was forced to resign. In May 1932 Janet reported to the *New Yorker* audience that Paris was still generally gay, but the following December she wrote that ten thousand Parisians had taken to the streets, screaming that "not one *sou!*" should be paid to the Americans, although the upper classes regretted the default. From then on Janet added the inevitable news of French economic and political turmoil to her letter, once calling such news "Political Addenda, Mostly Not Funny."

The return on her investments had trickled to almost nothing. Her sister Marie had been taking care of most of them but could offer little in the way of financial advice; she wasn't doing very well herself. In the spring of 1932 Janet heard that Lane, who had counseled her on her investments during their short marriage, was coming to Paris with his mother and his second wife. Janet went to meet him for cocktails, wearing a new hat and the black fur jacket she thought looked well on her. Ever polite and still a little awed by her, Lane said she looked as handsome as ever. She thought he looked a bit haggard: now working for Brown Brothers Harriman, he spent most of his time tending the Harriman family fortune. Though he'd bought 150 acres of land in the Berkshires for his weekends, he had spent the last two years without a vacation working in New York. He hardly ever painted anymore.

He asked about her mother and sisters and offered all of them his financial services. A few months later Janet took him up on his offer and gave him power of attorney over her investments. But there wasn't much he could do, given the condition of the stock market, she reasoned, so when her Liberty Bonds came due, she decided to buy gold coins. She put them all in a small sack, and Solita drove her to Orgeval. Janet climbed the wooden stairs to Noel's attic and tucked the bag inside an old chamber pot in the corner.

Politics and money had made life more exciting than usual, she wrote her mother that year; then, not twelve months later she complained to Gertrude Stein that she felt under constant pressure to keep up with everything she had to do and learn. She canceled engagements, often at the last minute; she had too much work, she apologized to painter Francis Rose, Gertrude's young protégé, who had invited Janet and Noel to the Mediterranean. The pressure made her edgy; she was afraid she wouldn't meet her deadlines, that she couldn't organize and present her material, that she didn't know enough. Pain shot through her arms and one leg. She took to bed for several days with a severe outbreak of sciatica, forcing her to "defect" — her word — and cancel plans to visit Gertrude and Alice in the country. She recovered quickly, but the cycles of anxiety and withdrawal would continue.

Because money arriving from America was worth less and less — Janet quipped that Americans in Paris might as well receive bananas, which they could at least eat — she accepted any jobs that came her way. Ralph Ingersoll, formerly with *The New Yorker* and now editor of *Fortune,* commissioned her to write something on French bankers, a piece that was eventually canceled but paid for in advance; she accepted all *New Yorker* assignments — profiles of Lily Pons, Max Reinhardt (never written), Igor Stravinsky, and Elsa Schiaparelli; and she accepted a position with the magazine *Arts and Decoration,* writing a monthly article for $100.[10] Pleased that her *New Yorker* salary was raised to $70 a letter, she tried, usually unsuccessfully, to send the money from these articles (she wrote at least five) to her mother, who was also suffering from the Depression.[11] But to make ends meet, in 1933 Janet sent *The New Yorker* a profile of the dressmaking firm Worth et Cie, two short stories, and a cartoon; and she rewrote her profile of hostess Elsa Maxwell five times before the magazine accepted it.[12]

The articles for *Arts and Decoration* often included the same items she used in her better-edited Paris letter — musical soirees sponsored by the Vicomte and Vicomtesse de Noailles, premieres, exhibits, the housewarmings of the Singer sewing machine heiress Mrs.

Daisy Fellowes — as well as items about characters she considered colorful, like the Montparnasse restaurateur Rosalie, who served Modigliani, Matisse, and Picasso on the condition that they finish everything on their plates. She described the attractions to be enjoyed at the French circuses and the sale to Sam Courtauld of recent paintings by Pavlik Tchelitchew, including a portrait of Noel Murphy — "a blond angel with a large white bow."[13] According to Janet, in Paris "talent is never allowed to hide under a bushel-basket" because the "high critical faculty . . . native to the aristocratic French mind" never fails to recognize and pay for its pleasures.[14] Cosmopolitan money, leisure, and taste continued to provide Janet with an income as their American chronicler. She was attracted to the events and pastimes of a leisure class that seemed to perpetuate itself regardless of the "exigencies," as Janet put it, of 1933.

But more and more she became caught up in the meaning of these exigencies. Early that year she, along with everyone else on *The New Yorker,* was forced to take a 10 percent pay cut, leaving her with $1,400 a year for twenty-three letters. By July, however, the exchange rate had dropped so far that Ross raised her back to $80 a letter to help her out. By the beginning of 1934 she was getting $105, for which she was enormously grateful. And she realized, with something of a shock, that for the first time in her life writing was her sole means of support.

Yet if fear of bankruptcy made these peculiar times, Janet told her family, at least some kind of change was afoot. No one knew its direction: Bolshevism, internationalism, nationalism. Everyone talked politics, and she too found herself involved in the speculation, analyses, the endless discussions — not just because she felt her job obliged her but because she was more and more interested.[15] Vaguely supporting some kind of redistribution of wealth, she declared that greedy bankers (she exempted Lane) should be the first group to be regulated. Insisting that she was no supporter of capitalism's inequalities, she was quick to disassociate herself from the Communist left and what she called her parlor Bolshevik friends. They demanded revolution, she said, and then cried the loudest when their stocks fell.

Claiming vaguely to prefer "nationalism" to "internationalism" and distancing herself once again from the left, Janet did not go so far as to say she was interested in the nationalism of the Third Reich. She was, however, definitely attracted to the pageantry of Nazis marching in their crisp uniforms, flags unfurled against the blue fall sky. Traveling through Germany with five other women, including Noel and Solita, in the autumn of 1933, she must have noticed the changes that had occurred since her last trip. When Janet and her friends stopped at a small guest house, Nazi soldiers crowded around their table at dinnertime, demanding to see that their papers were in order; if not, the soldiers threatened, they would be declared "light" and sent out of the country. In Murnau, Solita was told that she could not wear trousers; German women must wear skirts, and the Americans must dress like their German counterparts, who were also forbidden to use powder and lipstick or to smoke in public. Some towns posted "Jews Not Welcome" signs and in Nuremberg a young Jewish boy had to march through the streets with a placard tied around his neck. "I kissed a Christian girl," it said. "I promise never to do it again."[16]

Everywhere one went, Janet told her *New Yorker* audience with characteristic understatement, 1933 had been a "worrying kind of year."

When American broadcast correspondent William Shirer returned to Paris in January 1934 after a four-year absence, he found the French frustrated and resentful: "Rancour and intolerance poisoned the air. Insults and threats were hurled at each other by the Right and the Left. The former professed to fear the coming of Godless communism; the latter of totalitarian fascism."[17] Daily he saw rioting on the streets; not simply protests against particular government officials or policies, these were outbursts aimed at the heart of the parliamentary republican system.

At exactly this time *The New Yorker,* which was thriving despite the Depression, published Janet Flanner's "Those Were the Days," a profile of Worth et Cie.[18] As its title suggests, the profile was a somewhat nostalgic look at the dressmaking house, beginning with the innovations of its founder, Charles Frederick Worth, and concluding with the changes made by that inevitable curse "progress." The nineteenth century, with its small family enterprises catering to royal tastes, was over. The war had ended all that: "The Armistice, as we know now," Janet wrote, "settled nothing, least of all French dressmaking. For one thing, the gown called 'the creation' was over. As newcomer to the trade, Gabrielle Chanel, shrewdly smelling the machine age in the air, launched standardization as the style; women, to look fashionable, had to look alike. Formerly, as Worth's well knew, the only females who, unfortunately, had to look similar were queens, owing to the protocol about court trains. Furthermore, the war had killed fine French silk by killing the men who wove it."[19] The house of Worth had weathered most of the changes wrought by the twentieth century without losing any of its aristocratic appeal. But the old days — *"c'était les beaux jours"* — those good days of hard work, fine craft, real silk, luxury, and enough refinement to recognize its quality and mark — were forever lost. And Janet, though she described those days ironically, missed them.

Such wistful yearning for a lost elegance was one side of Janet's complex response to the bewildering, painful events of the present. Another part of this response was fear. On the evening of February 6, 1934, Janet was sitting at the Brasserie Lipp in the Boulevard Saint-Germain. A waiter she knew stopped by her table and told her she ought to hurry over to the Place de la Concorde. There was rioting, and it was bad. She left the brasserie half-heartedly, but once on the street, she allowed the crowds to push her back to Lipp's, where she and her friends ordered more beer. It wasn't until six the next morning that she learned there had been shooting and many deaths. A friend took her by car over to the Concorde, and she saw the tattered remains of the previous night, the bloodiest, everyone later agreed, Paris had seen since the Commune of 1871. The effect was profound; it revealed the perilous condition of the Third Republic and the anger and frustration smoldering just beneath the surface of French life.

Though no single event accounts for the new direction Janet's work took in the coming years, it's clear that the riots of February 6 decidedly altered her sense of Genêt's role. The ostensible cause of the rioting was the recent, ineptly handled Stavisky scandal. In 1926 financier Serge Alexandre Stavisky had been arrested for the embezzlement of nearly seven million francs but — probably because he had made important friends in the Justice Department — he was quickly released. While awaiting his trial, postponed nineteen times,

Stavisky continued to engineer swindles successful enough to net him two newspapers, one theater, and a stable of horses. But when he floated a loan of millions of francs' worth of valueless bonds, allegedly to finance a municipal pawnshop in Bayonne, he over-reached himself. The bonds came due, he couldn't make good, and the fraud, which implicated not only the mayor of Bayonne but several prominent politicians and a few editors of Paris newspapers, was uncovered. The public — spurred on by the right-wing paper *L'Action Française* — demanded that the government take some action.

At the height of the affair in January 1934, Stavisky suddenly disappeared, only to be found a few days later, shot to death. The police claimed Stavisky had killed himself just as they were breaking into his villa, but no one believed it; Stavisky's silence was too important to too many, including the police. The breach between the irate public and the government was made even worse when Premier Camille Chautemps refused to investigate, especially since it was alleged that several members of his government — and even members of his own family — had protected Stavisky. Incited in part by the Fascist leagues determined to overthrow the government, riots broke out nightly in Paris; the royalist Camelots du Roi, scattering marbles on the streets to trip the mounted police, joined forces with the Jeunesses Patriotes, outfitted in storm troopers' blue raincoats and berets, to mob the Ministry of Public Works.

Chautemps was forced to resign; he was replaced by Édouard Daladier, another Radical, also unable to deal with the situation satisfactorily. Daladier's actions annoyed almost everyone: he removed Chautemps' brother-in-law from his position as head of the Paris Parquet, the body responsible for not having prosecuted Stavisky in the first place, only to reward him with a high judicial office. He fired the director of the Comédie-Française (mainly because he'd produced a successful but antirepublican *Coriolanus*) and replaced him with the head of the Sûreté Générale, the national criminal investigation agency, which was also discredited by the scandal. Suspecting the right-wing prefect of Paris of having tolerated demonstrations against the government, Daladier removed him by making him résident-général of Morocco. This, it seems, was the last straw for the people.

On February 6, the day the Chamber of Deputies reconvened to vote on the new government, the people of Paris, not without the instigation of the press, took to the streets. Both Fascists and Communists, bitter foes in everything else, united briefly in what soon became an ugly riot; the police, trying to hold back the demonstrators, in a panic opened fire; rioters, armed with iron railings and sticks topped with razor blades, threw stones, bottles, and fiery rags soaked with gasoline into the buildings around the Place de la Concorde. Before morning casualties were high: thousands were injured and at least sixteen were dead. The tragic melee of "Bloody Tuesday" brought down Daladier's government.

Even after the new government of Gaston Doumergue patched together a tentative peace, everyone knew that a divided France had been brought to the brink of civil war. The Stavisky scandal was no mere footnote to the oddities of French political life. The Third Republic had been rocked by scandals before, and political factionalism was nothing new, but if there had been a remote, almost literary quality to other government scandals, there was nothing impersonal about the riots of Bloody Tuesday. Fascism and Communism could no longer be considered political abstractions; their ranks included fanatics like François Coty, who had financed one of the militantly right-wing groups on the street that night.

Janet was uncertain how to interpret what she was seeing; two city buses were still quietly burning near the Place de la Concorde on the morning of February 7. She considered violence of any kind, whether inspired by the right or by the left, intolerable, and she wanted to believe that "while Rome is capital of Italy, Vienna capital of Austria, and Berlin capital of Hitler, Paris is still capital of Europe for a kind of obstinate civilization, cerebral style, ideology, and suave, formulated, independent, liberty-loving living."[20] She wanted to believe that somehow this Paris would persist.

But Paris was changing. As Solita commented, "Nothing matters in France today but international money, the local gold standard, political riots, reforms, and Stavisky. The Paris Americans knew, and enjoyed, the cabarets, cocktails at the Ritz, the Folies-Bergère revues, the smart plays, good restaurants, dressmakers' collections, and the hoop-la on the Hill still exist. But no one cares and few go."[21] Both she and Janet reported that everyone read the newspapers from

morning till night to keep track of and try to make sense of events.
"Europe is undergoing some sort of change," Solita continued, "and
France is going along with it in spite of herself and in spite of her
disapproval of the changes everybody else has been making — including those of Franklin D. Roosevelt."[22]

By March, however, Janet was reassuring her readers — and herself — that in France, Fascism was "only a term, usually a reproach,
against the veterans and youthful patriotic societies."[23] Although the
Fascist leagues were the most rabble-rousing, she and Solita agreed
that "as a political party there is not real Fascism here, only a militant
emotionalism among war veterans and political club youths."[24] It's
hard to believe that both women could be so sanguine and naive;
perhaps they were trying to pretend that what they were seeing was
not as serious as they feared.

Certainly the focus and style of the Paris letter had started to shift.
Janet might still furnish social items to her *Arts and Decoration* audience, but in the wake of Bloody Tuesday she began to comment
more and more on the French political situation for *The New Yorker*.
When Ross said nothing, she interpreted his silence as encouragement. But she felt insecure. Offering only rudimentary political analyses, she still hid behind a mask of detachment, and she frequently
relied on others to provide the political acumen she thought she
lacked.

Years later, when describing the method she developed at this
time to cover political news, she insisted she was doing no more than
reporting events; if she gave any reactions to information, she said
she did so "in terms of the French reaction to it, like giving the
climate of French minds toward things French."[25] To a degree, this
meant she could summarize the various viewpoints — and there were
many — on any single event while believing she remained impartial.
She was, after all, an American woman summarizing the views of the
loquacious French, mostly men. She arranged these viewpoints so
that each would comment on another, usually negatively. This way
she appeared to give a range of opinions and analyses without specifically committing herself to any one, and she could demonstrate
the folly of each. Of course, she chose what to highlight and where;
she had her own opinions, and many of her friends regarded her as
one of the most opinionated people they knew.[26] But she strove in

her writing to appear as the unflappable, ever-ironic, objective Genêt; in this guise she did not predict outcomes, take sides, or search for causes. Obviously, this itself was a side, but Janet was not yet willing to admit that.

During this time Janet still thought she might write another novel. But no matter what she did, she remarked to her mother, she remained a journalist. And then she added — for the very first time — that she was beginning to like it.[27] With a small role to play in history, if only by virtue of chronicling it, Janet was apparently proud of the new Genêt, which also gave her the public reason she needed to explain why she had stopped writing fiction. "European and French politics, too, had started developing their appalling capacity for sounding like fiction, for sounding like horrifying thrillers," she would say more than once.[28] She had found her subject matter, her niche, her purpose.

But in the next fifteen years, she would on occasion grow dubious about the method she had developed. In her journal she wondered if her writing seemed slick and shallow, if her use of antitheses was tiresome, "surely the mechanical gimmick for an unfertile mind. By an antithesis one can get an effect instead of supplying a thought. Gibbon used it but I have no business to, since his serious business was a balancing of history; and all I am trying to do is to weather events."[29]

To earn some extra money, she agreed to write several crime pieces for *Vanity Fair*. She couldn't always depend on *New Yorker* profiles; she'd worked, for instance, on a profile of sports promoter Jeff Dickson, rewriting it five times, but it was never published. Then Frank Crowninshield, *Vanity Fair*'s editor, asked for a series on French murders; later she said she initially objected, claiming that Americans would not be interested in French murders because they were so different from American ones. Crowninshield didn't understand what she meant. "In France," she explained to interviewers, "nobody ever kills anyone he doesn't know."[30] However, she was in fact delighted to get the job. She'd write about the fall of Rome if someone asked, she commented to Hildegarde.[31]

The series began in June 1934 with "The Murder in Le Mans," about the trial of two sisters who'd gruesomely murdered their em-

ployers, two women. "Blood had softened the carpet," Janet wrote
of the grisly murder scene, "till it was like an elastic red moss."[32]
Janet's old friend Alec Woollcott, delighted with the piece, wrote
her a fan letter, saying he had "derived exquisite sadistic pleasure"
from it and had written Frank Crowninshield, "urging him to get you
to bathe us further in French blood."[33] By the end of the following
year, she had published four more pieces, in which she described
characters like Anatole Deibler, the French high executioner, and
several criminals, all in brilliant, arresting, and macabre detail. She
liked detective stories, she was a fan of Simenon, and she enjoyed
the melodramatic. But this was not what she considered her true
calling.

Instead, she wanted to try her hand at a London letter for *The
New Yorker*. If the idea was Ross's, it was one that pleased her. She'd
begun to reassess the content of her Paris letter and feared it or she
might be growing stale. Janet knew France was changing, and she
knew she was changing. Perhaps the parliamentary London of Queen
Mary looked more stable. Her friend Sam Weller, who had lived in
Paris in the twenties but had returned, fatally ill, to the United States,
encouraged her: "London will reawaken that great wicked insight of
yours into things. I had a feeling that the Paris job was doomed and
feared the New Yorker wouldn't know where to send you next."[34]
Her decision was also in part a financial one. "What frightful things
the economic situation brings about," Weller exclaimed when she
told him how costly Paris had become. "But what about Solita and
everything?" Weller asked. "Are you quitting the rue Bonaparte?"
No, she decided; she would stay in Paris and cross the Channel when
necessary. France was her home.

Many of the Americans who'd come to France full of hope and
illusion were quickly bumped into reality by the Great Depression,
according to Berenice Abbott, and many of them returned to the
United States.[35] But Janet did not. Each time her mother suggested
she might do better in America, Janet emphatically replied she'd
have no job and no income there.[36] She thought the best America
could offer her was an editorial post, which she wasn't suited for.
And she insisted she had the job she did precisely because she had
stayed in Europe. What's more, she believed she'd become especially

valuable to *The New Yorker* once she began substituting political news for gossip in her fortnightly letter.

Her mother must have suspected there was more to Janet's staying than money and a job. If she read between the lines of Janet's letters to her, she may have suspected that Janet feared America would rob her of everything she had created in the last ten years. "If you don't go home after ten years, you know you're hooked," she reflected many years later. "You're in the bird's cage, all right. And you won't go home. You won't want to go home. . . . There's a kind of gilt on the cage of life over there that is entrancing. Delightful. There's no sense of captivity."[37]

9

Peace in Our Time
1935–1939

> There is nothing I can say to say, except that as life is growing increasingly ugly it may be better to be away from it.
>
> Noel Murphy to Sara and Gerald Murphy,
> April 5, 1935

THAT THE NONSMOKING, teetotaling, celibate vegetarian Adolf Hitler ruled a nation of "sausages, cigars, beer and babies" gave Janet Flanner the striking contrast with which she began "Fuehrer," her three-part profile of the Nazi leader.[1] Examining the quirky habits of what she called her unphotogenic subject — his dress, diet, friends (very few) and private life (virtually nonexistent) — she recounted the highlights of his biography, including the political maneuvering responsible for his rise to power. She made Nazi ideology sound bogus and self-contradictory; she outlined the anti-Semitic points of its twenty-five-point platform; she summarized the illogical "earnest jumble" of *Mein Kampf,* which she read three times; and she talked about Hitler's taste in music and uniforms, art and automobiles.

Janet and Noel went to Germany at least once a year, usually to Bayreuth to hear Wagner and to Munich for Noel's singing lessons.

By the fall of 1935 they knew a number of people who could easily get them an invitation to the Nazi Congress Rally. One of Janet's best contacts was the half-American, half-German, Ernst "Putzi" Hanfstaengl, a good friend of Hitler's who'd subsidized him in his early post-prison days. Though considered by many as simply a jester in Hitler's court, playing *Die Meistersinger* on the piano to soothe the Fuehrer's frayed nerves, the well-connected Hanfstaengl was at present chief of the foreign press and could get Janet all the information she wanted — like what Hitler ate for breakfast. However, he probably couldn't arrange an interview.

That was all right with Janet. She said she'd rather be known as a tourist in Germany than as a foreign journalist; this allowed her to get material more easily from all kinds of sources, both official and unofficial.[2] Yet, since she was interested in reducing Hitler to human proportions, it's hard to imagine her not wanting to meet him to record, at the very least, her impressions, perhaps as Dorothy Thompson had.[3] Janet, however, was apparently nervous about interviewing the dictator. Insecure about her political acumen, she was also uncomfortable about being in Nazi Germany as a reporter; on several occasions she said she would be safer traveling as a private citizen, that no one would bother her if she were there just to look at scenery and drink beer. Her family, aware of her new assignment, was also concerned. Janet assured them by saying she'd be sure to stay away from Jews.[4]

In all likelihood she wouldn't have considered this remark — or any of her feelings — anti-Semitic. After all, she had protested Viennese anti-Semitism in the pages of the *New York Times*. Not realizing she'd adopted the unconscious attitudes of her background and class, she considered herself liberal and tolerant, which in many ways she was. But to her, any minority group was easily stereotyped: in her novel *The Cubical City* she described a Jewish theatrical agent as crude, his body like that of a pushcart vendor's; Jews had large noses (she joked with her family about whether her own nose suggested some "oriental" ancestors); she regarded Rebecca West's *Strange Necessity* as "jewish but unusual" and West herself as "a little Jewish."[5] In fact, she accepted stereotypes without giving them much thought and without thinking of them as particularly harmful, except when the discrimination resulting from them was flagrant, as in czarist

Russia, the subject of her early story, "The Portrait of Our Lady."
Her Semitic sympathies were apparently strong enough to offend
her mother, but in 1932 she flippantly wrote Mary that she'd be
pleased to know that she no longer liked Jews.[6]

Traveling in Germany in 1935, she was aware of the increasing
Nazi persecution of Jews, but this, like other "political" aspects of
Nazi Germany, was precisely the kind of issue she wanted to omit
from her profile. She intended to write a nonpolitical article, which
meant nonpolemical, for Janet considered politics a form of polemics.
She insisted she was above politics, that she was neither a debunker,
on the one hand, nor an advocate, on the other. She told herself that
her job demanded neutrality and that neutrality implied objectivity;
to be objective was to be fair, detached, bemused. Rather than balk-
ing at *The New Yorker*'s urbane, self-conscious elitism, she so identified with it that she asked her friend Horst (Bormann) to photograph her posing as the magazine's high-hatted Eustace Tilley, who
graced the cover of the annual anniversary issue. Seated in profile,
she peered at a copy of *The New Yorker* through her monocle. This
is the self-mocking, elusive, costumed position she wanted to assume,
but it was becoming harder and harder to maintain.

Genêt intended to treat Hitler no differently from her other profile
subjects. She had handled Elsa Schiaparelli, Elsa Maxwell, and Lily
Pons as if they were the architects of "civilization" (an important
word in her vocabulary); their products, be they sweaters, parties,
or a clear upper register, were civilized, and, in the case of someone
like Stravinsky, they actually re-created civilization by bursting its
"customary metric corset."[7] Hitler also represented a new epoch and
was packaging a new product in a very different way. Janet knew
that Hitler was different from anyone else she'd covered for the
magazine; the assignment was different in nature, the profile had to
be different in scope. She might present Hitler as a buffoon, as a
sometimes foolish, sometimes dangerous, mercurial, and pathetic
"self-taught" leader whose amazing oratory dazzled the German public, but she knew that Hitler "the man" didn't exist apart from Nazi
Germany. He was producing a new party, a new state, one that might
affect the future course of civilization. She could not coolly itemize
the Fuehrer's society connections and personal habits without giving
a small incisive chapter of German social history. As a result, the

Blood Purge of 1934, the anti-Semitic Nuremberg laws, and the "aristocratic" but terrifying SS hover over "Fuehrer" in ways impossible to imagine in her earlier, chattier profiles.

She'd earned the Hitler assignment partly because she'd so successfully written about England's Queen Mary for *The New Yorker*. Janet had been delighted and flattered when her editors asked her to write about the English monarch, interpreting it as an unassailable vote of confidence. In February 1935 she and Noel had set off for London, planning to spend several weeks in a small room on Half Moon Street. Janet brought her typewriter and banged out a list of questions for the queen's private secretary; she was promptly informed that the volume of similar requests made it impossible to answer hers and that the queen was not fond of articles of a personal nature. Undaunted, Janet pieced together information gleaned from British journalists who said they couldn't print all the information they had and from friends like Lady Juliet Duff, whom Janet had known in Paris. A houseparty was arranged so she could gather more, and she spoke to as many royal dressmakers and tradespeople as she could find. The resulting two-part profile was laden with details about the queen's taste in clothes and food, her jewels, her personal habits, and the slant of her handwriting.[8]

Katharine White thanked Janet for "a perfect profile," and Ross, praising it as "superb," sent her $750 for the two parts as well as a 40 percent increase to cover the fallen dollar. Solita was in Paris opening the mail when two checks for Janet dropped out of the *New Yorker* envelope. She immediately telephoned Orgeval to tell Janet she'd received over $1,100. Janet was so excited she couldn't eat for the rest of the day; she decided to open a savings account.

Dolly Wilde, however, said Janet's profile of the queen was pert.[9] As in the case of her Hitler profile, she balanced information in such a way that the finished product could be interpreted as satire, indictment, encomium, or none of these. Indeed, the Hitler profile finally avoided any point of view except that of a detached spectator too civilized to become involved with a peculiar and fanatical dictator.

Both the Hitler piece and the one on Queen Mary inevitably offended as many as they pleased. Editors at *Time, McCalls,* and *Colliers* congratulated Janet on "Fuehrer," asking her to write similar articles for them, but Malcolm Cowley of the *New Republic* greeted her coldly in the spring of 1936 and called her a Fascist to her face.[10] On the other hand, Raoul Fleischmann liked the piece, according to Janet, and said he learned to appreciate Hitler "the man." Many Jews complained, she wrote her mother, and evidently she understood why.[11] Nonetheless, she expressed surprise when she heard that in Germany her piece was considered pro-Fuehrer.

In her coverage of current political events, Janet was always careful to make it clear that she wrote for a reader who, as she put it, "is neither Left nor Right" but who, like her, refused political classifications. She resented what she considered the facile habit of labeling people by their views: if one weren't a Communist, one was immediately called a Fascist, or vice versa, she told Gertrude Stein.[12] She preferred terminology that bore no overt political meaning, using words like "cynical," "realist," and "idealist" to create an apparently depoliticized lexicon. All the same, each of her terms carried a particular meaning. "Cynical" affectionately described the "average" French person, who thought everyone in Paris crazy; "idealist" generally referred to the Marxists, and particularly to the reforms of the Popular Front and their socialist leader Léon Blum. Janet hadn't been particularly inspired by the 1935 Bastille Day rally of the newly formed Popular Front, a coalition of Communists, Socialists, and Radical-Socialists. Its militarism worried her, even though she later welcomed its long overdue reforms, such as the forty-hour work week. The promise of "bread, peace, and liberty," however, struck her as vapid, abstract, and ultimately impractical.

"Realist" was a positive term, and she applied it to Pierre Laval during his 1935 tenure as premier; Laval's "common sense" appealed to her. Calling him "no foolish optimist" in an article commissioned by *Forum* for its November 1935 issue, she said he had instituted an economic policy of deflation but opposed the devaluation of the franc; he stood firm against Germany's rearmament, forcing Britain and Italy to follow suit; he refused to let the French monitor the Saar plebiscite to return to Germany; he reconciled Great Britain and Italy, which had "sadly fallen out," she said, over Italy's intent to conquer Abyssinia. She couldn't foresee that Laval and the British foreign minister would hand over more than half of Abyssinia to Mussolini after he invaded it, but she was aware that Laval had delayed signing a military pact with Soviet Russia. If he must opportunistically play all sides to keep the peace, fine; after all, she declared, the man was not a theorist but a realist with a "sane economic view" of international affairs.[13]

Although she spoke well of Laval's politics, she did not always praise his person, especially when describing his mannerisms and tastes. Portraying him after the manner of her *New Yorker* profiles, with attention to his background, habits, appearance, and idiosyncrasies, she said that his face, "as alert and mobile as a gypsy horse trader's face," looked "dishonest." Yet the overall picture she painted was positive. She raised questions, for example, about Laval's personal finances, but then virtually dismissed them, since he apparently hadn't made money from the Stavisky scandal, just from foreign exchange.

Several of her friends admired Janet's political — or nonpolitical — stand. Gertrude Stein, for example, assumed that she and Janet shared a common perspective about the worsening situation in Europe. "It's funny," Stein wrote Janet in the late thirties, "that all these writers who are successful make lots of money and are snobbish are proletarian, while those of us who do not make money and have not been snobbish are conservative, I suppose it is natural, as Robinson Crusoe's father said to him, you my son were born under the most fashionable conditions, your father was neither rich nor poor, and I suppose if you are neither rich nor poor neither money nor position is on your mind."[14] Gertrude confided that if ever there was a war, neither she nor Noel was going to go (to war); England and France could do as they wished.

Janet herself was weary of France's political squabbles. They seemed endless, debilitating, dangerous, vacuous, and preeminently "male." It was men who arrogantly and stupidly presumed to govern, who abstractly theorized about the lives of others, particularly women. She called André Malraux's book *L'Espoir* "twice-over a man's book," difficult for women because it made war its subject.[15] Women respond to war differently from men, she argued, because they do not fall for philosophical abstractions over the meaning of armed conflict. Women know that war means only one thing — death.

But France was being pulled in several directions, and so, at times, was Janet, who was neither as uninvolved nor as unaffected as she liked to pretend. At the very least she wanted to believe that the values of the civilization she held dear would be maintained.

Glenway Wescott, who visited Janet and Noel in Orgeval during the spring of 1938, later remembered a conversation about leaving France: "And now little by little, in allusions amid what we had to say about politics, we were bidding each other an extraordinarily fond and significant kind of farewell. 'When are you sailing?' she [Janet] asked, and I told her. 'You know, you're quite right not to stay here,' she said. 'No one is going to be able to write fiction in France from now on. Do you think you will be able to, even at home, when the war gets going? Oh, I wish I could go home with you! How I envy you, in a way.'

"But," he continued, "she corrected herself. She did not envy me, she said; it was only her sentimentality and imagination. To stay in France as long as it was humanly possible was her fate. Because it was fate of course she herself did not altogether understand why it was. 'But I shall be the last to leave. The last Middle-Westerner on this peninsula of Europe, of Eurasia.' "[16]

She wasn't the last to leave, and although she stayed until 1939, she wasn't altogether happy about remaining. As early as 1936 she considered returning to the United States permanently.

In January of that year, just before "Fuehrer" appeared, she sailed for New York on the *Champlain*. By the time she reached Indianapolis to visit relatives, job offers were pouring in, she told her family. The press (with the prompting of her aunt, Anna Buchanan) besieged its native daughter, who handled herself with aplomb. A reporter from the *Indianapolis Star* described Janet as "chic and radiant, with a grand sense of humor and an oh-so-wise intelligence, that I could not figure after the rather abrupt interview who had been interviewed, Miss Flanner or myself"; her young cousins were taken with the monocle Janet had begun wearing in earnest.[17] It was with some confidence that Janet broached the topic of staying in the States to Katharine White and others at *The New Yorker*. They answered at once. They simply couldn't give her what she wanted: she was an expert on one place, Paris, and they didn't want her to leave. Only the Hearst Corporation, as it turned out, made her a concrete offer, so Janet, disappointed, sailed from New York on April 7. She didn't want to work for Hearst or another magazine. (When *Time* offered to make her their foreign correspondent in 1937, she wasn't interested.) She wanted to work only for *The New Yorker,* preferably in America. Instead she received a consolation prize: more European and London assignments at higher pay. She wasn't sure she liked this: the assignments would take more time and energy than the new salary could possibly cover. But she must have been more pleased than she let on. It was not that she wanted to leave France; she was just increasingly scared to stay.

For one of her first new assignments, Janet was sent to Berlin in the summer of 1936 to cover the Olympic Games. Protesting that she couldn't distinguish a handball from a football, she accepted, assuming this to be part of her expanded job and salary. She and Noel left for Berlin on July 3 in Noel's Ford. Germany looked even better than it had the previous year; Hitler had put the country on its best behavior for the games, and Janet and Noel were duly impressed. Decked out with banners and flowers, Berlin seemed well fed; the spectacular sports arena shone under the light of magnesium torches, and straight-backed German boys strutted in choreographed precision during the opening night festivities. It was thrilling, Janet reported, and even the German crowds were well mannered. She knew they had been skillfully tutored in how best to serve their own interests by accommodating the visitors: the SS, which Janet still called "aristocratic," rarely appeared in their uniforms, and persecution was not to be discussed. She called Nazi Minister of Propaganda Hermann Goering "apparently the most liberal official patron of the arts in Germany today,"[18] and she wasn't being ironic. Some friends believed that Janet had been seduced by the dazzling display of organized well-being.[19]

By that fall, Janet was shuttling back and forth between Paris and London for *The New Yorker,* juggling trains and steamers and trunks and finding time to write an occasional piece in another magazine when asked. But the strain began to show. The channel crossings were rough; it seemed she was constantly arriving in rainy London at midnight; her arm began to throb; distracted, she accidently threw a check from *The New Yorker* into the fire. After only four days in France in December, news of Edward VIII's abdication sent her back

to London with barely enough time to pack. And when she covered
George VI's coronation, straining hard over the guard rails to glimpse
his gold coach, she hurt a rib. For several days she typed in pain. By
July of 1937 she was so tired of this exhausting schedule that she
told her editors she was resigning her London post.

She didn't want to travel anymore; she wanted to stay in Paris and
perhaps write a book — nonfiction, a series of essays, something
"historical." It's now or never, she told her family. And it was from
Paris that she wanted to follow the "more or less semi-political news
or news which had politics, definitely, the way the seasons have hot
and cold."[20] Since the previous summer, when General Franco and
his rebel armies had risen up against the Popular Front alliance gov-
erning Spain, news was indeed political, whether broadcast from
London or from Paris. To many the Spanish Civil War epitomized
the conflict between Fascism and Communism; the Spanish Republic's fate symbolized the fate of European democracy. And many
private individuals considered the Republican cause an eminently
human one: the struggle of a people for their land and for self-
determination, against the "absentee landlords," as Ernest Hemingway called them, the Italians and the Germans.[21] The "Reds" might
be as bad as reported, Hemingway said, but they represented the
Spanish people.

France's Popular Front government was sympathetic to the Spanish
government but publicly supported a noninterventionist policy. It
soon became apparent, however, that both the rebels and the Re-
publicans were unofficially receiving men, money, and armaments
from other countries. Janet initially adopted the noninterventionist
position; too many hands in Spain, she felt, made both Spain and
Europe more dangerous.

In March 1937 Hemingway stopped in Paris on his way to Spain
as a correspondent for the North American Newspaper Alliance.
Waiting for the U.S. State Department to grant a visa to his traveling
companion, the American bullfighter Sidney Franklin, Hemingway
saw Janet and Solita almost daily, usually at the Hôtel Montana.
Franklin would unpack his matador costumes and swords and array
them over the bed, two chairs, and a small table. Hemingway, playing
bull, lunged at Franklin, who tossed his cape. Incredulous, Janet and
Solita crouched in the corner of the room. Hemingway, sweating

profusely, ushered the women out to a bar.[22] Although they liked Ernest, they thought his male histrionics, in the hotel room or on the battlefield, childish.

Franklin, however, gave Janet detailed information on the cost and decor of a matador's outfit as well as on the long and complicated routine of dressing. She incorporated much of this material into her "Letter from the Bull Ring," written after she went to the bullfights in Nîmes in July 1937. By then she was making her views about the war in Spain known — she deplored any justifications, political or otherwise, for the loss of human life. People in Spain were homeless and dying; nothing could justify that. That fall, when she attended a meeting held at the Albert Hall in London to raise funds for Basque refugee children, she decided that children were the true victims of political chicanery, and that supporting them was not a form of political partisanship. In a subsequent London letter she reported that generally England was "agreeably *démodé*" — taking sides on every issue was not "the fashion" there.[23]

Explaining to Katharine White that she had done nothing materially for the Spanish war — she did not give to causes as a matter of principle — she said she did want to help individuals, people like William Levick, who was then head of the makeup department at *The New Yorker*. Katharine had asked Janet to verify, if she could, the rumor that Levick's son had been killed in Spain while fighting on behalf of the Loyalists. With the help of Hemingway and a member of the Abraham Lincoln Brigade she met through him, Janet learned that it was true and that the young man was probably buried at Quinto. Sending White the news, she declared she didn't understand men at all — and never would understand men who killed.[24]

What was important to her was the avoidance of war. But it was hard to deny that war was possible and that if it came, no one would be exempt. Democracy seemed out of date, Janet kept writing publicly and privately; only totalitarian governments seemed able to act with brutal speed. When Germany invaded Austria in March 1938, Janet sat worriedly by the radio at Noel's and heard the ominous "Heil Hitlers" broadcast from Vienna. Soon it seemed Hitler would absorb Czechoslovakia without waiting for France or England to make up their minds about what to do. Yet she also felt that the rumors about Chamberlain's being pro-German were false, and that people in the know believed there would be no war. She wanted to believe this was true. War was too horrible, it was inconceivable, no matter what others wrote or felt. Perhaps, she tried to tell herself, the Anschluss would keep everyone safe.

But it was a spring of confusion and grief. While she was packing for London in April, she received a cable from her mother: Hildegarde had almost died in childbirth. A caesarean section had been performed after forty hours of labor, too late to save the baby and barely in time to save Hildegarde. Janet cabled her family, waited a day to see if there was any more news, and then gathered her notes and clippings and left Paris, feeling guilty because she was so far away from her mother and sisters.

With friends leaving France almost by the hour and urging her to do the same, Janet was uncertain what to do. There was nothing for her in America, and neither Noel nor Solita intended to go. She began to feel ill, and she was often depressed. Her arm was bothering her, her leg was sore. Sciatica forced her to carry a blanket for protection from drafts and to wear a wool sock under her stocking, even at the Opéra. Traveling with Noel from Paris to Megève to Antibes, she lugged woolen tights and trousers, two fur coats, and several blankets to make sure she was well insulated.

In the early summer of 1938 a diagnosis of severe kidney stones — the result of seventeen years of drinking white wine, her physician told her — improbably lifted her mood. She was glad to attribute her malaise to physical causes. Not a particularly heavy drinker, she was fond of wine, and she liked a cocktail or two, especially martinis. But she was willing to give alcohol up, at least temporarily.

Although she began to feel better, she remained unhappy about her work. Her London letters were terrible, she thought, and Katharine White's remark, that a so-called fan had said Janet sounded like a duchess out slumming, hadn't helped. And she was anxious about her profile, begun the preceding winter, of the American ambassador to France, William Bullitt. She felt unsure about everything. She'd undertaken a secret project (as she called it) of ghostwriting a serial biography of heiress Barbara Hutton for Elsa Maxwell at *Cosmopolitan,* but she confided to Katharine White that she was only doing it for the money — $3,000. She'd turned down an even better offer from *Cosmopolitan* the year before, and Katharine had thought her foolish, Janet reminded her, eager to justify her decision. At whatever price, writing for *Cosmopolitan* was beneath her.[25] But to her mother she explained that she had to swallow her intellectual snobbery; why not be expedient, she guiltily asked.

The travel that these pieces entailed further unsettled her. She took the night train to Cannes for the Hutton biography, stayed seven days, then returned to Paris to cover the French visit of the English king and queen for *The New Yorker*. Their cortege trailed down the Champs-Élysées as the city filled with cheering crowds ready to believe that good times had returned. She then repacked and took the night train back to Cannes, finished her work on the Hutton piece, and returned to Paris to help Carmel Snow of *Harper's Bazaar* with a fashion speech. She was exhausted.

She and Noel decided to take their annual holiday trip to the music festivals in Germany and Austria. It was much easier, Janet dryly noted, to get tickets this year. But it must have been a strange vacation. They stayed at the Hotel Fantaisie a few miles from Bayreuth and had a wonderful time. As the situation in Europe worsened, they needed to believe that in spite of everything, good food and good music remained and might even offer them shelter.

But in Austria it was harder for Janet to maintain her distance and equilibrium. The Vienna Symphony was playing in Salzburg as usual — for the last time. Janet knew this, and she knew that after the festival, the racial purge would continue.[26] In Vienna she noticed that the goods in the shops, and the shops themselves, were marked Aryan and non-Aryan; she bought Aryan stockings in the Jewish wholesale district and a non-Aryan washcloth in the retail center. At an anti-Semitic exhibition called "The Eternal Jew," she saw Austrian Christians eye the displays denouncing well-known degenerates like Karl Marx, Charles Chaplin, and Felix Mendelssohn. "These prints, photographs, models, electric signs, graphs, fine typography, and sales talks," wrote Janet, "are used not to make consumers buy a product but to make the public boycott a race."[27] The Anschluss might be good for Austria's economy, or so Janet had told her family, but Nazi racism was reprehensible.

They left Austria for Hungary so Janet could write a "Letter from Budapest." Passing large concrete roadblocks and barbed wire fences on the Czechoslovakian frontier, Janet scribbled notes and tried to sift local prejudices from facts, paranoia from portent. "History looks queer when you're standing close to it," she wrote in early September, after they'd returned to France.[28] Their trip had frightened her. The worst she'd heard about the Nazis seemed to be true: they wanted to gobble the world.

She sat by the radio in Noel's living room, listening to the French, English, and German versions of the Sudetenland crisis. Prime Minister Chamberlain and Hitler had agreed on a mid-September plebiscite for the Sudetenlanders to decide whether they would unite with Germany; Czechoslovakia declared the agreement completely unacceptable. The next week Chamberlain and Hitler met at Bad Godesberg, but Hitler surprised Chamberlain by rejecting the prime minister's peace plans — plans made irrespective of Czechoslovakia's wishes. Hitler insisted on a military occupation of the Sudetenland, and Chamberlain promised to deliver these demands to Prague. The Czechs responded by mobilizing, and France also ordered partial mobilization. Hitler announced he would invade Czechoslovakia. Britain, too, began to mobilize.

When Hitler announced the invasion plan, Janet and Solita packed several bags and "ignominiously," according to Solita, left the Hôtel Saint-Germain-des-Prés for Orgeval. The roads were clogged with cars loaded down with furniture, headed for presumed safety in coastal towns and mountain villages. At Noel's they waited for news, again sitting by the radio and listening for the telephone. Janet and Solita sorted and burned most of their letters. Ambassador Bullitt requested that Americans leave France, and the American embassy began making arrangements, although passage on most ships was already booked. Together, Noel, Janet, and Solita gathered cash in several currencies — French, British, American. They buried several pieces of their jewelry, Janet's gold coins, and Noel's family silver. They bought 150 gallons of gas in tins and stored much of it in tea kettles and champagne bottles. They bought sardines, noodles, sugar, brandy, matches. Cables from the United States implored them to come home.[29]

At Mussolini's behest, Hitler postponed the attack on Czechoslovakia and agreed to meet with Mussolini, Chamberlain, and Daladier (the prime minister of Czechoslovakia was not invited). At the end of that meeting in Munich during the latter part of September 1938, Hitler walked away with the Sudetenland. To many it seemed that France and England had simply sold Czechoslovakia out — and that France had lost her strength in eastern Europe in the bargain. But others were relieved, at least initially. When Premier Daladier returned to Paris, hundreds of thousands of jubilant Parisians cheered him at Le Bourget. Janet and Solita, grateful there was no war, returned to Paris.

After the crisis, French and British critics of the Munich pact — "parliamentary locusts" Janet called them — began eating away at the peace.[30] She resented them, believing the French had lost only prestige — not much of a sacrifice given the stakes. And she also resented that in the months to follow no one in France seemed particularly concerned about civilians, the people who would be most affected by war. Everyone seemed to be talking about poison gas. Hemingway shooed away Janet's fears, saying gas was too expensive to be used; if you wanted to worry, worry about those new German bombs without casings. They hit buildings and could tear out the guts of passersby a quarter of a mile away. Only the Union of French Women Decorated by the Legion of Honor seemed to be doing more than talking; they were recruiting female volunteers to staff bomb shelters in the event of an air raid.[31]

Janet's anxiety was evident in her profile of William Bullitt. She sent the piece to *The New Yorker,* but Katharine White returned the manuscript, which had missed its aim, she said. Janet agreed. With Solita's help, she rewrote it, convinced all the while that no one would like it, neither Bullitt's friends nor his enemies. She fretted that she'd made the piece boring by including too much, that she'd talked to too many of his friends, that she'd read too much, that she hadn't digested what she'd heard or read. Her interpretations seemed provisional, confused, full of desperate certainty.[32] To make matters worse, she couldn't decide how she felt about him. She'd handled him in her usual manner, combining words to both praise him on the one hand and criticize him on the other. But this played into her own ambivalence; it clarified nothing. Nonetheless, after several letters and revisions had passed between them, Katharine was pleased and Janet reasonably satisfied, or at least willing to put the profile behind her to resume the London letter.

In November she and Noel rented rooms in a small lodging house on Clarges Street, near Shepherd Market and Piccadilly, where she could write her letters as Noel prepared for a concert at the end of the month. Their Irish proprietress, Mrs. McCulloch, cooked most of their meals, her husband served the Scotch, and Janet tended the ice bucket when McCulloch and Janet's friend James Thurber, also a guest at the lodging house, could no longer find their way to the kitchen.[33]

For the moment life had returned to normal. If the weather was gray and changeable, Janet was now accustomed to it and to the channel crossings. And even in France life seemed more normal. The social and financial situation was apparently improving, Daladier looked stronger, and Finance Minister Paul Reynaud was restoring confidence in the franc. But despite the apparent calm on the surface, anyone looking beyond France's borders saw that the makeshift balance of power was flimsy. Mussolini was eyeing France's colonies; Barcelona had fallen to Franco. And France was not really stronger at all; it had lost both credibility and power.

The era of wishful thinking was over. Franco's victory would bring war, and Hitler, closer. The plight of the Spanish had, in a sense, come home. Spanish refugees clustered on the Left Bank, together with fugitives from Czechoslovakia, Rumania, Turkey, and Germany. Janet's writing about Spain was no longer detached. Disdainful of the Paris bourgeoisie who were frightened of losing their own comforts, she noted that they did nothing to help their compatriots in Spain. Rather, it was the French working class who sent supplies to Spain and raised funds any way they could — through bazaars, factory donations, left-wing party drives, even by passing a hat — to get food to the starving populace. She reported that her friend Diane Forbes-Robertson Sheean was appealing in England and Paris for money for the relief of Spanish women and children. Janet herself, along with Solita and their friend Russell Page, gave Nancy Cunard money and tins of food to take to Spain in January. Nancy got no farther than just inside the frontier, where she immediately distributed the goods.

In February 1939 Janet and Solita drove to Perpignan, the French town near the Spanish border where hundreds of thousands of refugees were waiting to see what would be done for them. The area swarmed with journalists, welfare workers, and French army officers. There was no lodging within a fifty-kilometer radius, and everywhere prices were inflated. Refugees, mostly women and children, lined the roads. Those few with documents and money were free to travel where they wished; the rest waited in concentration camps behind barbed wire, draped in the blankets they had brought with them. Around the camp Janet saw abandoned vehicles and horses and the scorched land, burned by the refugees to keep warm. "The whole scene was an unforgettable one," Janet wrote, "except to those living in it."[34] Human misery had touched her in a way that the political maneuverings of statesmen could not. Her sympathies were engaged by the plight of the people she saw — individuals caught by the machinations of history and diplomacy — and Janet may have recognized that she, too, had earlier been deceived by the very abstractions she deplored.

In March, when Germany occupied what was left of Czechoslovakia, disregarding the provisions of the Munich accord, Janet wrote that Paris was shocked. She and Noel sat once again by the radio in Orgeval, joined by Francis Rose, who had come to paint a mural on Noel's dining room wall.[35] On March 12 they listened to the coronation service of Pope Pius XII, then three days later heard the news of the German takeover. At the end of the month Franco defeated Republican Spain, and by Easter Italy had invaded Albania. Janet again prayed that the French and English would not fight. Yet Hitler's declarations of peace were less and less believable.

It was hard, she told Gertrude Stein, to find a story to trust — pride colored one version and anger another. In England that May, Janet found London divided about Chamberlain and Munich. She sent Stein a copy of Louis Bromfield's pamphlet *England, a Dying Oligarchy,* in which he offended the right by attacking the British policy of appeasement and offended the left by calling for a strong British leader to save the country from its continuing folly. She promised that her interpretation of the situation in her next London letter would be nothing like his.[36] She would be cool, dispassionate, seemingly neutral — even, perhaps, sympathetic toward Chamberlain. She did not want war.

She was working furiously, writing a weekly letter from Paris, traveling to London to write from there, working on articles for the *Woman's Home Companion,* gathering material for a profile of Pablo Picasso, and planning a trip to Alsace (later canceled) for a special *New Yorker* article. Janet had taken on much of this extra work in anticipation of a three-month absence from *The New Yorker* in the fall; she wanted to go back to America to see her mother, who was scheduled to have major surgery. She was also putting together an anthology of her writing, which was to include all her *New Yorker* profiles (as well as two pieces, not yet written, on Picasso and Mainbocher), an article on spies for *Harper's Bazaar,* and the pieces on French crime she had written for *Vanity Fair.* She wanted her old friend Alec Woollcott to write a preface, but when asked, he refused, explaining that even if he were not bound to Viking Press, he would not do it because no book was substantially helped by a preface written by anyone other than the author.[37] Janet decided to write an introduction herself, prophetically calling it "All Gaul Is Divided."

The summer of 1939 was one of fantastic costume balls, fiscal prosperity, crowded nightclubs, starry nights, and good theater. To mark the one hundred fiftieth anniversary of the French Revolution, on Bastille Day the British and French jointly displayed their military finery in a show of solidarity. Crowds danced through the streets and hung out of the windows to watch the spectacle that everyone hoped meant strength and peace. But underneath the gaiety Janet and her friends were worried.

By the end of August, with the signing of the Nazi-Soviet non-aggression pact, and the Germans readying for attack on Poland, Janet knew that war might be declared momentarily. Still, she and her friends could hardly believe it. Dick Myers wrote to his wife that "somehow I feel it [war] isn't coming now — Janet agrees with me — and there are amazing rumors about Italy — Mussolini ill — Italy weary of German domination, — rebellion of people who don't like the German alliance — etc — but nobody really knows anything."[38] The roads leading away from Paris again began to fill with evacuees; the city seemed to change overnight. People milled around the streets. "Soldiers with determined faces," Margaret Anderson recalled, "walked with aimless feet, a fat woman in the bakery told me about the last war. . . . We went back to the car, ashamed of its beauty, ashamed of the fresh white handkerchiefs in the side pocket where I had put them that morning."[39]

There were other worries. Pauline Pfeiffer Hemingway joined Janet and Noel in Orgeval for a few days; her marriage to Ernest had been disintegrating for some time, and she and her friends knew it. Djuna Barnes was sick in a Paris hotel; she had no money and was no longer writing. Margaret Anderson learned that Georgette Leblanc had cancer. Janet's mother, thinking of her daughter far away, the situation in Europe, and her operation, was frightened.

In Orgeval with Solita and Noel, Janet waited nervously for news. Margaret Anderson and Georgette Leblanc drove out on August 24. They stayed for a week, joined by other friends. Janet and Noel offered Dick Myers and his daughter Fanny shelter. "Some people here [at Noel's]" he wrote to Alice at home, "very optimistic but I trust the French reactions more. They are more logical. And they are *not* optimistic."[40] By night they covered the windows, and by day they stocked up on candles (which were sold singly), matches, sugar, soap, cotton, iodine, aspirin. Margaret later remembered that "everyone coming out from Paris brought news, as you bring candy to your hostess, and the one that predicted Paris would be bombed that night became the most exciting guest."[41]

On September 3, two days after Hitler's invasion of Poland, France and Britain declared war on Germany. Back in Paris for a day, Janet found most of the shops closed, their shutters pulled down. Restaurants, if not boarded up, stopped serving after eleven A.M. On the streets people carried mandatory gas masks. Some women used them to carry vegetables home from market, pedaling their bicycles and wearing ski trousers for comfort. Hotel proprietors escorted civilians into the bomb shelters for air-raid drills, locking them in until the all clear sounded. Otherwise the city was quiet.

Margaret returned to Orgeval briefly after Georgette's operation for cancer. She, Noel, Janet, and Solita sat by the radio from early morning to bedtime. In the afternoon the baker or butcher's wife would drive over, bringing goods and information. In the evening they strolled through the garden and looked up at the stars and the moon. Would the life they had known in Europe be destroyed? What would happen to each of them? Would they be separated? For how

long? Would they become what Margaret called "catastrophe people"? Perhaps, they thought, those who "had resources" should go
back to America and try to rescue the rest.[42]

Janet was going; she had planned to leave in October for three
months anyway. *The New Yorker* again asked her to stay, as it had at
least twice during the preceding year. This time she refused. Solita
was also going back to the States. But they would return soon, they
promised, maybe by the first of the year. In their own minds they
weren't so sure. Perhaps they didn't want to think that far in advance.
Janet paid the rent at their hotel through April, just in case. Margaret,
however, would not leave Georgette, and Noel would not leave
France. She had started working for J. P. Morgan's daughter, Anne
Morgan, who had founded American Friends for Devastated France
during the last war. Now it was called the Comité Americain pour
le Secours Civil, and Noel was helping them evacuate handicapped
people from Paris. I can do much here, she told Janet.

After breakfast, at five o'clock in the morning of September 16, Janet
and Solita loaded the back of Noel's car with thirty-five gallons of
gasoline and four suitcases. The three women drove out of Orgeval
on the misty country road and waited at the crossroads for Margaret,
coming to say goodbye. Too stupefied by events to feel anything,
they bade their farewells in the fog.[43] Back in the car, they wept.

They were headed for Bordeaux, at twenty kilometers an hour,
where they had no reservations on any American-bound ship. In
Chartres they saw planes flying overhead; in Tours, which was
crammed with soldiers, they pulled up to gas tanks, all marked empty,
and learned they had to apply for permission to buy more than four
gallons. Outside the city they saw the green Paris autobuses filled
with furniture, baggage, and medical supplies, as well as camouflaged
tanks, often decorated with flowers.

By the time they reached Bordeaux, more than 15,000 Americans
had passed through the city, all in search of passage home. The cafés,
hotels, cinemas, and churches were jammed, as were the post office
and the newspaper kiosks. They got a room in the Hôtel Majestic
and waited. Three weeks later, on October 5, they sailed for New
York.

10

Leave of Absence
1939–1944

BITTERLY LONELY and wearing a uniform, which she considered pretentious, Noel was working for Anne Morgan in Bléran-court, Aisne. She was driving truckloads of refugees, mostly pregnant women and old men, away from the war zones. Janet saw Noel's photograph in the *New York Mirror* and read Anne's account of their work: "My co-workers and I have seen thousands of people torn from their homes — thousands more in desperate want." At the front, fragments of a bomb hit one of her volunteers' cars — might it be Noel's? "She laughed," Morgan said, "and called it 'my car's baptism.' "[1]

"Now that everything is in print I can tell you what happened," Noel wrote Janet on June 1, 1940, less than a week before France fell to the Germans. "Friday May 10 we left (Blérancourt) for Givet at 9 p.m. I was alone in my Ford. There was a tidy new moon and thousands of troops, infantry, and cavalry going up (to the line.) They were all dusty, they would rest for 15 minutes, lying down on the road. I had to stop all the time. I arrived about 10 o'clock and slept in my car by the side of the river Meuse. At dawn a huge Henckel bomber flew 6 times around Givet. Evacuation began. Little bombing that day. The next day, Whitsunday, three thousand old men, women, and children were assembled in the Grande Palace and

23 bombers flew over. Everyone flung themselves flat on the ground, including Miss Morgan. The Germans bombed the railway station 200 meters away. It is true that the German fliers will leave their formation to machine gun refugees on the road. I've had too many times to hide in a ditch. On one of my trips I had a camion load of pregnant women. The English on duty ordered me to stop to get them out to lie in the ditch. It was hell, all fainting and vomiting, poor women, you can imagine."[2]

When the French Foreign Legion ambulancers helping them were caught and sent as prisoners to Germany, Noel and the other volunteers were forced to leave the old people behind and take only the children. The situation was desperate, Noel said, but she didn't want to give up; no matter what, she'd continue working. She hid Janet's money, drew up her will, and put her Tchelitchew drawings in a valise. If, she said, the "worst" should arrive in Paris, France would continue to fight in the south. "I shall remain in France," she declared, "wherever there is a France."[3]

Official Paris fell apart on June 10, three days after Janet received Noel's letter, and the French government moved to Touraine. In the next few days more than three million people fled the former capital, clogging the roads in an exodus that, according to Noel, approached biblical proportions. Yet the Germans were received with joy in many towns, Noel said. The French people "had been so disgusted with the conduct of their own army and soldiers that they welcomed order and efficiency and politeness," she wrote. On June 13 Paris was handed over to the Nazis as an "open city"; the next day the French government moved again, this time to Bordeaux, and German troops entered Paris, marching triumphantly down the Champs-Élysées. Three days later the octogenarian Marshal Philippe Pétain asked Hitler for an armistice.

Depressed by the country's moral collapse, Noel wrote that she believed all humanity, especially the French, was rotten. "There was nothing else for the French government to do but what it has done. It's no credit to the enemy to have walked through this country, but it is a credit to know when to do it and to have known how rotten France was, alas," she reported. She had seen French soldiers running away and officers stuffing their own household goods into military cars, leaving the foot soldiers behind. But "even I, after all I had seen, did not think it would last only ten days."[4]

Disgusted, she drove home at the end of the month. "When I finally heard no more firing, I mean from the Germans, there had been none from the French, I knew the war was over."[5] Still in uniform and carrying military pass papers, she arrived in Orgeval, which she said she never would have left except to try and "do some good." Janet thought Noel seemed more willing to return to America. Writing to Janet, her "Lovest," she said that her maid "Tsatsou [Tchatzu] refuses to leave Orgeval knowing what I do about previous occupations. I shall force her to come with me *when* I leave. She will be a dead weight and no chance of entering USA."[6] But more often she said, "I am staying. You should come."

It had been eight months since Janet had left France. Apparently expecting Noel to join her, she was angry when Noel refused. Noel wrote her brother-in-law Gerald, "I'm criticized for staying over here — there is anger . . . — [illegible] but work to do, and Janet and others say I am futilely pursuing Fred's shadow." But of course Janet's anger — her sense that Noel was abandoning her — reflected her own guilt over not returning. And by the time Noel unequivocally decided to remain in Orgeval, Janet had already broken with her in ways neither had anticipated.

In August 1940 Noel decided to stay. The village was desolate, but its few residents could provide her with milk and bread, and she was eating vegetables from her garden. If she tried, she said, she probably could bicycle to Paris occasionally. And she thought she could resume her singing — though the Germans would soon forbid non-Germans to sing *lieder*. But mainly she planned to stay close to home — she was finished with "good works." As for going back to the United States, that was impossible: "I'd be like an old fire horse on a farm!"[7]

She was also finished with governments and politics; she declared herself an anarchist. "Let the Germans have a whack at it & see what happens. We've proved a failure," she wrote Gerald Murphy, who passed the letter on to Janet. "What's the use of calling yourself the most intelligent race in the world & then believing all the propaganda so cleverly created by the Germans to further disrupt & pull the nation down? And what's the use of an old civilization that stumbles over itself to lick German boots?"[8] Gerald Murphy thought Noel had become pro-German, an idea Janet considered preposterous. Noel was as pro-French as ever, she insisted, just very unhappy, very tired, and incredulous at the course of events.

To Janet, Noel — and indeed all of France — seemed farther and farther away. "Come back to us soon," Gertrude Stein wrote from Bilignin. She and Alice disagreed about whether Janet would have liked being in France "for the darkest days"; Alice said no and Gertrude said yes. "Well until you do come back," Gertrude concluded, "Alice and I will continue to argue whether you would have liked being here."[9] Janet herself did not know.

Janet had arrived in New York in the crisp October of 1939. Almost immediately she had taken a bus to the *New Yorker* offices on Forty-third Street, where Daise Terry, the office manager, found a small space for her to work. It was inconvenient, but she didn't plan to stay long. She just wanted to finish her profiles of Picasso and Mainbocher, write a few letters, and then go out to California to see her mother, who was recuperating from surgery. She wrote Gertrude Stein that she'd be back in Paris by January.

Her rooms with Solita at the Hotel Earle on Washington Square were also temporary. They had moved in as soon as they arrived; friends had arranged what little there was to arrange. Soon they invited some people they hadn't seen in a long time to come by for drinks. But Solita, sitting darkly on the couch, was depressed, and Janet was tense, her face drawn.[10] Barely established in New York, they were between two worlds, wondering what would happen to those they'd left behind and when, or if, they'd return.

Janet, at least, had her work at *The New Yorker* to keep her somewhat occupied.[11] But never before had she experienced such pressure, she told Daise Terry. It was difficult to concentrate. The symbols of her life were gone; so were her friends, her community, her routine of work and pleasure. And there was no Gertrude Stein or Alice Toklas to provide the help she thought she needed with the Picasso profile; she used to watch Picasso from a distance when he sat at the Café Flore, but she'd never felt much affinity with him, nor did she care much for his recent work. She considered the painting "Guernica" propaganda, not art; the Spanish Civil War, she said, gave Picasso a "terrible, trite human tableau" which "distracted" him from "preoccupation with his own visions."[12] She had always believed it important to keep the lines separating art and politics clearly drawn, but never before had it seemed so crucial.[13]

Almost two months later, when Janet turned in her manuscripts, after postponing her trip to California more than once, it was obvious she wouldn't be back in France in January. And already A. J. Liebling, another *New Yorker* writer, had made himself reasonably comfortable in her Paris post. "I knew very little about Lady Mendl, Elsa Maxwell, Mainbocher and Worth the dressmakers, Mr. and Mrs. Charles Bedaux, or a number of other leading characters in Genêt's Paris dispatches," he later remarked, alluding to the difference between himself and Janet. "But since it seemed probable that they would lam anyway, Ross was willing to overlook this deficiency."[14] In fact Liebling wasn't altogether sure that Janet hadn't "lammed": it was hard for him to imagine "a reporter coming away from a story just as it broke."[15]

Aware of Liebling's criticism, which stung, Janet believed she hadn't begged off her responsibilities — technically. Justifying her decision, she reasoned that until now she'd always said yes to *The New Yorker*'s requests.[16] And her mother was ill, as everyone knew; Janet was on record as having requested a leave of absence long before Germany invaded Poland. But she was also aware that she hadn't wanted to stay in France if war was declared. She'd been ready to leave during the crisis of 1938, she was ready again in 1939 — more than ready, she'd been willing. And this time, of all times, she refused *The New Yorker*'s request that she stay. Nor did she return when Noel asked.

Daise Terry reported to Katharine White that once Janet was vacationing in California, she seemed in no hurry to get back to New York. From early December to early April Janet and Solita visited with some of the old Algonquin crowd who had settled in the golden sunshine; they went to parties and lunches, took a short trip to San Diego, visited the Hollywood studios. But if Janet was procrastinating, trying to forget what she had left behind or avoid thinking about what lay ahead, she still assumed she'd be going back to France fairly soon.

Clearly, however, she was reluctant, ambivalent. That spring she confided to Alec Woollcott that she had to figure out once and for all what her priorities were.[17] And then, not long after she returned to New York, she constructed an official story, explaining to Woollcott and others why she wasn't sailing for Europe: Ross refused to let her go. He wanted to know what Italy was going to do, she said, and didn't want to take responsibility for sending her to France until he knew she'd be safe.[18]

As unlikely as it is that Ross made the decision for her, he nonetheless got her to delay her return until events made the decision academic. Janet booked passage on the *Manhattan* just as Hitler started through Belgium in May. Passage was canceled, and the decision was made for her.[19] But it was obviously one that suited Janet, even though it left her feeling torn. Telling herself that the work she might do wasn't worth the risk, she also knew that in choosing to stay, she had chosen against France, her friends, Noel — even against her own work.[20] Her friend Russell Page, the British horticulturalist, wrote from London that he'd seen only one piece of Janet's since December: "Please get around to working. . . . One lives in the details of the day and week and month and dammed years and one *wants* one's friend's writing."[21]

Wake the Americans up, begged Noel.[22] Janet tried. Signed by Columbia Lecture Bureau, a division of Columbia Artists, she took to the stump with four lectures — "Midnight in Modern Europe," "The Vote, the Kitchen, and You," "Horizontal History," and "Famous People I Have Written About and Not Met, or My 14 Years in Paris." Her mother advised her on how to present herself: give the audience a chance to settle comfortably in their seats, let them see you before you begin, stay calm, end with a bang. Following her mother's directions, she talked about the war. History, she exhorted, was not just study of the past; history was happening now. Alec Woollcott was speaking out against American isolationism, and Janet, who had originally been angry at the English for declaring war — it was arrogant of them, she said, to pit bare fists against Germany's steel — now argued that something must be done to stop countries from taking over other countries.[23]

In June, when the "darkest days" overtook France, Solita wept. Janet could hardly believe the news. Grasping at straws, she weakly said that perhaps "some fusion" of France and Germany might help both countries.[24] The French would civilize the Germans — she didn't say what the Germans would do for France. Still clinging to neutrality, she declared that she backed both French governments, Pétain's and de Gaulle's; that way, no one could accuse her of being Fascist, Socialist, or pro-German.[25] But she wasn't joking, and this may well have been another way of expressing her divided feelings; she pretended she was above them.

One friend recalls that she initially supported the new regime in Vichy, thinking it France's only alternative, but changed her mind after she "got the facts."[26] Another said that Janet, who'd been considering a profile of General Maxime Weygand, had a knack for finding herself, at first, on the wrong side of things.[27] Whether this is true or not, in the occasional radio broadcasts arranged by Simon and Schuster as publicity for *An American in Paris,* her collection of profiles and crime pieces, Janet upbraided the democracies of Europe, accusing them of selfishness, of having been too short-sighted and garrulous, too complacent and comfortable, to see what lay in store for them.[28] She almost seems to be talking about herself.

By 1941, while still considering herself a pacifist, she had concluded that "we must be ready with the deep feeling and the real conviction that democracy is worth dying for, as our ancestors did."[29]

At the end of August 1940, the State Department forwarded to Janet a message from Noel — "Safe and well in Paris." That was all. Noel was virtually incommunicado. Nancy Cunard, in Mexico, heard about this and wrote Janet and Solita sympathetically, "That is the worst of ALL things, save death."[30] But by that time Nancy's condolences were overshadowed: Janet had fallen head over heels in love with another woman.

Early in June she and Solita had moved to the town of Croton-on-Hudson, not far from New York, but far enough to be cooler and much less expensive than Manhattan. Kathryn Hulme had found them the Tumble Inn, a quiet, comfortable, ramshackle hotel where Janet could write a few reviews of books about France for the New York *Herald Tribune* and begin a *New Yorker* profile of Thomas Mann. On weekends she would try to get away, either to Neysa McMein's home on Long Island or to Alec Woollcott's island retreat in Vermont, where he entertained friends, celebrities, and hangers-on. Generally surrounded by friends and colleagues, she was developing a routine of sorts. John Mosher, another writer for *The New Yorker,* invited her to spend the Fourth of July holiday at his summer home on Fire Island, whose beaches reminded her of le Lavandou. And it was there she met Natalia Danesi Murray.

In 1940 the thirty-eight-year-old Natalia, born in Rome, was living in New York with her young son Bill and her mother, Ester Danesi, former editor-in-chief for the Italian magazine *La Donna.* Divorced for several years, Natalia had once thought of herself as an opera singer and actress; now she worked for the National Broadcasting Company as an Italian language broadcaster. According to Arturo Toscanini, she had the most beautiful radio voice he'd ever heard. By all accounts, Natalia was stunning, a dark-haired, handsome woman whose ready laughter and volatile enthusiasms charmed many who met her. To Janet, she seemed sympathetic, adoring, devoted, and beautiful. Here was a woman who appeared undefeated and not bitter or jaded or disillusioned by what was going on in Europe. In fact, she seemed to represent the best part of Europe — exciting, civilized, impassioned, and liberty-loving — that Janet had left behind. Janet was smitten.

After the weekend on Fire Island when she met Natalia, Janet still wrote her family that she intended to return to France as soon as possible. She thought Germany's war with England would be concluded quickly, a new "set-up" (as she called it) arranged, and journalists welcomed back in all sections of France.[31] But now she mentioned going back to France much less often, and certainly Solita knew something important had happened. "Janet returns 'home,' " she confided to her daybook, uncharacteristically commenting that Janet "has new friend — Italian."[32]

Janet later lamented her cowardice in not returning to France and Noel, saying that her conscience always nagged at her, making her feel craven and useless.[33] But her admission of guilt was also her means of exorcising it. No one blamed her. And learning of Noel's final decision to stay in Orgeval barely a month after she met Natalia may have given her the justification she needed. Jokingly, she told Alec Woollcott she was thinking of practicing the Hindu custom of suttee. But, she added, she had no husband.[34] And, although she didn't say this, it was evident that she was in love.

Yet by the late fall, Daise Terry reported to Katharine White that Janet, who'd been given an office next to the telephone room on the nineteenth floor of the West Forty-third building, was "all over the place buzzing and yelling from one end of the hall to the other. She tells me she is losing her hair, coming out in handfuls as a result of war-worries."[35] Woollcott, however, was more amused than distressed by her agonizings: "At close range your life looks like a pin-tray of cigarette butts, stained with lip-rouge, and slightly dandruffical combings."[36] Janet sometimes agreed; her life too often struck her as disorderly, mismanaged, divided.

Janet did not tell everyone about Natalia. Neither she nor Solita explained very much to their new acquaintance Carson McCullers in New York or their old friend Nancy Cunard in Mexico; they kept their residence in Croton that summer and, for the time being, their apartment in Manhattan. For the next year or so, both Carson and Nancy wrote Janet and Solita jointly, and Nancy continued to address them as her "Darling Two." For a while Janet and Solita tried to pretend that nothing had changed — or would. They planned to spend the Christmas holidays together as usual, visiting Janet's family in California — almost as if they were a conventionally married couple wary of losing each other and the shared world they had built together. They were not just maintaining appearances: they were still bound by loyalty, respect, and affection. But Solita didn't trust Natalia Murray, whom she came to consider possessive, duplicitous, and cold. No doubt she was jealous, but she had dealt with Janet's lovers before; the difference seems to have been in Natalia's personality and the demands Solita sensed she'd make on Janet.[37]

In the beginning of December, Solita left New York to visit her family in Michigan and then drove out to California. Janet traveled later with her sister Marie and arrived at Hildegarde's on December 25. Gathered together for a family portrait, Janet and Solita looked away from one another. Solita observed that "Janet soon fled back to a new interest — six days later, in fact."[38] Already disconsolate about leaving France and friends, Solita knew she was also about to lose Janet.

*

Janet was uncertain what she should be writing, and *The New Yorker* was apparently not sure where to direct her. There had been talk of sending her to Washington as a permanent correspondent and, perhaps to test her political mettle, she was assigned a profile of Wendell Willkie. Calling it a "great trust" for the magazine to have asked her, a woman, she went to Indiana to interview the Republican presidential candidate. When the magazine hired the young writer John Bainbridge to help her collect information, Janet was pleased and excited.[39] However, after the profile was published, Alec Woollcott told her it was "dull, cluttered, and uncommunicative";[40] writer Stanley Edgar Hyman called it "tediously non-committal."[41] Others assumed that Janet backed Willkie and were annoyed. But the ever-loyal Hildegarde rose to her sister's defense: "My sister Janet voted for Roosevelt," she told Witter Bynner emphatically. "The article, though it had no partisanship, perhaps seemed to miss the objectiveness which it would, at less heated times, have achieved. It was meant merely as a portrait, not as a political piece, but did get her in rather badly with some of her Democratic friends."[42]

Some of her "Democratic friends" belonged to the eclectic group of writers, artists, and composers who frequented George Davis's modest brownstone at 7 Middagh Street in Brooklyn Heights. Janet misunderstood when Davis first told her about the arrangement there; she thought he said he ran a "bawdy house," not a boarding-house — and she didn't think the description wholly inaccurate. As an aspiring novelist living at the Hôtel Saint-Germain-des-Prés when Janet first lived there, George Davis had been so poor he had only carpet slippers to wear on his feet, as Janet recalled.[43] Now he was editor of *Harper's Bazaar* and a generous master of ceremonies at his unofficial Brooklyn colony.

Among its residents was Carson McCullers, the young, melancholy southerner who, with the publication in 1940 of her best-selling *The Heart Is a Lonely Hunter,* had become something of an overnight celebrity. Before very long she, Janet, and Solita had become good friends. The older women were fond of the fragile, strong-willed, and mercurial Carson, "full of the energy of affection," Janet recalled, and "an eccentric of the first water."[44] Solita frequently managed the details of Carson's life, making sure she got to her train on time or that she had enough money with her. Carson depended on her friends in a plaintive way, flattering and ingratiating herself — or trying.[45] Yet no matter how much Janet enjoyed being idolized by the talented young woman, she never allowed herself to be manipulated; she was always outspoken with Carson and did not hesitate to tell her to "face facts."[46] And Janet, aware from the first of Carson's and her husband Reeves's mutual destructiveness, warned their friend David Diamond not to get too close to the compelling couple.[47]

Both Janet and Solita listened to Carson's laments of unrequited love for the Swiss novelist and journalist Annemarie Clarac-Schwarzenbach, who had enchanted her. Clarac-Schwarzenbach was a friend of Erika Mann's, the oldest of Thomas Mann's six children and the one Janet admired most — "prince of the Manns" Janet called her. She thought Erika's brother Klaus, on the other hand, an egotist overly dominated by Erika.[48] Klaus, a liberal, a writer, formerly the editor of a literary exiles' review, *Die Sammlung,* in Amsterdam, was now eager to start a similar project in America, a "truly cosmopolitan magazine," he said, "devoted to creative writing and the discussion of all great, timely issues."[49] The Brooklyn colony — notably Carson, Wystan Auden, and George Davis — became involved in the planning of it. They decided Janet should be recruited to write for its first issue; Klaus, possibly referring to Janet, said he ought to use "big shots" to catch public attention.[50] In any event she consented, privately telling her family that the job was really a waste of time.

Decision, Mann's review, first appeared in January 1941 and contained Janet's hastily composed and confusing piece called "Paradise Lost." A nostalgic eulogy for democratic France, written without the sardonic humor characterizing most of her *New Yorker* pieces, it compared the France of the Third Republic to a beautiful dead woman — had she been ill a long time, Janet rhetorically asked, extending the metaphor, or had she been murdered?[51] It was an odd comparison, evidently containing more personal meaning for Janet than political meaning for the magazine. Janet had long associated France, conventionally, with a woman, and using the conceit again here, she may well have been struck by its ironic reference to her own life. Had she been thinking of Noel? Was it Noel who had been wronged, betrayed — or was Noel at least partly to blame for what had happened to their relationship?

But it was her work for *The New Yorker* that concerned Janet most.

Early in the summer of 1940, Harold Ross had suggested a story about France under occupation; Janet said she protested, commenting flippantly that no one knew any French who had been occupied. But she contacted William Bullitt in Washington and began gathering material; by December the result appeared in *The New Yorker* as "Paris, Germany." Gone was her cheekiness, gone was her detachment. The article was quiet, understated; she stressed the Germans' politeness and efficiency and their not very muted passion for "degenerate" goods. "Eyewitnesses say that some of the earliest German soldiers in their first free hour in Paris stuffed their mouths with oranges and bananas without taking the skins off and spread butter on their chocolate bars. All one Austrian soldier wanted of Paris was to eat tinned pineapple and to moon over Napoleon's tomb."[52] She presented life in Paris under the Nazis evenhandedly, telling how daily life accommodated itself to despair, defeat, and demoralization. As if taking the mantle of Genêt for the last time, she mentioned what was being served at the Ritz — but she was no longer footnoting the life of the smart set.

The article did not contain the conceit she'd used in "Paradise Lost," but it did have a personal meaning. The piece was an implicit indictment of Genêt, who could no longer chronicle the comings and goings of society from an olympian detachment. Now far from France, she began to drop the tone of neutral disinterest. Neutrality was no longer a sign of social and cultural superiority, which was itself suspect. And Janet was no longer willing to adjust to France's inevitable defeat.

As if to signal that Genêt could not continue in the same vein — ironic, accommodating, subdued, and ultimately helpless — her next *New Yorker* piece, "Soldats de France, Debout!" concerned the French Resistance. Janet examined the already legendary Charles de Gaulle and his army of Free French to find out if the legends were true. She discovered that this tall military man had been arguing for a modernized military since the 1930s, that he spoke beautifully but not often, despised politicians and politics, and, in resisting appeasement, offered the French an alternative to Marshal Pétain and his Vichy government. Even Janet saw him as larger than life, as the last hope of a divided and nearly vanquished nation. "Apparently he is like the carved prow of a ship," she wrote, "or the bronze statue of a soldier in a park; he has no more personality than either of them, yet represents, as they both do, something that men create either to follow or to remember something by, something that, in the flesh, can be hailed as a leader."[53] Presenting him without much irony and in energetic prose that made him seem a hero, she suggested that de Gaulle and the Free French might in fact salvage the civilization she had thought lost. She signed the article with her own name, and "Genêt" disappeared for four years.

While she was writing these eloquent and compassionate articles, she was still struggling with the profile of Thomas Mann. She continually put it off, this time to write more on occupied France for *The New Yorker*.[54] She'd also been working on a short piece for *Harper's Bazaar*, "The Lone Liberty Chorus," a brief sketch of four American broadcasters, including Natalia Murray, and another long piece on France and collaboration, "Blitz by Partnership," which appeared in *The New Yorker* in June.[55] Alec Woollcott wrote her immediately, partly to apologize for his harsh criticism of the Willkie piece and partly to praise her long-distance coverage of France. The recent article was a "journalistic masterpiece. Such fine, clean, sinewy, surgical prose!"[56] How, he wanted to know, did she get her information?

Janet told him she'd culled it from interviews with five people. But she was also using anecdotes differently, she noted. Instead of using them to make her subject appear slightly comic and endearingly human, she was trying to weave them into what she called theory.[57] She didn't mean that she was trying to write a theoretical piece; rather, she implicitly acknowledged that she was using storytelling techniques, substituting a strong narrative for much of the topical detail of her early Paris letters and her profiles. And she was not so opposed to revealing her point of view.

Having found her subject in pieces like "Blitz by Partnership" and "So You Are Going to Paris," published only two weeks apart, and having developed a new method of reporting, Janet was enjoying her writing again.[58] Marshaling the anecdotes of American expatriates recently returned from France or the information in some of their letters, she characterized life in Paris by drawing attention to the small, daily things. How one eats, washes, makes soap, how many hours one waits in line, what radio broadcasts one listens to, what one sells, and what one smuggles — all of this provided an impressive human document of struggle, adaptation, resistance, and collaboration.

Writing about France, not from the vantage point of a historian trying to sort out the reasons for its fall but as one who loved the country, she began to write much better than she had in "Paradise Lost" and the ill-fated Willkie profile. Knowing this, she felt increasingly confident about her subject, her range, her style.

When not addressing her *New Yorker* audience, she returned to themes first expressed in her *Indianapolis Star* articles written over twenty years before. She talked about the war and its causes in broad terms, blaming it on materialism and "selfishness and silliness." She again called her audience to self-sacrifice and idealism. In her lecture "Midnight in the Modern World," given in November 1941 at a convention of the New Jersey Education Association, she named Gabrielle Chanel and Serge Diaghilev as the two most important figures she observed while living in France. She concluded, according to the *New York Times* reporter, with the surprising judgment that "Chanel was a good influence. The Russian ballet was probably bad. Anyhow it summed up, in Paris, that instinct for hedonism, for pleasure, for spending which helped France to collapse."[59]

While she blamed "hedonism," which she often said had taken her to France in the first place, she also reaffirmed her faith in art. In her introduction to Marcel Vertès's album of drawings, *The Stronger Sex,* she declared that the "permanent pleasures" afforded by things of true beauty can only "grow in peace, which is the art man has now lost." Getting and spending, marching and fighting — these had nothing at all to do with the true beauties of civilization, which would, she insisted, survive.

Without the steady income from her fortnightly Paris letter, Janet worried about money. She was writing as many short pieces as she could but was constantly nervous that one of her projects would be "scooped," which occasionally did happen. At the same time she was trying to help a few friends place articles. Janet forwarded an article by Moura von Budberg in England to John Peale Bishop at the *Virginia Quarterly* and asked him also to look at a piece of Nancy Cunard's. Janet saw Nancy briefly during the summer of 1941 when she arrived in New York from Mexico without a visa and wasn't allowed to disembark. Nancy must have bribed an official to look the other way, for she walked down the gangplank and greeted Solita, Kay Boyle, and Janet, sitting on packing boxes, drinking beer, and waiting.[60]

Nancy urged Janet to send her a copy of the Mann profile. Janet had been agonizing over it for months; it was even harder to write than the profile of Hitler. And it depressed her. She complained to Alec Woollcott that she was like a hungry guest who feeds — and rather indiscriminately at that — on others' ideas.[61] She claimed she didn't know enough because she didn't have enough time to read. No, she decided, this wasn't the problem. The problem was herself: she simply wasn't creative or inventive, she didn't read enough or know enough and didn't have time to do much about it. All this seemed more critical, more apparent, in New York.

She finished the Mann profile in October 1941 and mailed the proofs to Carson McCullers in Georgia, asking Carson for some reason to destroy them after reading them. Carson complied; she didn't even show her mother, she assured Janet. She also said she liked the piece.[62] Janet was still anxious about it. She'd been re-searching and writing for over a year, often with the help of the various Mann children, who'd even arranged for Janet to meet their father once in Princeton. As it turned out, she liked neither Thomas Mann nor his writing; she found both stiff, studied, and pompous. In suggesting as much, however, she knew she would offend the many for whom Mann could do no wrong. But it was precisely this hero worship that accounted for much of what she disliked in him; the man who "endured the singular experience of being regularly described, while still alive, in terms usually reserved for the excep-tional dead" took "his symbolic eminence for granted."[63]

The title of the two-part profile, "Goethe in Hollywood," suggests Janet's bias: that Mann's so-called genius was a bit of a sham. Mann himself was outraged and insulted by what he called "embarrassing scribble about me and the people around me." Calling the piece "an insignificant piece of hackwork!" he wrote to his friend and translator Agnes Meyer that "it is truly a feat to be so cheeky and so boring. The combination is like the cross between indiscretion and false information which also distinguishes this piece of malice parading as biography. Every other fact is a falsehood."[64] He recalled the day Janet met him for lunch, admitting that he had been as "monstrously polite, stiff and buttoned up" as she characterized him; his only regret, he added, was that he had been polite. He was mollified, however, when his friends explained to him that the article was really a tribute, if merely by virtue of its size, and that it had appeared, after all, in a mere humor magazine. And he took comfort in the fact that at least one of his friends wrote an irate letter to both *The New Yorker* and Janet herself.[65]

Although Janet later remembered that only Glenway Wescott had defended her, this was not exactly true.[66] Shortly after the publication of the profile, she met journalist Irving Drutman at a party. He thought the piece impressive and even said he had cried when he read it. "I cried when I wrote it," she answered tartly.[67] Alec Woollcott, signing his letter "God," wrote that she must "feel more comfortable now that you have laid your Thomas Mann egg. You were heavy with that foetus ever since I can remember. If the result strikes you as a trifle dull, it is all the fault of Thomas himself. He is as interesting and artistic as Grant's tomb."[68] Erika Mann also liked the piece although, according to David Diamond, she commented that Janet wrote like a weasel.[69]

On the whole, Woollcott, whose criticism Janet trusted, preferred her Europe-in-absentia reports, like *The New Yorker*'s "Come Down, Giuseppe!" on the German presence in Rome.[70] Natalia Murray had made this one possible, providing Janet with letters, contacts, first-hand reports, and inspiration. And Solita still helped out. For example, after Solita joined the American Women's Voluntary Services, a training center and clearinghouse for women volunteers wishing to serve in community or war-related jobs, Janet decided to write a profile of its leader, Alice Throckmorton McLean, with Solita's help.

Solita meanwhile was aware that "in this year everything has changed nearly down to the roots of life," as she told Margaret Anderson, adding that she no longer wanted to write, she wanted an entirely new life, and she "must no more be homeless." She was not sure she could ever go back to Paris, "to those scenes where all is so changed, so lonely, where all my heart, in pieces now, will ever be."[71] But she had started a new page in her scrapbook. Writing "vita nuova" near a photograph of her new companion, the tall and stately Elizabeth Jenks Clark, Solita was ready to move on.

She and Lib Clark briefly moved to the West, and Janet wrote Solita often, confiding as she always had: her work dissatisfied her, the pieces she wrote simply for money sounded trivial and dull in her own ears. She thought she was working more slowly than ever and wasn't earning nearly enough to support herself in New York and send her mother a small check now and then. And with the United States' recent entrance into the war, the profile of Bette Davis that she was working on seemed singularly inappropriate.[72]

But despite the pressure she experienced in her work, by 1942 her life had become much more settled. Having left the apartment she and Solita had shared on East Forty-eighth Street to sublet part of Natalia's apartment, she began more and more to share Natalia's domestic life. She was happy with Natalia, she told Solita — at least during those periods when all went well between them, for occasionally it didn't. Solita herself was a bone of contention since Janet would not and could not fully break with her. Although both of them no longer pretended that the situation hadn't changed, Solita still gave advice and Janet still leaned on her, she said, as her oldest and most severe critic.[73] And Solita stayed a part of the Flanner family; she frequently sent Hildegarde news of her sister, letting her know if Janet was working too hard or "getting fat in tummy and behind too. It's the result of sitting and also sipping."[74]

Over and over, Janet told Solita she ought to be in France. She was suffering terrible pangs of conscience about Noel, and now the present seemed increasingly cut off from the past. Friends were older, feebler, more mortal and vulnerable. Neysa McMein fell and broke her back. John Mosher, who'd introduced Natalia and Janet, died in early September 1942. And later that month Janet learned that the Nazis had rounded up and arrested the American women still living in and near Paris, among them Noel Murphy.

Noel, along with the other Americans, had been classified by Germany as an enemy alien after the United States entered the war. Until September she had lived virtually undisturbed on her farm. Claiming that the Germans left her alone because she had no central heating, she was proud of the way she handled them. When a stray soldier climbed over her fence to pilfer her garden, she said she "shooed" him out of her yard in her best Schubert German. He sheepishly left the same way he arrived — over the fence. "Just like a German. It never occurred to him to walk out the gate."[75]

But Noel knew she was being watched; she'd been ordered not to leave Orgeval and to report weekly to the local police. Then, on September 24, she was told to pack her things. Taken to Paris, she and others like Sylvia Beach, writer Katherine Dudley, and former actress and broadcaster Drue Tartière, waited overnight under heavy guard. Over 350 women were put in an improvised dorm, with Nazi guards stationed everywhere, even in the bathrooms. The next morning the women were given a sausage, a small piece of cheese, and a loaf of bread before being quietly ushered into several waiting buses. They were not sure what was happening, just that they were being moved quickly so no one would notice.

They were taken by bus to a filthy train. The Germans apologized, blaming the French for its condition, and herded the women aboard. Now they knew where they were headed — an internment camp in the spa town of Vittel. As the train clattered through each station, several of the women dropped notes out of the carriage windows, hoping that someone might find and mail them, perhaps before they reached their destination. On the platform in Nancy the German Red Cross threw coffee dregs in their faces. But they arrived in Vittel, virtually without incident, the next morning. Noel was assigned to a room with five other women in the Grand Hôtel, a symbol of elegance now surrounded by barbed wire, where they waited, cooked, cleaned, and played solitaire to relieve the tension and boredom.[76] But she was more fortunate than most. Many of the women were eventually released, but not without pain and subterfuge: Drue Tartière, for example, used smuggled drugs to induce hemorrhaging, believing that her captors feared, above all else, cancer. She was right. Convinced she was stricken with uterine cancer, they released her in early December, the same day as Noel. Friends in Paris had apparently interceded on Noel's behalf.

Janet got official notice of Noel's release in February 1943 and sent the good news on to Gerald and Sara Murphy. Good news was scarce: the month before, Alec Woollcott had suffered a fatal heart attack. And Dick and Alice-Lee Myers's son was killed in Canada during a Royal Air Force training flight. History, Janet wrote to the

Myerses, would curse the "grown men" who could have prevented war as early as 1933.[77] As for Noel, Janet told Solita "I'll try not to grieve about my infidelity."[78] She couldn't make herself feel what she did not feel; she no longer loved Noel the way she had. And they were far apart, separated not just by the war but by all the complicated, ambivalent feelings that must have gone into their separation in the first place.

Janet claimed her heart was still in Paris. She had finished her profile of Bette Davis; it was informative but, as she had suspected, somewhat irrelevant. More interested in the stories told by the refugees still trickling into the United States, she compiled the saga of her friend Mary Reynolds into a *New Yorker* article that ran for three consecutive weeks.[79] Reynolds, the former companion of Marcel Duchamp, had left Paris just before the Nazis arrested Noel and the other American women. She traveled secretly through France, hiked across the Pyrenees to Spain, and made her way finally to Lisbon, where she eventually secured passage home by way of Liberia, Brazil, Trinidad, Puerto Rico, and Bermuda. The escape took seven months.

Flight and escape began to feel like recurring themes: Janet accused herself of always making evasive choices, of preferring flight to conflict in times of stress. She was engaged by the stories of those who were able to flee from the Nazis, thanks to the various underground organizations working throughout Europe. She wrote a short piece for *Home and Food* about a Belgian widow's harrowing escape to England in a rowboat and recounted some of the other stories of escape she'd heard.[80] She herself wanted to return to Europe as soon as possible — or at least she thought she did.

From the end of 1942 to the beginning of 1944, Janet immersed herself in the research and writing of an extended, four-part profile of Marshal Pétain, the eighty-seven-year-old head of Vichy France. Ross had lightly suggested the project without really knowing how long it would take or the kind of work it might entail. For fourteen months she read documents at the French Information Center Library, the French Institute, and the Office of Strategic Services in Washington and spoke to staff members at the French Military Mission there and in New York. When the profile was finished, Ross told Janet that he could not, in good conscience, call it anything but a "study." Never had he seen anything of its kind in any other magazine: "I don't know what the debutante subscribers and the younger married set will think about this, but our savant clientele will be profoundly impressed," he proudly wrote her. "I think your time was well spent and that probably you'll be offered a chair of French History at some Middle West University."[81]

Janet, too, was pleased with the profile. She had wanted to write something meaningful as well as dramatic, like her earlier "Escape of Mrs. Jeffries." She used her talents well in "La France et Le Vieux," a quasi-psychological piece that telescoped the history of the Third Republic.[82] By placing that saga and the oddities of French political history alongside Pétain's less than meteoric rise to power, she was able to weave together a sharp, incisive portrait of France and its waxen but symbolic leader. In Janet's cool prose, Pétain, jumping over a ditch specially dug for a publicity event, to prove he was fit to govern, emerged as a maladroit dupe.

Letters of congratulation and praise quickly came in. The publishing house Simon and Schuster decided to bring the articles together in book form, and when *Pétain: The Old Man of France* appeared in July 1944, all reviews were favorable. Although she was lightly criticized for not having considered Pétain in the context of the others responsible for his power, like Pierre Laval, her presentation of the Old Man was considered incisive, the prose sharp, the anecdotes entertaining, well placed, and witty.[83] She herself thought it the best work of her career.

Yet even with the success of the profile and the positive reviews of the book, she still felt useless in America, out of place — even "terrible," she confided to Gerald Murphy when she forwarded one of Noel's letters. She wanted to go back to Europe, and Natalia wanted to go to Rome. But if they went they would, in all likelihood, be separated for some indeterminate time.

That spring of 1944, before the Allied troops landed on France's Normandy coast on D-Day, Harold Ross had assigned Janet the task of writing a pocket guide for American soldiers. The project seemed reasonable, even somewhat important, and she told her family about it with a certain degree of pride. Later, when she met the general originally responsible for the project at a party, he confided to her that he didn't think the chapter on social diseases very strong. When she asked to see it, he said he was sorry, the document was top secret. I know what's in it, General, she answered. I wrote it.[84]

After Natalia received her uniform and commission from the Office of War Information and was sent first to Delaware for preparation and eventually to Rome, Janet felt even more useless and displaced. She stayed on in Natalia's apartment with Ester and young Bill Murray, and she frequently saw Solita and Lib Clark, now living together in New Jersey, as well as her sister Marie and other friends. She stayed busy, writing a three-part *New Yorker* article on the French-born American citizen Charles Bedaux, who had committed suicide before he could be indicted for treason, and emceeing the radio show "Listen: The Women." She hoped to make money or line up a more permanent job in radio, but the show was a disappointment. It took too much time and interfered with her writing, she said, and she never got to talk to the panelists; during the show, she was so nervous she could hardly concentrate on what anyone was saying, and afterward, everyone left.[85]

Janet was aware that she had changed in the last five years, and she wanted this change acknowledged. One incident more than any other suggests how her view of herself and of her professional obligations had altered. When her friend Horst first approached her in 1943 to write the text to accompany a book of his 1930s photographs, Janet was willing. But by the fall of 1944 she had changed her mind. She sent Horst a long letter explaining that she did not want to be associated with the Parisian society people who had reportedly become collaborationists; she had irrevocably decided that she did not want to have any part of "nauseating fashionable Fascism."[86] Horst, who had been sent to Fort Belvoir for military training, answered her letter, saying that if some of the portraits to be included in his book offended her (such as the one of the Vicomtesse de Noailles), he would consider suppressing them, but he thought she was over-dramatizing the importance of this "relative French non-entity" and forgetting about the other photographs in the volume — of people like Toscanini, Eve Curie, and Mrs. Harry Hopkins. "My idea was for you to bring out in your text how human values change," he told her. "If you have changed from a reporter to an arbiter and intransigent judge of humanity, I wish you luck. But I do not believe that one can wipe out the past by not talking about it or trying to forget it, much less by denying it."[87]

In her reply, late in September, she said she was in no way attacking his work, but as a good reporter and one who knew her profession, she felt she'd be forced to criticize too sharply some of the people he had photographed. The times, unlike the photos, had changed. Even though she had not known the fashionable Fascists of the photographs, she wanted to dissociate herself, not just from them but from her earlier role as their sometime chronicler. She wanted to make it completely clear that she had never participated in that world, even if she had reported for fourteen years on many of its pastimes and pleasures. She wasn't necessarily denying the past; she just didn't know what to do with it yet. By arguing that times had changed, she was declaring that she had changed — or at least that her role had, in terms of her responsibility as a reporter and her relation to the events she reported.

After her broadcasting contract for "Listen: The Women" ran out in October 1944, Janet intended to go to France for six months. She missed Natalia, and she worried when she did not hear from her. She also worried about her work and what might be in store for her in France. It was harder and harder to reimagine Europe. And she was not sure what she would say to Noel, who was expecting not only her return but the resumption of their relationship.

Harold Ross joked that he could arrange passage for her on a dynamite boat bound for Denmark. He was genuinely — and paternally — interested in her welfare and not altogether eager to see her leave. Janet appealed to her old friend Jane Grant, now editing the abbreviated wartime editions of *The New Yorker,* to find her passage. Grant arranged for Janet, who had never flown and was afraid of airplanes, to fly to London in November as an official army war correspondent for *The New Yorker.* She didn't know what to pack; the only thing she knew she'd be bringing was ignorance.[88]

11

A Charnel House
1944-1947

H ER GRANDMOTHER HAD PREDICTED that one day people
would move through the sky at unbelievable speeds, but Janet
wasn't prepared for the exhilaration of crossing the Atlantic in a mere
twenty-six hours. She was terrified. And fascinated, flying so close
to the ground over Scotland that she could count the sheep. She
arrived in London early in November 1944 and immediately wrote
Jane Grant to thank her for having arranged the flight: it had been
one of the strangest experiences of her life. She sent Solita news of
their friends in England and wrote Natalia telling her how much she
missed their life together. And to Noel she sent word that she had
arrived safely and would be in Orgeval in about ten days.

Nothing was the way she imagined it. She stayed several days at
Swan Court in a friend of a friend's spare room and spent most of
her days at the public relations headquarters at Grosvenor Square.
There she found typewriters, messages, tips, information, and ca-
maraderie. Her friends and colleagues, hailing her as "Miss New
Yorker," absorbed some of the shock she felt on finding London so
changed: the house in Piccadilly where she had stayed in the thirties
no longer existed. In its place was a large walled pond and a sign
warning passersby to keep out; on the wall hung a life preserver for
those who didn't bother to heed the warning. Tired, brave Londoners

carried on business as usual despite the long queues, the exorbitant cost of everything from taxis to food, and the blackouts, which frightened Janet at first.

Jane Heap, dressed snappily in a yellow hat with a green brim, treated her to sludgy coffee at Selfridge's; Madge Garland, the former fashion editor of the British *Vogue,* arranged to get her a pair of fur-lined boots, and Dick Myers and his daughter Fanny welcomed her with real Scotch. She filled in Nancy Cunard and Nancy's cousin Victor on friends like Djuna Barnes and Gene MacCown; she had lunch with Juliet Duff. She gathered material, tried to learn as much as possible about Paris, and prepared for what she heard were its appalling conditions. She bought woolen underwear, a new uniform, and a field jacket, as well as a bicycle, a hot plate, and an electric heater, figuring the best she could expect was cold and confusion.

By the last week of November she was in France. Sitting on the Paris-bound train, Janet must have recalled the morning five years before when Noel, slowly steering her car through the crowds lining the road, had driven her and Solita to Bordeaux. And she must have remembered the way Noel looked as they embraced and bade each other farewell. Janet could not have helped thinking of all this and much more as she boarded the small electric train for Saint-Germain-en-Laye that damp November afternoon.

Noel, in Orgeval preparing for Janet's arrival and busy as usual with the chores that filled her long days, certainly had her own reminiscences. She had been waiting for Janet for a very long time. At dusk she wheeled her bicycle onto the road. Although it had started to rain heavily, she pedaled quickly to the train station. Janet appeared, her hair short and white, deeper lines creasing her face. But one wonders what Noel saw — whether Janet looked older, slimmer, sadder; whether her voice had grown deeper and smokier; if seeing her in uniform struck Noel as odd, or whether years of occupation had made that seem ordinary. Janet, whose memory of Noel had been shadowed by five years of guilt and anxiety, immediately noticed that Noel was much thinner and stooped, her hands worn and gnarled. But Noel claimed she was in excellent health: a four-year regimen of home-grown vegetables and sour milk, of cleaning pigpens and pitching manure had cured her headaches.[1] Her laugh had not changed, and her sometimes abrasive humor still flashed across her handsome face.

Although she reported to her family that Noel was happy to have done her wartime duty as she saw fit, Janet hardly concealed her own anger, simultaneously directed at Noel and at herself.[2] Everyone, after all, had done the duty they'd seen fit to do, but who knew what that meant. Yet if Janet had planned to break off with Noel, she discovered she wasn't quite ready. Hemingway had apparently told Noel that Janet was involved with an Italian woman but hadn't said more, and Noel hadn't asked.[3] She "accepts without question like a hind that is beaten fact that I have an Italian friend," Janet wrote Solita a month later. "What a coward I am but how can I deliver that blow which she so obviously cowers [?] in order not to receive."[4]

Janet stayed with Noel for only three days. When she went back to Paris, she immediately went to the Hôtel Saint-Germain-des-Prés to see her old friends the proprietors, Louis and Melanie Doré. The hotel was decrepit and dirty. Melanie was dying of cancer, and Louis spent all his time nursing her. Is all Europe, Janet asked Solita, ill and dying?[5] Paris was rainy, cold, and muddy. Everywhere the destruction seemed senseless, avoidable. "Europe is a charnel house," she said, filled with "death, destruction, rot. French beginning to quarrel, they resent our not fulfilling promises, British resent our evasion responsibility in the international future affairs. The honeymoon was the liberation now it is over & the in-laws are back biting."[6] She saw their old friend Ilimaz Dadechkiliani, who had hid in a small town until the liberation. They laughed over his cynical, comic stories about the occupation until he got up to leave. Bowing and kissing her hand, he looked at her and said, "It was not funny. None of it. It was horrible."[7]

Janet would spend part of the week in Orgeval, where Noel met her at the small electric train station and put her bag on her bicycle. When she returned to Paris, she would hitchhike along the Route de Quarante Sous and stay at the Hôtel Scribe with the other foreign journalists. They recognized her as the small-boned, white-haired woman who cycled around the city: she often rode over to the rue Bonaparte to visit the Dorés and read them Solita's letters, or she stopped by the Flore, currently the favored café for writers and intellectuals, before picking up supplies, like champagne for Christmas, at the PX to bring back to Orgeval. It was a miserable winter, but her electric heater worked, and at the Scribe she could run a warm bath between eight and ten — if Hemingway didn't get there first, as he did at least once, to steal the bath water.

She saw Ernest frequently, either at her hotel or over brandy at the Deux Magots, where occasionally he read her his poems. She thought them superb, full of the "truth of a decade," but he seemed unwell. "But let *him* tell that to world," she told Solita. "I've seen a lot of him & love him far more even than ever —."[8] She met a number of people, correspondents like the "splendid" Helen Kirkpatrick, in Paris as the Chicago *Daily News* bureau chief, and the young British-born Monica Stirling, an American war correspondent for the *Atlantic Monthly,* who became Janet's closest friend at the hotel. In fact, her popularity with the press corps surprised her, but new friends didn't keep away sad memories or homesickness for former days. Nor could they allay her fears about her own work. The men billeted with her at the Scribe, she confided to Solita, thought her wise and insightful, but she considered their admiration a function of their inexperience. To herself she sounded as if she were merely repeating the same stale things she had said for fifteen years.[9]

When Harold Ross received her first Paris letter in December, he was moved enough to revive the "Genêt" signature. This, he said, is a historic moment in journalism.[10] Janet was annoyed, however, because editor William Shawn had rewritten it, substituting "I" for her editorial "we" and softening the anger with which she portrayed suffering individuals, crippled by cold and hunger, in a country where nothing short of a "revival of morality" could offset the effects of the war years. "For five years," she wrote, "Europe has been the victim of cannibalism, with one country trying to eat the other countries, trying to eat the grain, the meat, the oil, the steel, the liberties, the governments, and the men of all the others. The half-consumed corpses of ideologies and of the civilians who believed in them have rotted the soil of Europe, and in this day of the most luxurious war machinery the world has ever seen, the inhabitants of the Continent's capital cities have been reduced to the primitive problems of survival, of finding something to eat, of hatred, of revenge, of fawning, of being for or against something themselves or someone else, and of hiding, like savages with ration cards."[11]

The stories she heard and the pain she saw made her think that the two qualities necessary to the survival of France were strength and integrity — two qualities she doubted the French could muster. Nor was she sure, she confessed to Solita, that she herself could muster what was needed to portray all she saw and felt. "I know one thousand facts I cannot write," she sighed.[12] She worked on her next Paris letter for five days. Rereading it, she decided it was "dull, incoherent, introvert."[13] She tore it up, and for the first time in her life, she failed to send her letter to *The New Yorker*.

She was reworking the three-part piece on the industrialist Charles Bedaux and having it checked for accuracy by Bedaux's ex-secretary, now out of hiding.[14] But as a fortnightly Paris correspondent, she didn't know exactly what her place or her function should be in France or elsewhere in Europe, or even if she would ultimately stay. "The Philistine is he who passed by on [the] other side of [the] street," she told Solita, "but I really do not know what one can do by remaining on their side, do for them or oneself."[15] "Scooped" on Gertrude Stein's return to Paris and on Sylvia Beach's wartime activities, failing to go with Carmel Snow to Sarggermine for a story, Janet decided she was incapable of "huntsman's reporting."[16] Shawn told her to relax, but she couldn't.

Everything that had once seemed clear now was muddled. After years of occupation, the French were turning against one another, especially in reprisals against collaborators; many had already turned against America for entering the war so late or for not informing de Gaulle about D-Day until the eve of the invasion. People were suspicious of one another, unhappy, demanding, and greedy: "french also sad from head to foot. poor or rich, big or little. i can be wrong surely, but not without authority; i didnt make this up; they told me, they showed me, from melanie on up & down, doodle, rich, sad, bad, good, evil, saintlike, all. dishonesty, fear — all from nazis yes, but before was here, fear of losing money value, losing greed, comfort as they call it, indifferent to voice of mind, only body."[17] Janet felt dry and empty of hope, belief, and joy: "men & what [they] have done are too terrible. cannot love world or hope or believe or even sneer with satisfaction or cry."[18] Self-hatred, humiliation, collaboration — all were chilling.

Hildegarde and Solita did their best to keep her spirits up with frequent letters and with packages of supplies and food. Janet gave away much of what was sent, either in trade for favors or intelligence or to those who needed the precious cargo more. Noel and Tsatsou needed woolen underwear and socks, Janet wrote Solita, as well as handkerchiefs, cigarettes, tobacco, chocolate bars, vanilla, tea, canned fish, cooking oil, and rice. Mention Europe's fuel shortage to Gristede's Market in New York, Janet advised Solita; New Yorkers might consider slow-cooking brown rice a delicacy, but the faster white variety was better suited to the European situation.[19] She made sure that packages for others, like Noel, were sent to her at Supreme Headquarters Allied Expeditionary Force; otherwise they were consistently robbed. On receiving two packages from her sister that contained nothing but an envelope of soup, the stoic Noel wept in frustration.

The pain, the waste, the pervasive human suffering made Janet irritable and deepened her loneliness. She perceived herself as different from many of the Americans, at least the GIs and many of the journalists, flocking into Paris for a good time or a hot story or, worse, writing a manipulated, Pollyannaish one. Although she enjoyed being in demand and dining with old friends as well as new, she never seemed to have enough time. People rushed in and out of her room at the Scribe. Her temper soured. She angered quickly and criticized harshly. Then, in remorse, she flattered to assuage the feelings she hurt.

Her guilt about abandoning Paris and her friends, especially now that she could see what she'd been spared, made her impatient with reporters who hadn't known Paris before the war. "I am missing the war even here somehow; always I make evasive choices," she wrote Solita.[20] And she still could not tell Noel about Natalia. She merely said she didn't think she could permanently live in Europe — "i certainly will not not not not stay here more than one year; shall die in the bronx i hope & buried there."[21] She dropped further discussion of her plans.

Since Paris made her edgy, she decided she ought to travel. As she told Solita, travel was the necessary privilege of journalists. In January 1945 she went to Lyons, spending twenty hours in an unheated train, to cover the trial of Charles Maurras, the editor of *L'Action française* who had printed scurrilous anti-Semitic and royalist diatribes.[22] After the trial she returned to Paris to work on her letter for five days, then decided to visit the French soldiers stationed near La Rochelle, where fighting still continued. She dryly joked that to get there, she could get a southwest-bound train to Angoulême, one to Cognac, and then get out and ask directions to the war.

A Scottish captain she met at the Scribe volunteered to take her by jeep. Dressed in pink trousers, khaki beret, officer's field jacket, fur-lined red boots, and mittens, she took chocolate, cigarettes, gloves, tea, and soup to the soldiers she heard had fought near Marennes without guns or coats. The soldiers, touched by her genuine concern and charmed by her down-to-earth humor, gave her three baskets of oysters.[23] But on returning to Paris, she was not sure what to write in her letter from the Royan front: she'd seen nothing. When she asked Hemingway's advice, he told her, she reported to Solita, to write "it the way you saw it, dog (his new name for all) — There is never any other story." She said it was the best advice she'd ever heard. But, she insisted, she hadn't seen anything. "That is always all," he had answered.[24]

If Paris depressed her, Cologne, where German mortars were still exploding and buildings lay crumbled, did so even more. She found people starving, frightened, and still mouthing Nazi propaganda. Tirelessly she walked through all the rubble, constantly asking questions, switching from English to German with ease and insisting that she be taken to places not on the itinerary, such as a camp for displaced persons. Ed Tribble, the soldier escorting Janet and the other journalists through the ruined churches, was astonished by her energy. She was ebullient, enthusiastic, and genuinely concerned, he recalled, about everything she saw.[25]

After returning to Paris, she soon prepared to leave again. Headed for Nemours, south of Paris, she found herself in Verdun — only because her orders mistakenly read Trier, in Germany. From Verdun she flew by Piper Cub to Luxembourg, where she waited four days for her baggage. Circuitous and unexpected journeys were the norm,

she realized as she headed back toward Paris by way of Reims. Proud
that she, unlike the three WACs with her, didn't get sick when they
landed in a hailstorm, she braved the bumpy ride on to Creil.

Much of the material she gathered was too trite for *The New Yorker,*
she decided. But travel calmed her anxiety and assuaged her guilt in
a way that staying in Paris could not. Although it took its toll — she
began to weary, lose weight, feel constantly displaced and underre-
warded — she nonetheless could not stop. Paris fed her restlessness
and depression, she said, and traveling made her feel that she was
somehow part of what was happening and perhaps could do something to relieve the suffering she saw everywhere.[26] She learned
more, had more to write about.

In Paris she spent more and more time alone, except at night when
she would go to the hotel bar. Once in a while she would spend an
afternoon with Gertrude and Alice, who served unusually rich
lunches, including ice cream made with soldiers' chocolate. But she
still didn't know what she should be doing. At the end of January
she agreed to broadcast for the Blue Network, the forerunner of
American Broadcasting Company. She'd known about the job even
before she left America, for she had signed a contract with *The New
Yorker* promising not to use broadcast material in her letters, or vice
versa. But she had hesitated, even though the job intrigued her, until
she was offered $100 a week.

The night before her first dispatch, Hemingway tried to talk her
out of it. Thinking she had taken the job only for the money and
suspicious about the whole set-up, as he called it — he apparently
thought she'd be forced to propagandize — he offered to give her
as much money as she would earn. She was touched but, not sharing
his suspicions of a set-up, she politely refused. She began writing
her first copy the next morning at ten. At five that evening, she
nervously began to rehearse her 2,500-word manuscript. At six she
was on the air. As she finished speaking, she could hear voices
through her earphones. They were praising her report and her grand
voice. She was "in," she delightedly wrote Solita.

This was something she wanted to do; it provided her with a sense
of purpose, and she could use a tone quite different from that of her
written correspondence. If Janet spoke of issues similar to those she
covered in the *New Yorker* letters — the French reaction to domestic

problems, to de Gaulle, to the last of the Allied war effort, to food
shortages, and to bureaucracy — on the radio she dramatically added
the facts of daily life, facts which made the desperate mood of the
French clear. The broadcasts were more personal than professional,
or so she described them; in other words, she did not edit out her
feelings. By contrast, when she wrote for *The New Yorker,* she worked
"impersonally," she said, reporting everything she heard and saw.[27]
She assumed it was her duty to stay impartial and objective, insofar
as that was still possible. In the broadcasts, however, she voiced her
opinions as dramatically as she felt them. She decried the poverty
of Allied aid, which she would not do in her *New Yorker* pieces, and
itemized what the French had been doing without — windowpanes,
metal fillings for teeth, knives for peeling onions (the only available
vegetable), bed linens, pots and pans. All had been confiscated by
the Nazis. She broadcast the French response to de Gaulle's exclusion
from the Yalta conference, saying that since the Germans did most
of their fighting in what they considered their back yard — France —
then the French should have a stake in the peace. She liked the work,
at least at first, for she enjoyed the instantaneous communication,
and, in a phrase echoing Noel's of five years earlier, she said her
broadcasts might "do some good."[28] But over time her nervousness
on the air made her hands shake so badly she could hardly read her
copy.

That spring Solita, who was managing all Janet's finances, wrote
to say that Janet had saved only $400 since November. Janet was
incredulous. "I've been working and voyaging and watching and ob-
serving since November 6," she exclaimed. "This is April 15 . . . I
work like a fiend; these trips nearly kill one; most of the women
have had accidents of one sort or another, jeep in the ditch and slight
plane crash etc. Sleep without windows on cots or guard room floors;
I havent floor slept yet but by christ I am working hard and giving
Ross the last vestige of my strength. . . . It isn't worth it, I tell you,
to work like this and save no money."[29]

The next day Janet packed for a flight to Wiesbaden and Weimar.
She still wanted to travel, ostensibly to gather material for her *New
Yorker* letters and her broadcasts. Carrying a fleece-lined sleeping
bag lent her by Jimmy (Vincent) Sheean for sleeping on the floor of
the press camp, Janet endured another awful trip. The pilot didn't

know the Wiesbaden airstrip numbers, and his passengers couldn't help him because they knew only the name of the city. Twice they landed in Mannheim by mistake. Janet's sciatica flared up, and her arm hurt. By the time she got to Wiesbaden, she was exhausted and couldn't remember why she had come: "I have now realized that slips occur with this mad traveling. . . . but this all counts for experience & I become so nervous in Paris & so sunken."[30]

From seven in the evening till three in the morning, in the windowless apartment building rigged up as a press camp, she wrote a story about the French prison camp at Ravensbrück. She'd interviewed one of the French women recently released in exchange for four hundred Germans. Thirty thousand others, Janet wrote, still waited in Ravensbrück — if they were still alive.[31] The next day, from a caravan set up in an apple orchard, she broadcast on the condition of displaced persons. Back in Paris a week later — the day after VE Day — she described her visit to the concentration camp at Buchenwald.

It had been a quiet, blue day. Her guide was a thirty-year-old Jewish man from Prague, a former inmate, who took her from building to building, gently answering all her questions. Janet listened carefully. He showed her the gallows, the crematorium, the primroses of the Nazi officers, who were fond of flowers. She had been prepared for most of what she saw, even the ashes, but not for the dozen corpses, just discovered that morning, piled in a stiff, naked heap outside the crematorium. Their mouths were open as if they were still hungry. She sat down on the steps with her guide and was silent. "This," she wrote to Solita, "is beyond imagination."[32]

Janet had always been proud of her skeptical cast of mind, her ability to countenance alternative ways of viewing a situation, and choose what seemed the most rational, even if the least pleasant. She had used her skepticism to full advantage in her early letters, debunking conventions and deflating pretensions by deftly balancing incongruities. Behind her sardonic wit lay a deep belief in that thing she called "civilization," a belief in things created, things of beauty that spoke to the noblest aspirations of humankind. Now she was not sure what she could believe in. She was finding it harder and harder to place faith in "governments, politics, religion, God, and even man himself.

He is full of the wicked *proof* of the rightness of not purely believing in anything."[33]

At midnight on May 6 Janet wrote to her friends. The war ended as it had begun, she said, with "profound strangeness, unlike history's wars heretofore."[34] Crowds dispersed slowly, weary and grateful, but as afraid of peace as they had been of war. The next day she went to see Louis Doré in the shabby hotel on the rue Bonaparte and drank Armagnac in solemn celebration.

Having turned her broadcasts into a personal crusade about the plight of the returning prisoners of war, she despaired of getting results. The inefficiency with which the minister of deportees had handled the prisoners infuriated her; when one of the first groups arrived, no one had known they were coming, no food or flowers or cheers awaited them. They were greeted instead with disorganization and confusion. Janet considered the general incompetence appalling and said so. Only Parisian housewives and members of the Resistance arranged to meet the second group of returning prisoners with hot soup and clean clothes. No one knew who was alive or dead. No names had been taken or delivered. In exasperation, Janet claimed that she herself could have taken a count while at Buchenwald.

With the constant confusion, anger, delays, and an occasional freeze on news, Janet often was unable to get her copy to *The New Yorker* on time. Ross assumed that the broadcasts were interfering and reproached her for delivering only eight pieces between February and May while the biggest stories in Europe were hers for the taking. She answered his accusations in a seven-page letter, demanding to know who else, at the age of fifty-three and with comparable experience, had been traveling all over Europe at no small risk during those same four months.

Janet's feelings about her work were still confused. As it had so many times before, Paris became a metaphor for her state of mind, a way to articulate her thoughts. She said she was not sure she still loved Paris and didn't know whether she wanted to stay or leave. "I wish nothing had happened that has happened in all our lives," she wrote Solita.[35] Everything they both loved about France no longer existed. And though she wanted to believe the world could be restored to what it had been, or what she thought it had, she was losing faith, both in herself and in the world. The French had changed, Europe was changing; lacking the essential commodities, no one cared about moral niceties. People seemed to care more about their comforts and security, she said, than about freedom and liberty.[36] All Europe was engaged in a struggle for survival, but the struggle bred nothing but selfishness. Idealism hardly existed, especially among the occupying American armies, who regarded civilization "as a toilet."[37] She might be wrong about all this, she said, but she did not think so.

When she wasn't traveling, Janet still spent almost half of every week in Orgeval. She had the furniture from the Hôtel Saint-Germain-des-Prés moved to Noel's house; she had Noel's car repaired and requisitioned as a military vehicle; she brought her supplies from the PX; they planned holidays together. Noel, she knew, was very upset about the memoir being written by Drue Tartière, her fellow inmate at Vittel. Recounting her experience there and her subsequent hiding of Royal Air Force fliers, Tartière suggested in her book that Noel had been both an anti-Semite and a Nazi sympathizer, and she hinted that it might have been Noel who told the Germans about her Resistance work.

Janet was as angry at the allegations as Noel. Sensitive to the bitterness in France and grateful to the friend who had gotten Noel's letters to her during the war, Janet wrote Solita that Noel "wld strangle rather than have entertained a Nazi" but "nothing is black or white here. . . . A god-like kindness marked many collaborators, they had chance of doling out miracles & being thanked with tears of gratitude. A dangerous pinnacle. Few cld resist it, it was the reverse of a vice but probably vicious tho benign in effect on others."[38] But Noel, she vehemently affirmed, was not a collaborator. Janet cabled her friend Charlotte Seitlin at Simon and Schuster to warn that if the allegations against Noel in Tartière's book were not changed, there would be a lawsuit. If Noel *had* denounced Tartière, Janet maintained, Drue undoubtedly would have been taken to Ravensbrück.

Certainly Noel could be brutally forthright, and some of her opinions chafed; she defended German culture in a way that angered many. But Janet insisted that Noel admired only German music. Staunchly defending Noel in public, she admitted privately to Solita that Noel's statements about German culture and "pre-war people seems to me absurd and not realist. I am not interested," she continued, "in anybody preferring German lieder to US Kentucky hillbilly songs; I am interested in knowing in time which race has organized, fantastically, to represent an alliance with evil."[39] Janet was unequivocal in her feelings about Germans and Germany: *"I hate them,"* she wrote her sister from Nuremberg.

But Janet was capable of using this difference of opinion with Noel to ease her conscience about Natalia. She suffered at the sight of Noel, bent and burdened like an old horse, as Janet described her. And she suffered when Noel was gentle, kind, and understanding as much as when Noel was angry and jealous. By this time Janet had fully confessed her feelings for Natalia. She continued to depend on Noel for affection, support, and domestic comforts. But, divided and depressed, Janet longed for the life she and Natalia had shared in New York; they hadn't seen each other in almost a year. Nor would they see each other until the end of June, when Janet finally arranged transport to Rome.

Solita continued to manage Janet's affairs, send criticism of her broadcasts and writing, and understand the difficulty of her personal situation. "Only to you," Janet wrote her old friend, "can I tell the truth of my weaknesses."[40] She was devoted and loyal to all three women in different ways. Each gave her something she could not do without. She didn't want to hurt or disappoint any of them, and she would not — indeed, could not — consider rejecting one for another. This made her feel constantly guilty; when she experienced happiness, she felt it was purchased at another's expense. These were familiar feelings, especially regarding her mother and sisters, whom she often said she had abandoned.

Her work was her refuge. In the past she had explained to her family that she could not live near them because of her job. If she were a man, she once wrote her mother, she might feel less guilty when work took her away from those she loved.[41] Yet the work that took her away also protected her. For as much as Janet said she detested the separation, she also preferred it. Now, however, she felt more torn than ever because Natalia and Noel each wanted a commitment she could not give. Her feelings toward Noel had changed, and her relationship with Natalia, however passionate,

threatened her autonomy in ways that must have unconsciously reminded her of her relationship with her family.

Yet despite her ambivalence, Janet made it clear to Natalia that
she was not going to stay in either Rome or the United States. They
spent a happy month together in Italy, but when Natalia came to
Paris later that summer, both women were forced to confront the
fact that they might not be together again for a very long time. Again,
the ostensible reason was work. As for Natalia's coming to Paris to
live, that was impossible; Noel would not hear of it. She might be
able to accept Janet's relationship with Natalia from a distance, but
she demanded that Janet not bring her to Paris.[42]

After Natalia left, Janet continued to travel. She finished a *New
Yorker* letter Ross had wanted on wine, coal, and Cognac — a bore
and a bother, she said, and one that took time. Then in September
she went to Copenhagen, luxurious appearing, well-kempt, and
pretty, with its red brick churches and copper-green steeples. On
her way back to Paris she stopped in Bremen; shortly after, she
visited Wiesbaden again, then Frankfurt am Main, Mainz, and Mar-
burg, to collect material for a long *New Yorker* piece, eventually called
"The Beautiful Spoils," about the army's recovery of artworks stolen
and hidden by the Nazis.

She was busy. She hired a French stenographer to answer all the
fan mail she was receiving on "What's Wrong with France," an article
that criticized the American army's attitude toward the French. Her
piece on Charles Bedaux had been pirated by a French weekly; she
was angry that it had been translated into a French that deadened
her lively prose, and the piracy deprived her of the money she would
have earned from a legitimate reprinting. She decided to sue but
later dropped the case, feeling too tired. She had to get to Nuremberg
to cover the trial of Nazi war criminals and back to Munich to collect
more for her "Spoils" piece.

Her exhausting schedule was compounded by a gnawing malaise.
She was still homesick, she wrote Katharine White; this new Paris
was not her Paris.[43] As the holidays approached, she knew Solita
was going to California to celebrate with Janet's family; Natalia
was on her way to New York. And Janet, still working and scurry-
ing over Europe, was depressed and lonely. When she missed a

plane that subsequently crashed, she said she wished she had been on it.[44]

Stories were planned and stories were dropped and stories were missed as Janet moved around Europe. She planned a "Reporter at Large" piece, never written, about one man's underground work and his escape from several concentration camps. Travel, confusion, delays, and the many stories warm at her feet, as Ross once put it, made it difficult not to slip up on one story or cancel a second and unexpectedly write a third. She grew weary of what she called "high class hack writing," with its constant deadlines, pressures, and superficialities: "I want to write a book that will keep," she had told Solita, "like something in a box on a shelf."[45] To Natalia she confided that her "insolently sure-sounding reports" alarmed her.[46] And her schedule, with her regular letter, her intended "Reporter" pieces, her weekly broadcasts — all made reflecting, reading, concentrating, nearly impossible.

Early in 1946 she decided to quit broadcasting. Apologetically, she told her friends that a month's holiday had showed her how much the program had been interfering with the projects she now was eager to do. She even toyed with the idea of writing fiction again. Katharine White wrote and asked if Janet had any ideas for stories. Janet said she might like to try to write one or two, now that she had given up broadcasting, but she wasn't sure she had much "fictional sense"; then she added the phrase that became her standard explanation for having given up novel writing; all she could now see, she said, was a Europe "which is like nothing on earth except fiction."[47]

The New Yorker, meanwhile, wanted at least four more letters on the Nazi war trials. By the end of February 1946, Janet was back in Nuremberg, staying for several weeks in the villa that housed women of the press as well as clerks, typists, and stenographers. There were forty women in all, living in what Janet described as a kind of inefficient squalor; the army installed one bath and two urinals and then complained, she said, that women were difficult. If you give them urinals, you must find them difficult indeed, she replied.[48] Her grim humor amused her colleagues. One morning in the common dining room, Janet shocked several women at the breakfast table by

asking them to name which Nazi defendant·they would have slept
with had it been necessary.[49]

Janet's Nuremberg letters make clear how deeply she loathed what
she called the "unreconstructed" German mind, with its lack of conscience, racial bigotry, illogic, and brutal disregard for human life —
except, as she pointed out, that the Nazis on trial ironically did not
want to die for the cause that had killed millions.[50] All except Goering
jettisoned their own responsibility, blaming someone else, usually
someone higher in rank, like Hitler, for their crimes, or claimed they
had not really known what they were doing. For twenty-one hours
on the witness stand, Goering, with his dark humor and specious, intricate reasoning, alternately fascinated and horrified Janet, who detested his unconscionable brilliance. With "diabolical skill in drawing
on American and English history for familiar paradoxes and damaging
precedents," she told her *New Yorker* audience, he then devastated
the American prosecutor trying to match wits with him.

For all the praise she received for her Nuremberg letters — William Shawn cabled congratulations, and Harold Ross forwarded a
note from Alfred Knopf, who said her letters were the best reports
he had seen on the trial — Janet was not totally satisfied with them.
She did like her description of Goering but thought she should have
included in her report more of what he'd talked about — his plans
to take Gibraltar, the Mediterranean, and the Suez, or his plan to
goad Russia into fighting England. Thinking this material too cumbersome, she did not listen to her "inner voice" and therefore did
not describe his telling of that moment when the fate of the war,
according to her, was being decided: "As Goering spoke," she wrote
to Solita, "it seemed as if I were listening to the words, to the idea,
the moment indeed, when IF — the gigantic IF was being reported
upon, by which they might have won, or at least it was the moment
which seemed, as if on a clock, marked the minute when the time
turned against them & they began, as if it were a duty to history, to
lose the war."[51]

The writer May Sarton, who met Janet around this time, remembers that Janet "never rested on her laurels"; she struggled with all
her *New Yorker* letters and experienced extreme self-doubt about
each one. Helen Kirkpatrick Milbank likewise remembers how hard
Janet worked, often through the night, in the pressroom at Nurem-

berg.[52] And despite her reservations about the results, Janet herself felt she had done — and given — her best. She was therefore infuriated by the rumor she'd heard that Ross said he couldn't make Flanner stay in Nuremberg. He reportedly accused her of wanting to duck out, probably because fifty correspondents shared one bath. Indignant, she was half tempted to cable him another Nuremberg letter after she returned to Paris, just to make him pay for both the cable and a piece she knew he wouldn't print.[53]

Between the end of March and May, Janet wrote no *New Yorker* letters, but not because of her temporary anger at Ross; she was trying to work full time on "The Beautiful Spoils." By April she had finished the first part, subtitled "A.H., Linz," referring to Adolf Hitler, the intended recipient of 4,000 Old Masters, and Linz, their destination, where he planned to build a museum to honor his mother. She had also started the second part, "Collector with Luftwaffe," which discussed Goering's taste in art and intrigue, but this one was giving her trouble. She had gathered too many facts and was encumbered, she felt, with too many details.

By her own account, she had lost her powers of concentration and had become, as a result, short-tempered and impatient. Noel was doing everything she could, Janet reported to Solita, but she could not ward off the dark moods that left her angry with herself and her work. It seemed trivial; whatever drama she wrote into it was contrived and artificial. Her talent was small, her expectations too high, her laziness overpowering. And she despised making others, notably Natalia, suffer at the expense of a career that hardly seemed significant.

Janet readily admitted to Solita that she was painfully lonely. And she seemed to realize that behind her depression lay the need to make some decision about her relationships. In May Natalia, recently dismissed from her peacetime job with the United States Information Service, debated whether to stay in America, where she had been working for almost six months, or return to Rome. Janet promised she'd visit Natalia wherever she went. But she wouldn't promise more. When Natalia leaned toward staying in New York, Janet, remembering the difficulty of getting work there and believing she could not support herself financially or psychologically without *The New Yorker,* decided that she couldn't give up the security of her job as Paris correspondent.

Casting her feelings in public terms — an overintellectualizing habit that her friend Margaret Anderson, among others, criticized — Janet said that Americans were preoccupied with making money, and at their worst merely paid lip service to their heritage, which they did not really understand, being uncultivated and mentally unformed. She didn't want to return to that kind of environment, or live among those kinds of people.[54] As a result, France began to look less depressed and depressing. If she stayed, she could continue to write for *The New Yorker* and perhaps work on a book, a work of history — something solid, complex, and rewarding.

Natalia, also hoping to write a book, decided to return to Europe to begin research about the royal Italian House of Savoy. She would meet Janet in Paris in August, she said, and then Janet would join her in Italy in the fall. Janet was relieved but still troubled. That fall she confided to Solita from Rome, where she was staying with Natalia, that she frequently woke crying in the night. She missed Solita more than ever and couldn't help being reminded of the past. The hotel where they stayed many years earlier no longer existed, but, Janet confessed, "I always look at its absence, as near as I can locate it."[55]

Janet asked that Solita write to her at American Express; she did not want to anger Natalia, as mail from Solita would certainly do. She evidently asked that Noel do the same. Janet continued to try and protect her lovers from one another, though suspicious of her own motives in doing so. Noel asked whether Janet wasn't more afraid of herself than of any demand she, Noel, might make. In a letter to Solita, Janet called the question a "wise enquiry. I can think of many good questions but no answers because I keep hurting but don't want to give final death strokes, even to me."[56]

Work, despite the anxieties attending it, helped. After sending the completed draft of "The Beautiful Spoils" to *The New Yorker* and hearing from Shawn in September that he thought the piece not only eloquent and witty, as usual, but a major contribution to the rebuilding of Europe, Janet wept with joy. She had in fact wanted to preserve something of the civilization she saw crumbling. To learn that she had succeeded made all the work of the past twenty months worth the heartache and effort. With enthusiasm she turned to the work she'd outlined for herself during her stay in Italy — letters from Capri and Rome, at least, and possibly elsewhere in Italy, one from Trieste, and one from Vienna. As it turned out, she wrote the Capri, Trieste, and Italy letters that fall, and once back in France at the end of the year, she sent two Paris letters. Pleased, although she complained that she was working like a slave, she revised her "Spoils" piece again; she was again looking forward to writing, to traveling, to more writing — even to getting started on the book she was planning, a history of Europe covering the nineteenth and twentieth centuries. After her return, she decided her several months in Italy with Natalia had made her happy — and she was equally happy to be back in France.

In early 1947 Moscow said it would allow twenty American correspondents to visit the Soviet Union, and Janet wanted to be among them. She appealed to Jane Grant, the only one who in Janet's estimation could manage important tasks. Jane had arranged Janet's job in the first place, and her return to Europe in the second. Janet trusted Jane's powers of persuasion, her diplomacy, and her connections.

Janet proudly pointed out to the Soviet press attaché in Paris that *The New Yorker*'s circulation, though small when compared to the Hearst papers, almost equaled the *Herald Tribune*'s. The State Department, however, had ranked *The New Yorker* only forty-second on its list of seventy-three publications, and Jane Grant ultimately could not change that. Irate and hurt over the magazine's low rating, Janet immediately wrote Ross and Shawn about the unjust treatment. Rebecca West's work for the magazine on Nuremberg (which Janet thought better than her own) and John Hersey's "Hiroshima," she argued, had responsibly treated two of the most important consequences of the war, the legal prosecution of war crimes and the atom bomb. She herself had made an important contribution with her implicit analysis of the fall of France (the Pétain profile) and the three-part "Beautiful Spoils," which gave yet another example of destructive Nazi ideology.[57] These, and the war and postwar coverage of Europe and the Far East, she argued, entitled *The New Yorker* to a higher status than just that of a weekly humor magazine. Although she knew they wouldn't, she wished Ross and Shawn would protest the magazine's status to the State Department and to the chief of press for the delegation at Moscow. At the very least, a *New Yorker* correspondent should be placed on a waiting list, in the unlikely event one of the chosen journalists had to leave Moscow.[58]

The New Yorker's low rating clearly didn't match her sense of what it stood for; and an insult to the magazine was an insult to her, for if it was frivolous, then what was her twenty-two-year commitment to it? She had staked her reputation as a writer on *The New Yorker*. Whatever she thought of her own pieces as she wrote them, she was proud of the institution she represented.

And she trusted her editors' taste and judgment, even when they occasionally ruffled her. If they tempered her prose and softened her anger with cuts and slight changes, she usually protested and then succumbed, often because there was nothing she could do, being so far away. And she respected them. But in the third installment of "The Beautiful Spoils," the section entitled "Monuments Men," her editors had cut the story of the Monuments, Fine Arts, and Archives division of the Allied Forces. Though necessary, the cutting, she thought, had deprived the report of the drama, invention, hope, and excitement involved in the work of the Monuments men — protecting, inspecting, and locating stolen art.

With no possibility of a trip to Moscow, Janet began to feel restless again. Natalia had joined her in Paris for a few days in March, a pleasanter visit than some of their previous ones, Janet reported to Solita, but one that left her nonetheless exhausted with "emotional drags & aches."[59] Her book remained shapeless. She decided to ask British historian Denis Brogan if he would draw up an outline and bibliography for her so that she could try to block out a first chapter. But her anxiety about the project made her want to get away from Paris again. She decided to report on the ravaged parts of Europe she hadn't yet seen. She therefore put aside the book for *New Yorker* letters from Poland, Austria, and Berlin.

Carrying French francs, Polish zlotys, U.S. army scrip, American Express checks, and Austrian schillings, as well as her passport, French identity card and press card, U.S. Army card, and a fistful of other cards, military papers, and permits, she went to Vienna at the end of March 1947. She recalled the trip she had made with Solita after the First World War, when gold rings and jeweled boxes reminded them of the luxury of the recent past. This time there were no trinkets, no goods in shop windows, no pleasant evenings in the Opera House. Like the house where she and Solita had lived, the Opera House had been destroyed by Allied bombs. The gothic and baroque gravestones outside Saint Stephen's cathedral, which she and Solita had admired in the early twenties, remained intact, but the cathedral had been badly bombed by the Nazis. A curator at the Albertina Museum assured Janet that the damage was not as irreparable as it looked — if workers and mortar could be found for the repairs.

She stayed in the small, cheap hotel that served as a press camp and met a young American who gave her a good deal of material as well as several introductions. From Vienna she flew to Prague, where she stayed in the more modern section and saw delicatessens full of smoked salmon, sardines, and pickles. Although private homes received a ration of one pound of coffee per month, the coffee houses served the real thing, along with a newspaper in whatever language the coffee was ordered. She talked with government officials, some of whom she had met through William Bullitt years before, who helped her arrange a flight from Warsaw, her next stop, to Berlin. The Russians, she had heard, were making travel by train difficult.

Her Warsaw letters, which she herself liked, were pungent and compassionate. They dealt with the political future of Poland, which was being administered by Russia as an "absentee landlord," an image of Hemingway's and one she had used privately when predicting the loss of national self-determination in several European countries. She was, however, primarily concerned with what she saw — the ruins of war and its aftermath, with people drinking tubercular milk and taking shelter in ravaged buildings, people who had hardly forgotten the tragic insurrection of 1944.[60]

In her report of the Warsaw ghetto, she treated the Jewish uprising and subsequent German destruction of the ghetto as an event still connected to the present. Polish anti-Semitism persisted; it was, she noted, "not negligible" and certainly was motivating the remaining Jews, already fleeing the past, to leave Poland. Once again she implicitly campaigned against the treatment of displaced persons, especially the Polish Jews, the group most affected by the recent closing of the American Zone borders. Democracies, Janet felt, were everywhere threatened: "We sold one down the river at Munich and we could not save the other at Danzig. Nor does there appear to be anything much we can do today."[61] Always concerned in her letters with results rather than causes, she viewed the results of peace with mild derision. One Pole, she reported, asked her why America hadn't spoken up when their eastern border was claimed by Russia.

She finished writing her Cracow letter, a discussion of Polish Communism and nationalism, in Dahlem, a suburb of Berlin. In the town Hitler had thought an ideal locale for commuters, whose main street was called Uncle Tom's Cottage Street, she lived in one of the houses seized from the German bourgeoisie and assigned to the Allied press. The accommodations included a bedroom, salon, and bath, only two or three other journalists, a garden, and a housekeeper. Janet's housekeeper, an anti-Nazi vegetarian and nature healer, concocted salads that made her sick. But the quarters were comfortable and conducive to work, and Janet worked twelve to fourteen hours daily, sleeping little and feeling invigorated. In Aschaffenburg, she spent a weekend with Kathryn Hulme, now with the International Relief Organization, which had recently taken over from the United Nations Relief and Rehabilitation Administration. Then she was finally on her way home to Orgeval, where she planned to finish her Berlin letter.

Natalia, in the meantime, had decided to return to New York in September. Janet promised to join her later in the fall. She had not been back in almost three years, and she was ready, she hoped, to take a few months off to start her book. But when she did return to the United States, she still could not write the book that "would keep like a box on a shelf."

Soon, however, she received a token of gratitude for the work she'd done since returning to France; it was a bright ribbon, one she would wear on her lapel for the rest of her life. In the spring of 1948 Janet was invited to what she thought was a social reception. Too busy for what she considered simply a party, she declined. She later learned that the reception was a formal presentation ceremony at the Quai d'Orsay. Had she been there, she would have heard the commendation given Genêt for her years of scrupulous and passionate writing. That night Genêt was made a knight of the Légion d'Honneur.

12

Inventions Are Hastier
1948-1951

"HERS WAS TO BE a slow way of dying," said Hildegarde of Mary Flanner, "not of agony but of great tedium and frightening nervousness."[1] Kept alive by drugs — drugs for pain, drugs for sleep, drugs for the nausea the other drugs induced — Janet's mother sat in her chair by her bedroom window day after day, growing weaker and weaker, like an "old wind-battered grey moth," Janet wrote to Solita, "under a glass bell."[2] By December 3, 1947, Janet was convinced her eighty-four-year-old mother wouldn't survive another night.

Mary had been quite lucid at dinner. When Janet, who had come to California to be at her mother's side, mentioned Solita's name, her mother's face brightened in affectionate recognition. "Oh the dear girl," she said, "give her my love." And when Janet told her mother that Marie, who had also been ill, was moving to a new flat Janet was helping pay for, Mary smiled approvingly and called Janet a sweet child.[3] After dinner she retired, said goodbye to her grandson John and went to sleep. Janet read until around midnight, when she put down her book, Raoul de Roussy de Sales's *The Making of Yesterday*, and walked quietly into her mother's room. Mary was no longer breathing. Trembling, Janet returned to the living room. She didn't want to waken Hildegarde, who had asked not to be told

anything during the night, so she took out a sheet of paper and a
pen and at one-thirty began a letter. "Darling," she wrote Solita,
" . . . I am writing you first — You are the first to know." Turning
to the person she trusted most, the one she considered more reliable
than herself, she continued: "You knew her & my family of which
you were & are a part — You must not fail Hildegarde, darling —
She needs you."[4] So, apparently, did Janet.

Janet had written no letters for *The New Yorker* since the preceding
August; back in the United States, she was researching her book.
She'd settled on the Paris Commune of 1871 as her subject, and she
was reading, planning, thinking — and getting little done. She was
also gathering material for a profile of her friend Broadway producer
Cheryl Crawford. But as she was about to begin writing the profile,
in early January 1948, she found herself procrastinating "like a crab
that fiddles"; she felt that she was going nowhere: "I am nearly 56
years old and have known this condition, this set of conditions, to
operate, for at least 32 years of my 55."[5]
    Janet wrote this in a diary — her first, which she began less than
a month after her mother died. She was trying, by her own admission,
to reorganize her life, take stock of herself, and even, in a way, begin
again. Realizing that she, too, was mortal, she declared she could no
longer waste time, and in the same language she'd used in letters to
her mother over the years, Janet renewed the promises she'd made
to Mary: she'd work harder, concentrate more, do the things they
both believed she was capable of doing.
    "If I do not develop a will, a power of will this year, I never shall,
but my regrets at having failed will increase consciously and an-
nually," Janet wrote in her first journal entry.[6] She wanted to create
a pattern for her life, she said; the ability to take control of one's
life and shape it was "man's most civilized or civilizing ten-
dency. . . . It is the original formula of creation." With a pattern she
could overcome the fear, the confusion, the guilt that grew on her
like rust and made her feel like a failure in her own eyes. And the
diary, she hoped, would help discipline her, if she could find "the
will to keep it," by forcing her to preserve the thoughts that would
otherwise be lost, those ideas "contemporary to the day on which
they happened, when they were fresh like fruit, flowers or eggs."[7]

She thought about the January day she'd spent in New Jersey with Glenway Wescott and Monroe Wheeler in what she called their "phallic decorated house." Outside, the snow was deep and lined with rabbit tracks; inside, Janet and Glenway talked for an entire overheated afternoon. Agreeing that most recent fiction wasn't particularly good, Glenway said he thought the reason was self-censorship; if novelists wrote from their experience, he argued, they'd not only reveal too much about themselves, they'd probably be slapped with libel suits — especially if they were homosexual. Janet disagreed. She argued that recent novels weren't very good because no one writing paid attention to their inner lives, their daily emotions, their thoughts; no one kept diaries anymore or spent long evenings in contemplation of the day's events. As a result, she continued in the terms she'd used about herself, a writer fell back on tricks — contrivances of plot, for example — to give readers the "mere mechanics of emotions — the wheels that go round, not the small or great power that made them turn."[8]

Janet undoubtedly thought Glenway's observations interesting even as she refuted them. Surmising that her own writing lacked some essential but nameless quality, she felt that she had frequently censored herself, though not along the literal lines Glenway suggested. Perhaps, Janet wondered, she had erased "the major part of myself" and in so doing "wiped[d] out my report of everything else."[9] Although not given to extensive psychological analyses, she may have recognized her decidedly ambivalent feelings about her family and, in particular, about her mother, but she would not have supposed that these feelings necessarily inhibited her writing. She knew, of course, that as a lesbian, forced to conceal her sexual preference, "evasion" (her word) had become a way of life, but there is no direct evidence that she consciously linked this to the anxiety she experienced about her work. To Janet "evasion" had a very specific and tangible meaning: it referred to leaving her family in 1921, leaving France in 1939, leaving Noel in 1940, and always leaving Natalia.

A few weeks after her mother's death, Janet gazed out over Natalia's snow-covered terrace and tried to write the first sentence of her Cheryl Crawford profile. For a long time she couldn't come up with one. When she did, she confided to her diary that she had concocted nothing more than a "tired, inexpensive" contrast between musical comedy and literature — "surely the mechanical gimmick for an unfertile mind," she exclaimed.[10] "I LACK WILL POWER!" she declared over and over.[11] When she was able to work, however, she forgot herself and her accusations. "I love to look up at the clock over my bedroom door," she said, "& discover that an hour and forty minutes have gone by unobserved since last I looked because I was working & time didn't count, or rather I had missed its countings in what is for me the most satisfying oblivion."[12] The rewards of work were "lasting," she noted — unlike the "satisfaction of love, too brief and local to compete. There the man, usually, has the woman at a disadvantage. He has his work. She, or most of her in the world's millions, has only her memory, if it stays in shape, or a tender love achievement of which she was only half, after all. Man operates alone, woman by connection."[13]

Though happy with Natalia in New York that winter, Janet feared she was becoming passive, easily distracted, and undisciplined — a stereotypical female. "I plan to control myself and my chemistry," she said, "and then the chemistry makes me forget my plan to control it."[14] To explain her lack of will power, she reverted to traditional sexual stereotypes: men are generally active, women generally passive; men are either fools or beasts, but women are weak and dependent; where men create something solid and lasting in their work, women lose themselves in ephemeral relationships. Yet these stereotypes were traps and she knew it, because they finally failed to account for her or her feelings. Why can't there be a third sex, she once half-humorously asked her mother, a sex not dominated by muscle or the inclination to breed?[15]

To a certain extent Genêt allowed her to be that "third sex" in the public world. Neither masculine nor feminine, passive or active, Genêt was androgynous, anonymous, invented. The persona offered Janet security and identity; it gave her a form, a discipline, even what she later called a formula. It provided legitimacy, but in so doing, it may well have robbed her of her own voice; Janet on occasion suspected that Genêt kept her removed from the emotional sources her writing needed to give it ballast.[16] And she suspected that Genêt kept her not only from confronting her real thoughts and feelings but also from taking risks. She therefore wanted to create something that would be wholly and deeply hers — and something lasting. A book, not another novel, but a history, something solid, permanent, something to be proud of.

Yet Janet feared striking out on her own without *The New Yorker,* and the fear seemed to paralyze her, making her feel lazy and passive, easily distracted and out of control. As she tried to begin her book on the Paris Commune, she floundered. The feelings she experienced were by no means new to her. When she was writing *The Cubical City,* she had constantly complained that she worked slowly and with pain, that she struggled over every page, that she could write nothing but descriptions and that her descriptions were shallow. And she wrote this problem into her protagonist, Delia Poole. Passive but hard-working, pleasure-seeking but guilt-ridden, always feeling forced into subterfuges she hated but which gave her existence its structure, Delia wanted to take command of her life but couldn't. Even Delia's work gave her no lasting sense of accomplishment; a commercial artist who thumbed through the past in search of its loveliest and most exploitable visions, she recombined them into lavish sets decorating the Broadway stage. But she was only juggling surfaces. That she herself might be able to do no more than this worried Janet. Then in 1944, when she returned to Paris, this fear was replaced by a worse one. Unsure as to how she'd write about a world that had become unrecognizable, knowing that she could not write of Paris as she once had, and without any guidelines to instruct her, she was afraid she had nothing to say.

Having made no real headway on her book that winter, and ambivalent about staying in America, Janet was unable to see herself as the person she wanted to be. "What I know about me I do not wish to admit. So this knowledge is cancelled because of its unpleasantness. This basic evasion probably disbalances all my possibilities of self-information."[17] She feared she had ignored her inner life, preferring to skate on the surfaces of things; having failed to seek "news of" an "inner soul" she feared she would never be able to create anything she truly respected.[18]

On March 3, 1948, ten days before her fifty-sixth birthday, Janet sailed for France, alone. She said she felt old. The ship lurched, she slipped on the deck and cut her ankle. This, she thought, was symbolic: she lacked will power and muscular control, and her mind was slipping.[19] She wasn't really losing her memory, but she no longer felt confident of it; it was something else she could not regulate. "I forget everything," she complained to Solita. "My memory is like a piece of flypaper wh has dried & no longer catches the little flies or pretty insects either."[20] She hoped this birthday would be her last, she said — although she would still like to write the book on the Commune.

Noel had once surprised her by saying she'd like to remain absolutely observant, clear-minded, and conscious to the very end of her life. Janet wasn't so sure she agreed. Recalling their parents, Janet told Hildegarde, "I hope I don't live forever, and I hope I don't go mad."[21] As she approached the age her father was when he killed himself — an age Janet specifically described as "mortal" — she said that she herself felt limited, failed.

"The difference between 54 and 56 is," she declared on her birthday, "in my life, fatal."[22] And two months later, in a long and moving passage in her diary, she wrote, "There is a dividing line which is variable to different individuals, but upon which one's life sensibility passes its meridian, and to the body and the brain living that life, old age then sets in. In my 56th year only, have I crossed this meridian and now I know, degree by degree, that I am on the sliding, the downward slide. I try to discover what promoted this special discernment in me, what caused me to sigh 'Now' — meaning 'This is it, this is the incline, however slow, toward death.' I cannot find the exact reason or moment. I only know that before this year I was inclined upward, on to and toward perhaps ridiculous and imaginative and unattainable altitudes; they were hopes going upward and when reality, by day, was too slow and flat and agonizingly disappointing, a sort of fantasy substitute could lift me, even knowing it was false and of a dream quality and I could be relieved and inflated maybe to hope and believe in the uncertain. It was always attractive. Now that belief in this silly substitute has lost its means of being floated in my imagination and I feel doomed to my own limited reality. This should be the better because the truer state, yet I am desperate and homeless because I have now no place to go, to remove me from myself."[23]

The homeless feeling was attributable in large part to her mother's death: "the direct physical connection is finally cut," Janet observed.

"I am alone more than ever on the earth, I no longer have my ancestor — nothing but lovers."[24] Mary had believed in her daughters, encouraging them "to dream, we would be better than we are," as Janet once said.[25] And Mary had sacrificed a great deal for her children — or so her children were taught — so they might follow their artistic inclinations. These sacrifices made Janet feel unworthy, ungrateful, selfish — even duplicitous, for she was not who she was supposed to be. She felt like a fraud who had cheated her mother of everything Mary had a right to expect.

In her worst moments Janet thought she no longer belonged anywhere, with anyone. An American who had lived in Europe for as long as she had did not become a European, she once told May Sarton, but was no longer an American, either: "I am a spotted dog."[26] She had given up family and country, but without them she had nothing to define herself by. She considered altering her life in some radical way and thought of resigning from her job, returning to New York to live with Natalia, and writing her book there.

By April Janet was writing her Paris letter again, and at the end of the month she traveled to Rome to cover the Italian elections. She was active and feeling better, and the renewed activity helped restore her spirits. She spent part of the week in Orgeval, where she could relax in Noel's walled garden with old friends. She and Noel and Margaret Anderson would sit all afternoon beneath the fruit trees and talk. Afterward Janet would report to Solita, bragging a bit, that she had spoken with clarity and wisdom about European politics — and that she couldn't remember a word she'd said.

Much of the time that year she felt she couldn't work as quickly or as well as before; she needed peace of mind to concentrate and could find none. Even the loud dull drone of an airplane flying over the Opéra could disturb her. Working at her desk, she knew what the sound was, but nervously ran to the window anyway. One night she paused to admire the mist before entering her hotel. Suddenly she heard another noise, a resounding dry bang, which sounded as if it came from nearby. Frightened, the hotel porter ran out. "That was a bomb," Janet said calmly. "What an epoch," she commented to Solita. "Imagine my knowing a bomb when I hear it."[27]

"Inventions," she concluded, "are hastier than comprehensions."[28] Airplanes, bombs, the modern inventions men quickly made and thoughtlessly used, symbolized to Janet an age in which everyone hurried to produce something; an older world of contemplation and sensibility seemed to be slipping away. Even she hurried — she was not exempt from her own criticism — scrambling to get the information she needed and turn it into polished prose by a Tuesday deadline.

Determined to take control and make a decision once and for all, that spring or summer she wrote to Ross that she planned to resign by the beginning of 1949. Yet even as she typed, she must have known she couldn't leave *The New Yorker*. And she went on with business as usual, her pace never slackening. On her own initiative she went to Königstein, Germany, near Frankfurt, to cover the trial of Fritz Thyssen, the German industrialist indicted for supporting Hitler. She also visited Kathryn Hulme again in Aschaffenburg to get material for a letter on the displaced persons camp there. She and Kathryn listened to the sounds of the Berlin airlift overhead, and Kathryn answered so many questions that Janet envisioned a second piece. Her resignation letter had not altered her relationship toward her work; if anything, it had intensified it.

In September she wrote Ross again, saying she had changed her mind. She was staying on as the magazine's Paris correspondent.[29] Work "is now my second nature," she explained to Hildegarde, as if justifying her change of heart. Her decision to stay in Paris did not involve writing per se; it involved her job and her position, which gave her an automatic audience as well as the mandate she needed for writing.

The decision also involved Natalia, who had recently decided to move back to Rome. Janet was enormously relieved. She could spend three months or more with Natalia in Italy while working for *The New Yorker* as a Rome correspondent if Ross consented, which he later did. She could also leave undisturbed her arrangement with Noel, whom Janet had dreaded leaving. "I have used myself and people who loved me like victims in a series of emotional accidents," she had written sorrowfully the previous spring. "There has been blood, pain and groaning."[30]

When he learned that Janet had changed her mind, Ross cabled her immediately. They had not found — indeed, had not looked for — her replacement. He assured her she simply could not be replaced. Yet, he added, happy as he was, he was concerned about her. Kay Boyle had told him she looked very tired. Janet was in fact not feeling very well. She was complaining of headaches; she had dislocated her neck. She looked pinched, and she felt depressed and lonely. Hearing that her sister Marie, still living in New York, was again very ill with the heart ailment that had plagued her for several years, Janet wrote to Solita that she too knew "how awful it is to be lonely, even when you are with someone because you have lost yourself or lost love of yourself."[31]

Identifying with Marie, Janet said both she and her sister were incapable of giving or receiving love. The reason, she asserted, was that they did not love themselves: "Without any affection for oneself there is no communication with oneself & so I am lonely in my own heart each hour of the day & if awake at night. Nothing but regrets, errors, mistakes none of which can be loved I fancy poor Marie feels the same."[32] She considered calling Marie immediately but procrastinated, then decided against it. "I'm sure she wld start crying & that undoes me & her," Janet explained to Solita, compounding her sense of guilt. She sent several notes to the hospital and asked Solita to give Marie a check to cover her recent expenses. During the next few weeks Solita visited Marie twice, declaring she came in Janet's name.

In January 1949, the date Janet had originally targeted for leaving *The New Yorker* and one year after she had begun her journal, she declared, "I have manufactured journalism for nearly a quarter of this century. Nowadays everyone manufactures. Few create. If an individual knows the difference and I do, the failure to create leaves only one conclusion: one has manufactured."[33] "Inventions," she repeated a week later, "are hastier than comprehensions."[34] No longer, she said, could she hope to change: "One is old when one no longer believes in the possibility of change. Change won't come true, nor dreams by day, for I never dream at night and so I am wide awake for the rest of my life, eyelids open in shock and tears. I feel not only without faith in my future but I know my past has arrived and that it now becomes inescapable."[35]

Marie died the following fall when Janet was in Rome with Natalia. Hildegarde cabled the news, and Noel wired to offer Janet money if she wanted to go to New York or Indianapolis for the funeral services being held in each place. Janet didn't go. Named executrix of Marie's will, she assigned Solita the task of disposing of Marie's personal effects. Once again she turned to Solita, the person she trusted most, who had for all practical purposes become a part of her family.

When Janet returned to Paris in March of 1948, the city seemed haunted: "Such an air of doom hangs over Paris at night as brings back to me the nights, equally moon-lighted, in Bordeaux, Sept., 1939, when I was fleeing the war."[36] In the evening the streets were quiet. People were staying home and going to bed early. In Orgeval, Janet, Noel, and Noel's Czech housemate, Libousse Novak, listened to broadcasts about the Communist takeover of Czechoslovakia. They worried for Libousse's nephew, not the one studying in Paris but the younger one, in Czechoslovakia, who'd recently been attacked by a Communist classmate, who slashed his face. The boy, they thought, should leave Prague, but if he did, his father would surely lose both his ration card and his job. And his mother, an outspoken anti-Communist, might be arrested.

Decidedly anti-Communist herself, Janet equated Soviet Communism with Stalinism, and Marxism with Soviet totalitarianism. She could be quite narrow about this. When she and Mary McCarthy first met in Rome sometime after the war, she made "what I thought were very stupid remarks about Edmund Wilson," recalls McCarthy. "She said he was a Communist in her categorical way, and I took fairly sharp exception with it."[37] Janet believed that the Russians innately possessed what she called an "impulse for conquest," and although the economic damage they suffered during the war had temporarily suppressed it, it was always to be reckoned with.[38] She was therefore convinced that Soviet power in Europe must be politically and economically "contained." Yet at the same time she agreed with Monica Stirling, who said that anti-Communism was just as deforming as Communism.[39] People supported one side of something simply because they disliked its opposite, she complained to May Sarton, tired of the Cold War and the simplistic judgments it fostered.[40]

Writing a "Letter from Naples" in March 1949, Janet strongly criticized what she felt were the priorities of the Marshall Plan:

subsidizing hotels, not museums or excavations, and pandering to the comforts of tourists at the expense of culture.[41] The Naples letter was cut by her editors to temper her criticism of the Marshall Plan, which Ross decided was too oracular. Her job was reportage, he told her, not interpretation, and, anyway, he thought she was becoming more and more socialist. She agreed. Perhaps she had been a bit pontifical, and it was true that of late she had been far more engaged by the socialists than by any other political group. "I am a socialist," she declared (to herself). Socialism represented the future. As if it could reverse her sense that the past had arrived, she emphatically claimed, "Tomorrow is my party."[42]

With its pacifism, its plan of gradual reforms, and its humanism, socialism now represented the most "female-minded party," she noted.[43] She considered this "female-minded" aspect more important than the economic or political aspects of socialism. She was willing to embrace what she'd earlier denounced as socialism's impractical idealism, especially since men excluded women, as she told Hildegarde, and that was why they made wars "when women would never have done so."[44] She had heard that during the war, Italian women threw garbage out of the palace windows onto the heads of the *fascisti,* and she so liked the story that she copied it into her diary. It suggested to her that women were practical and humane, not given to abstract theorizing and the production of violence. If men exerted brute strength, the strength of ambition, conquest and war, women sustained life. "Men are strong and women are necessary," Janet concluded.[45]

Although she suspected that her views continued to worry her editors, she had their permission to begin a profile of Léon Blum, leader of the French socialists and, during the doomed Third Republic, France's first socialist and Jewish prime minister. He was a man Janet respected for his intellect, his idealism, his feminism, and his pacifism, and she very much wanted to do this profile. Blum was not exactly a substitute for her book, but he was an unusual man whose life began at the time of the Paris Commune and continued beyond the occupation; his life was bound to French history.

Because *The New Yorker* informally stipulated that profiles be written only about living figures, Janet remembered making sure that Ross promised he'd publish her piece even if Blum died while she was writing it. Later she said she could not imagine beginning the profile without such an assurance: she knew Blum was ill and wanted to warn her editors. In fact, he was recuperating from surgery in the spring of 1949 when Janet's friend Doda Conrad arranged an interview. Blum, who had only just begun receiving visitors, greeted them in his elegant green dressing robe, Janet reported. He talked to her about his views on Communism — unfavorable, she said — and the Fourth Republic, which he criticized. He seemed to be eulogizing France, she later wrote, but he still firmly believed in socialism and, of course, free speech. She liked him. He "had seen history, made history, and suffered from history."[46]

The work for the profile was underway. That summer Janet carried her notes for the piece wherever she and Natalia went. But she said she needed Solita's help with it, and offered to pay her passage from America to Paris in the fall.[47] After arriving in October, Solita moved with Janet into rooms at the Hôtel Vendôme and stayed seven weeks. She ran errands, visited the exhibits Janet wrote about for the Paris letter, typed as Janet dictated, and edited parts of the Blum profile. It was seven good and happy weeks — in spite of the death of Solita's teacher Gurdjieff — and Janet was depressed when Solita left. Their lives had been "deranged" by so much — time, distance, other lovers, she commented sadly.[48]

Shortly after Solita sailed, Janet moved to a red and white mansard room at the Hôtel Continental, rue de Castiglione, where she would live for the next twenty years. It was a tiny, cluttered affair, with a bed, a divan, a boulle buffet, and a pale wood chiffonier whose two missing bottom drawers Janet filled with books. She could see the Tuileries gardens from her high window, if she raised herself up to it, which one of her guests doubted she ever did.[49] Others who visited her over the years wondered how she could possibly find enough room to sleep, it was so jammed with books, newspapers, parcels, drawings, manuscripts, and miscellaneous papers. But she could walk out onto a small balcony and look over the city whenever she wished.

She continued to work on the Blum profile. That winter she sent Solita a copy of the first installment, and Solita wired that the profile in its present form was superb. But Janet thought it too cumbersome, cluttered, even too historical. She waited anxiously for Shawn's response. He cabled telling her that the piece possessed all the profundity of her work on Pétain and had a freshness of its own.

When Léon Blum died in March 1950, Ross wanted to cancel the profile. Janet reminded him that he had been warned about Blum's poor health and that he'd promised that he'd run the profile posthumously if necessary. Ross could not recall making any such promise, and neither she nor the *New Yorker* office had any memo relating to such a promise. More than two months passed. ("The longer ross waits to decide obviously the more he wastes time thus making sure blum will be indeed too very very dead to use in magazine," she told Solita.)[50] In the meantime Simon Michael Bessie of Harper and Row expressed interest in publishing the manuscript, and Janet contacted Blanche Knopf to see if she would consider it. But she wanted to know first what *The New Yorker* would do.

When Shawn wrote to her of the editorial decision, he encouraged her to finish the piece but said that in all likelihood the magazine would not run it.[51] However, they would pay her for it anyway. They did not, he reiterated, recollect any promise to print it. In addition, neither he nor Ross recalled consenting to a four-part profile; they would therefore pay her for what they remembered, which was three parts, unless she objected.

Of course, he added, she was free to sell the finished profile to another magazine if she wished. And they would certainly help her contact publishers if she desired. In fact, a book that contrasted Blum and Pétain might be even better; she could call it "Two Frenchmen," or, if she included her piece on Bedaux, "Three Frenchmen." (Janet thought both ideas "idiotic." As far as she was concerned, there was no need to drag Pétain in again.)[52] But Shawn insisted that Blum on his own was an unsuitable subject for *The New Yorker:* he was dead, for one thing, and the projected profile was too long, for another; in addition, Shawn added, Blum was a foreigner and a socialist.[53] It was the combination of these four elements, he stressed, that killed her piece.

Without *The New Yorker*'s, or at least Ross's and Shawn's, faith in the article, Janet found it difficult to complete. There was no reason, she finally concluded, to keep arguing. If Ross thought that Blum, being dead, was passé, then she would defer to his judgment. She thought it ridiculous to continue working on a piece that would never see print — that is, in *The New Yorker*. The matter of Blum was dropped; much of what she had written appeared in a Paris letter published on the first anniversary of his death. Janet was not able to step outside the magazine, either for the Paris Commune or for Léon Blum.

The issue behind the Blum misunderstanding was not really one of magazine policy, nor was it simply a matter of a misremembered promise. Janet was well aware that the battle over Blum was being fought for ideological reasons. Shawn was sending Janet a message, one made obvious by the comment at the end of his letter: the "mood of the country" had changed, and Janet seemed out of touch with it. He and Ross thought she ought to return to New York for a visit. Janet thought she knew what they meant; she was being asked to return because of her politics.

Janet arranged to sail on October 28, 1950. When she arrived at the *New Yorker* office, Ross turned to her gruffly and asked why she had come; he was working on the "damned Christmas issue" and couldn't talk to her before next year.[54] She reminded him that he himself had asked her to return — for "reorientation."

He finally did talk to her but didn't mention politics directly. He paced up and down his office, speaking in short outbursts. Janet realized he was disappointed that this war had not produced the happy stories or the comradely memories of the last one, his war. No one, he told her, could believe in the French any longer, not even her, he shouted, "and it shows in every go'damn word you write."[55] She answered that after the first few days of peace, no one had felt the same way about anyone anymore. She offered to resign. Ross mumbled apologies. She later thought he was worried about her, about what would happen to her if there were another war. But at the time she was confused, even hurt. Noting Janet's disappointment, Katharine White diplomatically referred to Ross's poor health.

She put the trip behind her, and returned to France, where there was work to do. She had begun a new profile before she left, a nonpolitical one that would certainly not come under the same editorial and political scrutiny as Blum had. This was a profile of Henri

Matisse, and Janet was excited. She hadn't written about a painter since her ill-timed Picasso profile in 1939, which she thought she'd ultimately botched. More enthusiastic about Matisse's work than she had been about Picasso's, she eagerly set out to interview him in the late winter of 1951. Janet carried enormous bunches of stiff red carnations from the nearby flower market in Nice to her hostess, the young writer Célia Bertin, who had helped arrange the meeting.[56]

Despite Janet's enthusiasm for the piece and Matisse's cooperation, the next few months were difficult. While working on the profile she went twice to Italy to be with Natalia. Natalia had been offered a job in New York with the publisher Arnoldo Mondadori and was considering a permanent move back to the United States. When she decided to sail in July, Janet again sank into a depression.[57] The self-recriminations returned: she was not fulfilling her own expectations; she had to struggle more and more with each sentence she wrote; she felt old; she could compose while talking but never while writing; sometimes she could not even recall what she said. "There is such a difference between wishing you were dead and wishing you were not alive," Janet wrote. "I wish both. I am at the depth of my comprehension of myself and of my strength to climb out of me, like a moat or a gutter."[58] She was disgusted with her continual intellectualizing of her emotions, but she could conceive of no other way to explain her feelings. Yet even this habit failed her at crucial moments, leaving her to "sit and weep," a slave to emotions she did not understand. She would go out on her balcony and look over the purplish foliage, her eyes filling with tears. "I suffer so from sheer sadness," she said, "that I can hardly stand being alive." Could she or would she, she wondered, "settle" her anguish with suicide.[59]

That fall she wrote Solita that she was exhausted from worry — "I dont start my [New Yorker] letters early enough, I know it, but cant control me. I am part crazy all the time."[60] She had written a Paris letter about the Supreme Headquarters, Allied Powers, Europe (SHAPE), located fifteen miles outside Paris, but after she mailed it, she couldn't sleep. It was no good, she thought, as she tossed and turned. At dawn, unable to bear it any longer, she got up and cabled Shawn not to run the letter. He cabled back reassuringly: it seemed fine to him.[61]

Calling William Shawn and Harold Ross her "most perfect gyro-
scopes," Janet completely respected and depended on their editorial
instincts. She had recently begun to think that Ross's editorial arteries
were hardening, as she put it, so she turned more and more to William
Shawn, whose skills she believed could get her out of any stylistic
problem. She did not, for example, think the writing of the second,
final, installment of the Matisse profile particularly good when she
mailed it to him in October, but she was sure he would take care of
it.[62] He did: "My choices of line history placing period explanation
etc were perfectly comprehended," she wrote Solita, "wh considering
that writing is less attractive in part 2 shows his skill in penetration."[63]

With the profile finished, Janet turned her attention to reading
Margaret Anderson's new volume of memoirs, *The Fiery Fountains*,
a book Solita had carefully edited. She was astonished at how Margaret made the reader "believe in love." The book also revived Janet's
memory of their years together in Paris before the war; as Margaret
put it, she "tried never to let a day go by without turning it into a
trance." ("Surely no egotist has ever written with such embroidered
placidity of her ego," Janet told Solita.[64])

But Janet genuinely admired the book and wrote to tell Margaret
so. At the end of her letter she apologized for what she feared might
have sounded like "stiff-gestured" praise. Harold Ross had died on
December 6, 1951, after undergoing surgery in Boston. "I am so
drowned, so hit, by Ross'es [*sic*] death that I reach unsteadily, stiffly
for words, like logs," she explained to Margaret. "I am out of my
element," she continued, "& trying to save myself which is what all
of us on the magazine feel —."[65] She remembered that on her last
visit to New York she had found him changed, distracted and un-
interested. Then she recalled one day when, on a whim, she'd decided
to drop by his office. As she entered, he looked up from his desk
and smiled; he'd just been thinking of her, he'd said, and should try
to see her more often. He asked if there was anything particular on
her mind. Janet said no, just that she saw him so infrequently, she
thought she'd come in to take a long look at him.[66]

Whatever their differences over the years, her basic feelings for
and trust in Ross had never altered. Ross had changed everything,
she told Kay Boyle. He had changed news because he had changed
the writing of it; he had changed laughter because he had changed

humor. And, she concluded, "he changed us." Without Ross, she told Katharine White, she again felt "homeless" — almost the same way she felt after her mother died.[67] After all, he had changed Janet Flanner by inventing someone for her to be. "The loss of my inventor," she confided to Kay, "is more personal than that of my procreator, by far."[68]

13

The Voices of Silence
1952-1955

JANET WAS NOT ALONE in viewing Harold Ross as a literary patriarch. Ralph Ingersoll, one of the first managing editors of *The New Yorker,* called him the "total father image" — idolized, imitated, ridiculed, criticized, but always defended.[1] Any successor of Ross's would have to not only wield a skillful editorial baton but also play paterfamilias to what Katharine White called the magazine's "family" of contributors. That William Shawn could do this shouldn't have surprised anyone. On the staff of the magazine since 1933, promoted by 1939 to managing editor, and by the time of Ross's illness groomed to take his place, Shawn was self-effacing, deferential toward writers, overwhelmingly courteous, and a talented, diplomatic editor. He was also, like Ross, a father figure, albeit one of a different kind. His style was less confrontational. More studious and withdrawn than Ross, less interested in humor, he'd express his displeasure more covertly. Ross might stride directly into a writer's office barking questions; Shawn would send a delicately worded memo. Certainly he would not threaten the fundamental integrity of the family; if anything, he would work diligently to strengthen its bonds.

Janet too felt that *The New Yorker* had become her family and sometimes went as far as to say she felt married to it.[2] But she was a bit wary of returning to New York during the first few months of its reorganization and so waited to sail until early February 1952, planning to spend time with Natalia in New York and visit Hildegarde in California. The trip went well, and Janet appeared composed and exuberant, as she always did in public; the *Los Angeles Times* reported that, dressed in a chic black velvet pants suit, "the gal's got charm."[3]

She returned in May to a Paris crowded with the activities of the First Congress of Cultural Freedom. Unable to get seats at the international writers' conference to hear André Malraux and William Faulkner speak, Janet and Kay Boyle stood in the balcony aisles to hear Malraux hold the audience spellbound, putting Faulkner to shame as far as they were concerned. Janet covered this event for *The New Yorker* as well as a myriad of other topical affairs — the annual rose show, the productions at the Opéra, and a book she had just finished reading, Marguerite Yourcenar's *Memoirs of Hadrian*. She also continued to comment on political events, for example, the Communist riots protesting the arrival of General Matthew Ridgway, Douglas MacArthur's replacement in Korea. She noted that the rioting equaled the 1927 demonstrations for Sacco and Vanzetti.

Most likely it was Nancy Cunard and Kay Boyle, not General Ridgway, who reminded Janet of 1927. They were both visiting Paris and joined Janet for a reunion of sorts. The three women, friends for over twenty-five years, were still bound by mutual admiration and affection; in particular Janet respected Nancy's and Kay's unswerving commitments to their visions of a better world, commitments unshaded by the doubts she frequently detected in herself. Yet she also thought they sometimes simplified complex issues by seeing them reductively, as matters of black and white, bad and good.[4] Of course, neither Kay nor Nancy would have agreed; they saw themselves as activists, champions of liberty and the disenfranchised. At the end of the war, when Nancy met Kay in London, the two of them proudly wearing the uniforms of Britain and America, respectively, Nancy looked at Kay and laughingly asked, "How in the world did we get on the side of authority?"[5]

Janet had first met Kay in the late twenties at a small party given by Djuna Barnes. The tall and majestic Kay was living in Raymond Duncan's commune of artists and hangers-on, desperately trying to support herself and her young daughter by selling sandals and scarves

in one of the colony's gift shops. Janet had briefly known the father
of Kay's child, the tubercular poet Ernest Walsh, and had disliked
him, Boyle recalls, because several years earlier he had wanted to
marry Hildegarde.[6] But Janet had liked the fiery Boyle (with hair
like "marble statues" Janet said); she was someone who had "viability
in her beliefs" — maybe having six children, Janet later speculated,
"gave her greater human belief in people than perhaps I had, having
no child."[7] Kay seemed never to hesitate to say exactly what she
thought; she would give whatever she had even when she had nothing; she appeared to face the world with courage and love. And Janet
respected Kay's ability to size up a situation squarely and feel, so it
seemed to Janet, undivided. Hers was a "Lincolnian" devotion to
democracy, of the sort, "she & I were brought up in, in the middle
west."[8]

In 1952, as the three friends sat over hot drinks and wine, they
talked about Senator Joseph McCarthy. Kay and her third husband,
Joseph Franckenstein, were themselves a target of the newest round
of witch hunts. An Austrian by birth who had left just before the
Anschluss, Franckenstein was an American war hero decorated by
the Office of Strategic Services. For his current job in the Liaison
and Security Office at the United States military installation in Bad
Godesberg, Germany, he needed a security clearance. Proceedings
had been initiated to grant him one, but then charges of a vague
nature had been leveled against him. The real issue, everyone suspected, was "loyalty." By signing Executive Order 9835 in 1947,
Harry Truman had established a loyalty and security program for all
federal employees and had revived the attorney general's list of "subversive" organizations.

Kay explained to Nancy and Janet that as she was not a State
Department employee, she ordinarily would not have been called
before the Consular Board in Bad Godesberg. However, she herself
constituted one of the charges against her husband: she was accused
of being a card-carrying Communist and of having endorsed so-called
subversive organizations, mainly because, as she recalled, she had
sent a ten-dollar check to a bill of rights rally in New York sponsored
by Eleanor Roosevelt and Paul Robeson. Janet, who thought the
allegations vicious and absurd, was happy to write a "character notice"
in support of Kay. "My word," she commented, "what have we come

to, giving statements out that we do not put silver spoons in our pockets at State department dinner parties."[9]

There seemed, however, no cause for undue alarm. That summer of 1952 Janet divided her time between Paris and Orgeval and continued to work on her fortnightly Paris letter. But again she wasn't feeling well. A recurring pain in her shoulder made writing difficult, and she complained of trouble with her liver and gall bladder. After she and Noel visited Nancy in her new home (a country wreck, Janet thought) at La Mothe Fénélon near Souillac, she apologized for having been so preoccupied; she hadn't talked or listened well, she explained, for she'd been ill, unable to eat for days and certainly not able to take much alcohol.[10] Worried, she tried not to inhale when smoking, but Noel finally insisted Janet see a specialist. He diagnosed a slight sclerosis of the liver, put her on a diet, and told her to stop drinking altogether. She did, temporarily.

The illness depressed her, leaving her breathless with the self-doubt that still assailed her. She had "wasted her life," she confided to Solita, making "events sound served in a glass with ice. I cld cry my eyes out too late —."[11] But the period of despair, though intense, was relatively short-lived and by August, when her health was better, so was her mood. She visited Natalia in Italy, and felt calmer and more soothed in her company. She preferred inviting Natalia to Paris only when Noel was away so that those two wouldn't berate each other — "a treat," she said.[12]

On returning to Paris and learning that Katharine White had nearly died of hepatitis that same summer, she immediately wrote Katharine a long, encouraging letter. She included Kay's latest news: Kay and Joseph were scheduled for a loyalty-security trial in Germany at the end of October. Janet reiterated that she thought the charges nonsensical and cruel.[13] Kay looked drawn and had lost fourteen pounds, Janet later reported to Solita, but was somewhat encouraged because she could present several impressive letters of character reference from friends and colleagues, including Drew Middleton of the *New York Times* and Janet. Yet the charges remained a grim sign of the times, all the more disturbing to Janet because she considered Kay a genuine democrat and a "bright guiding pillar of light."[14]

Janet offered to go to Germany to testify on Kay's behalf. In October Noel drove her to Bad Godesberg, the small, unbombed

town on the Rhine where Kay and Joseph lived in one of the modern
apartment buildings on the treeless streets — wide enough, Janet
was told, to use as runways in case the town had to be evacuated.[15]
The place seemed cold and unfriendly, the proceedings inane. The
day before her arrival, Joseph had been questioned about his employment as a swimming instructor in a New York summer camp,
later identified as a Communist-front organization. He told the
judges he occasionally took the boys on walks. What did he talk
about with the boys, the judges asked. About plant life and trees,
he answered. How, the judges pursued, did he, a foreigner, know
the names of American trees?[16]

At three in the afternoon on October 21, a car came to Janet's
inn to take her to the building near the Rhine where the hearing
was being held. She sat with an ashen Kay in the stenographer's room
until she was called and then walked into the courtroom, nodding
at the solemn group of judges, one who seemed made of wood,
another of cement.[17] Smiling comfortably, she instructed the gentlemen to please be seated.[18] Then, introduced as a *New Yorker* correspondent and a "known anti-Communist" by Kay and Joseph's
lawyer, Janet answered questions for about an hour on topics that
ranged from Kay's character to whether she thought Hemingway had
been political when he was in Spain. (She enjoyed telling friends that
she had suggested the judge read *For Whom the Bell Tolls* and decide
for himself; this, however, does not appear in the transcript of her
testimony.)[19] She outlined the atmosphere of Paris in the twenties
and then told her inquisitors that the American colony there had
been a demonstrably "non-political group." Among them, Kay had
served as "a central animation . . . sensitive to the development of
French literature and to French thinking." She made much of Kay's
being stamped with an indigenous midwestern libertarianism; in fact,
being with Kay, Janet said, was "like going back home without having
to take the boat."[20]

The members of the board then questioned Janet about Kay's
relationship with *The New Yorker,* about the ideological content of
Kay's writing, and about her support for the Loyalists in Spain. Janet
explained the difference between anti-Fascism and pro-Communism
to the judges, who struck her as singularly uninformed; she also
made sure to include them in her sweeping reference to people of

"good conscience" who naturally hated Fascism. When asked if Kay could be considered "politically naive," she tartly replied that Kay was "no milksop, somebody you wind around your finger like a little bandage." At the end of the hearing, the judges thanked Janet solemnly, one admitting he was a fan of her Paris letters.

She felt she had done well, that her testimony was strong, unequivocal, well-planned, and spirited. "My intention," she wrote Solita, "was to be as quick, strong & light as possible, to counteract gloom, to give a shock of differentness from Joseph and Kay, who had been in hearing all the day before & were paralyzed by melancholy."[21] She left Bad Godesberg as satisfied as she could be, under the circumstances.

But according to Kay Boyle, Janet's decision to testify was motivated by more than friendship or simple outrage at the whole investigation; she was also angry at *The New Yorker*'s lukewarm, waffling support of Kay.[22] Of all the letters in Kay's dossier from employers, friends, and colleagues, *The New Yorker*'s were the weakest, and they were the first the prosecution had asked to see. Worse, they appeared to damn with faint praise: William Shawn, who reportedly didn't write until Boyle's agent called him, finally sent a letter saying Kay was indeed employed by *The New Yorker* and that he had always taken her loyalty for granted; Gus Lebrano, the magazine's fiction editor and the one who had called Kay politically naive, said it was perfectly likely Kay had been the unwitting tool of a foreign power; Katharine White had not written at all.[23]

Janet had told no one on *The New Yorker* of her decision to testify. She later explained her actions to Katharine White by saying she had gone to Bad Godesberg simply as a friend, not as a representative of the magazine. This was true, and it's perfectly likely she didn't mention her decision because she thought it unnecessary and irrelevant. But it's also reasonable to assume that she wanted no one to know — she may have feared she'd be persuaded not to testify. In any event, when she returned from Germany, according to Boyle, she received a cable from William Shawn telling her that her action had jeopardized the reputation of the magazine. Janet was so upset, Solita told Kay, she cried all night and all the next day.[24]

Sometime that December Janet heard that the case against Kay and Joseph would probably be settled in their favor. But she also

heard that Kay was still being harassed. The American Civilian Occupied Forces in Germany announced a new regulation forbidding
government employees and their families from writing for publication. This regulation, which seemed directly pointed at Kay, also
affected her friend Sonia Tamara, foreign correspondent for the New
York *Herald Tribune.* Tamara's husband, Judge William Clark, chief
judge of the Court of Appeals under the Allied High Commission
in Frankfurt, was outraged. He protested the regulation, and the
clause was tactfully withdrawn, or at least never enforced. Then Kay
delivered news that affected Janet more personally: *The New Yorker*
had not renewed Kay's accreditation as a foreign correspondent.

What, Janet asked herself, did the magazine's fair-minded, noble,
and spirited disdain for McCarthyism mean if it did not mean action?
What, she asked herself, did the magazine represent? It was, after
all, no more than a group of people working together, united by
common concerns. But did it not also represent a dedication to good
writing and clear thinking, to freedom of speech and thought, and —
as Janet believed — to responsible action? She wondered if the magazine hadn't shirked its responsibilities to one of its writer-family.

She was deeply disturbed. Basic laws of civility, moral responsibility, and compassion had been breached. She considered that *The
New Yorker*'s handling of Kay's accreditation — indeed, the handling
of the entire trial — violated an almost sacred trust. Her pride in the
magazine and her pride in working for it were seriously threatened;
her disillusionment was, as she told Boyle, "like having fallen out of
love."[25] Early that winter, Janet saw Kay in Paris. "Kay," Janet had
said to her, "you know what I want to do; I want to resign. But you
have a husband, six children, a home; I just have *The New Yorker*.
Let's never speak of this again."[26] Boyle said they never did.

But if Janet did not want to resign, she did want the situation
clarified. She cabled Katharine White, instructing her to show the
cable to others, and wrote a long letter to explain what the magazine's
canceling of Kay's accreditation would mean to Kay and Joseph's
future. It was no less than the kiss of death, Janet argued, for in a
very real sense it branded Kay as a traitor and suggested that the
magazine wanted to discontinue its association with her. In fact, she
said, the magazine's action suggested out-and-out desertion.

In her answer White calmly listed the reasons for the unalterable decision. The magazine was not deserting Kay; everything that reasonably and honestly could have been done for her had been done. Nor did the letters of support written for Kay, White added, contain the "weakening over-statement" that some of the other letters of support had. (Katharine herself had not written, she regretted, because she was ill in Maine.) As for Kay's accreditation, it had originally been renewed years earlier even though Ross and the other editors felt they had not bought enough of Kay's material to warrant it. Ross had renewed because, as he told White, Kay "had 'so goddam many kids.' "[27] However, Ross did not know that Kay was not a full-time employee, which apparently she should have been to receive accreditation. Therefore, renewing the accreditation would constitute a fraud; it would be a "deception of our government," White argued, and would endanger all the magazine's foreign correspondents, Janet included. Moreover, it should not be forgotten that Shawn did renew Kay's first-reading agreement, "which should show Kay that we want to buy her work and consider her a member of our special contributors' family."[28]

The refusal to renew had not been handled abruptly or evasively, Katharine continued. The *New Yorker* office had not communicated to Kay directly because Kay herself had been communicating through her agent. The office merely followed suit. In addition, Katharine said that she and the other editors were miffed because Kay had never acknowledged the receipt of their letters; nor had she told anyone of the outcome of the hearing. Katharine also added that she wished that Janet had communicated more directly about her decision to testify. If she were trying to spare William Shawn, as Janet had said, then she was "entirely wrong . . . if you think Bill wants to be spared involvement in any contributor's or staff writer's personal problems and I do think you owed Bill the courtesy of letting him in on your decision."[29]

The disagreement was political and personal, institutional and familial. Janet had separated herself from the institution, or so she thought, with her individual act of conscience. She firmly believed that where institutions, for whatever reason, could not act, individuals still could. Shawn and White, however, felt obliged to remind Janet that her private actions had to be regarded institutionally. The individual was part of a family, and Janet was not a free agent. She herself had acknowledged to Katharine that *The New Yorker* was "my only family circle in all these expatriate years."[30] She did not want to lose that family and had to find a way to balance its demands with her own.

Janet responded at the end of March 1953 with a long letter addressed to both White and Shawn. It was a diplomatic letter, generous, kind, and unflinching. She ignored the technical arguments in the accreditation issue and instead discussed her and the magazine's involvement in the affair. Kay had initially contacted her, she said, because she was a close friend and "the only other member in Europe of the New Yorker family to which by pride & previous performance she felt she still belonged." Janet said she understood that Shawn did not know Kay well enough to have written much of a reference, but she could not agree that the letters of support sent in Kay's behalf from her non-*New Yorker* colleagues had been full of "weakening over-statement, as you say"; they were simply, Janet argued, the kind of evidence needed to counter the insane and solemn charges of disloyalty. Calling Kay "politically naive," as Gus Lebrano had, might have been considered humorous if the stakes were not so high. As it was, such a statement was a "poor, unliberal recommendation" from someone who did know Kay Boyle, and it was a poor recommendation from *The New Yorker*. "These, dear Katharine and Bill," she emphatically stated, "are the facts."[31]

Janet again stressed that she had gone to Bad Godesberg as a private individual, and that she had not told Bill Shawn so as to protect him when he was already carrying a heavy and complex burden at the magazine. "I don't know what there is about Bill," she wrote, "that makes some of us, makes me certainly, feel he must be protected from rough air though we really know he can stand like a rock." She hadn't wanted him to worry about whether or not he had acted adequately. And, she added, if she were to do it all again, she would behave no differently. In conclusion Janet urged that they all forget the entire episode. She said she definitely believed in White's and Shawn's good will and felt that their different opinions should not affect their friendship.[32]

Of course, the matter could not be immediately forgotten by anyone. Shawn was perturbed and offended. In a five-page, single-spaced letter in April — a "document," Janet called it — he outlined his motives and intentions: he had not known Miss Boyle as an "intimate friend" and could therefore not attest to her loyalty "sweepingly"; he would not write a "dishonest" letter, for it would be wrong, as he put it, to "testify falsely to somebody's innocence for fear he might later be proved innocent." "Constitutionally" unable to renew Boyle's accreditation, he reminded Janet that the magazine had in no way dissociated itself from Kay. Furthermore, he did not understand the uproar about the simple phrase "politically naive," since anyone not pro-Communist who was involved with "a pro-Communist organization" was obviously politically naive. Finally, he felt Janet should have consulted the magazine before going to Bad Godesberg, but he understood that in her "warm-heartedness," she had acted emotionally.[33]

That April Katharine also responded to Janet's charges; she could not drop any of the issues, especially since "we are in a position to be attacked from all sides — by the inveterate witch hunters, by liberals who are more interested in general principles than in specific facts, and even by you, whom we like to think we can count on in the pinches."[34] Janet realized that the whole matter had hit Katharine hard. She apologized to Katharine for having hurt Gus Lebrano, although she reiterated that even if his intentions were good, his letter was not. And she apologized for having sounded patronizing toward Shawn. But she did not change her position, and she did not countenance the excuse Shawn had given her — that she had acted emotionally.[35]

In the fall Katharine wrote again, saying that she was finally able to write her own letter — with Bill's permission, she added — to tell Janet how she felt. All the earlier letters had been public ones, Katharine confessed, "read and edited and fine-tooth-combed by all." She was writing now, more or less on her own, because she truly loved Janet and could not bear to lose her friendship: "You are really now my oldest friend and colleague and I simply cannot bear to have a rift between us now." She did not want to allow "these modern times and their tensions and . . . the feeling that every word one writes must be weighed and measured" to destroy their feelings for one another.[36]

In her reply Janet agreed with Katharine that McCarthyism poisoned everything and everyone it touched. She also agreed that technical arguments, the weighing and balancing of phrases, the scrupulousness of statement and rejoinder was an "apothecary-like" habit, capable at best of measuring feelings and actions in terms of profits and losses, advantages won or lost. In practice, this was a malicious way of protecting oneself from the Fascism ("which is what it is Kay [Katharine White], make no mistake") of McCarthyism. Then she added a striking analogy. She said she was ashamed of her country and particularly of those "best ones" who kept silent, as the French had in 1940.[37]

During this time Janet continued to cover French news for her Paris letter and was intending to write a *New Yorker* profile of Jean-Paul Sartre, whom she had met. She had obtained both his permission and the consent of the magazine but knew that Sartre's Communist affiliations might give Shawn grounds for canceling the piece. As it turned out, it was Sartre who withdrew permission first. He said he could no longer cooperate with her because the magazine had lately become reactionary.

Oddly enough, Janet assumed that he was not in fact annoyed with *The New Yorker;* despite Kay's recent experience, it was evidently still difficult for Janet to imagine anyone seriously criticizing the magazine as a whole. She assumed he was censuring her for one of her recent Paris letters. To give her readers a sample of what she saw as laughable and self-indicting propaganda, she had quoted the Communist newspaper *L'Humanité* at length in her flippant report on the French Communist party's denunciation of comrades Andrés Marty and Charles Tillon.[38] She joked that party members were invited to express their opinions only when their opinions didn't contradict party dogma. A condescending letter, it obviously wouldn't have pleased Sartre.

Janet, however, had already begun to worry that Sartre might not be a suitable subject either for her or for *The New Yorker* and had already written Shawn to that effect. When Sartre canceled, she had a new subject ready: André Malraux, who had impressed her and Kay when he spoke at the Writers Congress. Now that he was de Gaulle's right-hand man, he would be even more appropriate, and Janet was fascinated by his erudition, his former ties to the Left, and the shroud of mystery that seemed to envelop him. Her research did nothing to dispel the mystery or her respect for him. When she interviewed him for two hours at his home in Boulogne-sur-Seine, he rapidly covered so many topics, from Trotsky to German prisoner-of-war camps, from Nietzsche to Chinese music, from Lawrence of Arabia to the Spanish Civil War, that the stenographer she'd brought filled fifty-two typewritten pages.[39] Years later Janet said Malraux was the only genius she'd ever met.[40]

She was overwhelmed, not only by Malraux, but by the sheer volume of information surrounding him, information that gave away little about him. Malraux was willing to talk to her more as he learned to trust her, but no one, she discovered, wanted to dispel the man's myths — and that was what she had hoped to do. Those closest to him divulged little of a personal nature. Anecdotal information therefore had to be obtained from unexpected sources, including the staff of the Hôtel Continental, who were quite fond of Janet. One of the floor waiters, when he learned she was working on an article about Malraux, rushed to give her a picture postcard of the chateau where his brother had hid Malraux during the war; the brother also lent him money, she was told, which Malraux repaid as soon as the war was over.

She alternated work on Malraux with her Paris letters, suggesting to Shawn that as a sort of stunt she would do one describing seven of France's political parties. After she worked on it until nearly dawn for six days, the completed letter ran to seven columns, her longest ever, but she regarded the whole thing as dull and contrived. The United States Army did not agree; the Military Academy at West Point requested ten reprints of the article to use in a course on foreign governments. The National War College also requested reprints for required reading in a similar course.

She also went briefly to Strasbourg to cover the debates over the proposed European Defense Community, and in May she was collating the opinions of the French press for an anti-McCarthy letter. Although she did not explicitly state her personal views, it was obvious that she agreed with the outraged Europeans she quoted; she noted that the French Communists had "not lifted one stick of type" against McCarthy.[41]

The whirlwind visit to Germany of McCarthy's investigators Roy Cohn and David Schine, who presumably looked through all the loyalty-security hearing files, cost Joseph Franckenstein his job, even though both he and Kay had been cleared by the Consular Board. Kay and Joseph returned to the United States, but not before Kay visited with Janet and Nancy and Solita in Paris in June. Again the old friends sat together and talked over drinks at a café; again they heard shouts. Protestors were demonstrating in front of the American Embassy against the execution of Ethel and Julius Rosenberg. Janet thought she heard shots that night from her balcony.

After Kay left Paris, Janet wrote to her often, frequently reminding her of friends who wanted to help in some way. Thornton Wilder gave Janet a check for the Franckensteins, explaining that money earned from art should be shared by other artists. In courtly fashion he had entrusted Janet with the check because she knew Kay better, he said, and because he did not want to intrude.[42] Carson McCullers was also concerned. Although she and Kay were no longer the friends they once had been, she authorized Janet to deliver her own strong statement of support.[43]

Janet had stayed friendly with Carson and Reeves McCullers, who in the spring of 1952 had moved to a small house in the village of Bachvillers, near Paris, where Janet visited them at least once. Three strokes had numbed the left side of Carson's body and destroyed the lateral vision in her left eye, but her willfulness was unchecked. Janet still considered her brilliant and mercurial, but now Carson had become physically as well as emotionally demanding. One always had to draw the line with Carson, Kay said, and Janet was able to do this.[44] She might help Carson repack her clothes, but she would not be cajoled into giving her a bath.[45] And the spectacle of the couple's excessive drinking, their quarrels, and their self-destructiveness continued to trouble Janet, as it did all their friends. By the fall of 1953 their domestic situation had grown much worse: Carson was badgering Reeves; Reeves was drinking heavily and frightening her. When Janet visited Bachvillers, Reeves spent most of the time excusing himself to go to the well for a little refreshment — which turned out to be straight gin.[46] Yet if she disapproved of his drinking, she nonetheless appreciated the grace with which he carried his liquor; to her, he was the incarnation of the southern gentleman — composed and tactful, brave and kind.[47] But he was increasingly disturbed and lately had begun forging checks as well as frightening everyone who knew him.

When Carson eventually left him, the emotional, and sometimes financial, support of Reeves fell to his friends. David Diamond said he wouldn't be surprised to learn that Janet gave Reeves money during his last unhappy months. Janet had always been sensitive to the myriad of causes underlying Reeves's unhappiness and empathized with his suffering and confusion, his uncertainty about who he was and what he should be doing. He, in turn, felt very close to Janet, after his fashion. Do you think she will come to close my eyes when I die, he once asked David Diamond morosely.[48] Two weeks before his death, he called Janet at the Continental and said, "This is the man from across the River Styx."[49]

On the evening of November 18, 1953, Reeves called several friends, including Janet. All were engaged. One suggested he and Reeves get together the following night, but Reeves insisted it would be too late — he was "going west," he said.[50] The next day, after Reeves's body was found, Janet said she had received an extraordinarily large, beautiful bouquet of flowers from him, "the most beautiful flowers I ever received in my life."[51] David Diamond, then in Rome, recalled that Janet "was the only one who could tell me of Reeves McCullers' tragic death in such a way that did not leave me distressed or feeling guilty."[52] No one, she assured him, could have done anything.[53]

"His suicide seems to me to have been decided in the favor of dignity wh. his life no longer offered, . . . He had educated himself to such a point that he knew he had nothing to say & so told those fantastic lies —," observed Janet a few weeks later.[54] And we all recognized ourselves in Reeves, she told Carson; each of us recognized the "disorientation" we have all fought against.[55] But it's difficult to say exactly what part of herself she recognized — the need to appear outwardly composed, his strange, dislocated homelessness, or the frustration with talents never completely realized. Not long after Reeves's death, she began typing a Paris letter, "carefully worked out as usual," she commented, but one "which I could not praise even to myself —." Her "whole mature existence" sank, she said, as if she "did not have my 61 years besides to lean on."[56]

Janet's work, she knew, had in large part become her life; it structured her days, gave her purpose, and disciplined her — she who admired and felt in constant need of discipline. Hers was the kind of work that offered no restrictions: "Indeed," she commented, "it made implicit an expansion of mind & imagination." She blamed only herself for not having used the opportunities she was given. "I know I have never developed at all," she wrote in one of her darker moments. "Why did I not? How could I not have? What else was I doing to fill those years & days & hours, God help me? I do not know —."[57]

These reflections, written in early January 1954, were partly inspired by her decision to leave Paris for five months. Worried that when she returned, she would have no *New Yorker* job waiting for her, she worried about the time that lay ahead, months that would not be filled by her self-disciplining letters. Without the prod of her fortnightly letter, she feared she might again be engulfed by passivity. She assumed she didn't have "enough learning or history remembered or philosophy read or proved to have anything — literally anything at all — between me and approaching unemployment," and she must have feared, once again, that she'd be unable to change.[58]

Yet she was tired of the constant pressure of the Paris letters; in them she merely concealed her own ignorance with a "verbal writing glaze."[59] If the letters provided her with the discipline she feared she lacked, they also proved to her that the character behind them was weak. No doubt her recent argument with her editors sharpened her chronic sense of inadequacy. Knowing she was inextricably tied to the magazine and obliged to it, she also felt she had bartered away whatever talent she had, only to be rewarded for a "formula of fortnights."[60] And she admitted that she no longer intended to write a book on the Paris Commune or anything else.

Her ambivalence about her work was often reflected in her reaction to praise. When she completed a draft of the first part of her Malraux profile and received Shawn's cable complimenting her for having successfully handled Malraux in "profile terms," she was initially pleased.[61] On consideration, however, she thought it somewhat less than flattering: reducing Malraux to "profile terms" may have been necessary but was hardly praiseworthy. "I must accept that I write for a flash magazine," she observed to Solita. Then she became

Noel Haskins Murphy

Janet in the late 1930s

Marie, early 1940s

Harold Ross in Connecticut

Janet, early 1940s,
"my favorite tragic picture"

Photograph by Philippe Halsman 1946
© Yvonne Halsman 1989

Natalia Danesi Murray in her office at Rizzoli, New York

Janet with Ernest Hemingway at the Deux Magots

Kay Boyle, 1945

William Shawn

Janet in Rome, 1950s

Noel and Janet in Orgeval

Janet with her nephew John
Monhoff in California

Hildegarde (left) *and Janet*
on Janet's terrace at the
Hôtel Continental

Mary McCarthy interviewing Janet at the Continental, 1965

Janet with Alice B. Toklas, "the most widowed woman I know"

Janet outside the Tuileries

characteristically defensive: *The New Yorker* might not be the *Atlantic Monthly,* but its articles were better written.[62]

On occasion she thought her commitment to the magazine had cost her dearly, not only in professional development but in personal relations. At other times both her work and the arrangement of her personal life quite suited her, with Noel in Orgeval, Natalia in the United States, and Solita always available, wherever she was, to read, criticize, and comfort. Yet she basically lived alone, she told Solita, like a monk.[63] When she did not go to New York for Christmas, Janet wrote Solita, Natalia was very disappointed but took the rejection patiently; by now, she considered Janet's delays characteristic.[64]

When Janet finally went to New York and California for almost six months, she took her Malraux profile along. Simplifying her discussion of Malraux's book on art, *Les Voix du Silence,* and cutting her lengthy plot summaries of his novels in the overwritten second part, she had most of the profile finished by the summer of 1954. When she returned to France, she was free to reimmerse herself in the Paris letter and French politics — in particular, the fall of Dien Bien Phu, the government and personality of Prime Minister Pierre Mendès-France, and the final settlement of France's war in Indochina. Although she appreciated the human and political significance of the cease-fire, Janet regarded the "loss" of Indochina as a defeat for democracy.[65] She continued to worry over France's political future after the French Assembly virtually rejected the European Defense Community, which she had thought a good idea.

She was also troubled by matters more personal, in particular Kay Boyle's situation. Boyle, back in America and blacklisted, faced a new series of charges in Washington, which turned out to be the same charges as before. The McCarthy era was by no means over. Janet felt that she herself was reasonably safe. She reasoned that while she was on *The New Yorker,* no one would dare bother her, although if she were ever to leave, she too could be denounced. She decided to get her telephone, which she owned, back from the Hôtel Saint-Germain-des-Prés so she wouldn't have to take responsibility for anyone who might have used it during the last fourteen years, especially as she learned that it had been tapped. She also decided to have certain papers removed from her French dossier — papers that had amused her and Solita years earlier, when an irate customs inspector, angry that Janet had not tipped him, decided she was a Russian agent. ("Laugh yes" said Janet; "but Kay Boyle does not laugh now.")[66] The FBI was operating in Paris and reportedly could thumb through any American's file. Janet had saved her early passports, proving that in 1921 she had sailed directly from Constantinople to Marseilles, and she intended to have this fact recorded and put in her dossier. Nervous, she thought any incriminating papers the inspector might have left, ridiculous as they were, ought to be removed; she knew people who could help her, and did, for a fee.

Solita still kept Janet's accounts. Janet apprised her of all her expenditures, including the extra income she tried to give Noel, who lived more frugally than ever. "That's all I ever do do for her but she is so insistent, energetic squabbles so if I give her 345 francs extra bec. I can't make change," complained Janet.[67] Of late, Janet was trying to watch her expenses more carefully, "for I may need it," she wrote Solita, "to help friends."[68] One friend, the writer and translator Moura von Budberg, was out of work; Ernestine Evans faced possible blindness; Djuna Barnes was undergoing surgery; and Dorothy Caruso had cancer. "Everything is like death," Janet exclaimed, "because death is all around. I am beginning to fear it for the first time."[69] She twisted her ankle and had to stay in bed. "Age age age," she sighed.[70] She sent Djuna $150 through Solita, under the "misconception," Djuna said, "that art and recovery . . . should be saluted." Djuna thanked her, reminding Janet that such a sum was "an expensive folly on your part — you're a working girl! — remember?"[71]

When the proofs of her profile on Malraux arrived in September, she brought them to him, as she'd promised she would, for checking. He sat across a table from her in a lounging robe one night and marked the copy in red, black, or blue ink with carets, cross-outs, and the occasional large "No!" Janet returned home, chagrined to discover that his corrections made no sense at all to her except in those few cases where she remembered what he had said or what the pen tracks meant. Too ashamed to call him, she asked a friend of his to correct the errors.[72]

Meanwhile, she was constantly writing Stanley Eichelbaum, her "checker" at *The New Yorker,* who tracked down names, dates, and factual information and ran various and sundry fact-finding missions for her. Although Eichelbaum remembers her threatening to "boil him in oil" during the first days of their relationship, Gardner Botsford remembers that Stanley had a wonderful way of knowing exactly how and what Janet meant; he "had a feel for non-literal meaning she attempted."[73] And even after the Monday deadline for her Paris letter had passed, he would keep checking. Eichelbaum recalls that Janet could occasionally be crisp and testy if she felt her facts were being altered — even if they were actually quite mixed up and were just being corrected.

"How right you were that October might be the printing month — Or November?" Janet wrote Stanley impatiently when her Malraux piece was delayed.[74] *The New Yorker* didn't run Janet's two-part profile until November 6 and 13, 1954. But once in print, "The Human Condition" pleased her enormously — even though she was quick to point out that it had "cost" her two years and had nearly "ruined" her with worry and exhaustion.[75] The profile contained many of the issues she had been wrestling with during that time: loyalty, loneliness, age, the meaning of work and isolation. Outlining Malraux's colorful life, indicating the major themes of his novels, tracing his political development and its alterations, and trying to show what Malraux, formerly associated with the Left, and de Gaulle found in one another, Janet drew her subject as a complex, heroic, and contradictory figure — a profoundly disillusioned agnostic, a restless man of action and letters, a man never satisfied with easy consolations. Constantly wrestling with the demands of conscience, he defied death, lived alone, questioned everything. "As he walks," Janet wrote, "words and ideas rush from his brain and out of his mouth in extemporaneous creation, as though they were long quotations from books he has not yet written, and they flow at a rate that is almost the speed of thought, and sometimes faster than the ear can catch." "As a twentieth century thinker," she concluded, "he has illuminated his way through his investigations with his own intense blazing light."[76] She romanticized him as a creative thinker, not easily categorized, an elusive, brooding maverick, unbounded by any institution, struggling more heroically than most against time and human failing.

14

A Steady Conflagration
of Matches
1955-1959

JANET CALLED on Georges Braque at his rue Douanier studio on
January 28, 1955. It was four in the afternoon, a cold sunny day.
He looks like an Olympian workman, Janet thought, as Braque
greeted her and ushered her inside, where several paintings stood
on easels and nearly twenty lined the walls. Tall and slightly stooped,
he stood on small feet — too small for his height, Janet noted —
wearing socks as white as his hair, a loose jacket, and a scarf. He
coughed a little, talked without affectation, and calmly answered
questions "with the sure precision," Janet commented later, "of one
drawing a series of mental separate lines & forms. There is a generosity in his attitude toward his listener, he is donating, he is giving,
it is a nourrishing [*sic*] generous relation, it is almost impersonal as
if he were so purely himself that no undigested parts of his personality
now remained."[1] He looked and sounded like a very wise artisan,
she remarked, an expressive sage.

Seated in his studio, Janet commented on the sunlight streaming
through open draw-curtains — how did it happen that he had a southern, not a northern exposure in his studio, she asked. Modern artists
painted from their imaginations, Braque explained; they were not
affected by the physical direction of light, unlike the artists of the

nineteenth century, who painted from models and did not want the light to vary. The Impressionists, he added, painted light itself. How did he choose a subject, she inquired. He did not; a painting was caused by a rapport between him and the subject. "I do not paint to make a picture," he said, "I paint to paint." How did he explain the fact that the public, after a few years of rebellion, had finally understood cubism sufficiently to accept and even admire it? "Ils ont jamais compris, et ils ne doit pas comprendre, ils ont subi," he answered.[2] They looked together at some of the paintings and lithographs in his studio. Janet's eye caught the figure of a bird and asked if it was a duck or a swan. I paint a bird without genus, Braque gently responded.

It was a stupid question, Janet told Rosamond (Peggy) Bernier, who published the magazine *L'Oeil* with her husband Georges. Janet, somewhat nervous about the interview, had asked Peggy to accompany her. Afterward Janet asked if she might impose on her again to go over her notes. "Peggy darling," Janet scribbled on the bottom of two long typed pages, "write on the margin or back of page, or on another page, if you wish to be generous, whatever comes to you in memory, if these fragments suggest anything."[3]

Janet was interviewing Georges Braque for a *New Yorker* profile which, when finished, was to be published in a book-length collection of several of her pieces. The idea had been Simon Michael Bessie's. In the spring of 1954 he suggested she combine her profile of Matisse and her upcoming one on Malraux with the earlier one on Picasso, that she add to these the next one — the profile of Braque — and that she write an introduction linking them. The collection would be published by him at Harper and Row. She was interested. Early that summer, with Natalia acting as her literary agent, Janet signed a contract for the volume Bessie tentatively titled *Monuments and Men.*

Bessie had first met Janet — who reminded him of a Tiepolo — in the late thirties when he was working in Paris as a freelance journalist. He admired her work and called her "masterful at recreating the feel of a time and place; she is a wonderful observer — she *sees*. Nothing written on Paris in the twentieth century," he continued, "can afford to ignore what she has said, which is a real document, a record."[4] He also thought her an incredible researcher. Once, when they were all in Italy, Bessie had invited Janet and Natalia to a lunch of white truffles because Janet, he discovered, had never eaten any. Determined that she should know truffles, he ordered them with every course. Laughing and eating for the better part of the afternoon, Janet was delighted; almost immediately afterward, it seemed, she researched and wrote a definitive piece on truffles for *The New Yorker.* If her curiosity was piqued, Bessie concluded, there was apparently no stopping her.[5]

In the middle of January 1955, just before Janet interviewed Braque, Bessie tentatively asked her about publication dates for the collection; Janet responded that she was working hard — "damned hard" — but slowly. Writing a short piece for the *New York Times* magazine section on the new Faure regime and a short introduction to Daniel Talbot's collection *City of Love,* she had no time to work on the longer pieces.[6] In fact, it was difficult to find time even for the shorter ones. Events to be covered for her letter, people to be seen, copy to be cabled, as well as the additional writing she kept taking on — a piece on her old friend the painter Mark Tobey for *L'Oeil,* an introduction for a volume of Colette's short work — meant that she was falling behind on *Monuments and Men.*[7]

Again she confronted the questions that had nagged her all during her career. If she felt most invigorated when working, thriving on the pressure she constantly created for herself, she nonetheless wondered if she worked well only in bursts. She could work steadily for several days at a stretch in her small, crowded room; she could write through the night to make the next day's deadline. But could she sustain her energy, her enthusiasm, even her train of thought for a longer period? Could she plan her time in advance to outline a project and undertake, over a period, the research necessary for it? "I seem to live on in a steady conflagration of matches," she told Kay Boyle, "easily burnt out, but always relighted."[8]

And Janet was increasingly tired; she complained that her liver bothered her, and she still agonized over her complicated personal life.[9] Her various commitments made her feel guilty most of the time. Both she and Natalia may have slowly been accepting the limits of their relationship with fewer recriminations, but the situation, with Natalia living in New York, where she still worked for Mondadori, was far from resolved. Natalia often visited Italy, and Janet joined her there, but she simply could not choose between Noel and Natalia. She therefore pleased no one, least of all herself, and often disappointed Natalia.

She did spend September and October in Italy with Natalia, returning in November to finish her work on the Braque profile and to cover the French elections for her Paris letter. She was also interested in the career of Radical leader Mendès-France, whom she greatly respected, although in private she said she often thought him headstrong and tactless.[10] And she monitored the surprising rise of Pierre Poujade and his followers, so-called tax reformers of the Right, whose anti-Semitism, violence, hysteria, and even anti-Communism appalled her. Moreover, the agitation for home rule in North Africa was evolving into the tragic and bloody riots that would bedevil French politics and become the agonizing Algerian war. All this interfered, again, with Braque.

Janet planned to go to New York to see Natalia as soon as she finished the Braque piece, but when the first installment was completed in March 1956, she changed her mind, pleading work. New York would take her away from the continuing, painful drama of French politics: socialist Premier Guy Mollet, who had promised to end the war in Algeria, visited Algiers in February and altered his policy after being greeted by hostile, angry demonstrators pitching dung and tomatoes. Belligerence on both sides increased. By the end of May Mendès-France had resigned from Mollet's cabinet in disgust. To Janet it seemed that France's "strong" men — the other had been General de Gaulle — continued to withdraw from active political service while the country floundered. It was no time, she thought, for her to leave.

As it turned out, she postponed her trip to America for almost a year. Late that spring she finished the Braque profile, several months later than she had expected, and was still intent on a new Picasso piece, which she felt she could write only in France — especially because Solita was there and could help. She was quite far behind schedule. She wrote Michael Bessie to say she was mailing him her profiles of Malraux and Matisse and a revised "Beautiful Spoils," but she didn't have the Picasso piece ready. She apologized, but she proudly added that she had altered her profiles of Malraux and Ma-

tisse as well as "The Beautiful Spoils" to remove repetitions, make
them livelier, and add new corrections furnished by Malraux himself.[11]

She was mentally and physically exhausted and wanted Bessie to
know it. She painted a picture, probably true, of the pressure she
created for herself and the intensity with which she worked during
short periods. She said she completed half of the preface in a ten-
day stretch when she left her hotel room only once, for food. And
during this time she'd been furiously editing the Braque profile, until
she insisted that *The New Yorker* reschedule the publication date.
That done, she said she could probably finish the Picasso by the end
of June and suggested that *Men and Monuments* (she'd inadvertently
changed the book's title) be published without it, if that helped
matters.[12]

She felt guilty about her delays. Friends were worried about
her, she said; one, who had recently spoken to her by telephone,
wept when she heard how desperate Janet sounded. She took ten
days off — justifiably, she insinuated — and joined Noel and other
friends for a holiday looking at churches in Germany; she'd just
mailed the completed preface, rewritten twice. But she could not
continue working so hard, she concluded, and although she was still
not satisfied, her doctor had ordered her to rest.[13]

On July 9 Bessie cabled her to say that he simply must have the
Picasso by July 13 to meet the production schedule. Already several
deadlines had come and gone. He softened his urgent wire with a
letter to explain the constraints of an October publication schedule
and to apologize for having sounded so harsh. Janet, in reply, apologized again, saying she had rewritten the Picasso twice because she
thought the earlier versions glib and light. She worked slowly; perhaps she should not write at all. And if she didn't mean that literally,
she nevertheless believed that a publisher who undertook her book
was taking a risk.[14]

She was embarrassed about postponing *Men and Monuments* but
felt she had no alternative. For one thing, Hildegarde and her husband and their son John had arrived in Paris that summer for a visit.
One night Janet arranged that she and her sister dine with Solita and
Allan Ross MacDougall, an old friend who had been Isadora Duncan's secretary and was now editing Edna St. Vincent Millay's papers.

While Janet and Hildegarde sat with him over drinks in the bar of the Continental, Dougie, as he was called, entertained them with the last line Edna St. Vincent Millay wrote: "Handsome this day," he quoted, "no matter who has died." After they left the bar and went to the restaurant, where they had to wait for a table, Dougie said he was tired and would sit at a nearby table for a while. Janet then heard Solita cry out his name. She turned to look and saw MacDougall lying on the floor, dead.

At least Dougie had been with friends, commented Djuna Barnes in her dry way.[15] At their age, Janet said somewhat philosophically, one had to expect the death of friends.[16] She paid for Dougie's funeral and, with three other friends, declared him to be without family so that he might be buried as soon as possible. But friends were fragile, dry bones were cracking like old twigs, and company didn't always diminish the pain of loss. Dorothy Caruso had died the previous fall, with Margaret ministering yet again at the bedside of a dying lover. "I said to Noel," Janet wrote Solita, "how strangely we apply our sense of justice these days perhaps because we feel it so frustrated — My first reaction was to say, this is cruelly unfair, it's unjust — Neither Dot nor Margaret have merited this."[17]

Again she had to apologize to Bessie for being behind schedule. Canceling one of her Paris letters in August so that she could finish the Picasso profile by the end of the month, she was evidently pleased with the result, which was unlike anything she'd ever seen written about him. She had tried to treat Picasso psychologically, she said, sketching in his early background, his childhood and character, and then broadly summarizing his politics and his love affairs. She made reference to his various styles but did not discuss them, telling Bessie it was impossible to do so without illustration, and she didn't really deal with his work critically or analytically.[18] Virtually dismissing his political views, gliding over the war years, and attributing his Communism, somewhat ingenuously, to his having been poor, she treated Picasso as a magnetic and energetic personality, charming, witty, even generous.

Not long after she finished the Picasso piece, the Braque profile, simply called "Master," appeared in the October 6 and 13, 1956, issues of *The New Yorker;* it was, by far, the better of the two new profiles in *Men and Monuments,* partly because of Gardner Botsford's editing. He remembers having to untie the knots that occasionally occurred in her sentences and being able to do so to a large extent because he and Janet were well suited.[19] Although he didn't think her profiles as strong as her letters, and believed she agreed, he too thought the Braque a good piece. Certainly Janet's warmth toward her subject gave it the breadth and sensitivity the Picasso lacked.[20]

She herself was pleased and considered the Braque better than her profiles of Malraux and Matisse — "the malraux slopes down in part 2" she told Solita, "the matisse is too complicated and no real excitement in his life." Because she had in retrospect found the Braque material dull, "it was the extras that I put in the braque," she said, "that made it so thrilling, as shawn called it."[21] She was proud to win Shawn's approval, which she wanted Solita to hear; Solita, who more often than not supplied what Janet called a "repertory of praise," was just as likely to tell her not to stand on her "hind legs" begging for compliments when she thought Janet too dependent on flattery.

By the end of October she had heard from Stanley Eichelbaum that Shawn had decided to accept the Picasso article for publication. She said she did not have *The New Yorker* in mind when she wrote it, but she knew it might be suitable for the magazine and obviously hoped it would be taken. The news prompted her to expedite the work by checking the facts in the piece herself to help Stanley. Each morning she made comments in the margins of the draft and then in the late afternoon she'd work on her Paris letter, which often had to be redone at the last minute to include the latest news — usually about the Suez Canal crisis.

To be a good journalist, according to Janet's friend Sybille Bedford, one must have a quick-witted temperament to form opinions on the moment.[22] Janet certainly had this temperament, which had a negative as well as a positive side, and which created constant anxiety for her. Reporting important news that had not been commented on by any newspaper or relayed by any editorializing friend continued to make her anxious, as in the case of Wladyslaw Gomulka's sudden rise to power in Poland. When she had to draw her own conclusions, hoping she was right about them, she was still skeptical about her political insight, no matter how self-assured she sounded. And because she formed opinions rapidly and sometimes categorically, she did not always think issues through. Her temperament seemed to militate against her becoming the kind of writer she wanted to be. Her attention span was intense but limited, and she herself believed that this made for a certain fraudulence. After returning from a holiday with Noel in London, where she viewed a Braque exhibition at the Tate Gallery, she exclaimed, "How shocking that I had written so boldly from reproductions mostly, how like me too, reckless and usually lucky."[23]

To Solita she reiterated the familiar theme that she had not made sufficient use of her talent: "I suppose I might have been a modest historian," she wrote, half defensively, half in resignation. Yet she had chosen a direction and was becoming more reconciled to it: "But one cannot retrace life, its errors or its forward pass, not now," she concluded.[24] Implicitly she recognized that her best work was in the short form and that *The New Yorker* was its ideal outlet. According to Mary McCarthy, journalism didn't hamper her; the *New Yorker* format was perfect for her strong reactions, her vivid pictorial sense, her sharp metaphor, her common sense, and even the crushes she sometimes got on people and movements. "One couldn't be an intense admirer of Mendès and of de Gaulle at the same time," commented McCarthy. "Janet regarded these men as if they were actors, saw these people as if they were stars, in which case there would be no conflict between liking one and another. But this is not on the highest intellectual level and helped keep Janet a journalist."[25]

She was writing furiously, covering the Suez crisis, the Algerian atrocities, and the Soviet invasion of Hungary, which she protested with all her dramatic power. At the same time she wrote nineteen pages to be added to her Picasso profile. However, the new material threatened to delay the publication of *Men and Monuments*: the profile would have to be checked again and then edited by Gardner Botsford at *The New Yorker*. In late November Mike Bessie informed her that they were "now about to miss our third consecutive publication season, and it's really very difficult to keep the interest of the booksellers time after time."[26] Tired both of the delays and of feeling responsible for them, Janet decided that the Picasso article should appear in *Men and Monuments* without the benefit of Gardner Botsford's editing. All this meant that she again put off her trip to New York, first setting November 3 as her departure date, then November 20, then December 13.

Janet's profile of Pablo Picasso appeared in the magazine in edited form in March 1957, coincident with the publication of *Men and Monuments*. The magazine version, decidedly better written, differs little in substance, and only a few words were changed — "carnivorous" for "cannibal" to describe Picasso's malicious wit; but Gardner Botsford's fine reorganization clarified the sometimes confusing chronology of events and descriptions. *Men and Monuments* also included a new introduction, in which she discussed art generally to unify the various pieces in the book. Echoing some of the sentiments of her very early *Indianapolis Star* columns, but writing without their pomposity, she presented three main ideas — that there is no "permanent criterion" for defining art; that, notwithstanding, art was invariably the first thing seized during a war; and that since the Second World War art had become a choice and costly commodity for private investors and collectors.[27] Somewhat satirically, she noted that the significance of art could be measured by the intense responses it engendered, whether from the public, from collectors, or from looters, like the Nazis. Quoting from Malraux's *The Voices of Silence,* which characterized contemporary art as "an uneasy questioning of the scheme of things," she suggested that the most philistine of collectors, the Americans, had blatantly ignored most of these unsettling questions in their acquisitive pursuit. What was originally created to give pleasure, she concluded, was now high-priced merchandise.

On the author's information sheet Janet wrote that she had no biography, making it seem, as she increasingly suggested in her later years, that she had sprung into existence with the advent of *The New Yorker*. She mentioned that she had attended the University of Chicago for two years and then, she said, collapsing chronology, she began writing her Paris letter. Almost reflectively, she added, "I wonder for whom or what I would have written" if *The New Yorker* had not been invented to teach writers how to write.[28]

In this, her second book dedication (the first, *Cubical City*, she had dedicated to her mother), she paid tribute to another mentor, the father figure who had invented Genêt. For Harold Ross, she wrote, "creator of *The New Yorker,* for whom over years we wrote, and for whom we still write."

Janet fully expected that *Men and Monuments* wouldn't please the American critics. But Djuna Barnes wrote, in a letter addressed to "hoc genus omne" (Janet, Solita, and Elizabeth Clark), to say "I see strange, earnest young men dodging around corners *Men and Monuments* under arm."[29] The generally positive reviews of her book in America rather surprised Janet. Even Margaret Anderson declared that the profiles "seem to me prodigious, unique — for surely no one else can do just what you do," adding, characteristically, "In case this praise seems fulsome to you, I will take another position toward the first sentence of your preface: I don't agree." Margaret could not entertain the notion that, as Janet had put it, "there are no permanent criteria for declaring what art is and what it is not." But, Margaret continued, "since you hate argument, and since I've renounced such pleasure — . . . I'll spare you my propaganda. Congratulations on your accomplishment!"[30]

Gouverneur Paulding, in the New York *Herald Tribune,* praised Janet's writing, calling her style one of "disciplined naturalness." The director of the Guggenheim Museum, James Johnson Sweeney, writing in the *New York Times,* said that her type of journalism was lively, well documented, illuminating, and exemplary. Of all the reviews, the one Janet appreciated most came from Francis Henry Taylor, director of the Worcester Art Museum, who wrote in the *Saturday Review* that Janet, a "splendid, bright Medusa," had cast her withering gaze on the art world; "[for] the first time in living memory artists and their works pass before the scrutiny of an informed foreign correspondent — a reporter equally at home in world politics and literature with none of the inevitable bias of the professor or the critic. Her enthusiasms are those of the layman. . . . Where she shines most brilliantly is in the discovery of pertinent facts that no professional critic would even bother to find out."[31] She responded with a letter in which she thanked him and told him he had been alone in understanding her intentions — "you made a diagnoses [*sic*] of my inner mental workings, and more than that of my hopes, my patience, my searches, researches, the whole discipline and excitement of the private labor itself, performed as this magazine has taught us to do and then let us pursue, which only you recognized and summed up in your last line."[32]

When *Men and Monuments* was published in Britain by Hamish Hamilton, Janet's friend the critic Raymond Mortimer, writing in the London *Sunday Times,* argued that Janet had in fact invented the form other *New Yorker* writers tried to imitate. This "brilliant girl who left her native Indiana" had become the "shrewd wit with a knowledge of and curiosity about everything Parisian . . . almost everyone who has interested Paris during the last thirty-five years has been preserved in her amber prose."[33]

Not all reviews were so complimentary. The New York *Daily Telegraph* dismissed her prose as "New Yorkese, . . . a stream of personal and rather secondary information" that left "the reader sputtering in a spate of names, sums, anecdotes, and sheer gossip." By and large, however, she was applauded in America and criticized in Britain, where most of Mortimer's British colleagues were not as generous as he. Alan Bowness, in *The Observer,* thought she wrote fairly well but tended to be discursive and prolix; she was genuinely enthusiastic, occasionally sensible, frequently silly, never original. The *Manchester Guardian* called her articles "entertaining stuff unhandily written and mainly for Philistines." Others called her uncritical in her appraisal of the men she seemed almost to worship. The *Times Literary Supplement* called her a fine journalist who "sprinkled her pages with the financial pepper and salt of journalism" but who was completely out of her element in the quasi-philosophical, nonhistorical preface. Instead of unifying the pieces, it merely confused the book's direction and subverted its meaning.[34]

Most scathing of all was John Berger's piece in *The Spectator.* He said he intended to call the book's "bluff," with its dust-jacket claim that Miss Flanner was "an important and distinguished personality in her own right, creative and cosmopolitan." To the contrary, *Men and Monuments* showed only a "bright, magpie-like sophistication," the kind that turns art into a luxury commodity and does not understand art at all: "Miss Flanner writes with as little understanding as the philistine critics who helped to make the work unsellable; only she helps to make them more valuable."[35]

Janet was stung. Raymond Mortimer tried to be comforting, telling her that Berger's "outburst" could be explained by his communism.

Berger was, according to Mortimer, "the only writer of any ability in England, so far as I know, to belong to this discredited sect."[36] Mortimer offered a more personal explanation of Berger's reaction: he may have been annoyed by Mortimer's liking *Men and Monuments,* especially since Mortimer was given to teasing Berger. Basically, Mortimer was telling Janet not to take the review too seriously. But she did; she wondered if her book suffered from having been first published in *The New Yorker,* but as Mary McCarthy pointed out, the magazine stigma was "the price one pays for the price *The New Yorker* pays one."[37] Mostly, Janet felt that it was anti-American Britishers who savaged her.[38]

Janet left Paris for America in March 1957. She planned to stay for several months so as not to "always be away" for the rest of her life and to be near Hildegarde.[39] She had neglected her sister, she felt, for too many years, and since their mother's death was spending longer periods of time with Hildegarde's family in California. The two sisters took several trips together to visit the Monhoffs' new thirty-acre property, site of a home to be built on a Calistoga hillside overlooking the Napa Valley. Janet reported to Solita that they became laughing young girls again, driving up and down the California coast through dramatic dust storms, eating hotcakes by the side of the road, reminiscing about the past. That the sweet Hildegarde appeared overworked from housework, family responsibilities, and even her beloved gardening saddened Janet, as did the memory of her mother, who had for so many years lived in the little house adjacent to Hildegarde and Frederick's, which Janet refused to enter. Instead she slept securely on the bed prepared for her in Hildegarde's guest room, beneath an open window. Lulled to sleep in the chilly air by the song of a mockingbird, she was quite happy — "rare for me" she told Solita, "so often I am not."[40]

Janet thought she might do some writing while in America, but she wrote only one piece, a review of Sybille Bedford's first novel, *A Legacy,* for *The New Yorker.*[41] Janet had been so annoyed with Harper's when it refused to be Sybille's American publisher that she had written to Michael Bessie. That a first-rate novel of individual style, imagination, and "civilization" — still an important word to her — should be passed over for the tripe that merely made money was infuriating.[42] "It is humiliating to look at American novels or writing," she exclaimed to Solita, "and see how low we have sunk in the use even of our own language let alone that of the English."[43]

Paris remained Janet's spiritual home, even though in the next few years she divided her life, insofar as that was possible, into two geographic spheres. Paris represented the style, culture, and elegance she admired. She knew the city well and could find out whatever she wanted from any number of people, although she was beginning to complain that she didn't know as much about what was going on as in former days, when friends like Gene MacCown or Nancy Cunard could fill her in. But she was still able to close herself off with her work and not feel isolated; in fact, no matter how much time she spent alone, she was not isolated, for she spent part of almost every week with Noel and Libousse Novak in Orgeval. And Solita and Elizabeth Clark had bought a house not too far from Noel's, where they spent six months of the year, staying in Paris the remaining half year. Thus Solita, Lib Clark, Noel, and Libousse were at the center of Janet's life in France.

At sixty-five, her enthusiasm seemed boundless, her energy indefatigable. Journalist Benjamin Bradlee, who had known Janet since he was a rookie reporter, invited her to hear the Boston Symphony Orchestra perform an evening concert at Chartres Cathedral. She was unflappable, he recalled; the bats that had been awakened by the music didn't faze her at all as they swooped toward the audience. And when they retired to a café afterward, Janet entertained him with not only a history of cathedral music but a history of castrati as well.[44]

Janet liked the image she had created, living for thirty-five years in a hotel room with no possessions to speak of. Katherine Anne Porter visited Janet's room at the Continental and was "charmed" with it and "her entire scheme of living." Porter found "a real elegance in the whole thing. Also, more than a baffled admiration for *anybody* who can live ... years in a room, I should say, roughly, twelve by fifteen feet, and with all those objects, still have room to move about, keep a coherent and even pretty appearance, and even have the simple courage to keep things cleared out!"[45]

Gardner Botsford, who naturally called on Janet at the Continental whenever he visited Paris, said she was "the darling of the management, the waiters, room service, the bartenders, especially."[46] Late in the afternoon, he recalled, she would hold court in the bar, "sitting in a great big leather armchair at the end of the room, say, about four o'clock in the afternoon, and then all these people, every nationality, would be sitting on little funeral chairs in a line, and one could go up and talk to Janet, and everybody would move up one chair. And Janet knew them all, dealt with all their problems, promised to read their manuscripts, told them if their last piece was either good or no good."[47]

After returning to Paris in early June 1957 and resuming the Paris letter in July, Janet found her usual strength flagging. Although the problem was diagnosed as arteriosclerosis, she remained convinced that the ailment was simply muscular; nonetheless, she often complained to Solita that her memory lapses were "absolutely rampant since this foolish illness."[48] She briefly entertained the idea of writing on France for Doubleday's *Mainstreams of the Modern World* series, then dropped it; for the Berniers she undertook and then dropped a large, abundantly illustrated book on Paris similar to the one Mary McCarthy had written on Venice. Apprehensive, she decided it wouldn't be worth her while, financially or otherwise. Rosamond Bernier thought that Janet declined because the Paris book would simply have been too much for her.[49] Janet did write a piece for *L'Oeil* on Helena Rubenstein, who was so pleased that she gave Janet a ruby ring in thanks.[50]

By the late fall she was feeling better and was able to minister to Noel, who had been operated on for an arthritic toe that had become so gnarled she could hardly walk. Convalescing in a private clinic in a room that overlooked a garden, Noel entertained Janet and the nurses with her singing, but she was a difficult patient, berating the staff and refusing to eat. Noel hated being an invalid even more than Janet did.

Janet was well enough in December to go with Célia Bertin and Josette Lazar, a Romanian woman who wrote for the Paris bureau of the *New York Times* and gave Janet a good deal of her information, to visit Henri Cartier-Bresson and his wife near Blois, where the talk was books, editions, funny stories — "nothing but human talk," Janet said, "I had a wonderful time."[51] Then, wearing the red-and-white checked silk shirt Solita had given her for Christmas, she

celebrated New Year's with Marie-Louise Bousquet, Paris editor of
Harper's Bazaar and editor of the French *Vogue,* at Bernard Buffet's
chateau near Aix. Buffet was the subject of her next profile.

That winter Janet went to the south of France with Solita and Lib
to talk to some of Buffet's friends and to visit Margaret Anderson,
who lived near Cannes. The visit was a nostalgic and happy one, like
a "dream," Janet later told Solita. She lamented the trip to New York
she planned for March when, as she put it, she'd have to face reality.[52]
In a literal sense, she must have been referring to the legal action
recently taken against her and Harper and Row by the widow of Karl
Haberstock in Germany, who claimed that *Men and Monuments* contained libelous material impugning her husband's reputation as a
conscientious art dealer. The claim was eventually judged to have
no basis and was all but dropped by the fall of 1958, but not before
various official letters had passed back and forth between Haberstock's attorneys and those working for Janet and her publisher.

When she wrote to Solita about facing reality, she was also expressing the misgivings she invariably experienced when going back
to the United States. Although she gave way to sentimentality infrequently, a kind of nostalgia sometimes came over her; she had
exclaimed to Solita on one such occasion that "nothing can be the
same, my darling, as time changes it, with each human change, giving
deformities and looser relations."[53] Janet had learned how to com-
partmentalize her personal life, keeping present and former lovers
and friends away from one another, arranging itineraries and sched-
ules so as to prevent discord as much as possible and to protect
herself and others. Yet if Janet maintained that she felt no conflict
in her feelings — she loved each friend differently, she was loyal in
her devotion to each separately — she also frequently felt she was
living a lie. The smallest of subterfuges — asking Noel and Solita to
write her at her *New Yorker* office rather than at Natalia's apartment — disturbed her, and also evoked her history of subterfuge,
which had to undermine the pride she took in her forthright honesty.
She wanted to think of herself as others did, as "honest, outspoken,
kind, and good," and she regarded deceit as alien.[54] But she knew
she practiced it. During a New Year's celebration at Noel's in the
fifties, Janet and guests toasted their absent lovers. Later she said

softly to Sybille Bedford, one of those present, that "only you know the extent of my duplicity."[55]

That spring and summer of 1958, Janet seemed to be traveling between Paris and New York every other month. She had planned to stay in France for only a month, but Shawn asked her to stay at least until the first of June to cover the Algerian crisis that was bringing the country to the brink of civil war. The end of the Fourth Republic was obviously near. The French bombing of the Tunisian border village of Sakiet-Sidi-Youssef in February had turned public opinion against the government, and the last six months, said Esther Murphy, "have resembled nothing so much as the Queen's Croquet Party in Alice in Wonderland — but which nearly came to a denouement that would have been tragic and bloody."[56] As Janet quickly learned, much of France was ready to accept the return of General de Gaulle as the only solution to the political deadlock produced by the Algerian war.

Janet covered all this in elegant, eloquent Paris letters that drew on her despair over the protracted war and the crisis occurring when riots in Algiers and a military uprising did in fact usher de Gaulle into power. Janet climbed up and down the stairs to the visitors' gallery in the Assemblée Nationale as often as three times a day to listen to the near-tragic tumult: she heard the speaker of the assembly read, as the deputies jeered, President René Coty's letter calling on de Gaulle to form a new, legal government. At night she watched the demonstrators in the Champs-Élysées or on the Place de la Nation; she listened to the radio until the early hours of the morning and read all the newspapers and tracts proclaiming both the rebirth and the end of the republic. The streets were patrolled by special police carrying machine guns. She hardly slept.

On Sunday, June 1, the crowds in and around the assembly were so deep that her press card got her only as far as the nearby quays. Everyone waited for de Gaulle and the vote of the assembly which would turn the government over to him. At eight o'clock, after the results in favor of de Gaulle were announced, Janet hurried back to the Continental to finish her letter. On Wednesday, June 4, she worked through the night. The next morning, she flew to New York, and by Friday, June 6, she was working in the *New Yorker* offices, where she spent most of the day and half the night on her third Paris letter.

The letters documenting the crisis — dated May 25, June 1, and June 8 — were among the best she'd ever written in that she unsnarled the events of May 13 with precision and force and dramatized the critical events leading up to and including de Gaulle's takeover, which she seemed to welcome. (He is the "Frenchman of sacrifice," she wrote in her May 25 letter.)[57] That fall, as she continued to document the continuing Algerian crisis, she made clear her admiration for the rationalist general, descended, she said, from "long generations of privileged minds."[58] She considered his refusal to speak publicly about his intentions strategic and courageous; she did not seem bothered by his disdain for Algerian independence. The Algerians, she feared, would not be able to handle independence once it was given to them, Janet had confided to James and Helen Thurber the year before.[59] She also shared de Gaulle's disdain for *intégration*. Moreover, de Gaulle's invitation to the rebel Algerian army to debate with him in the French Parliament struck her as a fair, even superior, proposal, one "not comprehended by a primitive people, who might better grasp his brutally repressing them."[60]

Whatever socialist leanings Janet had had, or thought she had, in the late forties and early fifties were motivated as much by her desire for a credible political identity as by any theory or philosophy. Janet considered herself more sensitive to the human side of politics and its immediate impact on human lives than to its theoretical or philosophical aspects. She disparaged both Fascism and Communism, which she still associated with Stalinism; since the days of the Popular Front, which did not really inspire her, she had viewed any coalition of the left as generally naive, impractical, and perpetually divided. She considered, for example, the left's charge that de Gaulle's fiscal policies burdened the working classes an "old story," almost a tiresome one, about which little could practically be done.[61] The behavior of former socialist Guy Mollet, who had promised to end the Algerian war and then escalated it, not only disgusted her but struck her as typical.

By early 1959, however, she included in her Paris letter some of the French criticism of de Gaulle for his long silence on Algeria. Although Janet, too, began to worry over his silence, her criticism of the general did not curtail her respect for this educated, patriotic, even monarchical man. She continued to regard him in the same way she had during the war, as France's savior. Though she often treated him ironically, describing him in one instance as having a "dynastic-looking face," she justified her admiration by suggesting that without de Gaulle, France would revert to the Third Republic.[62] Many of her friends were convinced that Janet's admiration for him was insep-arable from her admiration for the majesty of his fluent prose; ac-cording to Michael Bessie, she appreciated "the elegance of his style and manner, that almost baroque quality about him."[63] She had learned very early in her life to respect the thespian strength of fine rhetoric, style, poise, and grandeur.

Determined to attend the 1958 commencement exercises at Smith College, where she was to receive an honorary degree, Janet had arrived in New York on Thursday, June 5, still writing her Paris letter on the consequences of the Algerian junta. She finished the copy Saturday noon, ran to have her hair washed, then boarded the Massachusetts-bound train with Natalia at two. Receiving the hon-orary degree meant a great deal to her.

The entire pageant delighted her: the pastoral Northampton set-ting, with gardens filled with pansies and orange lilies, the diplomas that looked like large old-fashioned passports, the gaily colored hoods worn by the faculty. Pleased that she was allowed to keep her own yellow and white velvet hood — not the cap and gown, "thank God — what to do with that later?"[64] — she had not anticipated the honor, which she attributed largely to the machinations of her friend Helen Kirkpatrick Milbank. But she heard that she'd been refused the honor three times before because she was not a "lady of letters," she was "just" a journalist. And she was aware that the Smith grad-uates had no idea who she was until *The New Yorker* was mentioned; only then did the crowd murmur approvingly.

In early 1959 Janet returned to New York twice — in February for investiture as a member of the National Institute for Arts and Letters and in April to speak at the Overseas Press Club and to talk with her editors at *The New Yorker*. At the urging of Glenway Wes-cott, Katherine Anne Porter had decided to nominate Janet for mem-bership at the institute. Porter, an honorary degree recipient at Smith

College with Janet, had switched caps with her when Janet's kept slipping down her nose. In her nomination, she called her friend "a brilliant annalist, a most scrupulous recorder of events, and accurate observer; she is generous in her judgements and yet judges with wonderful discrimination, and she can be shrewdly witty and caustic with frauds and second-raters; she has . . . a womanly tact that enables her to express very unpopular ideas without arousing resentment. . . . She's nobody's Yes-woman, she knows where she stands and what she believes and loves, and I'm pretty well convinced that she is naturally on the side of the angels." In fact, Katherine Anne told Glenway that the nomination was very hard to write because Janet "has so many virtues in her work, it is hard to arrange them."[65]

Once again recognition seemed to Janet to highlight her short-comings. She was proud of her *New Yorker* career, but she still could find her chosen work unfulfilling. Her profile of Bernard Buffet was a case in point. When Shawn originally suggested the piece, Janet consented, but over time grew ambivalent about it. Some of her hesitation was predictable: she always fretted when she began a new profile. Hiring a reporter from *L'Express* to help collect material had made the gathering of material an easier task; it was Buffet himself who was the problem. She wasn't as impressed with the young mil-lionaire painter as she had been when she first saw the retrospective of his paintings. He talked very little and said nothing of particular interest.

"Le Gamin," as the profile was called, did not see print until No-vember 1959, almost two years after she started it, a delay long enough to annoy Buffet himself.[66] Janet wasn't satisfied either, for different reasons. She wasn't sure she had handled the issue of the painter's celebrity well, although she wrote at length of the mer-chandising of Buffet and the boom in the postwar French art market; she discussed the controversy over the merits of his work and pointed out that the controversies themselves worked as publicity for the painter. But the profile lacked her enthusiasm. As in the second Picasso profile, she had not warmed to her subject. She was skeptical about Buffet's talent and never found him stimulating. As a result, "Le Gamin," written in large part without energy or conviction, was by no means up to the standards of her best work, and she must have known this. As it turned out, it was the last profile of hers to appear in *The New Yorker.*

But before the Buffet profile was published, Janet was considering another one. Natalia had handled the Italian actress Anna Magnani's press interviews in New York in 1953 and had accompanied the volatile actress to Hollywood the following year when she was working on the film *The Rose Tattoo.* In 1959 Natalia, with Magnani in New York for the filming of *Orpheus Descending* (later called *The Fugitive Kind*), was eager for Janet to write a piece on the actress for *The New Yorker.* Natalia could be one of Janet's prime resources, and the profile would obviously work to the advantage of everyone concerned.

Janet hesitated. Claiming she wouldn't be able to collect enough factual material for the typical profile, she approached Shawn with the idea of doing a generally psychological, or character, sketch. Shawn cabled his consent. But she still doubted whether she could handle it. Although many ideas for profiles were suggested and dropped — her friend Doda Conrad thought Janet ought to write about the queen of Belgium — it is not altogether clear why Janet was so unsure of this one. She cited her problems with Buffet, her inability to take interviews well enough, her slowness in writing, and the possibility that another magazine might run a piece on Magnani first; these were obviously excuses as well as reasons and may have concealed her wish not to become too entangled in Natalia's relationship with Magnani. Or Janet may have been jealous of it. Even more likely she was growing weary, more weary than she wished to acknowledge.

15

How Friends Grow Old
1960-1965

Think now how friends grow old —
Their diverse brains, hearts, faces, modify; . . .
Am I the same?
Or a vagrant, of other breed, gone further, lost —
I am most surely at the beginning yet.
If so, contemporaries, what have you done?

Nancy Cunard, *Parallax*, 1925

A T OUR TIME OF LIFE," Janet told Solita, "our friends are dying or going crazy or having terrible operations." Simply one more nail in our own coffin, observed Djuna Barnes.[1] Solita copied over Janet's wrinkled address book with all its markings — the small crosses penned in red ink next to names of the deceased, a small Star of David next to Gertrude Stein. "It is my doomsday book," Janet said, "of memory and love"; when friends remember one another, she added, they keep one another alive.[2]

In the spring of 1960 Janet was worried by rumors about Nancy Cunard. Nancy had been drinking more and more heavily and was often incoherent, violent, abusive, or raging — a "heroic figure in dilapidation," Raymond Mortimer called her. Thrown out of Spain after being jailed there for several days, she went to London; along the way she was kicked by train officials in France, she claimed, after she ate her ticket. Arrested in London while assaulting the police, who'd picked her up for soliciting, she threw her shoes at the magistrate sentencing her. In prison the medical officer deemed her mentally incompetent and transferred her to an East End hospital, where she tore the buttons off her clothes, tossed them into the bathtub, and wrote to everyone she could think of — Khrushchev, the prime minister, friends — for help. She was being imprisoned, she said, by Fascists.[3]

Raymond Mortimer told Janet that Nancy was irrefutably insane and had been committed; the "horrid job" had been done by Roger Senhouse, her publisher and friend. Mortimer visited Nancy at Holloway Sanatorium, outside London, in early July. He reported to Janet immediately, knowing how concerned she and Solita were. Nancy's room was plain, he said, but at least it looked out on several trees; she had said the food was good, and she was writing a great deal (frantically, Mortimer thought). On the whole she seemed lucid, but she talked at length about the illegality of her confinement and the conspiracy that led to it. Although she appeared more bored and indignant than unhappy, he did not doubt her insanity.

Nancy herself had kept in touch with Janet by letter, occasionally accusing the CIA, Allen Dulles, and the Home Office for the recent "chapter of my muck." She asked Janet to give ten pounds to Tomas Morales, the twenty-seven-year-old blacksmith she had taken up with in Spain, who was now on his way to France. When he showed up in Paris penniless, speaking only Spanish, and unable to get in touch with Janet right away, Nancy assumed that the hotel concierge had thrown him out. Janet eventually met him, lent him money, and oversaw his movements as best she could — although no one, least of all her, thought he should be encouraged to go to be with Nancy in London, as Nancy desperately wanted.

All this had to be handled delicately, for Nancy easily took offense if anyone suggested that alcohol might be the cause of her condition. Janet, comparing Nancy to Esther Murphy, made this mistake. "Thanks for the accusation," Nancy haughtily replied, adding that drink had nothing to do with her situation, which was political in nature. To a certain extent, some of her old friends, including Louis

Aragon in France and Walter Lowenfels in America, thought she had a point. Aragon's weekly newspaper, *Les Lettres Françaises*, told Nancy's story on its front page, noting that her "incarceration falls rather too neatly into place, explaining a life that has been upsetting for received ideas." And Lowenfels publicly questioned whether Nancy was not being confined — indeed, silenced — against her will. Janet took no public stand. She later told Nancy's biographer Anne Chisholm that she'd always thought Nancy's politics ridiculous and did not consider her institutionalization a political act.[4]

But Nancy's personal anguish affected Janet. Letter after tragic letter, filled with searing insights and brutal self-assessments, reminded Janet of Nancy's past courage and violent candor, her determination and obstinacy. Nancy was taking a personal inventory and finding that the only writings she cared about were her anthology *Negro,* some of her poems, and the pieces she had written during the exodus from Spain in 1939. "I have *loathed* my life," Nancy declared, "all of it, and spit on it, at present, for the future and on the past. It wasn't everyone I've said that to, but I certainly do repeat it to you and Solita and surmise both of you knew have known I have always felt that way."[5] She burned with a fury that consumed her; this, to Janet, was her greatness and her madness. Nancy threw herself into lost causes with quixotic blindness, identifying body and soul with the suffering and misery she'd seen in Spain, Mexico, Harlem, wherever.

But to Janet it was Nancy's writing, not her causes, that mattered. "A writer must have a talent for writing," Janet had recently told Hildegarde, "and a talent for survival."[6] Nancy had no talent for survival. At times Janet herself wondered what survival implied. "Wrapped in old sheets of typewriter paper," as she once ruefully remarked to e. e. cummings and his wife Marian Moorehouse, Janet felt she had insulated herself from the angry questions whose answers were hard to find.[7] Nancy had never done this, which was part of her allure: she was fearless and compassionate and committed. But, as Solita said, her anger caused her to "leave her home, her class, and her country; because of them, she never had time to profit by the experiences of love, of guilt or remorse."[8]

*

Late summer for Janet meant Natalia and Sperlonga, the charming Italian coastal village that had become the site of Natalia's new summer home, a small house with a rooftop terrace that overlooked the sea. Before she left Paris, Janet wrote in her letter for *The New Yorker* about the translation of Djuna Barnes's *The Antiphon* into Swedish, the spy trial of Gary Powers, what was being worn to *Carmen,* the French government's suppression of the press, Fellini's *La Dolce Vita,* de Gaulle's trip to London, and Nikita Khrushchev's visit to France. The last prompted Alice Toklas to remark to Anita Loos that Janet's "enthusiasm for the General has cooled but she has taken on very warmly Monsieur K."[9] According to Virgil Thomson, Alice was convinced that Janet was a Communist.[10]

Janet was certainly no Communist, even if she was rather sympathetic to Soviet Premier Khrushchev, referring to him laughingly as "our dear jolly Mr. K."[11] She had also become a bit more critical of de Gaulle as the Algerian war dragged on, and she wrote sympathetically the following fall of the "Déclaration des 121," the protest against the war signed by many well-known French figures in the arts.[12] The war entered its seventh miserable year. Regarding with relief de Gaulle's latest referendum on freedom for Algeria in January 1961, she anticipated a negotiated peace until March, when the peace talks stalled, slowed by the "virile pride," as she called it, of both sides.[13]

Reporting on the recently failed military coup and general strike, Janet observed the French anxiously waiting for paratroopers to fall from the Paris skies after Premier Michel Debré warned of the possibility. She herself lay in bed one night at the Continental, listening to the radio and laughing at Debré's absurd suggestion: if Algerian paratroopers landed in France, the French people should talk them out of their rebellion. But Janet, fantasizing about "hastily dressed French citizens" rushing out of their homes to win the paratroopers over with impeccable logic, suddenly sat up in bed. In her reverie, most of the soldiers seemed to be Germans.[14] She got up and began to type. She couldn't sleep anyway.

The Algerian war, the strikes, Nancy's state of mind, a mysterious burning pain in her hand — all took their toll. Then in July she was shaken by news of Ernest Hemingway's death. Not long afterward she saw Mary Hemingway and told her of the conversations she and Ernest used to have at the back table of the Deux Magots, where they always sat, near the door to the toilets down below. She recalled the time near the end of the war when Ernest had read Janet his poems about Mary — excellent, she thought, and full of feeling.[15] But Janet was upset that Mary was trying to hide the fact that Ernest had committed suicide. "I think it very shocking," she remembered saying to Mary, "that you didn't appreciate the fact that Ernest had killed himself because that was of vast importance to him." Janet recalled that Mary "gave a very weak reply," saying she had concealed his suicide because she felt it would look better.[16]

It was not a good summer for Janet. She feared she was losing her memory, and the pain in her hand, diagnosed as a nerve injury, had gotten worse. Writing was impossible. And although Janet "went right on living, talking, and thinking as hard as ever" according to Hildegarde, whom she was visiting, most of her energy was "spilling out in the injury."[17] Not until late fall did Janet return to Paris and to work. She reported to Hildegarde that she was much improved and that a short trip to Sperlonga with Natalia had soothed her nerves. Nonetheless, Alice Toklas remarked to a friend that Janet looked "thin and fidgety."[18]

She was having trouble sleeping. By night, as she stood on her balcony, looking down on the Tuileries skimmed in light mist, she heard bombs exploding on the nearby avenues; by day she saw the damage caused by nearly two hundred *plastiques*. Continued outbursts of violence and terrorism followed on the heels of the peace negotiations, and the seeming nonchalance of the French people toward both the Organisation de l'Armée Secrète (OAS) bombings and the police brutality angered Janet. The homes of several journalists were attacked. Nevertheless, Janet brushed aside Hildegarde's warning not to be too "sassy, even in the service of truth and the honor of history."[19] She maintained that the bombings didn't frighten her, they disgusted her.

Janet covered as many events as she could, from the funeral marches for those killed in the OAS bombings to the long-overdue Evian accord between France and the Algerian Front de la Libération Nationale. As usual, she was less concerned with broad political trends than with their daily manifestations. By placing specific and visual details in her narration of events, she portrayed the frustrated, divided, and violent mood of Paris and managed to turn it into high drama. With quiet fury she described the shattered glass covering the streets of Paris, the buildings bombed randomly and not so randomly; with mordant humor she told how the OAS had bombed the home of a Communist politician already dead for two years, and how she herself was told, when she telephoned the Palais de l'Élysée to ascertain the source for a reference in a recent speech, that no one in de Gaulle's press office knew anything about the speech.[20] She described the capture of ex-General Edmond Jouhaud, noting that he was wearing a false goatee and eating cookies. Covering the trials of Jouhaud and Raoul Salan, two generals responsible for the insurrection of April 1961, she turned the ironic twists of justice and history into macabre drama, as she had during the trials of Laval, Pétain, and the Nazi war criminals at Nuremberg.

Except for July, when she again joined Natalia in sunny Sperlonga, Janet stayed in France all during 1962, dividing her time between the Hôtel Continental and Orgeval, with Solita and Lib Clark nearby in both places. Orgeval continued to be Janet's private world, a world she protected and enjoyed. Some friends thought she was part owner of Noel's home, for she often talked as if it were hers.[21] She kept many of her papers there, some relics from her family's home in Indianapolis — a sleigh bed and a cupboard — and some of the furniture she and Solita had had at the Hôtel Saint-Germain-des-Prés. Noel cooked savory dinners, seasoned with herbs from her garden, and she and Janet and Libousse took their coffee beneath the fruit trees until the weather turned cold. But ever since Noel had fallen down the stairs several years before and had jammed two vertebrae together, her arthritis had worsened, frequently making movement quite difficult. There were still numerous guests, but many of the special friends who'd come for so many years were no longer there. Every loss was painful; the death of Esther Murphy, who collapsed in her Paris apartment, was particularly sad. Esther's health had not been good for some time, she was drinking a good deal, and she had been unable to write her books on Edith Wharton and Madame de Maintenon. This in particular, said Janet, was a tragedy.[22]

Because she had not realized all her own literary ambitions, Janet was especially sensitive to the unfulfilled desires of others. She never thought of her fortnightly letter as having lasting value, even when friends over the years encouraged her to think otherwise. Several suggested she publish her collected writings in book form. The suggestion, recalled Helen Kirkpatrick, was invariably met with Janet's usual modesty and lack of vanity — she could even characterize such an idea as pure "nonsense."[23] At the same time she did want recognition for her work; she still wanted to be considered a writer, not a journalist. Yet while Smith College had initially refused to give her an honorary degree because she was a journalist, Edmund Wilson reminded her that she couldn't get a Pulitzer Prize for *Men and Monuments* because the pieces did not qualify as journalism — they had never appeared in a newspaper. Her kind of writing could not be categorized. Worse: because the major body of her work had appeared in a magazine, even if it was *The New Yorker,* her finely wrought prose was ultimately disposable.

Earning recognition for her work became all the more important because she had never written her book on the Paris Commune, and deep down she must have known she would not write the other books she still planned — one on de Gaulle, for instance. She always insisted that she did not have the time or the financial ease to do what she wanted to do, but she also knew she had profoundly resisted these projects. Mary McCarthy speculates that fear of rejection and fear of disapproval may have kept Janet from straying too far from *The New Yorker*: "She could handle disapproval from people she disapproved of herself but if she got involved with different groups with different standards, I think she might have been afraid of them."[24]

When Professor Carlos Baker, Hemingway's official biographer, contacted Solita, she inveigled Janet into writing a memoir of their old friend for him. She assured Baker that Janet "will surely in time (her own!) send you a reminiscence of Ernest," but warned him that Janet was "a last minute writer."[25] And when she was asked to write about herself, she adamantly refused. Michael Bessie recalls plaguing Janet for years for a book of memoirs. No, she had answered, she wrote only of the moment — and only for *The New Yorker.*[26] Memoirs did not interest her; everything she had to say was in her Paris letters. After so many years spent studiously avoiding the word "I," she was hardly about to embark on a project in which the first person was essential. Moreover, she must have thought that writing her memoirs would make public her private life, and this she would not do. Her life had been an eminently private one, devoted to concealment, not revelation, and the conscious crafting of an identity. In her remaining years Janet was not inclined to drop the mask she'd carefully fashioned, even if that had been a real possibility, which it wasn't. Her public persona had become completely dependent on — and took strength from — her private one.

Michael Bessie then approached her with a different idea: a book of her selected writings from Paris. Although Janet would not think of marketing herself to earn the praise she wanted, the more commercially minded Natalia, acting as Janet's unofficial publicist and agent, did. She urged Janet to think seriously about Bessie's suggestion, and Janet finally agreed to put her forty years of Paris correspondence between hard covers with Atheneum, the publishing house Bessie helped form when he left Harper and Row.

On March 14, 1963, Janet was in New York having lunch with William Shawn. Later that afternoon, Michael Bessie remembers, he got a call. Janet had had a few drinks and was elated. She said she was speaking for Shawn (who was too shy to speak himself); he had just consented to edit a book of her Paris letters if Bessie was still interested in publishing them. Bessie couldn't believe it. Was she sure? This was going to be a great deal of work, and it was an unusual decision for "one of the world's busiest men." But when Janet put Shawn on the phone, he confirmed the story.[27] Janet was thrilled and touched. She knew that Shawn's willingness to edit the letters was indeed a compliment. As E. J. Kahn, Jr., put it, Shawn consented because he regarded her as special, as sweet, as generous and kind, and as no ordinary writer.[28]

Janet had returned to the United States that year at the beginning of February with three projects in mind: the memoir for Carlos Baker's biography of Hemingway; a tribute to Sylvia Beach, which *Mercure de France* had requested; and a *New Yorker* profile of Ethel Merman. As usual, she felt so at sea in New York without her regular Paris letter that she got no work done on any of the pieces.[29] She was more successful during a six-week visit with Hildegarde at the Monhoffs' new house in Calistoga. She went with Stanley Eichelbaum, then living in San Francisco, to Lake Tahoe to see Ethel Merman and worked on a twelve-page draft of the profile about the singer with, as Janet said, an androgynous name. But the first draft was overwritten, and she never finished it — whether because *The New Yorker* canceled it or because she just lost interest is not clear.

It may very well have been the latter. Back in Paris by the beginning of June, Janet was again involved in the pathetic affairs of Alice Toklas, whose health had been deteriorating since the time two years before when Toklas had gone to Italy and returned to Paris to find the walls of her apartment stripped bare: Gertrude's collection of modern art had been impounded. Stein's heirs had taken inventory of the collection while Toklas was away and discovered that several Picasso drawings were missing. Alice had sold the drawings, for Gertrude's will had specified that items from the collection could be sold either to publish her work or to provide for Alice's maintenance. Nevertheless the heirs, arguing that Alice's prolonged absence had endangered the paintings, obtained a court order to remove the entire collection. It was subsequently deposited in a vault at the Chase Bank.

To help Alice, Janet had decided to include the story of Gertrude's collection in her Paris letter. Alice was a bit nervous, fearing Janet might be indiscreet, so Janet wrote a five-page draft and then read it to the nearly blind Alice over the telephone. The piece ended touchingly with Alice's own statement about the lost pictures: "I am not unhappy about it. I remember them better than I could see them now."[30] The story of the pictures' removal appeared in the December 5, 1961, Paris letter and earned congratulations even from Margaret Anderson, Janet's perennially harsh critic. Margaret, strolling one day in the Orgeval garden with Janet, said Janet must have been swamped with appreciative letters. Janet grimly replied that she hadn't received a single one.

Now, with only memories of the pictures, Toklas faced losing the flat as well. When the building was sold, she assumed she would not be evicted, but while she was in Rome, the owner of the building had sued for possession of her flat, claiming it had been left vacant. Both Janet and Monroe Wheeler cabled André Malraux, minister of cultural affairs, asking him to intervene; Virgil Thomson also interceded on her behalf, and the eviction was stayed, at least temporarily.

Janet and Doda Conrad and Virgil Thomson were still trying to sort out Alice Toklas's financial situation: her maid had not been paid for months; numerous household expenses needed attending to; her home at the rue Christine was again in jeopardy. Toklas's recent hospital bills had been paid by Janet and other friends, all of whom considered the whole matter deplorable; at eighty-six, penniless, half blind, and half deaf, Alice was denied access to the estate Stein had left for her maintenance. Her friends hoped they could sell one or two of the confiscated pictures so that she could live properly. But this required a series of letters to the Stein lawyers, written by Janet and Doda Conrad. With their help, Alice was finally installed in a new home on the rue de la Convention.

Writing to Alice from Abano to apologize for not having dropped by before leaving, Janet explained that unhappiness "has eaten my time like acids."[31] Several friends had taken ill; one had slipped in the bathtub, injuring her hip, and was now bedridden; another had taken an overdose of drugs; Kay Boyle's husband was dying of cancer at the age of fifty-three. And Natalia's visit to Paris that summer was strained. Natalia wanted more of her time, and as usual Janet offered promises: she would stay in Paris six months each year if Shawn consented and spend the rest in New York with Natalia. But she did not return to the United States until the fall of 1964, over a year later.

Despite her work helping arrange Toklas's affairs, Janet was not good at managing the humdrum details of her own life. If there was something warm and wise, enthusiastic, and generous about her — if she was a woman of great dignity, as her friends believed — she was never able to fend entirely for herself. The small contrivances of daily life — locks on doors, bottle openers — perplexed her. As Sybille Bedford put it, she could not even manage the breakfast egg.[32] Solita and Noel and Natalia willingly took care of many everyday concerns for Janet. Noel cooked for her; Solita saved her money, edited much of her writing, and packed her clothes before she sailed for New York in September. Natalia waited for her.

Janet's energy at seventy-two seemed unflagging, but some friends felt she was growing slightly out of touch with Paris. She didn't seem as interested or as well informed as previously, partly because of her

arteriosclerosis and memory lapses. Rosamond Bernier recalls that
Janet would often call to ask about the latest exhibits — what should
I see, she would ask, what is good? Writing continued to be a great
struggle, and often Janet would insist that *this* time she would not
be able to finish her letter.[33] She always did, but not without agonizing
over each word. She'd always worked this way, but now her energy
seemed to sag. And she was finding more in Paris that she did not
like: the physiognomy of the city was changing, and so was its eloquent language, now invaded by American slang. Janet abhorred all
slang, even the word "okay." To her, a culture's style of writing or
speaking reflected its style of thinking, and American writing, in
particular, was nothing more than "a melange of freudianism and
advertising, our complete absence of an idea or thought, just action."[34]

By contrast, she was still intrigued by the high-toned rhetoric of
Charles de Gaulle. Despite her growing disenchantment with the
president, the peculiar psychology of the man who, like Henry
Adams, often spoke of himself in the third person appealed to her.
In a preface (edited by Solita) for Pierre Viansson-Ponté's *Les Gaull-
istes,* she roughly outlined the features of the de Gaulle phenomenon,
using de Gaulle's own question — "How can you govern a country
which has two hundred and forty-six different kinds of cheese?" —
as her point of departure. She was intrigued by the paradoxical leader,
whom she described as looking like a melted candle; in him she
found braininess mixed with pride, egoism, and theatricality. As Mary
McCarthy put it, Janet was "stage-struck" by characters like de
Gaulle.[35]

To conclude the proposed volume of Paris letters Shawn was editing, Janet suggested a longish piece on de Gaulle, comparing the
Third, Fourth, and Fifth Republics. The prospect of surrounding de
Gaulle, in all his lonely grandeur, with the controversy he had inspired excited her. She could use her old friend Pierre de Massot as
a source on the Communists' reaction to the general, and for a comparison between the Fourth and Fifth Republics, she could tap
Georges Bernier, who believed that the prosperity of the Fifth Republic came from the Fourth.[36]

Shawn thought this a fine idea. The day after her arrival in New
York in the fall of 1964, the two of them met for lunch at the

Algonquin (packed with "nobodies," she said, "in pretense of being somebodies") to go over his work on the letters.[37] He had already edited the ones written between 1925 and 1935 but happily agreed with her decision to jettison them. She thought they were "trash." (She had not as yet reread them.) They reminded her of a past she was not altogether comfortable remembering, filled, or so it seemed to her, with brash insolence and ignorance. She felt that only the letters written after she had returned to Paris in November 1944 were worth preserving. Shawn concurred, nodding slowly. He told her, Janet reported to Solita, that she possessed a "dual writer's personality, juvenile and adult." The juvenile part had been the peculiar legacy of Harold Ross, a "meretricious early glitter which Ross'es [*sic*] lack of culture had imposed."[38] Whether or not Janet swallowed the formulation whole, she did agree that her later letters represented her "maturing style and thoughts over this last 2 decades."[39]

She had work to do in America. She had promised Carlos Baker she would give a talk at Princeton, and she still hadn't written her memoir of Hemingway; but she wrote neither during her visit to Hildegarde. California was not conducive to work; her solicitous sister hovered over her, making cherry pies and apple crumbles and taking her to the Calistoga spa, where a Seventh Day Adventist massaged her tired feet. But she continued to write letters, sometimes daily, to Solita and Noel. (Noel sometimes annoyed Janet by sending mail to Natalia's flat rather than to the *New Yorker* office.) She'd also been writing to Nancy Cunard and sending her small gifts — clippings, articles, a copy of Nabokov's *The Defense,* which Nancy loved.

In the fall of 1960 Nancy had been released from the sanatorium and had returned to her home in France, her mental condition greatly improved. But she was definitely ill: she suffered from vertigo, she could not eat, her legs were swollen, she could barely walk or breathe. She had emphysema and would not recover. Her letters were "so tragic," Janet said to Solita in 1963, "as to be a new kind of personal documentation."[40] The only thing that seemed to give her any kind of relief was her writing, so Janet and Solita arranged to send her a new typewriter.

Nancy wrote to Janet in Paris, in early January 1965, thanking her for the slim jersey she'd sent for Christmas. Two months later, on March 9, the eve of Nancy's sixty-ninth birthday, a taxi driver carried her, raving, into Solita and Lib's house in Orgeval. A few days earlier, after quarreling with her long-time friend Jean Guérin, himself an invalid, Nancy had left his home in the middle of the night, in the arms of a servant, as she could barely walk. She made her way to Nice, lost all her money, got into a fight, and was arrested. When she showed up in Orgeval, she sat for twenty-two hours in a pale blue armchair, spilling wine and ashes, tearing at her clothes, and refusing the food Solita tried to give her, calling for more to drink. Lib watered the Scotch, and Solita telephoned Janet, who arranged to meet Nancy at a doctor's office in Paris. Lib and Solita carried Nancy out to the taxi, giving the cab driver strict instructions. Janet waited at the doctor's office for four and a half hours, pacing, calling Solita to see if she'd heard anything, calling the hotel to see if Nancy had left any messages. There were none, and Janet never saw her again. Later Janet learned that Nancy had gone to a small hotel, where she kicked several guests before burning her manuscripts on the hotel carpets. She then crawled to the street — she could hardly stand — and was picked up by the police. They brought her, unconscious, to a hospital ward, where she died on March 16, three days after Janet's seventy-third birthday.[41]

"She seemed really to evanesce at the last, simply to slip from sight, our poor ⅓ darling Nancy, so soiled, so decayed, so violent in her febrile rage against the life she made —" Janet wrote to Solita.[42] When they heard nothing from Nancy's family, Janet and Solita offered to pay for the funeral. Then the family sent a solicitor to make arrangements.[43] Of all the thousands of people Nancy knew, only six attended the rites. Two years later Solita, discovering that Nancy's ashes were left at Père Lachaise unmarked, arranged for a plaque to be put up.

Three months before Nancy's death, Janet had been eager to begin a profile of playwright Eugene Ionesco, which she'd suggested to Shawn. She was feeling better than she had in a while; although her eyes had been bothering her, clouding over with tears whenever she tried to write, her oculist reassured her by saying her condition had nothing to do with age. Her spirits good, she took pills for high blood pressure and the slow creep of arteriosclerosis, allowing her to feel reasonably fit and ready for work.

She had flown back to Paris in December to save time, for she wanted to resume her fortnightly letter as soon as possible (Solita and Josette Lazar were saving clippings for her) and to finish the de Gaulle letter, which would close *Paris Journal,* by December 16. She did complete it, but gradually stopped work on the Ionesco profile. According to Solita, Janet was "run to earth by her articles, proofs of coming collection of 20 years' war articles (& politics) and also (now) a long article on General de Gaulle which she has no time for, but over-tempted into doing."[44] The proofs for *Paris Journal* had arrived, and Solita was working hard for "*Janet* of course, book binder and such."[45] When Professor Hugh Ford asked her to contribute to a memorial volume on Nancy, Janet could offer only the obituary she'd written in the Paris letter.

And Janet was also still taking care of frail, impoverished Alice Toklas, who, her friends believed, was entitled to whatever small pleasures they could give her. Alice preferred strawberries from Fauchon's, so Janet kept an old Fauchon box handy to be filled with ripe fruits bought more cheaply in the neighborhood. "It drives me mad," Janet exclaimed, "that Alice is driven to the generous charity of her friends when she is in reality an HEIRESS."[46] That summer of 1965 Janet rode with her to and from the hospital when Alice had a cataract removed from her right eye; Virgil Thomson speculated that Alice was making sure she'd see Gertrude clearly when the time came. Thornton Wilder helped out with the hospital and surgeon's bills, but Alice's affairs were still a mess, and her expenses came to about seven hundred dollars a month.

Janet planned to finish going over the proofs for *Paris Journal* by the end of the summer of 1965; then she would discontinue the Paris letter for a month or so in order to write a ten-thousand-word pamphlet on de Gaulle for Avon publishers. At the same time she was planning a small volume on Picasso for the Time-Life artists series. Josette Lazar would help with the de Gaulle pamphlet, and Janet could spend part of her summer holiday with Noel gathering material in the south of France. This she did, but by August she had abandoned both projects.

Even though she had been genuinely enthusiastic about it, she quit the de Gaulle project when her editor at Avon left. It's not altogether clear why she dropped both pieces completely, although she did say, regarding the Picasso, that the work would simply be too taxing at her age. But she gave up on it for other reasons as well: she really did not like Picasso's work and did not like writing about it. "Over all those years since [cubism], his styles have troubled (baffled) me," she confessed, "have seemed ugly and almost always indubitably excellent compositions. I don't see how I could write in the jargon of praise which todays critics and viewers of his late paintings sincerely accord him."[47] The project and the price offered for it had attracted her initially, but she admitted they couldn't keep her interest. Nor could she handle that work and continue to do her Paris letters — "familiar ground and formula," as she called them.[48]

Whatever ambivalence Janet may have felt on canceling her extra work, particularly the piece on de Gaulle, was offset by the upcoming fall publication of *Paris Journal*. William Shawn had written a preface, which Janet thought terrific but much too glowing to use. She cabled him saying that it would only make their "mutual" book vulnerable to adverse criticism. But she'd been pleased when he said that her work had created "the FORM wh. all other foreign letters consolidated by copying *my* copy —."[49]

Reviews of *Paris Journal* began appearing in November. Alan Pryce-Jones, in the New York *Herald Tribune,* complimented Genêt's "perfectly natural prose, witty but unfrilled" by saying that "like a conjurer, she pulls out of her hat whatever is going to divert her audience; but, unlike the conjurer's, her rabbits are still alive after twenty years." Ben Bradlee, Jr., in the *Washington Post,* called her a "paragon of foreign correspondents — the one with a first class brain, plus the best senses in the business." Oscar Handlin, reviewing for *The Atlantic,* was not so effusive: "Read in sequence these pieces are less satisfying than when they stood alone," he argued, because the "same style is not altogether appropriate" from 1944 to 1964. Similarly, Donald Keene in the *New York Times,* although he largely praised *Paris Journal,* thought her pieces lost something important in the transition from magazine to book form: "Rather than objectivity about events which no longer excite and which are too fragmentarily related to rank as history, the reader might prefer more of Miss Flanner herself."[50]

The most loving and considered of all the reviews came from Janet's old friend Glenway Wescott. He was sensitive to the general fate of most journalistic writing — "Posterity reads old books if they are good enough, but not old magazines or newspapers" — and sensitive to Janet's special contribution to it. "Her great quality is her immediacy and candor of impression — a greatness that journalism is inherently capable of (and history is not, as a rule)." At the same time, he argued, she went beyond mere reporting by telling "tremendous tales nevertheless," narrating the trials of Pétain and Laval, at the start of *Paris Journal,* and the trial of General Salan, at its end. Together she and William Shawn had created an intricate, balanced volume haunted by de Gaulle in the same way that de Gaulle haunted the entire postwar period in France. Without preaching, haranguing, or moralizing — "her mind seems inclined to microcosm rather than macrocosm, and her pages consist of juxtapositions of details rather than flexings of intellect" — Janet re-created the drama and inconsistencies of twenty years of French life in a prose that read like poetry. To Wescott she was "the foremost remaining expatriate writer of the Twenties," a survivor teaching others how to survive.[51]

16

Paris Was Yesterday
1966-1978

But it is day by day that we go forward; today we are as we were yesterday and tomorrow we shall be like ourselves today. So we go on without being aware of it, and this is one of the miracles of that Providence which I so love.

Madame de Sevigné, 1687

... be kind darling, this may be your last chance. The remainders of great love affairs in one's life demand special refuge & handling with tender remembering hands, do not fail because to fail would be to lacerate.

Janet Flanner to Solita Solano, 1966

JANET TOOK WELL to publicity. At times, however, she felt it demeaned her: television brought her more fame than forty years of hard work had.[1] Yet she performed obligingly when Atheneum, the publisher of *Paris Journal*, sent her on a round of interviews and television programs soon after she arrived in New York in January 1966. Describing herself as "a reliable old war horse," she appeared first on NBC's "Today" show — a "breakfast show for the gentry," she called it — and then taped a half-hour broadcast for PBS in which she and Alfred Kazin discussed Truman Capote's new documentary novel *In Cold Blood.* "I looked rather like a grey owl, fluffed up for snow," she observed, adding, "Alfred was better than I, more literary and he *talked* more, he apologized later, and a good thing he did as he recalled all the appropriate literary murder references including Cain & Abel — That enraged me that I hadn't thought of it first!"[2] She was, however, generally pleased with herself. After being interviewed by Eric Goldman, professor of history and consultant to President Lyndon Johnson, for NBC's "Open Mind," she claimed she had been "pretty good in spots and all over very reliable, good, personal, gay, & filled with information."[3]

In early February *Paris Journal* was nominated for a National Book Award in the category of Arts and Letters. Proud that her book was nominated, "a high honor in itself," she didn't expect to win; she thought Alfred Kazin's *Starting Out in the Thirties* the obvious choice.[4] But the judges picked *Paris Journal,* calling it enlightened and humane, "a unique narrative of the culture of a nation in transition." Janet, delighted, handled the official and unofficial press conferences deftly, fielding questions, calling de Gaulle a Shakespearean whose love for France was incestuous, and quipping airily about the $1,000 prize money, already spent but not to be scoffed at. Appearing completely at ease with her new moniker, America's Tocqueville, she could not resist pointing out privately that her four decades of work were "nothing compared to the success of the BOOK and its award — One was ephemeral, the latter compact and tangible."[5] Perhaps, she conceded, "all who favored making a book of my Paris letters were right & I wrong."[6]

Janet gave the first acceptance speech at the awards ceremony on March 15 on the stage of New York's Philharmonic Hall before a crowd of 1,200. A gasp of pleasure could be heard in the audience as the small woman, carefully dressed in a white blouse and black satin skirt, approached the podium. She smiled and said she found herself in the "most delightful circumstances possible for a writer. Writing, good writing, good prose writing is an odd profession and life work because it is so peculiarly balanced." The prose writer struggles to describe "an event over which one has had no control in the first place — . . ." with the "justifiably right words." Once those words are found, the agonized search is momentarily forgotten; the writer is euphoric. "The prose writer," she concluded, "is in a very mild way manic and depressive, down, up, up, down."[7]

Honors of one sort and another continued to arrive; she received the Indiana Authors' Day award from the Indiana Writers Conference, was invited to a White House reception for presidential scholars, and was elected a Daughter of Mark Twain by the Mark Twain Association. She was pleased, but not unreservedly. Although gratified by the national recognition she was getting so late in life, she definitely felt she deserved it. She considered herself a good writer, and she had come to believe that she had invented the form she exploited so well. However, that a collection of her Paris letters had brought her recognition when her personal ambitions remained unfulfilled must have seemed ironic; she suspected that she clung to the form she had created long after it had turned into a formula. Sometimes the books she had not written rose up to taunt her, accusing her of having bartered her talent for the security of *The New Yorker*. Winning the National Book Award reminded her yet again, she wrote Natalia, of the time she believed she had wasted: "I merely copy myself year after year in *The New Yorker,* getting better with practice in copying me, but not expanding."[8] As a result, when she returned to France that spring of 1966, it was with renewed determination to write her book on de Gaulle.

After six months in the United States, she felt displaced in Paris, and her letters did not go smoothly. Josette Lazar was again helping with research on de Gaulle, but Janet wasn't getting very far with the book. She repeated a talk on Colette she'd given at Rizzoli's bookstore in New York to a group of Sarah Lawrence students studying abroad, but she was tired of giving interviews. By summer, however, she was refreshed by the company of a new friend, the writer Mary Frances Kennedy Fisher, who had come to Paris to write on "Foods of the World" for Time-Life Books. Having taken the room adjoining Janet's, Fisher spent a good deal of the summer "happily puffing around Paris on errands for her, fending off her fans at concerts, sampling a new batch of Sancerre in a cool cellar under the Luxembourg, with an ancient vintner she had known for countless years."[9] Beautifully dressed, with her Legion of Honor ribbon pinned to her lapel, Janet would appear each day with a series of tasks for her new assistant. "The pace almost killed me," Fisher would later recall. "And Janet always travelled by Métro or on foot." Janet would not, however, take Mary Frances to Noel's, where she went each weekend, returning to Paris with large bouquets of garden flowers, golden marigolds and dark red roses. Fisher knew that Orgeval was a special place for Janet, where she relaxed, and Janet guarded it jealously.[10]

Most of her friends understood how complicated her private life was. One commented that Janet was like a sailor with a lover in every port; another said she was under such constant pressure that it was a blessing when Natalia wasn't around. But all her friends protected her and respected the discretion with which she conducted her personal affairs. And all enjoyed her mischievous side; she loved ribald humor and was not above an occasional lewd remark herself. Even in her seventies, she amused friends who might have expected a woman of her age to be more sedate. At a concert one night she drifted off to sleep just before a young man, stark naked, streaked through the audience. Michael Bessie didn't think she'd seen him, but later asked her what she thought. "Well-hung," she retorted.[11] Her friend and *New Yorker* colleague Philip Hamburger remembers that after the breakup of his first marriage, she came by his office to cheer him. "Whatever happens," she merrily told him, "keep your cock up."[12]

Hamburger also remembers that Janet was not sympathetic to any flamboyant display of sexuality, be it heterosexual or homosexual. She was shocked by the overt homosexuality in New York, which to her showed a definite lack of propriety and class. Love, she felt, was a question of being genuine, not a matter of show.[13] In public life, one must be circumspect. "Circumspect in writing, she is outspoken in talk," said composer Ned Rorem, who met Janet at one of Rosamond Bernier's parties. Indeed, Rorem's *Paris Diaries,* which weren't particularly discreet, had shocked her. "What on earth," Rorem remembers her asking, did his Quaker parents think about his "pornographic diary?" He said she then looked at him "reproachfully through her monocle, resembing a hip and handsome Amazon disguised as George Washington playing Greek tragedy."[14]

After winning the National Book Award, she was asked to write

several pieces for different magazines, including one on Les Halles
for *Life,* as well as a preface to Robert Phelps's edition of Colette's
writings about physical pleasure and homosexual love. Janet found
the latter a more difficult task than she had anticipated; she wasn't
even sure she approved of the book. Meeting Phelps one January
evening in a smoky lesbian bar in Paris, where she was apparently
well known, Janet confided that the preface was giving her trouble.
She was not sure "how far she dared go."[15] She could certainly not
use her accustomed methods, which in this case might disclose information she did not want disclosed. For assistance she called on
Colette de Jouvenal, the writer's daughter, and her old friend Germaine Beaumont.

Janet had been seeing Germaine more in recent years than she
had before the war, when they quarreled over Janet's "absenteeism"
(Janet's word, used apparently to characterize the change that took
place in their relationship once Janet met Noel).[16] But Germaine
had been one of the first people Janet called on after the war, and
in 1954, twenty-five years after Janet had translated Colette with
Germaine's help, they'd gone to Colette's funeral together. Thanks
to a friend of Germaine's, they sat among the academicians in the
second row. "Could you have dreamed that I should be present
before her catafalque & its resplendent flowers," Janet had excitedly
written Solita.[17] Now they saw one another occasionally at Natalie
Barney's for tea.

Janet called on Germaine ostensibly to refresh her memory about
Colette and pick up some more anecdotes. But she didn't really need
more information; after all, she had been writing and lecturing about
Colette a great deal in the past months. She needed to know how
to handle a subject that made her uncomfortable. Yet when she
finished the piece in March 1967, the publisher praised it for having
struck the "right tone," for having said neither too much nor too
little.[18] She too was satisfied with the result: a short publishing history
of *The Pure and the Impure* followed by a discussion of its content,
making it clear that although she had not liked the book at first, she
had come to consider it a "serious analysis of sex . . . wherever found
or however fragmented and reapportioned."[19]

Natalia, now vice-president of Rizzoli's New York office, came to
Paris in May, impatient with Janet's refusal to leave the Paris letter —

and with her refusal to admit Natalia more fully into her life.[20] After she left, Janet wrote, promising that she would leave for America again by the end of June and stay for almost six months. This time she kept her promise. But soon after she arrived in New York, her friends in France began urging her to return to Paris. She explained to them, characteristically, that she simply could not leave until she had finished her introduction to Jane Grant's memoirs, which had to be edited and checked twice by the *New Yorker* staff; she also was writing a review of Monica Stirling's *The Summer of a Dormouse*. The pattern of her excuses had not changed.

Late in 1967 Janet's sciatica returned, making her peevish and irritable. Although she was back in Paris, what she saw and read gave her little pleasure, and writing her letter was difficult. She disliked most of the new plays; she did not understand long-haired youth; and the politics of the New Left annoyed her, although she regarded the United States' escalating involvement in Vietnam as shameful, wrong, and tragic. The world seemed more and more incomprehensible, with its burgeoning skyscrapers, its ugliness, its continuing violence, its youth subculture, its scatological language. Turning away from it all in her Paris letter of January 3, 1968, she lovingly wrote about the Ingres exhibition at the Petit Palais. The exhibition was "like a pivot, turning public taste backward in time, manner, and subject matter."[21]

Janet, like the public she described, also craved a turning backward. Writing of Les Halles for *Life* magazine, she recalled the "fabulous Paris 1920s and 1930s, when we were all younger and Paris seemed much older than now, with hardly a modern touch and not a single skyscraper."[22] Over time the smells of vegetables, horses, and fresh flowers had been replaced by the stench of gasoline fumes, and even that would soon disappear, she wrote, when the markets were razed. The same sentiment appeared in a piece for *Holiday* magazine, where she described the Bois de Boulogne as the once "famous and fashionable pleasure garden" now "passé in its romanticism." The twentieth century had encroached on its serene respectability, first between the wars when motorists went there for "al fresco pleasures" and then more tragically in 1944, when the Germans shot thirty-five members of the Resistance "against the forest trees."[23]

Janet was romanticizing the past, just as she always had. Attracted to beauty, elegance, and "civilization," she had found that Paris best symbolized all three. But now Paris did not look or even sound the same: the "franglais" she heard spoken everywhere struck her as "dangerous"; the French were losing their "creative function."[24] Only de Gaulle continued on as the "classic frenchman such as france has hardly seen since the days of montaigne."[25]

For these reasons, in part, she was sympathetic to de Gaulle's handling of the national crisis that exploded in the spring of 1968. When the head of the Sorbonne called in the Paris police on May 3 to break up a meeting of striking students, the gendarmes responded quickly and brutally, arresting several students, injuring others, and revealing to many the repressive side of the Gaullist regime. For the next week street fights erupted throughout the Latin Quarter, where barricades lined streets that smelled of burning rubber and tear gas. The teachers' federation declared a sympathy strike, left-wing trade unionists and many intellectuals supported the students, and by May 17, ten million workers walked out of their jobs.

Janet tried to be sympathetic to the protesting students but could not. Neither the May 13 demonstrations against the government nor the subsequent strikes won her support. To her the destruction of everything from plane trees to automobiles was no more than wanton violence. Although she detested the police brutality, she was horrified by the students' disrespect for venerable institutions like the Théâtre National de l'Odéon, which they slept in, scattering their garbage throughout. They were a generation of malcontents, she wrote, and agreed with the *Le Monde* editorial calling the riots nothing more than nihilistic tribal warfare.

Mary McCarthy recalls that at the time she was "very eager for Janet to go to the Sorbonne and also to the Odéon and cover this." McCarthy arranged for some students to take Janet around and show her, for example, their various headquarters. But McCarthy doubts that Janet went. "She was scared," said McCarthy. "Also, she was too conservative; it was a mixture. And, she had been propagandized, by whom I don't really know, but people who had told her that the Sorbonne was terribly filthy. . . . That was not the thing that one should be concentrating on."[26]

In the main Janet considered herself uninformed about the recent violence, or so she wrote Kay Boyle from Orgeval — and she stayed that way.[27] Three years later, when questioned on a television talk show about de Gaulle and his handling of the student demonstrations, she repeated what she had written in her Paris letters of May and June 1968 — that he (like her) had been "uninformed," especially about the danger of the demonstrations, which she called "foolish fracases which the students were having at night." When asked why she had supported de Gaulle, she answered sharply that "I was there, for one thing" and then vividly described the troops sent in to dispel the students. They had been beautifully outfitted, she said without apparent irony, wearing tall boots and carrying big shields.[28]

In extra letters for *The New Yorker,* Janet treated the crisis topically, telling her readers what was happening in graphic detail — so much so that Philip Hamburger commented that she managed, yet again, to get the things nobody else got.[29] She did not, however, try to analyze what lay behind the crisis or to predict where it might lead. She treated it in immediate terms, the terms in which she experienced it. But the crisis depleted her physically and emotionally. The world seemed to have gone mad.

During that troubled spring Solita, who occasionally came to stay with Janet at the Continental, was worried. Janet was in constant physical pain. Solita reported to Kay Boyle in July that "my own darling Janet is 'losing ground' — inevitable with hardening of the arteries; no cure; thank heaven she doesn't understand *anything* medical. Weakness, walking difficult, memory reduced, and such *distress* on her poor marked face. This *must* be her last year of the writing struggle. She now takes 7–8 days to do what was done in 3–4. And in anguish. But her result is as good, often better than her former letters."[30] In August, thinking she had had a nervous collapse, Janet was admitted to the American Hospital in Neuilly for observation. Later she realized she had suffered a small stroke.

She would not stop working. She kept on until the end of October, when she returned to New York and was forced to rest. In November she told Solita that she felt "extremely well, no question but what no work has been my salvation."[31] In Natalia's apartment she was happy and comfortable. But everything having to do with politics or literature still enraged her. In America, Nixon's election prompted her to write that "the country got what it deserved; inauspicious third grade candidates," and most of the novels she read made her "stomache [*sic*] rise —."[32]

For New Year's she and Natalia went to Puerto Rico, where she was fascinated by the "hillsides, all dripping with the frequent rain which several times daily simply drops out of the sky in vertical sheets."[33] Quiet and comfortable, she nonetheless worried that her weakness made her poor company. She had always been spry, but now Natalia didn't think her strong enough for a day's outing to the nearby islands, so Janet stayed indoors, writing letters and listening to Tebaldi on the phonograph. But she fretted that her decision to recuperate in New York might have deeply offended Noel and even Solita — "dearest I shall be back soon," she wrote to Solita in early January 1969, explaining "this has been a bad time for the oldest friends I know but my duty and my necessity of heart were clear —."[34]

Janet resumed her life in France and the Paris letter in March with only one major change; she moved to the posh Hôtel Ritz, complaining all the while about its price. Solita, in Paris to help Janet, disliked the paneled white and gold room with its pink satin divan instead of a bed. However, the surroundings were ultimately unimportant; she had work to do. Solita, at eighty-one, still assisted Janet in collecting, sorting, typing, and editing, just as she had for more than four decades. She took umbrage when people didn't comprehend all that she did. Hugh Ford remembers that one day after he had lunch with the two women, he and Solita watched Janet walk away. Solita was very concerned about Janet's health and thought she was becoming too frail to stay in Paris alone. Ford commented that Janet probably needed a secretary. Solita bristled. "I will let that comment pass," she said coldly, turning on her heel. She abruptly got into a taxi and left. Bewildered, Ford learned only later the extent of her devotion, secretarial and otherwise, to Janet.[35]

Solita had become the architect of the collection of papers she and Janet would jointly donate to the Library of Congress. When John Broderick, chief of the library's Manuscript Division, first asked Janet in early 1966 if she would present her papers to the library, she politely replied that she had none. Undeterred, Broderick wrote again in July of that year. This time Solita answered him, as "Genêt's

friend amateur sec'try, and *guardian* of the thesaurus: birth to retirement . . . to tell you only: pay no attention to Janet Flanner's
statement: 'I have no papers, no material.' Well, *I* have . . . Janet
Flanner knows I am writing to you and what I have told you. Consents
to being bullied."[36] In 1967 Broderick visited them in Orgeval, where
he also met Lib Clark and Noel. He remembers that Janet was initially
a bit cool until she heard a familiar sound, the jingle of change in a
man's pocket; it reminded her of Harold Ross, who'd always kept
his pockets loaded with silver, she told Broderick. From then on
they got along quite well.[37]

Solita clearly enjoyed preparing her own and Janet's papers, going
over their scrapbooks, filing the many documents Janet had in fact
saved, and interesting other friends in the collection. According to
Hildegarde, Solita harvested everything Janet ever wrote and probably became more interested in Janet than in herself.[38] Even during
the spring of 1969, while slowly recuperating from surgery, Solita
still helped Janet prepare the Paris letter, as well as the introduction
she was trying to write for the reissue of Margaret Anderson's *Fiery
Fountains.*

Margaret had retired to Le Cannet in the south of France, where
she had nursed Georgette Leblanc in the earliest days of the war.
Living as a recluse, suffering from emphysema, never complaining,
and in constant touch with Solita, Margaret was aware that Janet had
been ill and had not wanted to pressure her about the often postponed introduction. In late May Janet finally sent it to Margaret,
who said it was too cerebral. Yet, she admitted to Solita, it gave her
"good material" for her "argumentative nature."[39] However, one
annoying detail must be corrected: Janet had written that Margaret
always wore one glove only, to hide her left hand. Margaret impatiently replied that she had never covered her left hand, which was
her favorite. She had worn a glove on her *right.*

The slight changes Solita made in the copy infuriated Janet, who
was by this time "red of face" and snapping at everyone. She was
"worn out — falls asleep all the time," Solita reported to Margaret.
"Can't take a drink — even one. Look & acts *ill.* Forgets *everything.*"[40]
Nevertheless, Solita got Janet ready for a trip to Italy to see Natalia,
and from there to New York and California. When she returned to
France in the fall, Janet was more relaxed but still weak and occa-

sionally irritable. She moved back into the Continental, deciding that the Ritz was much too expensive. Even if *The New Yorker* agreed to pay for a first-class berth, recalls Sybille Bedford, Janet would still take a second.[41] But the modernized Continental frustrated her and she decided to return to the Ritz, accompanied temporarily by Solita. Slowly she was recovering her strength and exuberance.

Janet still presented a composed, witty, and energetic face to the world. Ned Rorem, who turned extracts of *Paris Journal*, selected by Robert Phelps, into a piece for chorus and orchestra, saw Janet in October 1969. Janet was moved by his setting her words to music — "Nobody's ever done that to me before," she told him when she invited him to dinner one night.[42] He fondly recalled that "three hours were passed over a shrimp bisque, soles meunieres, and a kilo of raspberries in thick cream, a long time considering we took no wine. Tonight as always Janet churned midwestern reticence into continental clarity."[43] She showed no sign of irritability or of waning powers. Nor had her sense of humor diminished. After they finished dinner, she called the waiter. Rorem protested, saying, " 'You can't pay, dear Janet. I'm a gentleman.' 'So am I,' she answered." He accompanied her back to her room at the Ritz, where he noticed the aquamarine nightgown which, as he recalled, "earlier in the evening, a chambermaid had laid out on the narrow Spartan bed. 'I'll probably die here,' said Janet without passion, but with the straightforward poignance of one born in 1892."[44]

Janet continued writing Paris letters for the first half of 1970 with an eye toward their inclusion in a second volume of *Paris Journal*, also to be edited by Shawn and published by Atheneum. Enthusiastic about the new collection, she decided that this one would also end with a tribute of sorts to de Gaulle, this time an obituary. Writing from Calistoga in November 1970, she called the majestic de Gaulle "a profound believer in a better, civilizing world."[45] Remembering his brooding grandeur, she admitted she'd become a full-fledged Gaullist.

"Janet flies back from New York today," Solita wrote Kay Boyle on February 1, 1971, proud that her friend was "back to work at 78."[46] Work, however, was almost immediately interrupted. Janet fell and cracked two ribs, and not long after she became violently ill with what she believed was food poisoning. Disgusted, she retired to Orgeval and work on the proofs of *Paris Journal: 1965–1971*.

Noel's companion, Libousse Novak, said Janet lay in bed chortling over her work, enjoying it as if it had been written by someone else and she were reading it for the first time.[47] She was impressed with Shawn's editorial choices: "that he did [the editing] so quickly, and didn't even tell me he was at work on it is a miracle of kindness and goodness," she had commented the preceding December.[48] Delighted by his praise of her work — "transcendental writing," he had called it — she hoped volume two would be as good a book as the first. Now, reading the proofs, she was convinced it was.

She was not so sure about the value of a collection of her early writing. Natalia and her friend Irving Drutman, a journalist and former press agent, had been urging Janet to publish a volume of *New Yorker* pieces from the twenties and thirties, those Janet and Shawn originally thought too jejune to be included in the first *Paris Journal*. Finally she acquiesced. "Viking will pay a good advance," she rationalized to Solita.[49] Regarding her early letters as flippant and sophomoric, she thought Viking's enthusiasm misguided. "We shall see which is wiser," she remarked.[50]

Michael Bessie remembers that he had been lukewarm to the idea when Irving Drutman approached him because at the time, he didn't really understand why someone other than Janet would edit the material. What he neglected to consider, he said, was that she really didn't want to, or couldn't. He also sensed Janet and Natalia were both disappointed with the distribution, promotion, and sales of the second *Paris Journal*. They believed, or Natalia did, that the first volume had created an audience that Atheneum had not adequately exploited.[51] This, recalls Bessie, may have resulted in their going elsewhere — to Roger Straus and then to Viking, which bought the idea that would become *Paris Was Yesterday* even before *Paris Journal: 1965–1971* came off the press in August 1971.

For her summer holiday that year, Janet went with Natalia to Dubrovnik, Yugoslavia, which she described to Lib Clark as a "handsome clean medieval town of white stone, fifteenth century houses with green shutters and marvelous ice cream at the cafes — . . . The Red Flag flies on the flag pole on the town square but the Catholic cathedral had plenty of candles lit and women at prayers so god still reigns!"[52] From there they went to visit Monica Stirling in Lausanne and then on to Venice. Janet was exhausted: "This has been a fine trip visibly, but otherwise I am too old and weary for it really and too much of a burden to look after."[53] Natalia had not left her side, making sure, as she would increasingly in the years to come, that Janet was eating properly, resting, not drinking too much, and taking her medication.

But the constant supervision meant Janet was never alone — "it is natural but exhausting," she commented — and could not freely write to Noel or Solita. "Forgive silence please," she begged Solita, whom she had not written in a few weeks, "I have too little energy to arrange subterfuges etc."[54] The small deceptions of almost thirty years had not ended. However, Janet's lovers were now linked by their common concern over her unsteady health. In October Noel passed through New York en route to Paris from California. She and Natalia, with Janet describing herself as "squashed in between," had dinner and went to the opera. It was the first time they had all spent an evening together.[55]

Complaining of pains in her left arm from a "damned angina" which depressed and fatigued her, she went in to the *New Yorker* office only once a week. She wrote to Solita and Noel less often, saying she felt unambitious and tired. The preface for *Paris Was Yesterday,* was proceeding with difficulty because she suffered from memory lapses and had to depend, long distance, on Noel and Solita for the details she needed: "What was the apertif we used to drink at the Magots, it was a mixture of some sort of cinzano & fruit juice?" she asked Solita. "Write and tell me please — You have so wonderful a memory."[56]

Her letters to Solita began to fill nostalgically with the places and people they had known — Nancy Cunard crossing the Accademia Bridge in Venice, her face streaked with mascara; driving on the Saw Mill River Parkway to Ross's house in Stamford, Connecticut; Janet excitedly forgetting her new *Guide Bleu* the day she and Solita first visited Chartres. "Memories," her preface to *Paris Was Yesterday* began, "are the specific invisible remains in our lives of what belongs in the past tense."[57] Yet she was slightly startled by what she called the "eulogistic" quality of the reviews of *Paris Journal: 1965–1971* that fall. The press photos made her look like Noah's wife, she thought. Regardless, she was pleased: "It is critical acclaim such as I have never received so grandly in the past and which I frankly deserved!!! Volume II of the Paris Journal is really fascinating even for me to reread — wonderfully well-written."[58]

Not all the press was favorable. John Ardagh, Paris correspondent for the London *Times,* wrote in the New York *Herald Tribune* that he could not "fully recommend her latest book to anyone wanting to taste the flavor of the France of these recent years" because her information seemed second-hand, "based mainly on her intelligent reading of the press," albeit "sifted through her long experience of France." Her coverage of the May 1968 riots — "the main event since 1965" — was particularly weak, he noted, as it omitted "acute analysis of their deeper causes and results. . . . Miss Flanner, like de Gaulle himself and other gifted people, has not been entirely spared the onslaught of time."[59]

Janet made fewer public appearances on behalf of the second *Paris Journal* than she had for the first, but when she did, she seemed to enjoy herself thoroughly. One of her most memorable appearances was on Dick Cavett's television interview program, aired on December 12, 1971. Wearing a smart dark suit, a scarf neatly tied at her neck, and white gloves, she laughed heartily, her head thrown way back, and frequently addressed the audience directly, as if she and it were co-conspirators. She appeared completely at ease, except for her right hand, the one that usually held her cigarette, which kept slapping the side of her chair. Her fine enunciation made it seem that she always knew what she was talking about; she dodged subjects adroitly and earned the gallant respect of Norman Mailer, another of Cavett's guests: never had he seen anyone handle the "obdurate art" of television so well, he told her publicly. Later he wrote that "she had a nice crust to her personality. It was like the crust on good bread that lets out agreeable sounds when a piece is broken off for you. . . . It hardly mattered how much she said since she could give you a lesson in deportment by the clearing of her throat."[60]

Shortly after that appearance, Janet finished the preface for *Paris Was Yesterday,* a reminiscent piece about her life in the twenties and her friends. She recollected her conversations with Hemingway about suicide, the publication of *Ulysses,* the lunches in Senlis with

Louis Bromfield, who decorated the table with flowers dazzlingly arranged in Brueghel-like bouquets; she sketched Sylvia Beach, Djuna Barnes, Scott Fitzgerald, and Picasso; she described the "immutably French" Paris that enchanted Americans with its beauty. But it was the first part of her preface, the part about Hemingway, that she liked best.

Containing "all I could record — putting much of it on Earnest and the Bals Musettes & sunsets on the Seine," the preface was to be printed in *The New Yorker*. An "odd inclusion for them," she commented, and one she did not entirely approve of for the magazine: "It is too intimate about Hem and Nancy & my father's suicide —."[61] When Gardner Botsford saw it — Janet had sent it to *The New Yorker* for editing — he said it should appear in the magazine. Printed in the March 11, 1972 issue, it earned so much praise from her colleagues that she decided it was the most popular piece she had ever written.

In fact, its popularity bothered her: it seemed to obscure everything else she had produced for so many years. "Coming as late in my life as it does," she told George Wickes, "I was pretty astonished and pretty indignant, too. But there it was. In the corridor (that means in the corridor of *The New Yorker* . . .), it aroused more interest and corridor appreciation than any other thing I've ever written. I never wrote anything else that pleased everyone else as much as that did. And then they say 'oh, write another.' And I said, 'Well, really, you know. You expect me to produce another absolutely brand new Picasso incident and also an absolutely brand new Marcel Proust incident? You're out of your minds. Those things are rare, and in fact I'd forgotten I knew them.' "[62]

The piece appeared two days before Janet's eightieth birthday. She was in New York. Her cousin Stephen Buchanan, also in New York, happened to remember her birthday and on a whim called the *New Yorker* office. To his surprise, Janet answered and quickly invited him to drop by; he was one of the Buchanans she rather liked. As they sat in her office and chatted, she told him that she had recently seen Hildegarde. The two of them, she said, had decided to have the Flanner name removed from the family undertaking business, which was still called Flanner and Buchanan. Stephen Buchanan was shocked: "I had to tell her that you can't do that so easily." He explained to her that the Buchanan heirs owned the name as well as the business and would not give it up without a fight. "Besides," he added, "it was an honorable association which had a great deal of prestige associated with it." Her father, he reminded her, was a "man well ahead of his time," a man who had brought many reforms to the business. Janet listened carefully, and the matter was dropped.[63]

In public Janet often talked of her father's philanthropy, but she still declined to mention his business, referring to him as a real estate developer or the founder of Flanner House. According to Buchanan, she was probably still angry at Frank Flanner, still ashamed of him. But the preface to *Paris Was Yesterday*, the memories it stirred, the many interviews after its publication, her recent visit with Hildegarde — all this reawakened the past for Janet, who generally did not speak of her family and took pains to avoid relatives when they visited France. She did talk about Hildegarde to friends but hardly ever mentioned Marie; many were not even aware she had had an older sister; when Mary McCarthy asked what happened to her, Janet merely replied, "She died."[64] As Janet would have it, she was a midwesterner whose life began at the age of thirty, when she first went to Paris.

Paris Was Yesterday was a critical hit, amply and favorably reviewed. Most reviews mentioned Genêt's long and loving residence in France, her perspicacious wit, her genteel iconoclasm. Convinced that the second volume of *Paris Journal* was her last volume of consequence, she was rather surprised that *Paris Was Yesterday* did not embarrass her as she had suspected it would: "I am *not* ashamed of those early letters on the whole as I expected to be," she told Solita, "they have pith —."[65]

This time the reviewers agreed heartily. Anatole Broyard, writing for the *New York Times,* called the book a "bouquet of epiphanies"; he quoted so many of its pungent descriptions that he irritated Margaret Anderson into exclaiming that Janet "has no judgment about anything, just fireworks in saying anything at all. That is what the public most adores — look at the Times review: just her wit and brilliant ease of writing."[66] George Wickes, writing for the *New Republic,* more carefully examined the style of *Paris Was Yesterday* to show how it revealed a "different aspect of her [Genêt's] art," more literary than historical, and all the more remarkable considering the frequent gloom of her subject matter. "For *Paris Was Yesterday* is not merely elegiac, it is downright funereal. . . . It smells of mortality throughout, the work of a biographer with a touch of gallows humor and an unfailing curiosity about all the circumstances that turn men into dust."[67]

Emphatically announcing that, unlike Wordsworth, she had no intimations of immortality, she returned to Paris in the spring of 1972, "trailing a cloud of glory at 80," as Solita put it. Still traveling back and forth between the United States and France, she could not be satisfied with one place. She would not choose between her friends nor give up her work. She was, in fact, quite busy, with writing (a preface for Hugh Ford's projected book on small presses in Paris in the twenties), with television (the taping of an interview with Mike Wallace for CBS's "Sixty Minutes"), and with friends like Josette Lazar, who was helping her gather material for an article on de Gaulle's home at Colombey-les-Deux-Églises.

But in August a debilitating attack of uremia cut short her work on de Gaulle. She was hospitalized in Neuilly; her condition was grave, and the illness persisted through the fall; on her release from the American hospital in September, she went to Noel's in Orgeval. Her face was scored with deep lines, her eyes ringed in circles. As she was too weak to travel alone, Noel brought her back to New York in November; Hildegarde joined her there in February while Natalia was away. At the beginning of March 1973 Hugh Ford reported on Janet's recovery: "Yes, I noticed a slowness in her walk, and perhaps she hasn't regained all the weight she must have lost, and her face has preserved the signs of what she has gone through. I saw these things and was saddened. However, I also saw, even more vividly, her grit, indomitableness, her great will to carry on. To my question about how she felt, she replied, 'A little listless and a little restless; I feel I want to be working.' "[68]

Ford, as well as many others, found her memory to be "uncertain, unpredictable, undependable." All the work they had done together the previous July in Paris had vanished. "I had to begin again," he said, "gently, slowly, telling her of the plans we had made, of the substance of the book, of some of the people she thought she would include in the Introduction. With the mention of every name, of every press, of every book, out would come a rush of memories, vivid and colorful and exact."[69] But at the same time she could not see the relationships among these memories, and coordinating all the information seemed almost impossible. Ford persisted, and so did Janet.

Despite her sometimes frail condition, Janet insisted on working. Like her memory, her writing was unsteady; she wrote a short, disconnected piece about Dolly Wilde for *Prose* magazine.[70] Yet at times she felt, appeared, and wrote quite well. To many younger colleagues, like Katharine White's son Roger Angell, she still seemed assured and confident; she had a sense, he recalls, of what the world should be; she did not fall back on cynicism; her opinions might be strong, but she never alienated anyone, for she never attacked persons.[71] She was still witty in public. When she attended a party given for her by the French consul general in November 1972, she handled the huge crowds easily. She saw friends, went to her *New Yorker* office regularly, and started other pieces. She also worried about Noel, who had taken ill and was slowly recovering in Orgeval.

But Janet was too old and sick to take care of Noel; she couldn't even go to France unless Noel were well enough to take care of her. In June of 1973 Noel was better. She promised to take Janet for short trips in her car, so Janet left New York, assuring Natalia she'd come back in the fall. "If I do not, Natalia will leave me and I don't blame her —," she confided to Solita. "In the thirty or more years since I met her I have never spent any lengthy time with her — I am a *brute*."[72] But Noel did not understand that Janet could not — would not — leave Natalia. If she did, she would lose "her forever," Janet complained, "which I cannot afford to do —."[73]

She still felt torn about her relationships. "I have made a cruel mess of my life and of my dearest friends," she wrote Solita sadly, "I never meant to — I have been a fool —."[74] But even Solita, her confidante, was hurt when Janet asked her to destroy their joint checks, a radical change. No longer managing Janet's money, she felt as if she were being erased from Janet's life. Janet was spending more and more time in New York, away from both Noel and Solita.

Natalia cared for her with gentle, conscientious devotion. Fanny Brennan recalls having lunch with the two of them at Natalia's apartment, Janet reaching for the cookies she wasn't supposed to have and Natalia delicately moving them away.[75] When they visited the novelist Célia Bertin, then living in Boston, Natalia would leave very careful instructions each time she went out about everything, from what Janet should have for breakfast to when she should sleep. Each morning when she was out, Natalia would call around eleven to see if Janet was awake, what she had eaten, how she was.[76]

During this visit Janet was very disoriented; she associated Célia Bertin with France, not America. She had entirely forgotten Célia's husband and the advice she'd given Célia before their wedding: Janet had said she'd feel more secure if Célia married, because someone would then take care of her. This had struck Célia as odd. Now Janet said something similar. Célia was talking to her about people they both knew to help Janet get her bearings. When she mentioned Henri Cartier-Bresson, Janet snapped to attention and said yes, she knew him; as a matter of fact, she continued, she'd always been scared by the way both Célia and Henri lived — that is, without security. She had had *The New Yorker* for security, she continued, but they, living from hand to mouth, had had nothing.[77]

Janet tried to live as normally as she could, but the extent of her frailty couldn't be denied. In Paris, Jim West, Mary McCarthy's husband, called to invite Janet to dinner one night. Janet declined, saying she was already in her nightgown. But he was planning to take her to Prunier, he protested. She said she'd be right down. Walking to the restaurant, she stopped to take a nitroglycerin tablet, then half a block later she stopped for another.[78] When Noel took Janet to England to meet Natalia for the British publication of *Paris Was Yesterday* in the summer of 1973, Janet and Natalia stopped by Sybille Bedford's for a drink. As they were leaving, Sybille suggested that they walk to the corner instead of calling for a cab; the cabs were always slow in coming, she said. But by the time they got to the corner, Janet was exhausted.[79]

That fall Noel accompanied Janet to California and left her in Hildegarde's care. There she learned of Margaret Anderson's death. William Shawn suggested she write an obituary, which she willingly took on, calling it a "fanciful" piece. For despite her memory lapses and weakness, she was still able to produce an excellent and penetrating character study of her impassioned friend and rival, a woman of unrelaxed high standards whose contribution to literature Janet considered incalculable. (According to Janet, Margaret wrote quite "carelessly, especially for one always critical of how others wrote!!!!")[80] But her respect for Margaret was genuine: "Do tell her of my admiration, for what she has meant in American writing and publishing," Janet had said in 1969 when Solita was visiting Margaret in Le Cannet. "I admire her for all she created by acts as I did not."[81]

To some, Janet seemed to have become increasingly susceptible to flattery. Compliments pleased her more and more, and yet all the public attention of the last few years had not offset her own private, damning evaluation. She felt she'd had a good life but had opted for security. And Margaret's death reminded her of "all my failings, my weakness, my lack of vigor for work when I had so much talent I did not use —."[82] Again she turned to Solita, asking her forgiveness for not having done what Margaret, in a different way, had.

In the mid-seventies Irving Drutman was putting together a companion volume to *Paris Was Yesterday,* a thin picture-book-type collection of her early London letters, called *London Was Yesterday,* for which Janet had written an introduction.[83] She was also writing an afterword to *The Cubical City,* to be reissued as a "lost" work of American fiction by Southern Illinois University Press. It was a difficult task, for in her estimation the novel had little literary value. But the reprint was a success, and she was surprised. "Who would have thought it would have been successfully revived," she wrote Solita, "a novel which had so little life of its own to begin with — had you not driven me by your energy & indeed your ambition for me I would never have started it, let alone completed it —."[84]

Writing these pieces helped anchor her, not only because they focused her memory but because she felt so rootless. Physically frail, she lived "like a drifter," she said, as she traveled from Orgeval to California to New York and back to Orgeval. Her failing memory was becoming more obvious. In April 1974, she saw some of the Murphy family, whom she had known for years, at the Museum of Modern Art opening of Gerald Murphy's one-man show. She seemed to enjoy the show, Gerald's daughter Honoria Donnelly recalls, but she did not remember Honoria or Gerald or the connection between them. "This is very nice," Janet said simply.[85]

During the next year her failing health further ravaged her mem-

ory, although she performed remarkably well when called upon to
make publicity appearances or do television interviews. She still went
to her *New Yorker* office when she could, and Natalia diligently did
everything possible to keep her spirits up. But each excursion was
difficult. One night in the winter of 1975, after dinner with Lillian
Hellman and Ned Rorem, Janet had a heart seizure in the elevator.
But she was undaunted. She planned to return to France in the
summer and take up her Paris letter again.

She did return, but in Orgeval in June she suffered another attack.
Convalescing at Noel's, she tried to write. Finally, in late August,
she dispatched her final Paris letter. In it appeared all the subjects
she had written about for fifty years — politics, the arts, the local
scene, nature, the weather — but it was a farewell to them, written
elegantly from memory and conviction. Paris, she said, or at least
the Place Saint-Germain-des-Prés, where she had spent so many
years, looked as it had when she first came there in the twenties;
somehow it had preserved itself, despite all the modernizations and
improvements; somehow René, the headwaiter of the Deux Magots,
was still there, delivering vermouth cassis and gossip. She saw Léon
Blum and the socialists standing behind the politics of 1975, reminding both workers and the government of what had and had not
changed. Art, too, looked very much as it had in 1934, and it still,
Janet confessed, baffled and enchanted her. She remembered that
in 1934, when asked what a certain picture by Max Ernst meant, she
had politely refused to answer. Now, she said, if asked again, she
would say "what I could have said so long ago: 'I do not know what
this art means, except that it springs impromptu from the civilized
imagination of man.' "[86]

But not all of the letter was written retrospectively. For two long
paragraphs she lyrically described the roses in Noel's garden, bloom-
ing in grand profusion as they had bloomed all those many summers
before. The brilliant clusters, so alive, were her tribute to Noel and
their years together. One patch, in particular, she loved best of all:
"It blooms with a medley of colors and confusions — a garden of
errors and survivors of mistakes, left to chance and to their floral
fate, frequently bursting with inappropriate rich colors, like bad em-
broidery." This, she said, was the garden "so impoverished when
compared to the great lines of incarnadined blossoms in the well-

tended gardens of our neighbors — this final mixed garden, collected over the years in our rich rural corner of the Ile-de-France, is my favorite floral harvest."[87]

Caring for Janet, who needed constant attention, was becoming increasingly difficult; Solita, living in Orgeval with Lib Clark, was quite frail, and the arthritis Noel had battled for years was overtaking her, stooping her shoulders and slowing her walk. Quipping that "the chassis is gone but the motor still kicks over," Noel would be completely paralyzed by the end of her life, lying abed on the second floor of her home, waiting to be carried downstairs to the garden.[88]

When Janet left France in October 1975, it was clear she could live there no longer. Almost as though she divined that Janet would not return, Solita died a month later. She was eighty-seven.

Janet did return to Orgeval in the summer of 1976 for a short visit, and at times she appeared to be her old self, crisp and witty and in full command of all the "important" things, said Hildegarde — the memories of her friends and family and her first years in Europe.[89] According to Thomas Quinn Curtiss, who visited her then, she adamantly refused to discuss the upcoming American presidential elections, and as always, if she did not want to do something, she did not do it.[90]

In New York Natalia ministered to Janet's every need with infinite patience and skill and unflagging good spirits. Natalia's extraordinary devotion comforted Janet's friends, who were saddened by her worsening condition. When she could, Janet went to her *New Yorker* office, but she was sometimes testy and invariably confused. Her frailty shook her confidence. Upon meeting theater critic Edith Oliver in the corridor one day, she leaned close, touched her shoulder, and whispered, "Where am I?"[91] But if one got her talking about a specific subject, Philip Hamburger remembers, the years would slip away; she might look out the window and say, "The sky is pure Constable."[92]

Hildegarde came to New York to visit Janet for several weeks in the early summer of 1977. She found her sister living in retirement, her memory a shambles. However, accompanied by Natalia, she made a public appearance as late as 1978, at the Rutgers University symposium on women, the arts, and the 1920s. Looking old and tired, she clearly did not know where she was and could not recognize her old friends. She was given no microphone, and she did not speak. But Berenice Abbott said that despite the confusion, Janet seemed to enjoy herself.[93]

The night of November 7, 1978, Janet died en route to Lenox Hill Hospital in Manhattan. Natalia had been with her when she had awakened, frightened, clutching her breast and crying out, sure that this was the end.

Almost ten years later, all Janet's friends — those who had known her well and those who hadn't — said they still missed her. At his desk at *The New Yorker,* Roger Angell leaned back, closed his eyes, and smiled. When Janet turned around and looked at you, he said, a warm light shone on your face. Kay Boyle recalled Janet's words: When I die, she had said in that husky voice, let it not be said I wrote for *The New Yorker* for fifty years. Let it be said that once I stood by a friend.

NOTES
BIBLIOGRAPHY
INDEX

Notes

In the notes, the following abbreviations are used:

JF	Janet Flanner	MHF	Mary Hockett Flanner
HFM	Hildegarde Flanner Monhoff	HRHRC	Harry Ransom Humanities Research Center at the
SS	Solita Solano		University of Texas, Austin

I. YOUNG GIRL

1. Jacob Piatt Dunn, *Representative Citizens of Indiana* (Indianapolis: B. F. Bowen, 1912), p. 30.
2. Interview with HFM, July 15, 1985.
3. Ibid.
4. Flanner-Buchanan scrapbooks, courtesy of Brian K. Buchanan.
5. Anna Flanner Buchanan, "What My Mother Told Me . . . My Father and his Family," unpublished manuscript, pp. 5–6, courtesy of Brian K. Buchanan.
6. Henry Beeson Flanner to Anna Beeson, December 12, 1842, Henry B. Flanner Collection, Indiana Historical Society Library.
7. Buchanan, "What My Mother Told Me," pp. 4–5.
8. For all of the information in the account of Henry's life, I am indebted to Buchanan, "What My Mother Told Me," pp. 2–3.
9. Ibid., p. 8.
10. Henry Beeson Flanner to William Darlington, March 1862, Indiana Historical Society.
11. Buchanan, "What My Mother Told Me," p. 9.
12. Henry Beeson Flanner to Orpha Annette Tyler Flanner, January 19, 1863, Indiana Historical Society.
13. Buchanan, "What My Mother Told Me," pp. 13, 15.
14. Ernest P. Bicknell, *Indianapolis Illustrated* (Indianapolis: Baker Randolph Lithograph and Engraving, 1893), p. 17.
15. Telephone interview with Stephen F. Buchanan, March 22, 1987.

16. Eleanor Goodall Vonnegut, "A Friendship" (1974), p. 3, Eleanor G. Vonnegut Collection, Indiana Historical Society Library.

17. Hildegarde Flanner, "Wildfire!" *The New Yorker,* September 23, 1974, p. 36.

18. See JF, *The Cubical City* (New York: G. P. Putnam's Sons, 1926; reprint, Carbondale: Southern Illinois University Press, 1974), p. 140.

19. Hildegarde Flanner, *Different Images: Portraits of Remembered People* (Santa Barbara: John Daniel, 1987), p. 98.

20. Ibid., p. 98; Vonnegut, "A Friendship," pp. 3–4.

21. Interview with HFM, July 15, 1985.

22. JF to MHF, August 1925, courtesy of John Monhoff.

23. Mary Hockett Flanner, *Bargain Day* (New York: Samuel French, 1911), p. 3.

24. Telephone interview with Stephen F. Buchanan, March 22, 1987.

25. Interview with HFM, July 15, 1985.

26. Phil Casey, "Janet Flanner, the Lady Known as Genêt: A Rarity among Journalists," *Washington Post,* July 2, 1972, p. 5.

27. "Flanner House," *Indiana Recorder,* July 7, 1945, p. 29.

28. Casey, "Janet Flanner," p. 5.

29. See Mary McCarthy, "Conversation Piece," *New York Times Book Review,* November 21, 1965, p. 89. See also JF, interview with Mary McCarthy, 1965, typescript, p. 2, Vassar College Library.

30. Telephone interview with Christin Keller, April 16, 1987; telephone interview with Stephen F. Buchanan, March 22, 1987.

31. Vonnegut, "A Friendship," p. 2; telephone interview with Allegra Stewart, May 12, 1987.

32. Interview with HFM, July 15, 1985.

33. Hildegarde Flanner, *Different Images,* p. 101.

34. Interview with HFM, July 15, 1985.

35. *The Chronicle,* Tudor Hall yearbook, 1906, p. 29, courtesy of Park-Tudor School, Indianapolis.

36. Hildegarde Flanner, *Different Images,* pp. 98–99, 102.

37. JF, Afterword, *The Cubical City* (reprint, Carbondale: Southern Illinois University Press, 1974), pp. 431–33.

38. Information on the early days of Tudor Hall was provided by Lucille C. Dunne, secretary for the alumni.

39. JF to Harrison G. Dwight, n.d., Amherst College Library.

40. Margaret Anderson, *The Strange Necessity* (New York: Horizon Press, 1969), p. 116. See also JF, Afterword, *Cubical City,* p. 433.

41. JF to Katharine White, February 3, 1950, and October 3, 1952, Bryn Mawr College Library.

42. *The Chronicle,* 1909, courtesy of Park-Tudor School, Indianapolis.

2. THIS HARD GEMLIKE FLAME

1. See, for example, JF, *Darlinghissima: Letters to a Friend,* ed. Natalia Danesi Murray (New York: Random House, 1985), p. 63; John Bain-

bridge, *Another Way of Living* (New York: Holt, Rinehart and Winston, 1968), pp. 15, 16; and Mary McCarthy, "Conversation Piece," *New York Times Book Review,* November 21, 1965, p. 89.

2. Bainbridge, *Another Way of Living,* pp. 16–17.
3. Jeannette Nolan, *Hoosier City* (New York: Julian Messner, 1943), p. 206.
4. Telephone interview with HFM, October 3, 1986.
5. Ibid.
6. McCarthy, "Conversation Piece," p. 89.
7. Telephone interview with HFM, October 3, 1986.
8. See Lillian Faderman and Brigitte Erikkson, *Lesbian-Feminism in Turn-of-the-Century Germany* (Naiad Press, 1980), pp. iv–v; Lillian Faderman, *Surpassing the Love of Men* (New York: William Morrow, 1981), p. 250; Carroll Smith-Rosenberg, *Disorderly Conduct: Visions of Gender in Victorian America* (New York: Oxford University Press, 1986), pp. 265–81.
9. Bainbridge, *Another Way of Living,* p. 23; JF, quoted in "Then and Now," *Paris Review* no. 33 (Winter/Spring 1965), p. 162.
10. JF, "The Portrait of Our Lady," *Chicago Literary Monthly,* April 1913, pp. 15–23.
11. JF, "The Portrait of Our Lady," unpublished manuscript, p. 1, Library of Congress.
12. Ibid., p. 5.
13. This version of the story is almost the same as the earlier one: after the boy finds a poster of the dancer in the street, he brings it home to hang in his window. As it happens, Therese Manet inadvertently saves the boy and his family. That night a regiment of "devout" soldiers eager to kill a few "Jewish swine" sees the picture and, mistaking Manet for the madonna, assumes the home belongs to a Christian. The soldiers decide to leave the house unharmed, but not before one of them peers more closely at the poster and is repulsed by the boy.
14. Telephone interview with HFM, October 3, 1986.
15. Telephone conversation with John Monhoff, December 9, 1987.
16. Jacob Piatt Dunn, *Representative Citizens of Indianapolis* (Indianapolis: B. F. Bowen, 1912), p. 471.
17. Telephone interview with Christin Keller, April 16, 1987.
18. Telephone interview with HFM, January 28, 1987.
19. Interviews with HFM, July 15, 1985; John Monhoff, December 8, 1987; Stephen F. Buchanan, March 22, 1987.
20. Telephone interview with Stephen F. Buchanan, March 22, 1987. Telephone interview with Allegra Stewart, May 12, 1987.
21. JF, *The Cubical City* (New York: G. P. Putnam's Sons, 1926; reprint, Carbondale: Southern Illinois University Press, 1974), p. 140.
22. Telephone interview with HFM, January 28, 1987.
23. JF, interview with George Wickes, 1972, tape courtesy of George Wickes.

24. JF, Introduction, *Paris Was Yesterday* (New York: Viking Press, 1972), p. viii.
25. "Questionnaire," *The Little Review,* May 1929, p. 33.
26. JF to SS, June 1950, Library of Congress.
27. Telephone interview with HFM, October 3, 1986.
28. JF, *Cubical City,* p. 181
29. JF to SS, September 25, 1946, Library of Congress.
30. Nott Flint, *The University of Chicago: A Sketch* (Chicago: University of Chicago Press, 1905), p. 8.
31. Joseph Regenstein Library, *One in Spirit* (Chicago: University of Chicago Press, 1973), p. 29.
32. Interview with Fanny Myers Brennan, February 22, 1985.
33. Ibid.
34. JF, *Cubical City,* p. 139.
35. Henry Mencken, "The Flapper," *Smart Set* 45 (February 1915): 1–2.
36. Harold Bloom, ed., *Selected Writings of Walter Pater* (New York: Columbia University Press, 1974), p. 60.
37. JF to SS [1956], Library of Congress.
38. McCarthy, "Conversation Piece," p. 90.
39. JF, About the Author, *An American in Paris* (New York: Simon and Schuster, 1940).
40. See, for example, "Genetics," *Time,* April 22, 1940, p. 97; G. Y. Dryansky, "The Genteel Iconoclast," *Women's Wear Daily,* April 22, 1968, p. 12; and Steve Saler, "Janet Flanner: Last of a Writing Generation," Baltimore *News American,* December 13, 1971, pp. 1A, 5A.
41. McCarthy, "Conversation Piece," p. 90.
42. See Phil Casey, "Janet Flanner, the Lady Known as Genêt: A Rarity among Journalists," *Washington Post,* July 2, 1972, p. 5; Carol Elrod, "Two Hoosiers Prominent in Expatriate Scene," *Indianapolis Star,* November 4, 1979, sec. 6, p. 1; Gwen Mazer, "Lifestyle: Janet Flanner," *Harper's Bazaar,* October 1972, p. 131.
43. Telephone interview with HFM, October 3, 1986.
44. See McCarthy, "Conversation Piece," p. 91; and Casey, "Janet Flanner," p. F5.
45. Telephone interview with HFM, October 3, 1986.
46. Telephone interview with Chris Connelly, April 27, 1987.
47. Ibid.
48. JF, "Impressions in the Field of Art," *Indianapolis Star,* July 7, 1918, sec. 6, p. 3.
49. JF, "Impressions," April 14, 1918, sec. 6, p. 38; December 16, 1917; April 2, 1918, sec. 2, p. 14.
50. JF, "Impressions," January 13, 1918, sec. 6, p. 26; December 30, 1917, p. 28; February 17, 1918, p. 38; June 9, 1918, p. 5.
51. JF, "Impressions," January 6, 1918, sec. 3, p. 20.
52. JF, "Impressions," November 18, 1917, sec. 6, p. 4.
53. JF, "Impressions," January 20, 1918, p. 20.
54. JF, "Impressions," April 2, 1918, sec. 2, p. 14.

55. JF, "Impressions," January 13, 1918, sec. 6, p. 26; January 20, 1918, sec. 6, p. 20; April 2, 1918, sec. 2, p. 14; August 4, 1918, sec. 6, p. 34.

56. JF, "Impressions," August 4, 1918, p. 35.

57. She expressed this conflict as early as 1908, when she wrote "Marks," a short farcical play, for the Tudor Hall yearbook. In the play, Work-for-its-own-sake and Report Card struggle for the soul of a tired student. Work tells the student she slaves for worthless symbols and false rewards. The student protests that good grades win her the esteem of her family (and make it easier for her to ask for spending money). But she and Report Card, who has come along to take part in the debate, lose the argument, and the repentant student promises never to work just for good grades again.

58. JF, "Impressions," March 3, 1918, p. 34.

59. Interview with Fanny Myers Brennan, February 22, 1985.

60. "Eddie" [apparently George Rehm, Lane Rehm's brother] to JF, circa 1950s, Library of Congress.

61. Letters of Richard Myers, Alice-Lee Myers, Hilmar Baukhage, and William Merrill to Lane Rehm, courtesy of Fanny Brennan.

62. JF, *Cubical City*, pp. 41–42.

63. Telephone interview with Stephen F. Buchanan, March 22, 1987.

64. Robert Tucker, "Former Reviewer for *Star* Pens *American in Paris*," *Indianapolis Star*, April 28, 1940.

65. JF, "Comments on the Screen," *Indianapolis Star*, July 14, 1918, sec. 6, p. 1.

3. SHE WHOM THE GODS HAD MADE

1. JF to SS, November 20, 1951, Library of Congress.

2. Matthew Josephson, *Life among the Surrealists* (New York: Holt, Rinehart and Winston, 1962), pp. 44–51.

3. On the New Woman, see Carroll Smith-Rosenberg, "The New Woman as Androgyne," in *Disorderly Conduct: Visions of Gender in Victorian America* (New York: Oxford University Press, 1986), pp. 245–96.

4. G. Y. Dryansky, "The Genteel Iconoclast," *Women's Wear Daily*, April 22, 1968, sec. 1, p. 12.

5. See Malcolm Cowley, *Exiles Return* (New York: Viking Press, 1951), p. 50; and Franklin P. Adams, *The Diary of Our Own Samuel Pepys* (New York: Simon and Schuster, 1935), p. 271, from column of December 31, 1920.

6. Dale Kramer, *Ross and The New Yorker* (Garden City: Doubleday, 1952), p. 22.

7. Anita Loos, *A Girl Like I* (New York: Viking Press, 1966), p. 147.

8. Marc Connelly, *Voices Offstage* (New York: Holt, Rinehart and Winston, 1968), p. 111.

9. JF to Alice-Leone Moats, February 17, [1930s], Boston University Library.

10. Anita Loos, *But Gentlemen Marry Brunettes* (New York: Boni and Liveright, 1928), pp. 38, 40, 42.

11. Richard Myers to Stephen Vincent Benét, March 26, 1925, courtesy of Fanny Brennan.

12. Edna Ferber, *A Peculiar Treasure* (New York: Doubleday, Doran, 1939), p. 291.

13. Anita Loos and Helen Hayes, *Twice Over Lightly* (New York: Harcourt Brace Jovanovich, 1972), p. 6.

14. Ferber, *Peculiar Treasure,* pp. 292–93.

15. Connelly, *Voices Offstage,* p. 82.

16. Telephone interviews with Célia Bertin, July 24, 1987, and Thomas Quinn Curtiss, June 16, 1987.

17. JF, interview with Mary McCarthy, 1965, typescript, p. 5, Vassar College Library.

18. JF to SS, May 17, 1945, Library of Congress.

19. See JF, *The Cubical City* (New York: G. P. Putnam's Sons, 1926; reprint, Carbondale: Southern Illinois University Press, 1974), p. 21.

20. JF, *Darlinghissima: Letters to a Friend,* ed. Natalia Danesi Murray (New York: Random House, 1985), p. 486.

21. Telephone interview with Thomas Quinn Curtiss, June 16, 1987.

22. Jane Grant, *Ross, The New Yorker, and Me* (New York: Reynal, 1968), p. 223.

23. JF, "In Transit and Return," *Century,* 1920, pp. 801–13.

24. "As It Was," unpublished manuscript, Library of Congress. Solita dated the story as 1912, calling it "Janet's earliest story," but her dates were often wrong. It is possible, though unlikely, that the story was first written soon after Janet returned from Berlin, during the year of Frank Flanner's death, and then revised more than once.

25. JF to SS, January 31, 1974, and March 29, 1973, Library of Congress.

26. Before meeting Janet in 1918, Solita was called variously Salita Solana and Salita Solano. She apparently began to change her name when she turned twenty-one and settled on Solita Solano just before taking the job at the *Tribune.*

27. Interview with Warren S. Wilkinson, August 21, 1986.

28. SS, *Statue in a Field* (Paris: 1934), p. 25.

29. Postcard, n.d., JF/SS scrapbooks, Library of Congress.

30. Interview with Warren S. Wilkinson, August 21, 1986.

31. SS scrapbooks, Library of Congress.

32. Telephone interview with Elizabeth Jenks Clark, January 17, 1988.

33. JF/SS scrapbooks, Library of Congress.

34. Sir Herbert Tree to SS, July 1, 1917, Library of Congress.

35. SS to Alexander Woollcott, December 22, 1915, Houghton Library, Harvard University.

36. See Sherwood Ross, *Gruening of Alaska* (New York: Basic Books, 1968), pp. 38–39.

37. News item (1919) enclosed in letter from SS to Carlos Baker, August 29, 1964, courtesy of Carlos Baker.

38. H. L. Mencken to SS n.d., Library of Congress.
39. George Jean Nathan to SS, November 8, 1920, Library of Congress.
40. Adams, *Diary of Our Own Samuel Pepys,* p. 254, from column dated May 30, 1920.
41. SS, *Statue in a Field,* p. 8.
42. SS, marginal notation in SS/JF scrapbooks, Library of Congress.
43. Interview with Fanny Brennan, February 22, 1985; interview with M. F. K. Fisher, July 13, 1985.
44. Interview with HFM, July 15, 1985.
45. Interview with Fanny Brennan, February 22, 1985.
46. Interview with Philip Hamburger, October 8, 1986.
47. "Eddie" [George Rehm] to JF, December 18, [1950s], Library of Congress.
48. Interview with HFM, July 15, 1985.
49. Ibid.

4. BUT, I MUST DARE ALL

1. Quoted in John Bainbridge, *Another Way of Living* (New York: Holt, Rinehart and Winston, 1968), pp. 16, 21.
2. Ibid., p. 16.
3. Ibid., p. 18.
4. JF to SS, April 4, 1973, Library of Congress.
5. JF, "Hoi Polloi at Close Range," *New York Tribune,* November 20, 1921, sec. 5, p. 2.
6. Ibid.
7. See, for example, Malcolm Cowley, *A Second Flowering* (New York: Viking Press, 1973), p. 4; and Paul Fussell, *The Great War and Modern Memory* (New York: Oxford University Press, 1975), chap. 1.
8. SS, "Constantinople Today," *National Geographic* 41 (June 1922): 647.
9. Ibid., pp. 663, 671.
10. Interview with Virgil Thomson, December 31, 1985.
11. JF, "Lament in Precious Shape," in miscellaneous writings, Library of Congress.
12. JF, Letter to the Dramatic Editor, *New York Times,* June 4, 1922, sec. 6, p. 1.
13. SS, "Vienna — A Capital without a Nation," *National Geographic* 43 (January 1923): 79, 86, 95.
14. JF, "Impressions in the Field of Art," *Indianapolis Star,* April 2, 1918, sec. 2, p. 14.
15. JF, "Hoi Polloi at Close Range," p. 2.
16. JF, "Weather: Wise and Foolish," *Seven Seas,* April 1933, pp. 17, 29–30.
17. "Paris in the Twenties," *The Twentieth Century,* CBS television program, April 17, 1960.
18. Quoted in "Then and Now," *Paris Review* no. 33 (Winter/Spring 1965), p. 169.

19. See Sandra M. Gilbert, "Costumes of the Mind," *Critical Inquiry* 7 (1980): 408–17, for a discussion of the male modernist's response to World War I and its impact on women.

20. Quoted in Bainbridge, *Another Way of Living,* p. 16. See also JF, Foreword: Three Amateur Publishers, in *Published in Paris: American and British Writers, Printers, and Publishers in Paris, 1920–1939,* ed. Hugh Ford (New York: Macmillan, 1975), p. xiii; and JF, "Why Do Americans Live in Europe?" *transition* 14 (Fall 1928): 98–119.

21. JF, Last Will and Testament, September 8, 1923, Library of Congress.

22. "Questionnaire," *The Little Review,* May 1929, p. 32.

23. SS, "The Hotel Napoleon Bonaparte," draft, Library of Congress; and John C. Broderick, "Paris Between the Wars: An Unpublished Memoir by Solita Solano," *Quarterly Journal of the Library of Congress,* October 1977, p. 308.

24. Quoted in Broderick, "Paris Between the Wars," p. 309.

25. Margaret Anderson, *The Fiery Fountains* (New York: Horizon Press, 1951), p. 33.

26. JF, note on SS's typescript of "The Hotel Napoleon Bonaparte," Library of Congress.

27. Telephone interview with Berenice Abbott, May 6, 1987.

28. Quoted in Noel Riley Fitch, *Sylvia Beach and the Lost Generation* (New York: W.W. Norton, 1983), p. 135.

29. JF, "Oscar Wilde's Niece," *Prose,* Spring 1973, p. 40.

30. Anita Loos, *A Girl Like I* (New York: Viking Press, 1966), p. 237.

31. Ibid., pp. 240–44.

32. Anita Loos to SS, April 24, 1974, Library of Congress.

33. See, for example, "Diary of an American Art Student in Paris," *Vanity Fair,* November 1922, pp. 44, 106, 108; and JF, "Why Do Americans Live in Europe?" pp. 98–119.

34. Ezra Pound, "The Island of Paris: A Letter," *The Dial* 69 (1920): 406.

35. Elizabeth Eyre de Lanux, "Letters of Elizabeth," *Town and Country,* December 15, 1922, p. 34.

36. Kay Boyle and Robert McAlmon, *Being Geniuses Together* (San Francisco: North Point Press, 1984), p. 163.

37. See Leo Litwak, "Kay Boyle — Paris Wasn't Like That," *New York Times Book Review,* July 15, 1984, pp. 1, 32–33.

38. See Janet Scudder, *Modelling My Life* (New York: Harcourt, Brace, 1925), p. 231; and Sisley Huddleston, *In and About Paris* (London: Methuen, 1927), p. 1.

39. See Harold Stearns, *A Street I Know* (New York: Lee Furman, 1935), p. 258.

40. Anderson, *Fiery Fountains,* p. 36.

41. Interview with Fanny Myers Brennan, February 22, 1985.

42. Interview with Roger Angell, June 19, 1987.

43. JF to Alice-Léone Moats, [1930s], Boston University Library.

44. Basil Woon, *The Paris That's Not in the Guidebooks* (New York: Brentano's, 1926), pp. 267–68.

45. See Hugh Ford, ed., *The Left Bank Revisited: Selections from the Paris Tribune, 1917–1934* (University Park: Pennsylvania State University Press, 1972), p. 113.
46. JF to MHF, May 24, [1924], courtesy of John Monhoff.
47. Bryher, *The Heart to Artemis* (New York: Harcourt, Brace, and World, 1962), pp. 207–8.
48. JF, *Paris Was Yesterday* (New York: Viking Press, 1972), p. x.
49. SS to Carlos Baker, February 18, 1962, courtesy of Carlos Baker; SS to Margaret Anderson, n.d., Library of Congress.
50. Interview with Fanny Myers Brennan, February 22, 1985.
51. JF to Carlos Baker, December 7, 1966, Library of Congress.
52. Ibid.
53. JF and SS to Carlos Baker, December 27, 1966, Library of Congress.
54. Telephone interview with HFM, January 28, 1987.
55. Interview with Hugh Ford, May 16, 1986.
56. JF to MHF, November 20, 1923, courtesy of John Monhoff.
57. Correspondence of JF to MHF, March–August 1924, courtesy of John Monhoff.
58. Ibid.
59. See Jane Grant, *Ross, The New Yorker, and Me* (New York: Reynal, 1968), p. 223.
60. SS to MHF, December 5, 1923, courtesy of John Monhoff.
61. JF to MHF, n.d., courtesy of John Monhoff.
62. JF to MHF, May 19, [1924], courtesy of John Monhoff.
63. JF, *The Cubical City* (New York: G. P. Putnam's Sons, 1926; reprint, Carbondale: Southern Illinois University Press, 1974), p. 166.
64. Ibid., p. 421.
65. Ibid., p. 312.
66. Mercy Wellington may have been partly modeled on Mercedes de Acosta, a friend of Janet's, who married Abram Poole in 1920; some circumstances of her marriage resemble Delia's. See Mercedes de Acosta, *Here Lies the Heart* (New York, Reynal, 1960), pp. 106–9, presumably edited by Solita. Another model for Mercy Wellington may have been Sally Farnham, a sculptress Janet knew who lived near Neysa McMein.
67. JF, *Cubical City,* p. 349.
68. Ibid., p. 318.
69. Ibid., pp. 229–30. For a recent, provocative discussion of the mother-daughter bond from a psychoanalytic viewpoint that may bear on the relationship between Janet and Mary Flanner, see Nancy Chodorow, *The Reproduction of Mothering: Psychoanalysis and the Sociology of Gender* (Berkeley: University of California Press, 1978); see also Adrienne Rich, *Of Woman Born: Motherhood as Experience and Institution* (New York: W. W. Norton, 1976). For an overview of the literature on the mother-daughter relationship in psychoanalytic and literary theory, see Judith Kegan Gardiner, "Mind Mother: Psychoanalysis and Feminism," in Gayle Greene and Coppelia Kahn, *Making a Difference: Feminist*

Literary Criticism (London: Methuen, 1985), pp. 113–45; and Marianne Hirsch, "Mothers and Daughters," *Signs: Journal of Women and Culture in Society* 7, no. 1 (Autumn 1981): 200–222.

70. JF, *Cubical City*, pp. 137–38.

71. See, for example, JF, *Paris Was Yesterday*, p. xxiii; and "Then and Now," p. 169.

72. JF, *Cubical City*, p. 45. This description may refer to the association of lesbian with prostitute found in nineteenth-century French literature; it is likely that she was familiar with this association. See Elyse Blankley, "Renee Vivien and the City of Women," in *Women Writers and the City: Essays in Feminist Literary Criticism,* ed. Susan Merrill Squier (Knoxville: University of Tennessee Press, 1984), p. 49: "Writers and artists have long regarded lesbians and prostitutes as twin exfoliation of the same rootstock. . . . The sapphist/whore connection was . . . well understood by the turn of the century."

73. See Adrienne Rich, "Compulsory Heterosexuality and Lesbian Existence," *Signs: Journal of Women in Culture and Society* 5, no. 4 (Summer 1980): 659.

74. For a brief overview of JF's view of America and what she called "aesthetic ignorance," see Bainbridge, *Another Way of Living,* pp. 17–18.

75. JF, *Darlinghissima: Letters to a Friend,* ed. Natalia Danesi Murray (New York: Random House, 1985), p. 44.

76. SS to MHF, December 5, 1923, courtesy of John Monhoff.

77. Telephone interview with HFM, January 28, 1987.

78. JF to MHF, June 26, 1925, courtesy of John Monhoff.

5 . PARIS FRANCE

1. SS, "The Hotel Napoleon Bonaparte," in John C. Broderick, "Paris Between the Wars: An Unpublished Memoir by Solita Solano," *Quarterly Journal of the Library of Congress,* October 1977, p. 313.

2. Transcript of "60 Minutes," CBS television program, April 22, 1973.

3. See Shari Benstock, *Women of the Left Bank: Paris, 1900–1940* (Austin: University of Texas Press, 1986), pp. 8–20, 24–30.

4. Margaret Anderson, *My Thirty Years' War* (New York: Covici, Friede, 1930), p. 266.

5. SS, "Hotel Napoleon Bonaparte," p. 309.

6. "Paris in the Twenties," *The Twentieth Century,* CBS television program, April 17, 1960.

7. Transcript of "60 Minutes," April 22, 1973.

8. JF, memo, n.d., Library of Congress.

9. "Paris in the Twenties"; "When This You See, Remember Me," film documentary on Gertrude Stein, Del Mar, California, 1971.

10. Interview with Virgil Thomson, December 31, 1985.

11. Linda Simon, *The Biography of Alice Toklas* (Garden City, N.Y.: Doubleday, 1977), p. 224.

12. Most accounts, derived from Solita's, date the meeting as 1923, but that fall Janet was in California and New York. Janet's letters to her family suggest that they met Nancy in the fall of 1924.
13. Hugh Ford, ed., *Nancy Cunard: Brave Poet, Indomitable Rebel, 1896–1965* (Philadelphia: Chilton, 1968), pp. 78, 76.
14. See Anne Chisholm, *Nancy Cunard* (Harmondsworth, England: Penguin Books, 1981), pp. 103 and 110–120, for a discussion of the differences between Cunard and Iris March.
15. Nancy Cunard to SS, April 20, 1963, Library of Congress.
16. HFM to the author, September 2, 1986.
17. Nancy Cunard to JF, [early summer 1924], [fall 1925], Library of Congress.
18. Interview with HFM, July 15, 1985.
19. See JF to Nancy Cunard, February 3, [1963], HRHRC.
20. See JF to Sylvia Beach, October 4, 1958, Princeton University Library. In fact, however, the hat she wore that night belonged to her barber.
21. Telephone interview with Berenice Abbott, May 6, 1987.
22. Ibid.
23. Nancy Cunard, *G.M.: Memories of George Moore* (London: Rupert Hart-Davis, 1956), p. 162.
24. Ibid., p. 163.
25. Daphne Fielding, *Those Remarkable Cunards: Nancy and Lady Emerald* (New York: Atheneum, 1968), p. 77; and SS, manuscript drafts of "The Hotel Napoleon Bonaparte," Library of Congress.
26. SS to Marie Flanner, [1925], Library of Congress.
27. Marginal note by HFM on letter of JF to MHF, September 14, 1925, courtesy of John Monhoff.
28. Interview with HFM, July 15, 1985.
29. Interview with M. F. K. Fisher, July 14, 1985.
30. Hildegarde Flanner, *The Hearkening Eye* (Boise, Idaho: Ashanti Press, 1979), p. iv.
31. Hildegarde Flanner, "Wildfire!" *The New Yorker,* September 23, 1974, p. 36.
32. Interview with HFM, July 15, 1985; correspondence of JF and HFM, n.d., courtesy of John Monhoff.
33. See SS, "Both Banks of the Seine," *D.A.C. News,* March 1932, p. 51; George Wickes, *The Amazon of Letters* (New York: Putnam, 1976); and George Wickes, "A Natalie Barney Garland," *Paris Review* 61 (Spring 1975): 110, 118.
34. William Carlos Williams, *Autobiography of William Carlos Williams* (New York: New Directions, 1967), p. 229.
35. SS, "Hotel Napoleon Bonaparte," p. 309.
36. Quoted in Wickes, "Natalie Barney Garland," pp. 117–18.
37. Quoted ibid., p. 131.
38. W. G. Rogers, *Ladies Bountiful* (New York: Harcourt, Brace and World, 1968), p. 44.
39. Quoted in Wickes, "Natalie Barney Garland," p. 109.

40. JF, interview with George Wickes, June 8, 1972, tape courtesy of George Wickes.

41. See Miron Grindea, "Combat with the Amazon of Letters," *Adam* no. 299 (1964), p. 9.

42. Wickes, "Natalie Barney Garland," p. 124.

43. See Wickes, *Amazon of Letters,* p. 253.

44. Dolly Wilde to JF, [1920s], Library of Congress. There is reason to believe that Janet and Dolly had a short-lived affair and that Janet was occasionally jealous of Dolly's devotion to Natalie.

45. JF, interview with George Wickes, June 8, 1972.

46. See JF, Foreword: Three Amateur Publishers, *Published in Paris,* ed. Hugh Ford (New York: Macmillan, 1975), p. xii; and Benstock, *Women of the Left Bank,* p. 231.

47. Quoted in Djuna Barnes, *Interviews,* ed. Alyce Berry (Washington, D.C.: Sun and Moon Press, 1985), p. 388. See also Kay Boyle and Robert McAlmon, *Being Geniuses Together* (San Francisco: North Point Press, 1984), p. 31.

48. Morrill Cody, *This Must Be the Place* (New York: Lee Furman, 1927), p. 312.

49. Djuna Barnes to JF, postcard, n.d., McKeldin Library, University of Maryland.

50. Andrew Field, *Djuna: The Life and Times of Djuna Barnes* (New York: G. P. Putnam's Sons, 1983), p. 240.

51. Kathryn Hulme, *Undiscovered Country* (Boston: Atlantic–Little, Brown, 1966), pp. 37–39.

52. Edward Burns, ed., *Staying On Alone: The Letters of Alice B. Toklas* (New York: Liveright, 1973), p. 208.

53. See Margaret Anderson, *My Thirty Years' War* (New York: Covici, Friede, 1930), p. 36.

54. Ibid., p. 36.

55. Quoted in Margaret Anderson, *The Unknowable Gurdjieff* (1962; reprint, New York: Samuel Weiser, 1970), pp. 28–29.

56. Interview with HFM, July 15, 1985.

57. Solita's first novel, *The Uncertain Feast* (New York: G. P. Putnam's Sons, 1924), earned F.P.A.'s approval — "An elegant book, to say the least, / Is Solita Solano's *The Uncertain Feast*" — as well as William R. Benét's, who called Solita "the first of our feminine realists to be absolutely ruthless, in the sense that Theodore Dreiser and Ben Hecht are ruthless." (See F.P.A., "The Conning Tower," *New York World,* October 9, 1924; and W. R. Benét, *Saturday Review of Literature,* November 1, 1924, p. 243.) Eugene Jolas wrote in *transition* that Solita was one of those "seeking the quiescent atmosphere of an Old World civilization in order to realize their creative dreams." Of *The Uncertain Feast,* he commented chauvinistically that "although written by a woman, it has not the usual feminine garrulity that makes women writers produce enormous volumes without feeling or insight." (See Hugh Ford, ed., *The Left Bank Revisited: Selections from The Paris Tribune,*

1917–1934 [University Park: Pennsylvania State University Press, 1972], pp. 260–261.)

Her second novel, *The Happy Failure* (New York: G. P. Putnam's Sons, 1925), did not receive such high praise; it and her next, *This Way Up* (New York: G. P. Putnam's Sons, 1927), suffered at the hands of New York critics who thought that Solita capitalized on the "scandalous temerity of the 'younger generation' of 1920." Lillian Hellman was one of the few to disagree: "Miss Solano has evidently escaped the palsy of admiration which strikes so many Americans when they come to write of Paris. If in the past you have been a little weary of those panegyrics, you will hail this book [*This Way Up*], which treats Paris as though it were founded by human beings and which drops it to a level slightly lower than God." (See review of *The Happy Failure, New York Times,* August 30, 1925, p. 24; and Lillian Hellman, "Books," New York *Herald Tribune,* October 8, 1927, p. 22.)

58. JF to e. e. cummings, July 20, [1956], Houghton Library, Harvard University.
59. Margaret Anderson to Coburn Britton, n.d., Library of Congress.
60. JF to Margaret Anderson, [1929], Library of Congress.
61. JF to SS, October 29, 1973, Library of Congress.
62. Letters of Richard Myers, courtesy of Fanny Myers Brennan; interview with Virgil Thomson, December 31, 1985.

6. A GENTLEMAN OF THE PRESS IN SKIRTS

1. Garreta Busey, "Living One's Own Life: *The Cubical City*," New York *Herald Tribune,* December 12, 1926, p. 3.
2. JF to MHF, December 4, 1926, courtesy of John Monhoff.
3. She sent the sketch to *The New Yorker,* which published it in the issue of November 27, 1926, pp. 30–31.
4. Jane Grant to JF, [June] 1925, Jane Grant Papers, University of Oregon.
5. The editors, *The New Yorker,* February 21, 1925, p. 2.
6. Jane Grant to JF, [June] 1925, Jane Grant Papers, University of Oregon.
7. Lionel Trilling, "*New Yorker* Fiction," *The Nation,* April 11, 1942, p. 425.
8. Dale Kramer, *Ross and The New Yorker* (Garden City: Doubleday, 1952), p. 121.
9. "Letter from Paris," *The New Yorker,* October 5, 1929, p. 73.
10. "Letter from Paris," *The New Yorker,* October 24, 1925, p. 30.
11. Ibid.
12. "Letter from Paris," *The New Yorker,* July 31, 1927, pp. 41–43.
13. "Letter from Paris," *The New Yorker,* June 12, 1926, p. 49.
14. "Letter from Paris," *The New Yorker,* April 3, 1926, pp. 51–52.
15. Jane Grant, *Ross, The New Yorker, and Me* (New York: Reynal, 1968), p. 224.
16. See correspondence of JF to MHF, 1925, especially December 18, 1925, courtesy of John Monhoff.

17. David Diamond to the author, July 24, 1987. In her earliest Paris letters, she did occasionally use the first-person pronoun.
18. Telephone interview with Thomas Quinn Curtiss, June 16, 1987.
19. JF, *Paris Was Yesterday* (New York: Viking Press, 1972), p. xvi.
20. Telephone interview with Chris Connelly, April 27, 1987.
21. "Two Get Divorces in Paris," *New York Times,* April 1, 1926, p. 6.
22. Nancy Cunard to JF, n.d., Library of Congress.
23. Nancy Cunard to JF, September 3, [1926], Library of Congress.
24. Interview with Anne Chisholm, October 23, 1986.
25. Anne Chisholm, *Nancy Cunard* (New York: Alfred A. Knopf, 1979), p. 150.
26. JF to MHF, February 29, 1927, courtesy of John Monhoff.
27. JF to SS, July 1971, Library of Congress. Interviews with Sybille Bedford, October 22, 1986; and Rosamond Bernier, August 6, 1987.
28. JF to SS, July 1971, Library of Congress.
29. Hugh Ford, ed., *Nancy Cunard: Brave Poet, Indomitable Rebel, 1896–1965* (Philadelphia: Chilton, 1968), p. 76.
30. Jane Heap, "Lost: A Renaissance," *The Little Review,* May 1929, p. 6.
31. Ralph Ingersoll, *Fortune,* August 1934, p. 97.
32. Interview with Kay Boyle, July 16, 1985.
33. Quoted in Brendan Gill, *Here at The New Yorker* (New York: Random House, 1975), p. 389.
34. SS, "The Hotel Napoleon Bonaparte," *Quarterly Journal of the Library of Congress* 34 (October 1977): 311.
35. "Isadora," *The New Yorker,* January 1, 1927, p. 18; reprinted in *An American in Paris* (New York: Simon and Schuster, 1940), p. 180; and in *Paris Was Yesterday* (New York: Viking Press, 1972), p. 35.
36. See "The Egotist," *The New Yorker,* October 29, 1927, pp. 23–25; reprinted in *American in Paris,* p. 219, and in *Paris Was Yesterday,* p. 151. "Dearest Edith," *The New Yorker,* March 2, 1929, pp. 26–28; reprinted in *American in Paris,* p. 193, and in *Paris Was Yesterday,* p. 176.
37. "The Egotist," p. 23.
38. "Dearest Edith," p. 28.
39. "California — Dunt Esk" was signed "J.F."
40. Quoted in Leo Litwak, "Kay Boyle — Paris Wasn't Like That," *New York Times Book Review,* July 15, 1984, p. 2.
41. Interview with Simon Michael Bessie, November 11, 1986.
42. "Questionnaire," *The Little Review,* May 1929, p. 32.
43. Interview with Simon Michael Bessie, November 11, 1986.
44. JF to MHF, November 17, [1927], courtesy of John Monhoff.

7 . NOELINE

1. Interview with Sybille Bedford, October 22, 1986.
2. Edmund Wilson, *The Twenties* (New York: Farrar, Straus, and Giroux, 1975), p. 355.

3. Richard Myers to Stephen Vincent Benét, January 19, 1932, courtesy of Fanny Myers Brennan.

4. Richard Myers to Stephen Vincent Benét, March 7, 1932, courtesy of Fanny Myers Brennan.

5. See Simon Hodgson, "Sublime Governess," *New Statesman* February 22, 1963, p. 268.

6. Ibid.

7. Richard Myers to Stephen Vincent Benét, June 24, 1930, courtesy of Fanny Myers Brennan.

8. Drue Tartière, *The House near Paris: An American Woman's Story of Traffic in Patriots* (New York: Simon and Schuster, 1946), p. 105.

9. Francis Rose, *Saying Life: The Memoirs of Sir Francis Rose* (London: Cassell, 1961), p. 71.

10. SS, "Both Banks of the Seine," *D.A.C. News,* September 15, 1933, p. 36.

11. Glenway Wescott, "The Frenchman Six Feet Three," *Harper's Magazine,* July 1942, p. 136.

12. Wescott, "Frenchman Six Feet Three," p. 136.

13. Noel Murphy, interview with Honoria Murphy Donnelly, June 1981, tape courtesy of Honoria Donnelly.

14. Honoria Murphy Donnelly, *Sara and Gerald* (New York: Holt, Rinehart and Winston, 1984), p. 133.

15. "Mrs. H. S. Haskins's Will Filed," *New York Times*, May 16, 1928, p. 26.

16. Edmund Wilson, *The Fifties* (New York: Farrar, Straus, and Giroux, 1986), p. 376.

17. Noel Murphy, interview, June 1981, tape courtesy of Honoria Murphy Donnelly.

18. Ernest Hemingway to JF, April 18, 1933, Princeton University Library.

19. See Margaret Anderson to SS, [1970s], Library of Congress.

20. Diane Forbes-Robertson Sheean to the author, March 11, 1987.

21. SS, "Both Banks of the Seine," *D.A.C. News,* February 20, 1932, p. 50.

22. Diane Forbes-Robertson Sheean to the author, March 11, 1987; telephone interview with Ruth Mills, March 27, 1987.

23. Interview with Virgil Thomson, December 31, 1985.

24. Telephone interview with Elizabeth Jenks Clark, December 8, 1986.

25. Interview with Mary McCarthy, October 26, 1987.

26. SS, notes on sessions with Gurdjieff, February 29, 1936, Library of Congress.

27. Kathryn Hulme, *Undiscovered Country* (Boston: Atlantic–Little, Brown, 1966), p. 40.

28. JF to Kathryn Hulme, September 1, 1966, Library of Congress.

29. Ibid.

30. JF to MHF, August 15, 1933, courtesy of John Monhoff.

31. "Letter from Paris," *The New Yorker,* September 2, 1933, pp. 43–45.

32. Interview with Sybille Bedford, October 22, 1986. See also corre-

spondence between JF and Sir Francis Rose, Fales Collection, Bobst Library, New York University; correspondence between JF and Gertrude Stein, Beinecke Library, Yale University.

33. SS, "Both Banks of the Seine," *D.A.C. News,* March 1932, p. 50.
34. JF to MHF, [December 1928], courtesy of John Monhoff.
35. See ibid., for example.
36. See Gabrielle Colette, *Chéri,* trans. Janet Flanner (New York: A. & C. Boni, 1929); Gabrielle Colette, *Mitsou,* trans. Jane Terry, introduction by Janet Flanner (New York: A. & C. Boni, 1930); and Gabrielle Colette, *Claudine at School,* trans. Janet Flanner (London: V. Gollancz, 1930).
37. JF to MHF, September 5, 1931, courtesy of John Monhoff.
38. Margaret Anderson to Coburn Britton (?), n.d., Library of Congress.
39. There may have been a fourth story in the series, for during this time *The New Yorker* apparently rejected one. She mentions the rejection in her correspondence with her mother but does not describe the story.
40. JF, "Tchatzu," *The New Yorker,* March 19, 1932, pp. 18–20; "Oh, Fire!" *The New Yorker,* November 5, 1932, pp. 19–20; "Venetian Perspective," *The New Yorker,* August 25, 1934, pp. 17–19.

8. C'ÉTAIT LES BEAUX JOURS

1. "Perfume and Politics," *The New Yorker,* May 3, 1930, p. 25; reprinted in *An American in Paris* (New York: Simon and Schuster, 1940), p. 131.
2. Stanley Edgar Hyman, "The Urban New Yorker," *New Republic,* July 20, 1942, p. 91.
3. Quoted in Valentine Lawford, *Horst: His Work and His World* (New York: Alfred A. Knopf, 1984), p. 63.
4. Interview with Virgil Thomson, December 31, 1985.
5. See JF, "Behind the Seams," *Ladies' Home Journal,* April 1929, p. 22.
6. JF, "Fashions in Spies," *Harper's Bazaar,* May 19, 1938, p. 125.
7. See "Letter from Paris," *The New Yorker,* December 14, 1929, p. 54; reprinted in *Paris Was Yesterday* (New York: Viking Press, 1972), p. 59. "Come as Somebody Else," *The New Yorker,* November 23, 1933, p. 27; reprinted in *American in Paris,* p. 212.
8. Katharine S. White, memo to Harold Ross, Wolcott Gibbs, St. Clair McKelway, and Ik Shuman, September 8, 1937, Bryn Mawr College Library.
9. Originally published as "A Reporter at Large: Über Alles," *The New Yorker,* January 9, 1932, p. 48; reprinted in *Janet Flanner's World: Uncollected Writings, 1932–1975* (New York: Harcourt, Brace Jovanovich, 1979), p. 5.
10. Like *The New Yorker, Arts and Decoration* was published by the Hanrahan Group. A typical advertisement for it ran in *The New Yorker,* January 21, 1932, p. 45:

Decoration and The Art of Living: Decoration is an end in itself — and it is a means to a further end. The end in itself, quite ample in itself, is *beauty*. But decoration is a means to a further end: *the art of gracious living*. . . .

This is to treat decoration not as a static but as a dynamic concern; as a subject of human interest *turning around people who count*. . . .

There is beauty in Arts and Decoration and dignity, too — the dignity of the true aristocrat. And there is excitement in it, too — the excitement of ideas that make for spaciousness, of ideas which make for enlargement of the social sphere.

11. See JF to MHF, April 2, 1932; April 11, 1932; June 12, 1932; May 28, 1935.

12. One of the short stories, "Tchatzu," was accepted (see Chapter 7); the other, unidentified, was not.

13. See JF, "Spring Scene in Paris," *Arts and Decoration,* June 1933, p. 62.

14. JF, "Patrons for the Arts," *Arts and Decoration,* January 1933, p. 48.

15. See JF to MHF, February 23, 1934, courtesy of John Monhoff.

16. SS, "Both Banks of the Rhine," *D.A.C. News,* December 1933, pp. 32–35.

17. William L. Shirer, *The Nightmare Years: 1910–1940* (Boston: Little, Brown, 1984), p. 83.

18. JF, "Those Were the Days," *The New Yorker,* January 20, 1934, pp. 17–20.

19. Ibid., p. 19.

20. "Letter from Paris," *The New Yorker,* July 7, 1934, pp. 67–68.

21. SS, "Both Banks of the Seine," *D.A.C. News,* April 1934, p. 32.

22. Ibid.

23. "Letter from Paris," *The New Yorker,* March 31, 1934, pp. 65–68.

24. SS, "Both Banks of the Seine," *D.A.C. News,* April 1934, p. 34.

25. Quoted in John Bainbridge, *Another Way of Living* (New York: Holt, Rinehart and Winston, 1968), p. 22.

26. See, for example, Joan Givner, *Katherine Anne Porter* (New York: Simon and Schuster, 1982), p. 383.

27. JF to MHF, August 15, 1933, courtesy of John Monhoff.

28. Draft for speech delivered before the American Institute of Arts and Letters annual meeting, May 1959, New York, Library of Congress. See also JF to Katharine White, February 12, 1946, Bryn Mawr College Library.

29. JF, "Day and Night Thoughts," edited journal, January 9, 1948, Library of Congress.

30. Quoted in "Genetics," *Time,* April 22, 1940, p. 97.

31. Telephone interview with HFM, October 3, 1986.

32. Janet Flanner, "The Murder in Le Mans," *Vanity Fair,* June 1934, p. 73; reprinted in *American in Paris,* p. 304; and in *Paris Was Yesterday,* p. 99.

33. Alexander Woollcott to JF, May 21, 1934, Library of Congress.

34. Reginald [Sam] Weller to JF, May 31, 1934, Library of Congress.

35. Telephone interview with Berenice Abbott, May 6, 1986.
36. Interview with HFM, July 15, 1985.
37. "Paris in the Twenties," *The Twentieth Century,* CBS television program, April 17, 1960.

9. PEACE IN OUR TIME

1. See "Fuehrer," *The New Yorker,* February 29, 1936, pp. 20–24; March 7, 1936, pp. 27–31; and March 14, 1936, pp. 22–26. The profile is reprinted in *Janet Flanner's World: Uncollected Writings, 1932–1975* (New York: Harcourt Brace Jovanovich, 1979).
2. "The Girl about Town," *Indianapolis Sunday Star,* March 29, 1936, p. 15.
3. See Dorothy Thompson, *I Saw Hitler* (New York: Farrar and Rinehart, 1935).
4. "The Girl about Town," p. 15; and JF to MHF, August 12, 1935, courtesy of John Monhoff.
5. JF, *The Cubical City* (New York: G. P. Putnam's Sons, 1926; reprint, Carbondale: Southern Illinois University Press, 1974), p. 109; JF to MHF, December 1928; and January 20, 1929, courtesy of John Monhoff.
6. For example, JF to MHF, June 12, 1932, courtesy of John Monhoff.
7. See "Russian Firebird," *The New Yorker,* January 5, 1935, pp. 23–28.
8. See "Her Majesty, The Queen," *The New Yorker,* May 4, 1935, pp. 20–24; May 11, 1935, pp. 28–32.
9. Quoted in JF to MHF, May 28, 1935, courtesy of John Monhoff.
10. Interview with HFM, July 15, 1985; also JF to MHF, October 27, 1937, courtesy of John Monhoff.
11. JF to MHF, [March–April, 1936], courtesy of John Monhoff.
12. JF to Gertrude Stein, [1939], Beinecke Library, Yale University.
13. See "Pierre Laval: France's One-Man Government," *Forum,* November 1935, pp. 272–75.
14. Gertrude Stein to JF, [Spring 1939], Library of Congress.
15. "Letter from Paris," *The New Yorker,* January 29, 1938, pp. 53–54.
16. Glenway Wescott, "The Frenchman Six Feet Three," *Harper's Magazine,* July 1942, p. 135.
17. Telephone interview with Stephen F. Buchanan, March 22, 1987; "Girl about Town," p. 15.
18. "Letter from Berlin," *The New Yorker,* August 1, 1936, p. 40; August 15, 1938, pp. 39–41; August 22, 1936, pp. 64–67.
19. Interview with Sybille Bedford, October 22, 1986.
20. JF, interview with George Wickes, 1972, tape courtesy of George Wickes.
21. See Carlos Baker, *Hemingway: A Life Story* (New York: Avon, 1980), p. 382.
22. See Baker, *Hemingway,* pp. 383–84.

23. "Letter from London," *The New Yorker,* November 27, 1937, p. 60; reprinted in *London Was Yesterday* (New York: Viking Press, 1975), p. 105.
24. JF to Katharine White, January 12 and January 28, 1938, Bryn Mawr College Library.
25. See JF to Katharine White, July 10 [1938], Bryn Mawr College Library.
26. See "Letter from Bayreuth," *The New Yorker,* September 3, 1938, pp. 48–49; "Letter from Salzburg," *The New Yorker,* September 10, 1938, pp. 55–56.
27. "Letter from Vienna," *The New Yorker,* September 17, 1938, p. 69; reprinted in *Janet Flanner's World,* p. 42.
28. "Letter from Budapest," *The New Yorker,* September 24, 1938, p. 63; reprinted in *Janet Flanner's World,* p. 46.
29. See SS, "Both Banks of the Seine," *D.A.C. News,* December 1938, pp. 46, 48.
30. See "Letter from Paris," *The New Yorker,* October 22, 1938, pp. 82–84, reprinted in *Paris Was Yesterday* (New York: Viking Press, 1972), p. 1.
31. See "Letter from Paris," *The New Yorker,* November 19, 1938, p. 49; see also SS, "Both Banks of the Seine," *D.A.C. News,* December 1938, pp. 46, 48; and SS, miscellaneous notes, n.d., Library of Congress.
32. See "Mr. Ambassador," *The New Yorker,* December 10, 1938, pp. 30–33; and December 17, 1938, pp. 22–27.
33. See JF, Introduction, *London Was Yesterday,* p. 6.
34. "Letter from Perpignan," *The New Yorker,* March 11, 1939, p. 82; reprinted in *Paris Was Yesterday,* p. 201.
35. See Francis Rose, *Saying Life: The Memoirs of Sir Francis Rose* (London: Cassell, 1961), p. 389.
36. See JF to Gertrude Stein, [May 1939], Beinecke Library, Yale University.
37. See Alexander Woollcott to JF, July 26, 1939, Houghton Library, Harvard University.
38. Richard Myers to Alice-Lee Myers, August 25, 1939 (F. M. Brennan).
39. Margaret Anderson, *The Fiery Fountains* (New York: Horizon Press, 1951), p. 171.
40. Richard Myers to Alice-Lee Myers, August 27, 1939 (F. M. Brennan).
41. Anderson, *Fiery Fountains,* p. 172.
42. Ibid.
43. Ibid., p. 176.

10. LEAVE OF ABSENCE

1. "Air Terror Told by Miss Morgan," *New York Mirror,* May 19, 1940, p. 4.
2. Noel Murphy to JF, June 1, 1940, Library of Congress.
3. Ibid.

4. Noel Murphy to Gerald and Sara Murphy, June 25, 1940, courtesy of Honoria Murphy Donnelly. The Murphys sent a copy of the letter to JF, and it is in the Library of Congress.

5. Ibid.

6. Noel Murphy to JF, n.d., courtesy of Honoria Murphy Donnelly.

7. Noel Murphy to Gerald Murphy, August 2, 1940, courtesy of Honoria Murphy Donnelly.

8. Ibid.

9. Gertrude Stein to JF, [June 1940], Beinecke Library, Yale University.

10. Interview with David Diamond, June 30, 1987.

11. Solita's job with the *D.A.C. News* had ended when she was no longer a foreign correspondent.

12. See "One-Man Group," *The New Yorker,* December 9, 1939, p. 35. Here her meaning is purposely obscure: partly she is applauding Picasso's burgeoning social conscience; partly she is satirizing it. Although she withholds her own opinion about "Guernica," she makes clear her belief that art should have nothing to do with political sentiment.

13. For example, after reading John Peale Bishop, "The Discipline of Poetry," *Virginia Quarterly Review* (summer 1938), she told Bishop she agreed with its thesis, that art should remain aloof from contemporary morality; she also told him she did not agree with Edmund Wilson's view in *The Triple Thinkers* that literary techniques "are tools, which the masters of the craft have to alter in adapting them to fresh uses."

14. A. J. Liebling, *Liebling Abroad* (New York: Wideview Books, 1981), p. 21.

15. Ibid., p. 20.

16. Correspondence of JF to MHF, 1939–1940, courtesy of John Monhoff.

17. JF to Alexander Woollcott, [spring 1940], Houghton Library, Harvard University.

18. See ibid.; and JF to MHF, [spring 1940], courtesy of John Monhoff.

19. Interview with HFM, July 15, 1985.

20. When she met Janet twenty years later, the writer M. F. K. Fisher recalls that Janet still seemed to feel guilty about not being in France during the war. Interview with M. F. K. Fisher, July 14, 1985.

21. Russell Page to JF, April 13, [1940], Library of Congress.

22. Noel Murphy to JF, June 1, 1940, Library of Congress.

23. Telephone interview with HFM, January 28, 1987; see also JF to MHF, 1940, courtesy of John Monhoff.

24. JF to MHF and HFM, [June 1940], courtesy of John Monhoff.

25. JF to MHF, August 18, 1940.

26. Interview with David Diamond, June 30, 1987.

27. Telephone interview with Thomas Quinn Curtiss, June 16, 1987. In the spring of 1940, Supreme Commander Weygand had issued orders that spelled certain defeat for France; he also urged the government to cling to Paris, apparently more intent on preserving his notion of domestic harmony than on fighting the Germans.

28. See also "Look at the Calendar: Will We Talk Democracy to Death in the Country?" *Harper's Bazaar,* August 1940, pp. 68, 109.

29. "World's Ills Laid to Money Worship — Janet Flanner Tells New Jersey Teachers Conditions Here Like Those in France," *New York Times,* November 10, 1941, p. 13.

30. Nancy Cunard to JF and SS, September 12, [1940], Library of Congress.

31. For example, JF to MHF, July [1940], courtesy of John Monhoff.

32. SS, Daybook, summer 1940, Library of Congress.

33. JF to SS, [1943], Library of Congress.

34. JF to Alexander Woollcott, [August 1940], Houghton Library, Harvard University.

35. Daise Terry to Katharine S. White, Saturday, [November 1940], Bryn Mawr College Library.

36. Alexander Woollcott to JF, January 8, 1942, Library of Congress; and Beatrice Kaufman and Joseph Hennessey, eds., *The Letters of Alexander Woollcott* (New York: Viking Press, 1944), p. 299.

37. SS to HFM, [1940], courtesy of John Monhoff; telephone interview with Doda Conrad, August 21, 1987.

38. SS, Daybook, December 1940, Library of Congress.

39. JF to MHF, [1940], courtesy of John Monhoff.

40. Alexander Woollcott to JF, June 6, 1940, Library of Congress. The profile of Wendell Willkie, "Rushville's Renowned Son-in-Law," appeared in *The New Yorker,* October 12, 1940, pp. 27–45.

41. Stanley Edgar Hyman, "The Urban New Yorker," *New Republic,* July 20, 1942, p. 91.

42. HFM to Witter Bynner, November 23, 1940, Houghton Library, Harvard University.

43. Irving Drutman, *Good Company* (Boston: Little, Brown, 1976), p. 101.

44. Quoted in Virginia Spencer Carr, *The Lonely Hunter: A Biography of Carson McCullers* (New York: Carroll & Graf, 1975), p. 123.

45. Ibid, p. 123; and interview with Kay Boyle, July 16, 1985.

46. Interview with Kay Boyle, July 16, 1985.

47. Interview with David Diamond, June 30, 1987.

48. Carr, *Lonely Hunter,* p. 123; interview with David Diamond, June 30, 1987.

49. Klaus Mann, *The Turning Point* (London: Victor Gollancz, 1944), p. 256. As it turned out, the magazine *Decision* was discontinued, much to Mann's regret, two years later.

50. Mann, *Turning Point,* p. 266.

51. See JF, "Paradise Lost," *Decision* 1, no. 1 (January 1941): 35–38.

52. JF, "A Reporter at Large: Paris, Germany," *The New Yorker,* December 7, 1940, p. 58; reprinted in *Janet Flanner's World: Uncollected Writings, 1932–1975* (New York: Harcourt Brace Jovanovich, 1979), p. 56.

53. JF, "A Reporter at Large: Soldats de France, Debout!" *The New Yorker,* February 1, 1941, p. 20.

54. See JF, "A Reporter at Large: Le Nouvel Ordre," *The New Yorker,* March 15, 1941, pp. 38–47.

55. JF, "The Lone Liberty Chorus," *Harper's Bazaar,* March 1, 1941, pp. 81, 131–132; and JF, "A Reporter at Large: Blitz by Partnership," *The New Yorker,* June 7, 1941, pp. 42–54.

56. Alexander Woollcott to JF, June 6, 1941, Library of Congress.

57. JF to Alexander Woollcott, July 1, [1941], Houghton Library, Harvard University.

58. Janet Flanner, "A Reporter at Large: So You're Going to Paris!" *The New Yorker,* June 21, 1941, pp. 36–48.

59. As reported in "World's Ills Laid to Money Worship — Janet Flanner tells New Jersey Teachers Conditions Here Like Those in France," *New York Times,* November 10, 1941, p. 13.

60. See Hugh Ford, ed., *Nancy Cunard: Brave Poet, Indomitable Rebel* (Philadelphia: Chilton, 1968), p. 80.

61. JF to Alexander Woollcott, [fall 1941], Houghton Library, Harvard University.

62. Carson McCullers to JF, [October 1941], Library of Congress.

63. JF, "Goethe in Hollywood," *The New Yorker,* December 13, 1941, p. 31; December 20, 1941, p. 32; reprinted in *Janet Flanner's World,* pp. 165, 187.

64. Thomas Mann to Agnes E. Meyer, December 16, 1941, in *The Letters of Thomas Mann,* ed. Richard Winston and Clara Winston (New York: Alfred A. Knopf, 1971), pp. 380–81.

65. Ibid., p. 381; and Thomas Mann to Caroline Newton, January 10, 1942, ibid., p. 386.

66. See JF, *Darlinghissima: Letters to a Friend,* ed. Natalia Danesi Murray (New York: Random House, 1985), p. 147.

67. Drutman, *Good Company,* p. 269.

68. Alexander Woollcott to JF, January 8, 1942, Library of Congress.

69. Interview with David Diamond, June 30, 1987.

70. JF, "A Reporter at Large: Come Down, Giuseppe!" *The New Yorker,* January 17, 1942, pp. 46–58; reprinted in *Janet Flanner's World,* pp. 221–31.

71. SS to Margaret Anderson, 1942, Library of Congress.

72. JF to SS, n.d., courtesy of John Monhoff; also JF to Alexander Woollcott, n.d., Houghton Library, Harvard University. The Bette Davis profile appeared in *The New Yorker,* February 20, 1943, pp. 19–29; reprinted in *Janet Flanner's World,* pp. 188–200.

73. JF to SS, [1950s], Library of Congress.

74. SS to HFM, April 30, [1942], Bancroft Library, University of California, Berkeley.

75. Noel Murphy to Honoria Murphy Donnelly, taped interview, summer 1982, courtesy Honoria Donnelly.

76. Drue Tartière, *The House near Paris: An American Woman's Story of Traffic in Patriots* (New York: Simon and Schuster, 1946), pp. 98–115.

77. JF to Alice-Lee Myers and Dick Myers, n.d., courtesy of Fanny Brennan.

78. JF to SS, [1943], Library of Congress.

79. See JF, "The Escape of Mrs. Jeffries," *The New Yorker,* May 22, 1943, pp. 23–28; May 29, 1943, pp. 40–47; and June 5, 1943, pp. 50–67; reprinted in *Janet Flanner's World,* pp. 63–92.
80. JF, "Run for Your Life," *Home and Food,* October 1943, pp. 14–15, 31.
81. Harold Ross to JF, January 31, 1944, Library of Congress.
82. See "La France et Le Vieux: From the Empress Eugénie to the A.E.F.," *The New Yorker,* February 12, 1944, pp. 27–40; "La France et Le Vieux: Hero of Verdun," February 19, 1944, pp. 27–43; "La France et Le Vieux: Versailles to Vichy," February 26, 1944, pp. 28–41; "La France et Le Vieux: Maréchal, Nous Voilà!" March 4, 1944, pp. 37–63.
83. See, for example, Theodore Draper, "Man of Vichy," *New York Times Book Review,* July 9, 1944, pp. 4, 16.
84. See Jane Grant, *Ross, The New Yorker, and Me* (New York: Reynal, 1968), p. 14.
85. JF to MHF, August 2, 1944, courtesy of John Monhoff.
86. See Valentine Lawford, *Horst: His Work and His World* (New York: Alfred A. Knopf, 1984), pp. 220–21.
87. Ibid., p. 222.
88. JF to Jane Grant, November 15, 1944, Jane Grant Papers, University of Oregon.

11. A CHARNEL HOUSE

1. JF to SS, November 22, 1944, Library of Congress.
2. JF to MHF, November 25, 1944, courtesy of John Monhoff.
3. See JF to SS, November 22, 1944, Library of Congress.
4. JF to SS, January 3, 1945, Library of Congress.
5. JF to SS, December 26, 1944, Library of Congress.
6. JF to SS, January 3, 1944, Library of Congress.
7. JF to SS, December 26, 1944, Library of Congress.
8. JF to SS, postcard, [winter 1945], Library of Congress.
9. JF to SS, February 7–8, 1945, Library of Congress.
10. JF to SS, January 22, 1945, Library of Congress.
11. "Letter from Paris," *The New Yorker,* December 23, 1944, p. 42; reprinted in *Paris Journal, 1944–1965* (New York: Harcourt Brace Jovanovich, 1977), p. 8.
12. JF to SS, [July] 1945, Library of Congress.
13. JF to SS, January 3, 1945, Library of Congress.
14. The articles on Bedaux appeared as "Annals of Collaboration," *The New Yorker,* September 29, 1945, pp. 28–47; October 6, 1945, pp. 32–45, October 13, 1945, pp. 32–48.
15. JF to SS, January 22, 1945, Library of Congress.
16. JF to SS, January 3, 1945, Library of Congress.
17. JF to SS, [February 1945], Library of Congress.
18. JF to SS, February 7–8, 1945, Library of Congress.

19. JF to SS, April 14, 1945, Library of Congress.
20. JF to SS, January 3, 1945, Library of Congress.
21. JF to SS, February 7–8, 1945, Library of Congress.
22. See, for example, "Letter from Lyon," *The New Yorker,* February 12, 1945, pp. 60, 62–65.
23. Interview with HFM, July 15, 1985.
24. JF to SS, postcard, [winter 1945], Library of Congress.
25. Interview with Ed Tribble, November 26, 1985.
26. JF to SS, April 24, 1945, Library of Congress.
27. JF to SS, May 17, 1945, Library of Congress.
28. JF to MHF, January 7, 1946, courtesy of John Monhoff.
29. JF to SS, April 15, 1945, Library of Congress.
30. JF to SS, April 24, 1945, Library of Congress.
31. "Letter from Paris," *The New Yorker,* May 5, 1945, p. 50.
32. JF to SS, April 16, 1945, Library of Congress.
33. JF, "Day and Night Thoughts," p. 8, n.d., Library of Congress.
34. JF to SS, Margaret Anderson, Dorothy Caruso, and Elizabeth Clark, May 6, 1945, Library of Congress.
35. JF to SS, April 24, 1945, Library of Congress.
36. JF to SS, [spring 1945], Library of Congress.
37. Ibid.
38. JF to SS, June 17, 1945, Library of Congress.
39. JF to SS, [spring?] 1945, Library of Congress.
40. JF to SS, January 3, 1945, Library of Congress.
41. JF to MHF, April 22, 1945, courtesy of John Monhoff.
42. Telephone interview with Doda Conrad, August 21, 1987.
43. JF to Katharine White, February 12, 1946, Bryn Mawr College Library.
44. JF to SS, December 23, 1945, Library of Congress.
45. JF to SS, [spring 1945], Library of Congress.
46. JF, *Darlinghissima,* p. 68.
47. JF to Katharine White, February 12, 1946, Bryn Mawr College Library.
48. JF to HFM, March 22, 1946, courtesy of John Monhoff.
49. Helen Kirkpatrick Milbank to the author, July 16, 1986.
50. See "Letter from Nuremberg," *The New Yorker,* March 16, 1946, pp. 92–94; March 23, 1946, pp. 78, 80–84; March 30, 1946, pp. 76, 81–82; reprinted in part in *Janet Flanner's World: Uncollected Writings, 1932–1975* (New York: Harcourt Brace Jovanovich, 1979), pp. 98–122.
51. JF to SS, April 17, 1946, Library of Congress.
52. Telephone interviews with May Sarton, October 12, 1986; Helen Kirkpatrick Milbank, August 10, 1986.
53. JF to SS, [1946], Library of Congress; see also JF to HFM, [1946], courtesy of John Monhoff.
54. See JF, *Darlinghissima,* pp. 84–85.
55. JF to SS, September 25, 1946, Library of Congress.
56. Ibid.
57. See "Annals of Crime: The Beautiful Spoils," *The New Yorker,* February

22, 1947, pp. 31–48; March 1, 1947, pp. 33–49; and March 8, 1947, pp. 38–55.
58. JF to Harold Ross and William Shawn, March 5, 1947, Jane Grant Papers, University of Oregon.
59. JF to SS, March 23, 1947, Library of Congress.
60. See "Letter from Warsaw," *The New Yorker,* May 31, 1947, pp. 58, 60–63; "Letter from Poland," *The New Yorker,* June 21, 1947, pp. 46, 48–49, 51; reprinted in *Janet Flanner's World,* pp. 131–40.
61. "Letter from Cracow," *The New Yorker,* July 12, 1947, p. 51.

12. INVENTIONS ARE HASTIER

1. Hildegarde Flanner, *At the Gentle Mercy of Plants* (Santa Barbara, Calif.: John Daniel, 1986), p. 40.
2. JF to SS, December 4, 1947, Library of Congress.
3. Ibid.
4. Ibid.
5. See JF, "Day and Night Thoughts," January 2, 1948, pp. 1–2; January 8, 1948, p. 5, Library of Congress.
6. Ibid., January 1, 1948, p. 1
7. Ibid., March 14, 1948, p. 11; January 1, 1948, p. 1; January 24, [1948], p. 8.
8. Ibid., January 24, [1948], pp. 7–8.
9. Ibid., January 16, 1948, p. 5.
10. Ibid., January 16, 1948, p. 5. The first sentence of the profile finally read: "Miss Cheryl Crawford, producer of the Scotch-plaid musical comedy 'Brigadoon,' now in its second year on Broadway, is a small, scholarly Middle Westerner of austerely chiselled character and countenance who likes serious books, can recite all of Keats' odes from memory, and talks as little as possible."
11. JF, "Day and Night Thoughts," January 8, 1948.
12. JF, notes and memoranda, n.d., Library of Congress.
13. JF, "Day and Night Thoughts," January 7, 1948, p. 4.
14. Ibid., January 3, 1948, p. 2.
15. JF to MHF, March 22, 1946, courtesy of John Monhoff.
16. See JF, "Day and Night Thoughts," [February 1948], pp. 10–11.
17. Ibid., January 16, 1948, p. 5.
18. Ibid., [February 1948], p. 11.
19. Ibid., March 8, 1948, p. 12; March 13, 1948, p. 13.
20. JF to SS, November 4, 1948, Library of Congress.
21. Telephone interview with HFM, January 28, 1987.
22. JF, "Day and Night Thoughts," March 13, 1948, p. 13.
23. Ibid., May 29, [1948], pp. 17–18.
24. Ibid., March 12, 1948, p. 13.
25. JF to MHF, [summer or fall 1945], courtesy of John Monhoff.
26. JF to May Sarton, [1954–55], Berg Collection, New York Public Library.

27. JF to SS, November 1948, Library of Congress.
28. JF, "Day and Night Thoughts," [February 1949], p. 19.
29. JF to HFM, October 9, [1948], courtesy of John Monhoff.
30. JF, "Day and Night Thoughts," June 1, [1948], p. 18.
31. JF to SS, November 4, 1948, Library of Congress.
32. Ibid.
33. JF, "Day and Night Thoughts," January 1, 1949, p. 23.
34. Ibid., [February 1949], p. 19.
35. Ibid., January 1, 1949, p. 23.
36. Ibid., March 16, 1948, p. 14.
37. Interview with Mary McCarthy, October 26, 1987.
38. JF, "Day and Night Thoughts," n.d., p. 9. She was greatly influenced
    by Drew Middleton's series of articles in the *New York Times* on the
    Soviet Union, which she'd read the preceding February.
39. JF, "Day and Night Thoughts," May 20, [1948], p. 17.
40. See JF to May Sarton, August 1948, Berg Collection, New York Public
    Library.
41. See "Letter from Naples," *The New Yorker,* March 12, 1949, pp. 66,
    68, 70–71.
42. JF, "Day and Night Thoughts," October 14, [1951?], p. 22.
43. Ibid.
44. JF to HFM, October 9, [1948], courtesy of John Monhoff.
45. JF, "Day and Night Thoughts," February 1949, p. 19.
46. See "Letter from Paris," *The New Yorker,* March 31, 1951, pp. 74, 78–
    82, on the death of Léon Blum; reprinted in *Paris Journal, 1944–1965*
    (New York: Atheneum, 1965), p. 145.
47. Judge Worrall Mountain to the author, July 1986.
48. JF to Nancy Cunard, November 1949, HRHRC.
49. Interview with Simon Michael Bessie, November 11, 1986.
50. JF to SS, [spring 1950], Library of Congress.
51. William Shawn to JF, May 29, 1950, Library of Congress.
52. JF to SS, [June] 1950, Library of Congress.
53. *The New Yorker* changed its policy somewhat the following year when
    it published Alva Johnston's four-part profile of the deceased architect
    Addison Mizner, who was not, however, a foreigner or a socialist. See
    Alva Johnston, "The Palm Beach Architect," *The New Yorker,* Novem-
    ber 22, 1952, pp. 48–93; November 29, 1952, pp. 46–94; December
    6, 1952, pp. 48–64; December 13, 1952, pp. 42–85.
54. JF to Jane Grant, December 9, 1951, Jane Grant Papers, University of
    Oregon.
55. Quoted in JF to Katharine White, November 1, 1953, Bryn Mawr
    College Library.
56. Telephone interview with Célia Bertin, July 24, 1987.
57. Solita did not learn of Janet's most recent bout of depression until 1968,
    when she was typing out entries from Janet's diary. "We [Solita, Eliz-
    abeth Clark, and Noel] were all here with you in Paris," Solita wrote
    angrily in the margin, "and you said not a word to me or other friends!!"

58. JF, "Day and Night Thoughts," August 29, 1951, p. 20.

59. Ibid.

60. JF to SS, October 19, 1951, Library of Congress.

61. Ibid.

62. The finished profile, timed to run during a Matisse show at the Museum of Modern Art, set Matisse amid his canvases and placed the canvases within the various credos of late nineteenth-century and early twentieth-century painting. It was filled with interesting anecdotes. For example, the dove Picasso painted as an emblem for the Communist party's Stockholm poster originally belonged to the "anti-Communist" Matisse, who had given the bird (a pigeon) to his neighbor Picasso. Janet told the story, both the apocryphal and the ascertainable parts, of how Matisse had come to design the Chapel of the Rosary for the Dominican nuns. She presented a striking portrait of the eighty-two-year-old Matisse lying in bed while his hands busily created fanciful designs, and she contrasted the prices his paintings then fetched with the prices (if any) the outraged public originally offered for his work. It was a conventional story of struggle and success, of philistinism and endurance. Janet reiterated that Matisse had been called a bourgeois, not a bohemian — which seemed to be an important point for her — and that he was able to join decoration and beauty. In all, the profile is airy and offers no particularly novel insights, but it is full of highly wrought, colorful visual detail. See "King of the Wild Beasts," *The New Yorker,* December 22, 1951, pp. 30–46; December 29, 1951, pp. 26–49.

63. JF to SS, November 20, 1951, Library of Congress.

64. JF to SS, December 5, [1951], Library of Congress.

65. JF to Margaret Anderson, December 13, 1951, Library of Congress.

66. JF to Kay Boyle, December 27, 1951, Morris Library, Southern Illinois University at Carbondale.

67. JF to Katharine White, December 13, 1951, Bryn Mawr College Library.

68. JF to Kay Boyle, December 27, 1951.

13. THE VOICES OF SILENCE

1. Ralph Ingersoll, *Point of Departure* (New York: Harcourt, Brace and World, 1961), p. 164.

2. See JF to Kay Boyle, February 3, [1953], Morris Library, Southern Illinois University at Carbondale.

3. *Los Angeles Times,* March 31, 1952, p. 8.

4. See, for example, JF to SS, June 17, 1945, Library of Congress.

5. Kay Boyle, "Nancy Cunard," in *Nancy Cunard: Brave Poet, Indomitable Rebel,* ed. Hugh Ford (Philadelphia: Chilton, 1968), p. 80.

6. Interview with Kay Boyle, July 16, 1985.

7. JF to SS, [November], 1952, Library of Congress.

8. Ibid.

9. JF to Kay Boyle, [June 1952], Morris Library, Southern Illinois University at Carbondale.

10. JF to Nancy Cunard, [1952], HRHRC.
11. JF to SS, July 7, [1952], Library of Congress.
12. JF to SS, [January] 1953, Library of Congress.
13. JF to Katharine White, October 10, 1952, Bryn Mawr College Library.
14. JF to SS, [October 1952], Library of Congress.
15. Ibid.
16. Ibid.
17. Ibid.
18. Interview with Kay Boyle, July 16, 1985.
19. JF to SS, [November] 1952, Library of Congress.
20. A copy of Janet's testimony is in the Kay Boyle Collection, Southern Illinois University at Carbondale, and in the Flanner/Solano Collection, Library of Congress.
21. JF to SS, [October 1952], Library of Congress.
22. Interview with Kay Boyle, July 16, 1985.
23. Ibid.
24. Ibid.
25. JF to Kay Boyle, February 3, 1953, Morris Library, Southern Illinois University at Carbondale.
26. Interview with Kay Boyle, July 16, 1985.
27. Quoted in Katharine White to JF, March 20, 1953, Library of Congress.
28. Ibid.
29. Ibid. To clarify matters, White enclosed a copy of William Shawn's letter to Kay Boyle, March 11, 1953 (Library of Congress).
30. JF to Katharine White, November 1, 1953, Bryn Mawr College Library.
31. JF to Katharine White and William Shawn, March 30, [1953], Library of Congress.
32. Ibid.
33. William Shawn to JF, April 24, 1953, Library of Congress.
34. Katharine White to JF, April 27, 1953, Library of Congress.
35. JF to Katharine White, May 12, 1953, Library of Congress.
36. Katharine White to JF, October 18, 1953, Library of Congress.
37. JF to Katharine White, November 1, 1953, Bryn Mawr College Library.
38. See "Letter from Paris," October 14, The New Yorker, October 25, 1952, pp. 114–19.
39. JF to Nancy Cunard, September 23, 1954, HRHRC.
40. She made this remark on "The Dick Cavett Show," PBS television program, December 12, 1971.
41. See "Letter from Paris," The New Yorker, May 30, 1953, pp. 82, 84–87.
42. JF to Kay Boyle, [October–November 1952], Morris Library, Southern Illinois University at Carbondale.
43. JF to Kay Boyle, [November 1952], Morris Library.
44. Interview with Kay Boyle, July 16, 1985.
45. JF to Katharine White, November 1, 1953, Bryn Mawr College Library.
46. JF, interview with Virginia Spencer Carr, March 3, 1972, transcript, Duke University Library.

47. Ibid.

48. Interview with David Diamond, June 30, 1987.

49. JF, notes and memoranda, December 1953, Library of Congress. In 1972 Janet told Virginia Spencer Carr that this message came with the bouquet of flowers she received from Reeves the day he died. However, her diary entry shows that Reeves delivered this message himself about two weeks before he died. He probably did send the flowers, however, although Janet may have misremembered this as well.

50. Virginia Spencer Carr, *The Lonely Hunter* (New York: Carroll and Graf, 1975), p. 402; interview with Kay Boyle, July 17, 1985.

51. JF, interview with Virginia Spencer Carr, March 3, 1972.

52. David Diamond to the author, May 26, 1987.

53. Interview with David Diamond, June 30, 1987.

54. JF, notes and memoranda, December 22, 1953, Library of Congress.

55. JF to Carson McCullers, December 5, 1953, HRHRC.

56. JF, diary, January 6, 1954, Library of Congress.

57. Ibid.

58. Ibid.

59. Ibid.

60. Ibid.

61. JF to SS, December 10, 1953, Library of Congress.

62. Ibid.

63. Ibid.

64. Ibid.

65. JF to Kay Boyle, July 21, 1954, Morris Library, Southern Illinois University at Carbondale.

66. JF to SS, [November 1954], Library of Congress.

67. JF to SS, [fall 1954], Library of Congress.

68. Ibid.

69. JF to SS, [1954], Library of Congress.

70. JF to SS, August 1954, Library of Congress.

71. Djuna Barnes to JF, August 23, 1954, University of Maryland Library.

72. JF to Simon Michael Bessie, January 6, 1956, Columbia University Library.

73. Telephone interview with Stanley Eichelbaum, August 20, 1985; interview with Gardner Botsford, November 15, 1987.

74. JF to Stanley Eichelbaum, September 1954, Library of Congress.

75. JF to Nancy Cunard, September 23, [1954], HRHRC.

76. "The Human Condition," *The New Yorker,* November 6, 1954, pp. 45–81; November 13, 1954, pp. 46–100; reprinted in *Men and Monuments* (New York: Harper and Brothers, 1957). The quotations are from p. 2 and p. 56.

14. A STEADY CONFLAGRATION OF MATCHES

1. JF, notes from an interview with Georges Braque, January 28, 1955, Library of Congress.

2. Ibid.

3. Ibid.

4. Interview with Simon Michael Bessie, November 11, 1986.

5. Ibid.

6. See JF, "In Defense of the French," *New York Times,* March 6, 1955, sec. 6, pp. 12, 30, 32, 34; and Daniel Talbot, ed., *City of Love* (New York: Dell, 1955), pp. 6–8.

7. See JF, "Tobey, Mystique errant," *L'Oeil,* no. 6, June 15, 1955, pp. 26–31; and JF, Introduction, Gabrielle Colette, *Seven* (New York: Farrar, Straus, and Cudahy, 1955), pp. v–xv.

8. See JF to Kay Boyle, March 22, 1955, Morris Library, Southern Illinois University at Carbondale.

9. JF to May Sarton, Berg Collection, New York Public Library.

10. JF to James Thurber, January 18, [1956], Ohio State University Library.

11. JF to Simon Michael Bessie, June 3, 1956, Columbia University Library.

12. Ibid.

13. JF to Miss Shaeffer at Harper and Row, June 9, 1956, Columbia University Library.

14. JF to Simon Michael Bessie, July 13, 1956, Columbia University Library.

15. Djuna Barnes to SS, July 24, 1956, Library of Congress.

16. JF to SS, [November or December 1953?], Library of Congress.

17. JF to SS, November 10, 1955, Library of Congress.

18. JF to Simon Michael Bessie, August 24, 1956, Columbia University Library.

19. Interview with Gardner Botsford, November 15, 1985.

20. See "Master," *The New Yorker,* October 6, 1956, pp. 49–83; October 13, 1956, pp. 50–97.

21. JF to SS, October 25, [1956], Library of Congress.

22. Interview with Sybille Bedford, October 22, 1986.

23. JF to SS, October 25, 1956, Library of Congress.

24. Ibid.

25. Interview with Mary McCarthy, October 26, 1987.

26. Simon Michael Bessie to JF, November 26, 1956, Columbia University Library.

27. See JF, Preface, *Men and Monuments* (New York: Harper and Brothers, 1957), pp. xi, xiv, and xviii.

28. Book Information Sheet, Harper and Row Collection, Columbia University Library.

29. Djuna Barnes to JF, May 16, 1957, Library of Congress.

30. Margaret Anderson to JF, March 31, 1957, Library of Congress. She did, however, take up the argument again in the third volume of her autobiography: see Margaret Anderson, *The Strange Necessity* (New York: Horizon Press, 1969), p. 40.

31. Francis Henry Taylor, "French Ideas, American Dollars," *Saturday Review,* May 11, 1957, p. 17.

32. JF to Francis Taylor, May 14, 1957, Library of Congress.

33. Raymond Mortimer, "Eminent Artists of Our Own Time," *Sunday Times* (London), June 30, 1957.

34. See the New York *Daily Telegraph,* June 21, 1957; *Manchester Guardian,* August 27, 1957; Alan Bowness, *The Observer,* June 23, 1957, p. 13; "An American in Paris," *Times Literary Supplement,* July 5, 1957, p. 408.

35. John Berger, *"Men and Monuments," The Spectator,* July 1957, p. 114.

36. Raymond Mortimer to JF, July 25, 1957, Library of Congress.

37. Mary McCarthy to JF, August 4, 1957, Library of Congress.

38. JF to Djuna Barnes, February 8, 1958, McKeldin Library, University of Maryland.

39. JF to Nancy Cunard, November 27, [1957], HRHRC.

40. JF to SS, [March] 1957; [April] 1957, Library of Congress.

41. See "Books: Yesterday's World," *The New Yorker,* April 27, 1957, pp. 136–41.

42. JF to SS, January 7, 1956, Library of Congress.

43. Ibid.

44. Interview with Benjamin Bradlee, July 21, 1986.

45. Quoted in Glenway Wescott to JF, January 11, 1967, Library of Congress.

46. Gardner Botsford, interview, spring 1967, Oral History Collection, p. 45, Columbia University Library.

47. Ibid., p. 45.

48. JF to SS, Thanksgiving [1957], Library of Congress.

49. Interview with Rosamond Bernier, August 6, 1987.

50. See JF, "De Diverses Formes de Beauté," *L'Oeil,* October 1957, pp. 24–30.

51. JF to SS, December 7, 1957, Library of Congress.

52. JF to SS, March 1958, Library of Congress.

53. JF to SS, July 7, [1952], Library of Congress.

54. Interview with Kay Boyle, July 16, 1985.

55. Interview with Sybille Bedford, October 22, 1986.

56. Esther Murphy to Gerald Murphy, June 1958, courtesy of Honoria Murphy Donnelly.

57. See "Letter from Paris," *The New Yorker,* May 31, 1958, p. 68; reprinted in *Paris Journal, 1944–1965* (New York: Atheneum, 1965), p. 369.

58. See "Letter from Paris," *The New Yorker,* October 25, 1958, pp. 164–170; reprinted in *Paris Journal, 1944–1965,* pp. 390–95.

59. JF to Helen and James Thurber, November 24, 1957, Ohio State University Library.

60. See "Letter from Paris," *The New Yorker,* January 22, 1958, p. 112.

61. See "Letter from Paris," *The New Yorker,* January 10, 1959, p. 109.

62. JF, interview with Mary McCarthy, typescript, p. 37, Vassar College Library.

63. Interview with Simon Michael Bessie, November 11, 1986.

64. JF to SS, June 10, 1958, Library of Congress.

65. Katherine Anne Porter to Glenway Wescott, May 3, 1958, Library of Congress.

66. See "Le Gamin," *The New Yorker,* November 21, 1959, pp. 57–108.

15. HOW FRIENDS GROW OLD

1. JF to SS, [November/December 1953?]; Djuna Barnes to SS, September 7, 1960, Library of Congress.
2. JF to Kay Boyle, September 23, 1963, Morris Library, Southern Illinois University at Carbondale.
3. See Anne Chisholm, *Nancy Cunard* (New York: Alfred A. Knopf, 1979), pp. 408–10.
4. Interview with Anne Chisholm, October 23, 1986.
5. Nancy Cunard to JF, July 19, 1960, Library of Congress.
6. Quoted in HFM to James Rorty, June 15, 1960, University of Oregon Library.
7. JF to e. e. cummings and Marian Moorehouse, July 20, [1956?], Houghton Library, Harvard University.
8. SS, "Nancy Cunard: Brave Poet, Indomitable Rebel," in *Nancy Cunard: Brave Poet, Indomitable Rebel,* ed. Hugh Ford (Philadelphia: Chilton, 1968), p. 77.
9. Alice Toklas to Anita Loos, May 8, 1960, in *Staying On Alone: Letters of Alice B. Toklas,* ed. Edward Burns (New York: Liveright, 1973), p. 382.
10. Interview with Virgil Thomson, December 31, 1985.
11. JF to SS, n.d., Library of Congress.
12. See "Letter from Paris," *The New Yorker,* October 26, 1960, pp. 163–64.
13. See "Letter from Paris," *The New Yorker,* March 18, 1961, p. 130.
14. Unedited copy for Paris letter, April 27, 1961, Library of Congress. See also "Letter from Paris," *The New Yorker,* May 6, 1961, pp. 125–28; reprinted in *Paris Journal, 1944–1965* (New York: Atheneum, 1965), pp. 477–81.
15. JF to SS, postcards, n.d., Library of Congress.
16. JF, interview with George Wickes, June 8, 1972, unedited tape courtesy of George Wickes.
17. HFM to Alice Toklas, March 2, 1962, HRHRC.
18. Alice Toklas to Princess Dilkusha de Rohan, November 26, 1961, in Burns, *Staying On Alone,* p. 408.
19. HFM to JF, 1961, Library of Congress.
20. See "Letter from Paris," *The New Yorker,* February 7, 1962, p. 120.
21. Telephone conversation with Stanley Eichelbaum, August 20, 1985.
22. JF to Gerald Murphy, November 25, 1962, courtesy of Honoria Murphy Donnelly.
23. Helen Kirkpatrick Milbank to the author, July 16, 1986.
24. Interview with Mary McCarthy, October 26, 1987.
25. SS to Carlos Baker, n.d., and September 24, 1963, courtesy of Carlos Baker.
26. Interview with Simon Michael Bessie, November 11, 1986.
27. Ibid.
28. Interview with E. J. Kahn, Jr., July 18, 1985.
29. JF to SS, March 1, 1963, Library of Congress.

30. Quoted in "Letter from Paris," *The New Yorker,* December 16, 1961, p. 109.
31. JF to Alice Toklas, July 13, [1963], HRHRC.
32. Interview with Sybille Bedford, October 22, 1986.
33. Interview with Rosamond Bernier, August 6, 1987.
34. JF to SS, January 7, 1956, Library of Congress.
35. Interview with Mary McCarthy, October 26, 1987.
36. JF to SS, October 26, 1964, Library of Congress.
37. JF to SS, September 1964, Library of Congress.
38. Ibid.
39. Ibid.
40. JF to SS, May 6, 1963, Library of Congress.
41. SS to Kay Boyle, March 24, 1965, Morris Library, Southern Illinois University at Carbondale.
42. JF to SS, March 31, 1966; Library of Congress.
43. SS to Hugh Ford, March 18, 1965; April 20, 1965, courtesy of Hugh Ford.
44. SS to Hugh Ford, April 20, 1965, courtesy of Hugh Ford.
45. Ibid.
46. JF, notes and memoranda, July 6, 1965, Library of Congress.
47. JF to Maitland A. Edey, August 27, 1965, Library of Congress.
48. Ibid.
49. JF to SS, September 21, 1964, Library of Congress.
50. Alan Pryce-Jones, "Janet Flanner's Crow's Nest View of Paris," New York Herald Tribune, November 12, 1965; Benjamin Bradlee, "Paragon of Correspondents Provides Excellent History," *Washington Post,* November 16, 1965, p. 18; Oscar Handlin, Review of *Paris Journal, 1944–1965, The Atlantic,* December 1965, p. 146; Donald Keene, "Letters from France," *New York Times Book Review,* November 21, 1965, p. 5.
51. Glenway Wescott, "The Tri-Colored Rainbow," *Book Week,* New York Herald Tribune, December 19, 1965, pp. 1, 8.

16. PARIS WAS YESTERDAY

1. See, for example, JF to SS, January 19, 1966; January 26, 1966, Library of Congress.
2. Ibid.
3. JF to SS, January 26, 1966, Library of Congress.
4. Other nominees included R. W. B. Lewis's *Trials of the World,* Lionel Trilling's *Beyond Culture,* and René Wellek's *History of Modern Criticism.*
5. JF to SS, March 17, 1966, Library of Congress.
6. JF to SS, February 1, 1966, Library of Congress.
7. Acceptance speech delivered at the National Book Award ceremony, March 15, 1966, and draft, Library of Congress.
8. JF, *Darlinghissima: Letters to a Friend,* ed. Natalia Danesi Murray (New York: Random House, 1985), p. 398.

9. M. F. K. Fisher, Foreword, *The Alice B. Toklas Cook Book* (New York: Harper and Row, 1984), p. xi.

10. Interview with M. F. K. Fisher, July 14–15, 1987.

11. Interview with Simon Michael Bessie, November 11, 1986.

12. Interview with Philip Hamburger, October 8, 1986.

13. Ibid.

14. Ned Rorem, *Setting the Tone* (New York: Coward-McCann, 1983), pp. 132–34.

15. Interview with Robert Phelps, July 11, 1987.

16. JF, interview with George Wickes, June 8, 1972, tape courtesy of George Wickes.

17. JF to SS, August 1954, Library of Congress.

18. H. D. Vursell to JF, March 7, 1967, Library of Congress.

19. JF, Introduction, Gabrielle Colette, *The Pure and the Impure,* trans. Herma Briffault (New York: Farrar, Straus, and Giroux, 1967), pp. v-vi.

20. See JF, *Darlinghissima,* p. 397.

21. "Letter from Paris," *The New Yorker,* January 13, 1968, pp. 96–100.

22. JF, "The Departed Glory of Les Halles," *Life,* May 12, 1967, p. 82.

23. JF, "A Promenade for Strollers, Dreamers, Sportsmen, Even Lovers," *Holiday,* January 1964, pp. 44–45, 90.

24. JF, notes, [1968], Library of Congress.

25. Ibid.

26. Interview with Mary McCarthy, October 26, 1987.

27. JF to Kay Boyle, July 1, 1968, Morris Library, Southern Illinois University at Carbondale.

28. "The Dick Cavett Show," PBS television program, December 12, 1971.

29. Quoted in a letter from William Maxwell to JF, May 21, 1968, Library of Congress.

30. SS to Kay Boyle, July 1, 1968, Morris Library, University of Southern Illinois at Carbondale.

31. JF to SS, November 11, 1968, Library of Congress.

32. Ibid.

33. JF to SS, January 6, 1969, Library of Congress.

34. Ibid.

35. Interview with Hugh Ford, May 16, 1986.

36. SS to John Broderick, July 20, 1966, Library of Congress.

37. Interview with John Broderick, July 30, 1987. See also John Broderick, Prefatory Note, "Paris Between the Wars: An Unpublished Memoir by Solita Solano," *Quarterly Journal of the Library of Congress* 34 (October 1977): 306–7.

38. Interview with HFM, July 15, 1985.

39. Margaret Anderson to SS, June 23, 1969, Library of Congress.

40. SS to Margaret Anderson, [June 23, 1969], Library of Congress.

41. Interview with Sybille Bedford, October 22, 1986.

42. Telephone interview with Ned Rorem, June 24, 1987.

43. Rorem, *Setting the Tone,* pp. 132–34.

44. Ibid., p. 133.
45. "Letter from Paris," *The New Yorker,* November 21, 1970, pp. 111–12; reprinted in *Paris Journal 1965–1971* (New York: Atheneum, 1971), p. 413.
46. SS to Kay Boyle, February 1, 1971, Morris Library, Southern Illinois University at Carbondale.
47. Interview with Mary McCarthy, October 26, 1987.
48. JF to SS, December 28, 1970, Library of Congress.
49. JF to SS, November 5, 1971, Library of Congress.
50. JF to SS, October 22, 1971, Library of Congress.
51. Interview with Simon Michael Bessie, November 11, 1986.
52. JF to Elizabeth Jenks Clark, [July 1971], Library of Congress.
53. JF to SS, [July 1971], Library of Congress.
54. Ibid.
55. JF to SS, September 22, 1971, Library of Congress.
56. JF to SS, November 5, 1971, Library of Congress.
57. JF, *Paris Was Yesterday* (New York: Viking Press, 1972), p. vii.
58. JF to SS, November 5, 1971, Library of Congress.
59. John Ardagh, "Autre Temps," *Book World,* New York *Herald Tribune,* November 21, 1971, p. 10.
60. Norman Mailer, *Pieces and Pontifications* (Boston: Little, Brown, 1982), p. 67.
61. JF to SS, January 12, 1972, Library of Congress.
62. JF, interview with George Wickes, June 8, 1972, tape courtesy of George Wickes.
63. Telephone interview with Stephen F. Buchanan, March 22, 1987.
64. JF, interview with Mary McCarthy, 1965, typescript, Vassar College Library.
65. JF to SS, [spring] 1972, Library of Congress.
66. Margaret Anderson to SS, July 21, 1972, Library of Congress.
67. George Wickes, "One for Bastille Day," *New Republic,* July 15, 1972, pp. 23–25.
68. Hugh Ford to SS, March 3, 1973, Library of Congress.
69. Ibid.
70. See JF, "Oscar Wilde's Niece," *Prose* 6 (Spring 1973): 37–42.
71. Interview with Roger Angell, June 19, 1987.
72. JF to SS, March 29, 1973, Library of Congress.
73. JF to SS, April 4, 1973, Library of Congress.
74. Ibid.
75. Interview with Fanny Brennan, January 24, 1985.
76. Telephone interview with Célia Bertin, June 24, 1987.
77. Ibid.
78. Interview with Mary McCarthy, October 26, 1987.
79. Interview with Sybille Bedford, October 22, 1986.
80. JF to SS, December 20, 1973, Library of Congress.
81. JF to SS, November 18, 1968, Library of Congress.
82. JF to SS, October 29, 1973, Library of Congress.

83. The venture, an obvious attempt to capitalize on the success of *Paris Was Yesterday,* was ill-advised at best. Out of their original context, the selected London letters read poorly, and the accompanying photographs served mainly to highlight the superficiality of the text, prompting one reviewer to exclaim that "what is unforgivable, and also unreadable, is ignorance disguised by that knowing, nudging loutishness which one still looks for today in the more elevated society columns" (Benny Green, "Old Flanner," *The Spectator,* August 23, 1975, p. 253).

84. JF to SS, [1974 or 1975], Library of Congress.

85. Interview with Honoria Murphy Donnelly, July 22, 1986.

86. "Letter from Paris," *The New Yorker,* September 29, 1975, p. 110; reprinted in *Janet Flanner's World: Uncollected Writings, 1932–1975* (New York: Harcourt Brace Jovanovich, 1979), p. 3.

87. Ibid., p. 109.

88. Noel Murphy, interview with Honoria Murphy Donnelly, June 1981, tape courtesy of Honoria Donnelly.

89. Interview with HFM, July 15, 1985.

90. Telephone interview with Thomas Quinn Curtiss, June 18, 1987.

91. Interview with Edith Oliver, September 26, 1986.

92. Interview with Philip Hamburger, October 8, 1986.

93. Telephone interview with Berenice Abbott, May 6, 1987.

Bibliography

BOOKS BY JANET FLANNER

The Cubical City. New York: G. P. Putnam's Sons, 1926. Reprint, Carbondale: Southern Illinois University Press, 1974.
An American in Paris. New York: Simon and Schuster, 1940.
Pétain: The Old Man of France. New York: Simon and Schuster, 1944.
Men and Monuments. New York: Harper and Brothers, 1957.
Paris Journal: 1944–1965. New York: Atheneum, 1965.
Paris Journal: 1965–1971. Volume 2. New York: Atheneum, 1971.
Paris Was Yesterday, 1925–1930. New York: Viking Press, 1971.
London Was Yesterday, 1934–1939. New York: Viking Press, 1975.
Janet Flanner's World: Uncollected Writings, 1932–1975. New York: Harcourt Brace Jovanovich, 1979.
Darlinghissima: Letters to a Friend. Edited by Natalia Danesi Murray. New York: Random House, 1985.

UNCOLLECTED ARTICLES BY JANET FLANNER

"In Transit and Return." *Century,* October 1920, pp. 801–13.
"Hoi Polloi at Close Range." *New York Tribune,* November 20, 1921, p. 2.
"California — Dunt Esk." *The New Yorker,* November 27, 1926, pp. 30–31.
"Behind the Seams." *Ladies Home Journal,* April 1929, pp. 22–23.
"What Americans Are Seeing in Paris." *Arts and Decoration,* November 1930, pp. 56, 90.
"Tchatzu." *The New Yorker,* March 19, 1932, pp. 18–20.
"Oh, Fire." *The New Yorker,* November 5, 1932, pp. 19–20.
"New Patrons for the Arts." *Arts and Decoration,* January 1933, pp. 48–49, 63.
"Music and Dancing in Paris." *Arts and Decoration,* February 1933, p. 49.
"Kaleidoscope of Paris." *Arts and Decoration,* April 1933, pp. 46–47, 56.
"Weather: Wise and Foolish." *Seven Seas,* April 1933, pp. 17, 29–30.
"Spring Scene in Paris." *Arts and Decoration,* June 1933, pp. 32–33, 62.

"Revue . . . Paris' Decorative Scene." *Arts and Decoration*, November 1933, pp. 47–48, 50–51.

"Those Were the Days." *The New Yorker*, January 20, 1934, pp. 17–20.

"Paris Review." *Arts and Decoration*, May 1934, p. 47.

"Things Women Never Tell Men." *Vogue*, June 1, 1934, pp. 61, 97.

"The Big Ten." *Harper's Bazaar*, October 1934, pp. 71, 148–49.

"Venetian Perspective." *The New Yorker*, August 25, 1934, pp. 17–19.

"Lengths Women Have Gone To." *Vogue*, November 15, 1934, pp. 56, 84.

"The Women They Like to Dress." *Harper's Bazaar*, September 1935, pp. 107, 145, 148.

"Pierre Laval: France's One-Man Government." *Forum* 94 (November 1935): 272–75.

"Burning Questions." *Vogue*, May 1, 1936, pp. 74, 148–50.

"Boom Shot of Hollywood." *Harper's Bazaar*, October 1936, pp. 106–7, 183–84.

"Fashions in Spies." *Harper's Bazaar*, May 19, 1938, pp. 86–87, 124.

"Mr. Ambassador." *The New Yorker*, December 10, 1938, pp. 30–33; December 17, 1938, pp. 22–27.

"The Generation That Knows Nothing Else." *Woman's Home Companion*, October 1939, pp. 16–17, 53–54.

"Girls Raised in the Great Tradition." *Woman's Home Companion*, October 1939, pp. 16–17, 118.

"One Man Group." *The New Yorker*, December 9, 1939, pp. 32–37.

"Behind the Maginot Line." Review of *France at War* by Somerset Maugham. New York *Herald Tribune*, book section, May 12, 1940, p. 4.

"History Tramps Down the Champs-Élysées." Review of *Paris France* by Gertrude Stein. New York *Herald Tribune*, book section, June 23, 1940, p. 1.

"Let's Look at the Calendar: Will We Talk Democracy to Death in the Country?" *Harper's Bazaar*, August 1940, pp. 68, 109.

Review of *Romantic Rebel* by Selizia Seyd. New York *Herald Tribune*, book section, September 8, 1940, p. 5.

"The Voices of France." Review of *They Speak for a Nation*, edited by Eve Curie and others, New York *Herald Tribune*, book section, June 23, 1940, p. 5.

"Rushville's Son-in-Law." *The New Yorker*, October 12, 1940, pp. 27–45.

"Paradise Lost." *Decision* (January 1941): 35–38.

"The Lone Liberty Chorus." *Harper's Bazaar*, March 1, 1941, pp. 81, 131.

"Soldats de France, Debout!" *The New Yorker*, February 1, 1941, pp. 19–24.

"Le Nouvel Ordre." *The New Yorker*, March 15, 1941, pp. 38–47.

"Blitz by Partnership." *The New Yorker*, June 7, 1941, pp. 42–54.

"So You're Going to Paris." *The New Yorker*, January 21, 1941, pp. 36–47.

"Come Down, Giuseppe!" *The New Yorker*, January 17, 1942, pp. 46–54.

"The Triumph of Timidity." *Glamour*, May 1942, pp. 52, 84.

"Ferox, Mendox, ac Praedator." *The New Yorker*, April 1, 1942, pp. 24–32.

"General and Mrs. Douglas MacArthur." *Ladies Home Journal*, June 1942, pp. 15, 59–60.

"Ladies in Uniform." *The New Yorker*, July 4, 1942, pp. 21–29.

"Guinea Pigs and the Mona Lisa." *The New Yorker*, October 31, 1942, pp. 44–58.

"Run for Your Life." *Home and Food*, October 1943, pp. 14–15, 31.

"What's Wrong with France?" *Overseas Woman*, October 1945, pp. 32–40.

"Annals of Collaboration." *The New Yorker*, September 29, 1945, pp. 28–47; October 6, 1945, pp. 32–45; October 13, 1945, pp. 32–48.

"In Defense of the French." *New York Times Magazine*, March 6, 1955, pp. 12, 30, 32, 34.

"Tobey, Mystique errant." *L'Oeil*, June 15, 1955, pp. 26–31.

"De Diverses Formes de Beauté." *L'Oeil*, October 1957, pp. 24–30.

"Recipes of Alice Toklas." *New Republic*, December 15, 1958, p. 20.

"Le Gamin." *The New Yorker*, November 21, 1959, pp. 57–108.

"Sylvia Beach: The Great Amateur Publisher." *Mercure de France*, 1963, pp. 46–51.

"A Park for Strollers, Dreamers, Sportsmen, Even Lovers." *Holiday*, January 1964, pp. 44–45, 90.

"Oscar Wilde's Niece." *Prose* 6 (Spring 1973): 37–42.

GENERAL

Abbott, George. *Mr. Abbott*. New York: Random House, 1963.

Abbott, Lyman. "What Is Christianity?" *Arena* 3 (1891): 46.

Adams, Franklin P. *The Diary of Our Own Samuel Pepys*. New York: Simon and Schuster, 1935.

"Air Terror Told by Miss Morgan." *New York Mirror*, May 19, 1940, p. 4.

Alajalov, Constantin. *Conversation Pieces*. Introduction and commentary by Janet Flanner. New York: Studio Publications, 1942.

Aldington, Richard. *Life for Life's Sake*. New York: Viking Press, 1941.

Allan, Tony. *Americans in Paris*. Chicago: Contemporary Books, 1977.

Anderson, Margaret. *My Thirty Years' War*. New York: Covici, Friede, 1930.

———— *The Fiery Fountains*. New York: Horizon Press, 1951.

———— *Traits and Portraits*. London: Routledge and Kegan Paul, 1962.

———— *The Unknowable Gurdjieff*. 1962. Reprint, New York: Samuel Weiser, 1970.

———— *The Strange Necessity*. New York: Horizon Press, 1969.

Ardagh, John. "Autre Temps." *Book World*, New York *Herald Tribune*, November 21, 1971, p. 10.

———— *The New France*. Harmondsworth, Eng.: Penguin Books, 1973.

Bainbridge, John. *Another Way of Living*. New York: Holt, Rinehart and Winston, 1968.

Baker, Carlos. *Hemingway: A Life Story*. New York: Avon, 1980.

Baragwanath, John. *A Good Time Was Had*. New York: Appleton-Century-Crofts, 1962.

Barnes, Djuna. *Ladies Almanack*. Paris: 1928.

——— *Interviews*. Edited by Alyce Berry. Washington, D.C.: Sun and Moon Press, 1985.

Barney, Natalie. "Traits and Portraits." *Mercure de France*, 1963.

Beach, Sylvia. *Shakespeare and Company*. 1956. Reprint, Lincoln: University of Nebraska Press, 1980.

Beaton, Cecil. *The Wandering Years: Diaries 1922–1939*. Boston: Little, Brown, 1961.

Behrman, Daniel. "Genêt . . ." *Realité,* June 1965, pp. 56–59.

Benét, William R. "The Cubical City." *Saturday Review of Literature,* November 1, 1924, p. 243.

Benstock, Shari. *Women of the Left Bank: Paris, 1900–1940*. Austin: University of Texas, 1986.

Berger, John. "Men and Monuments." *The Spectator* (1957): 114.

Bernikow, Louise. *Among Women*. New York: Harmony Books, 1980.

Bernstein, Burton. *Thurber*. New York: Dodd, Mead, 1975.

Bicknell, Ernest P. *Indianapolis Illustrated*. Indianapolis: Baker Randolph Lithograph and Engraving, 1893.

Bishop, John Peale. "The Discipline of Poetry." *Virginia Quarterly Review* 14:3 (Summer 1938): 343–56.

Boyle, Kay, and Robert McAlmon. *Being Geniuses Together*. San Francisco: North Point Press, 1984.

Bradlee, Benjamin. "Paragon of Correspondents Provides Excellent History." *Washington Post,* November 16, 1965, p. 18.

Brassai. *The Secret Life of Paris of the 30's*. Translated by Richard Miller. New York: Pantheon, 1976.

Brinnin, John Malcolm. *The Third Rose: Gertrude Stein and Her World*. New York: Praeger, 1959.

Broderick, John C. "Paris Between the Wars: An Unpublished Memoir by Solita Solano." *Quarterly Journal of the Library of Congress* (October 1977): 306–14.

Bryher [Annie Winifred Ellerman]. *The Heart to Artemis*. New York: Harcourt, Brace and World, 1962.

Burns, Edward, ed. *Staying On Alone: The Letters of Alice B. Toklas*. New York: Liveright, 1973.

Busey, Garreta. "Living One's Own Life: *The Cubical City*." *New York Herald Tribune,* December 12, 1926, p. 3.

Callaghan, Morley. *That Summer in Paris*. New York: Dell, 1964.

Carr, Virginia Spencer. *The Lonely Hunter: A Biography of Carson McCullers*. New York: Carroll and Graf, 1975.

Caruso, Dorothy Park. *A Personal History*. New York: Hermitage House, 1952.

Casey, Phil. "Janet Flanner, the Lady Known as Genêt: A Rarity among Journalists." *Washington Post,* July 2, 1972, p. 5.

Charters, Jimmie. *This Must Be the Place: The Memoirs of Jimmie the Barman as Told to Morrill Cody.* New York: Lee Furman, 1937.

Chase, Edna Woolman. *Always in Vogue.* Garden City, N.Y.: Doubleday, 1954.

Chisholm, Anne. *Nancy Cunard.* New York: Alfred A. Knopf, 1979.

Chodorow, Nancy. *The Reproduction of Mothering: Psychoanalysis and the Sociology of Gender.* Berkeley: University of California Press, 1978.

Churchill, Allen. *The Improper Bohemians: A Recreation of Greenwich Village in Its Heyday.* New York: E. P. Dutton, 1959.

Colette, Gabrielle. *Chéri.* Translated by Janet Flanner. New York: A. & C. Boni, 1929.

——— *Claudine at School.* Translated by Janet Flanner. London: Victor Gollancz, 1930.

——— *Mitsou.* Translated by Jane Terry. New York: A. & C. Boni, 1930.

——— *Seven.* New York: Farrar, Straus, and Cudahy, 1955.

——— *The Pure and the Impure.* Translated by Herma Briffault, Introduction by Janet Flanner. New York: Farrar, Straus, and Giroux, 1967.

Connelly, Marc. *Voices Offstage.* New York: Holt, Rinehart and Winston, 1968.

Cowley, Malcolm. *Exiles Return.* New York: Viking Press, 1951.

——— "The Twenties in Montparnasse." *Saturday Review,* March 11, 1967, pp. 51, 55, 98–101.

——— *A Second Flowering.* New York: Viking Press, 1973.

Crosland, Margaret. *Colette: The Difficulty of Loving.* Introduction by Janet Flanner. Indianapolis: Bobbs-Merrill, 1973.

Cunard, Nancy. *Black Man and White Ladyship.* London, 1931.

——— *G.M.: Memories of George Moore.* London: Rupert Hart-Davis, 1956.

——— *These Were the Hours.* Carbondale: Southern Illinois University Press, 1969.

Davidson, Cathy, and Esther Broner, eds. *The Lost Tradition.* New York: Frederick Ungar, 1980.

Davis, Linda. *Onward and Upward: A Biography of Katharine S. White.* New York: Harper and Row, 1987.

de Acosta, Mercedes. *Here Lies the Heart.* New York: Reynal, 1960.

"Diary of an American Art Student in Paris." *Vanity Fair,* November 1922, pp. 44, 106, 108.

Donnelly, Honoria Murphy. *Sara and Gerald.* New York: Holt, Rinehart and Winston, 1984.

Draper, Theodore. "Man of Vichy." *New York Times Book Review,* July 9, 1944, pp. 4, 16.

Dreiser, Theodore. *A Gallery of Women.* New York: Liveright, 1929.

Drutman, Irving. *Good Company.* Boston: Little, Brown, 1976.

Dryansky, G. Y. "The Genteel Iconoclast." *Women's Wear Daily,* April 22, 1968, p. 12.

Dunn, Jacob Piatt. *Representative Citizens of Indiana.* Indianapolis: B. F. Bowen, 1912.

Earnest, Ernest. *Expatriates and Patriots.* Durham, N.C.: Duke University Press, 1961.

Eisenstein, Hester, and Alice Jardine, eds. *The Future of Difference.* New Brunswick, N.J.: Rutgers University Press, 1985.

Evans, Ernestine. "Now That One Looks Back." *Virginia Quarterly Review* 17:1 (Winter 1941): 43–52.

Eyre de Lanux, Elizabeth. "Letters of Elizabeth." *Town and Country,* December 15, 1922, p. 34; February 15, 1925, p. 30.

F.P.A. "The Conning Tower." *New York World,* October 9, 1924.

Faderman, Lillian. *Surpassing the Love of Men.* New York: William Morrow, 1981.

Faderman, Lillian, and Brigitte Erikkson. *Lesbian-Feminism in Turn-of-the-Century Germany.* Tallahassee, Fla.: Naiad Press, 1980.

Ferber, Edna. *A Kind of Magic.* Garden City, N.Y.: Doubleday, 1963.

——— *A Peculiar Treasure.* New York: Doubleday, Doran, 1939.

Field, Andrew. *Djuna: The Life and Times of Djuna Barnes.* New York: G. P. Putnam's Sons, 1983.

Fielding, Daphne. *Those Remarkable Cunards: Nancy and Lady Emerald.* New York: Atheneum, 1968.

Fitch, Noel Riley. *Sylvia Beach and the Lost Generation.* New York: W. W. Norton, 1983.

Flanner, Hildegarde. "Wildfire." *The New Yorker,* September 23, 1974, pp. 36–40.

——— *The Hearkening Eye.* Boise, Idaho: Ashanti Press, 1979.

——— *Brief Cherishing.* Santa Barbara, Calif.: John Daniel, 1985.

——— *At the Gentle Mercy of Plants.* Santa Barbara, Calif.: John Daniel, 1986.

——— *Different Images: Portraits of Remembered People.* Santa Barbara, Calif.: John Daniel, 1987.

Flanner, Mary Hockett. *Bargain Day.* New York: Samuel French, 1911.

——— *The Christmas Burglar: A Play in One Act.* New York: Samuel French, 1913.

Flanner, William. *A Brief Memoir of William Flanner of Stillwater Quarterly Meeting.* Edited by Abigail Flanner. Mount Pleasant, Ohio: J. P. Flanner, 1860.

Flint, Nott. *The University of Chicago: A Sketch.* Chicago: University of Chicago Press, 1905.

Ford, Hugh. *Four Lives in Paris.* San Francisco: North Point Press, 1986.

Ford, Hugh, ed. *Nancy Cunard: Brave Poet, Indomitable Rebel, 1896–1965.* Philadelphia: Chilton, 1968.

——— *The Left Bank Revisited: Selections from the Paris Tribune, 1917–1934.* University Park: Pennsylvania State University Press, 1972.

——— *Published in Paris: American and British Writers, Printers, and Publishers in Paris, 1920–1939.* Foreword by Janet Flanner. New York: Macmillan, 1975.

Freedman, Estelle B., ed. *The Lesbian Issue: Essays from Signs.* Chicago: University of Chicago Press, 1985.

Fussell, Paul. *The Great War and Modern Memory.* New York: Oxford University Press, 1975.

Gardiner, Judith Kegan. "Mind Mother: Psychoanalysis and Feminism." In *Making a Difference: Feminist Literary Criticism,* ed. Gayle Greene and Coppelia Kahn, pp. 113–45. London: Methuen, 1985.

"Genetics." *Time,* April 22, 1940, p. 97.

Gilbert, Sandra M. "Costumes of the Mind," *Critical Inquiry* 7 (1980): 408–17.

Gill, Brendan. *Here at the New Yorker.* New York: Random House, 1975.

Gilliam, Florence. *France.* New York: E. P. Dutton, 1945.

"The Girl about Town." *Indianapolis Sunday Star,* March 29, 1936, p. 15.

Givner, Joan. *Katherine Anne Porter.* New York: Simon and Schuster, 1982.

Glassco, John. *Memoirs of Montparnasse.* New York: Oxford University Press, 1970.

Goodspeed, Thomas. *A History of the University of Chicago: The First Quarter Century.* 1916. Reprint, Chicago: University of Chicago Press, 1972.

———— *The Story of the University of Chicago Press, 1890–1920.* Chicago: University of Chicago Press, 1925.

Gordon, Ruth. *Myself among Others.* New York: Atheneum, 1971.

Grant, Jane. *Ross, The New Yorker, and Me.* Introduction by Janet Flanner. New York: Reynal, 1968.

Green, Benny. "Old Flanner." *The Spectator,* August 23, 1975, p. 253.

Hahn, Emily. *Romantic Rebels: An Informal History of Bohemianism in America.* Boston: Houghton Mifflin, 1967.

Hamburger, Philip. *The Oblong Blur and Other Odysseys.* New York: Farrar, Straus, 1949.

Handlin, Oscar. "Reader's Choice." *Atlantic,* December 1965, p. 146.

Hanfstaengl, Ernst. *Unheard Witness.* Philadelphia: J. B. Lippincott, 1957.

Hayes, Helen, and Anita Loos. *Twice Over Lightly: New York Then and Now.* New York: Harcourt Brace Jovanovich, 1972.

Hellman, Lillian. "Books." New York *Herald Tribune,* October 8, 1927, p. 22.

Hemingway, Ernest. *A Moveable Feast.* New York: Scribners, 1964.

Hirsch, Marianne. "Mothers and Daughters," *Signs: Journal of Women and Culture in Society* 7, no. 1 (Autumn 1981): 200–22.

Hobhouse, Janet. *Everybody Who Was Anybody.* London: Weidenfeld and Nicolson, 1975.

Hodgson, Simon. "Sublime Governess." *New Statesman* 65 (February 22, 1963): 268.

Hoffman, Frederick. *The Little Magazines.* Princeton: Princeton University Press, 1947.

Hoyt, Edwin P. *Alexander Woollcott: The Man Who Came to Dinner.* London: Abelard, 1967.

Huddleston, Sisley. *In and About Paris.* London: Methuen, 1927.

————*Bohemian Literary and Social Life in Paris.* London: George G. Harrap, 1928.

Hulme, Kathryn. *The Wild Place*. Boston: Little, Brown, 1963.

—— *Undiscovered Country*. Boston: Atlantic–Little, Brown, 1966.

Hyman, Stanley Edgar. "The Urban New Yorker." *New Republic,* July 20, 1942, pp. 90–92.

Imbs, Bravig. *Confessions of a Young Man*. New York: Henkle-Yendale House, 1936.

Ingersoll, Ralph. "The New Yorker." *Fortune,* August 1934, pp. 72–86, 90, 92, 97, 150, 152.

—— *Point of Departure*. New York: Harcourt, Brace and World, 1961.

Joseph Regenstein Library. *One in Spirit*. Chicago: University of Chicago Press, 1973.

Josephson, Matthew. *Life among the Surrealists*. New York: Holt, Rinehart and Winston, 1962.

Kahn, E. J., Jr. *About the New Yorker and Me*. New York: G. P. Putnam's Sons, 1979.

Kaufman, Beatrice, and Joseph Hennessey, eds. *The Letters of Alexander Woollcott*. New York: Viking Press, 1944.

Keats, John. *You Might As Well Live*. New York: Simon and Schuster, 1970.

Keene, Donald. "Letters from France." *The New York Times Book Review,* November 21, 1965, p. 5.

Kenner, Hugh. *The Pound Era*. Berkeley: University of California Press, 1971.

Klaich, Dolores. *Woman + Woman: Attitudes Toward Lesbianism*. New York: Simon and Schuster, 1974.

Kohner, Frederick. *Kiki of Montparnasse*. New York: Stein and Day, 1967.

Kraditor, Aileen. *The Ideas of the Women's Suffrage Movement*. New York: Columbia University Press, 1965.

Kramer, Dale. *Heywood Broun*. New York: Current Books, 1949.

—— *Ross and the New Yorker*. Garden City, N.Y.: Doubleday, 1952.

Krutch, Joseph Wood. "The Profession of a New Yorker." *Saturday Review of Literature,* January 20, 1954.

Laney, Al. *The Paris Herald*. New York: Greenwood Press, 1947.

Langer, Lawrence. *The Magic Curtain*. New York: E. P. Dutton, 1951.

Lawford, Valentine. *Horst: His Work and His World*. New York: Alfred A. Knopf, 1984.

Liebling, A. J. *Liebling Abroad*. New York: Wideview Books, 1981.

Litwak, Leo. "Kay Boyle — Paris Wasn't Like That." *New York Times Book Review,* July 15, 1984, pp. 1, 32–33.

Loeb, Harold. *The Way It Was*. New York: Criterion Books, 1959.

Longstreet, Stephen. *We All Went to Paris*. New York: Macmillan, 1972.

Loos, Anita. *But Gentlemen Marry Brunettes*. New York: Boni and Liveright, 1928.

—— *A Girl Like I*. New York: Viking Press, 1966.

Lottman, Herbert R. *The Left Bank*. Boston: Houghton Mifflin, 1982.

Lovett, Robert Morss. *All Our Years: The Autobiography of Robert Morss Lovett*. New York: Viking Press, 1948.

McCarthy, Mary. "Conversation Piece." *New York Times Book Review,* November 21, 1965, pp. 5, 89–91.

Macdonald, Dwight. "Laugh and Lie Down." *Partisan Review* 4 (December 1937): 44–53.

Mailer, Norman. *Pieces and Pontifications.* Boston: Little, Brown, 1982.

Mann, Klaus. *The Turning Point.* London: Victor Gollancz, 1944.

Marsh, Ed. *A Number of People.* New York: Harper and Brothers, 1939.

Maxwell, Elsa. "The Truth About Barbara Hutton." *Cosmopolitan,* October 1938, pp. 22–25, 134–36; November 1938, pp. 46–49, 94–97; December 1938, pp. 50–51, 105–9; January 1939, pp. 56–57, 134–35.

Mazer, Gwen. "Lifestyle: Janet Flanner." *Harper's Bazaar,* October 1972.

Mellow, James R. *Charmed Circle.* New York: Praeger, 1982.

Mencken, H. L. "The Flapper." *Smart Set* 45 (1915): 1–2.

Mortimer, Raymond. "Eminent Artists of Our Own Time." London *Sunday Times,* June 30, 1957.

Mott, Frank Luther. *A History of American Magazines,* vol. 5. Cambridge, Mass.: Harvard University Press, 1968.

Nolan, Jeannette. *Hoosier City.* New York: Julian Messner, 1943.

O'Conner, Richard. *Heywood Broun: A Biography.* New York: G. P. Putnam's Sons, 1975.

Ostriker, Alicia. *Writing Like a Woman.* Ann Arbor: University of Michigan Press, 1983.

Overton, Grant M. *The Women Who Make Our Novels.* New York: Moffat, Yard, 1922.

Parry, Albert. *Garrets and Pretenders.* New York: Covici, Friede, 1933.

Porter, Benjamin S., ed. *Poets and Poetry of Indiana, 1800–1900.* New York: Silver, Burdett, 1900.

Pound, Ezra. "The Island of Paris: A Letter." *Dial* 69 (1920): 406–11.

Pryce-Jones, Alan. "Janet Flanner's Crow's Nest View of Paris." New York *Herald Tribune,* November 12, 1965.

Putnam, Samuel. *Paris Was Our Mistress.* Carbondale: Southern Illinois University Press, 1947.

Ray, Man. *Self-Portrait.* Boston: Little, Brown, 1963.

Rich, Adrienne. "Compulsory Heterosexuality and Lesbian Existence." *Signs: Journal of Women in Culture and Society* 5:4 (Summer 1980): 659.

——— *Of Woman Born: Motherhood as Experience and Institution.* New York: W. W. Norton, 1976.

Rogers, W. G. *Ladies Bountiful.* New York: Harcourt, Brace and World, 1968.

Rorem, Ned. *Setting the Tone.* New York: Coward-McCann, 1983.

Rose, Sir Francis. *Saying Life: The Memoirs of Sir Francis Rose.* London: Cassell, 1961.

Ross, Ishbel. *The Expatriates.* New York: Crowell, 1970.

Ross, Sherwood. *Gruening of Alaska.* New York: Basic Books, 1968.

Sachs, Maurice. *The Decade of Illusion: Paris, 1918–1928.* New York: Alfred A. Knopf, 1933.

Saler, Steve. "Janet Flanner: Last of a Writing Generation." *News American,* December 13, 1971, pp. 1A, 5A.

Scudder, Janet. *Modelling My Life.* New York: Harcourt, Brace, 1925.

Secrest, Meryle. *Between Me and Life: A Biography of Romaine Brooks.* Garden City, N.Y.: Doubleday, 1974.

Seitz, William C. *Mark Tobey.* Garden City, N.Y.: Doubleday, 1962.

Sheean, Diana Forbes-Robertson, and Roger W. Straus, eds. *War Letters from Britain.* London: Jarrolds, 1942.

Sheean, Vincent. *Between the Thunder and the Sun.* New York: Random House, 1943.

Shirer, William L. *The Nightmare Years: 1930–1940.* Boston: Little, Brown, 1984.

Simon, Linda. *The Biography of Alice Toklas.* Garden City, N.Y.: Doubleday, 1977.

Smith-Rosenberg, Carroll. *Disorderly Conduct: Visions of Gender in Victorian America.* New York: Oxford University Press, 1986.

Sokolov, Raymond. *Wayward Reporter: The Life of A. J. Liebling.* New York: Harper and Row, 1980.

Solano, Solita. "Constantinople Today." *National Geographic,* June 1922, p. 647.

——— "Vienna — A Capital without a Nation." *National Geographic,* January 1923, pp. 76–102.

——— *The Uncertain Feast.* New York: G. P. Putnam's Sons, 1924.

——— *The Happy Failure.* New York: G. P. Putnam's Sons, 1925.

——— *This Way Up.* New York: G. P. Putnam's Sons, 1927.

——— "This Way Up." *transition* 6 (September 1927): 68–74.

——— *Statue in a Field.* Paris, 1934.

Squier, Susan Merrill, ed. *Women Writers and the City: Essays in Feminist Literary Criticism.* Knoxville: University of Tennessee Press, 1984.

Stearns, Harold. *The Street I Know.* New York: Lee Furman, 1935.

Stearns, Harold, ed. *Civilization in the United States.* New York: Harcourt, Brace, Jovanovich, 1922. Reprint, Westport, Conn.: Greenwood Press, 1971.

Stein, Gertrude. *The Autobiography of Alice B. Toklas.* New York: Harcourt, Brace, 1933.

——— *Paris France.* London: B. T. Batsford, 1940.

——— *Two: Gertrude Stein and Her Brother and Other Early Portraits.* Introduction by Janet Flanner. New Haven: Yale University Press, 1951.

Stewart, Donald Ogden. *By a Stroke of Luck.* New York: Paddington Press, 1975.

Talbot, Daniel, ed. *City of Love.* New York: Dell, 1955.

Tartière, Drue. *The House near Paris: An American Woman's Story of Traffic in Patriots.* New York: Simon and Schuster, 1946.

Teichmann, Howard. *Smart Aleck.* New York: William Morrow, 1975.

Taylor, Francis Henry. "French Ideas, American Dollars." *Saturday Review,* May 11, 1957, 17.

"Then and Now." *Paris Review* 33 (Winter-Spring 1965): 158–70.

Thompson, Dorothy. *I Saw Hitler.* New York: Farrar and Rinehart, 1932.

Thomson, Virgil. *An Autobiography.* New York: Alfred A. Knopf, 1966.

Thurber, James. *The Years with Ross.* Boston: Little, Brown, 1957.

Toklas, Alice. *What I Remembered.* New York: Holt, Rinehart and Winston, 1963.

—— *The Alice B. Toklas Cook Book.* Foreword by M. F. K. Fisher. New York: Harper and Row, 1984.

Trilling, Lionel. "*New Yorker* Fiction." *The Nation,* April 11, 1942, p. 425.

Tucker, Robert. "Former Reviewer for *Star* Pens *American in Paris.*" *Indianapolis Star,* April 28, 1940.

Tyler, Parker. *The Divine Comedy of Pavel Tchelitchew: A Biography.* London: Weidenfeld and Nicolson, 1969.

Vertès, Marcel. *The Stronger Sex.* Introduction by Janet Flanner. New York: Hyperion Press, 1941.

Viannson-Ponté, Pierre. *The King and His Court.* Translated by Elaine P. Halperin. Introduction by Janet Flanner. Boston: Houghton Mifflin, 1964.

Vivien, Renée. *A Woman Appeared to Me.* Translated by Jeanette Foster. Tallahassee, Fla.: Naiad Press, 1977.

Ware, Caroline F. *Greenwich Village 1920–1930.* Boston: Houghton Mifflin, 1935.

Warshow, Robert. *The Immediate Experience.* New York: Atheneum, 1975.

Wertenbaker, Lael Tucker. *Death of a Man.* New York: Random House, 1957.

Wescott, Glenway. "The Frenchman Six Feet Three." *Harper's Magazine,* July 1942, pp. 131–40.

—— *Images of Truth.* New York: Harper and Row, 1962.

—— "The Tri-Colored Rainbow." *Book Week,* New York *Herald Tribune,* December 19, 1965, pp. 1, 8.

Wheeler, Kenneth W., and Virginia Lee Lussier. *Women, the Arts, and the 1920's in Paris and New York.* New Brunswick, N.J.: Transaction Books, 1982.

"Why Do Americans Live in Europe?" *transition* 14 (Fall 1928): 98–119.

Wickes, George. *Americans in Paris.* Garden City, N.Y.: Doubleday, 1969.

—— "One for Bastille Day." *New Republic,* July 15, 1972, pp. 23–25.

—— *The Amazon of Letters.* New York: G. P. Putnam's Sons, 1976.

—— "A Natalie Barney Garland." *Paris Review* 61 (Spring 1975): 110, 117–18.

Williams, William Carlos. *Autobiography of William Carlos Williams.* New York: New Directions, 1967.

Wilson, Edmund. *The Triple Thinkers.* New York: Harcourt, Brace and World, 1938.

—— *The Wound and the Bow.* Boston: Houghton Mifflin, 1941.

—— *The Twenties.* New York: Farrar, Straus, and Giroux, 1975.

—— *The Fifties.* New York: Farrar, Straus, and Giroux, 1986.

Winston, Richard, and Clara Winston, eds. *The Letters of Thomas Mann.* New York: Alfred A. Knopf, 1971.

Wolff, Charlotte. *Love Between Women*. New York: Harper Colophon, 1972.

Woodress, James. *Booth Tarkington: Gentleman from Indiana*. New York: Greenwood Press, 1969.

Woon, Basil. *The Paris That's Not in the Guidebooks*. New York: Brentano's, 1926.

Index